THE COLLECTED
WORKS OF
JEREMY BENTHAM

General Editor
F. Rosen

CONSTITUTIONAL LAW

The writings collected here lend credence to Bentham's claim, in *Constitutional Code*, that his ideas were appropriate 'for the use of all nations and all governments professing liberal opinions'. The essays, dating mainly from late 1822 and early 1823, are based exclusively on manuscripts, many of which have not been previously published. Bentham here attempts to legislate for an Islamic state, and offers advice to another in the process of throwing off Islamic rule. The Writings for Tripoli include the famous 'Securities against Misrule', in which Bentham draws up a constitutional charter with an accompanying explanation of its provisions. He also discusses the social, political, and religious institutions of the country, and proposes a scheme for the introduction of constitutional reform both there and in the other Barbary states. The Writings for Greece include a rare commentary on the first Greek Constitution of 1822, and advice and warnings to the Greek legislators against the temptation of 'sinister appetites'. The main theme in both groups of writings is the efficacy of representative institutions and the publicity of official actions in preventing the abuse of government power.

The Collected Works of Jeremy Bentham

The new critical edition of the works and correspondence of Jeremy Bentham (1748–1832) is being prepared and published under the supervision of the Bentham Committee of University College London. In spite of his importance as jurist, philosopher, and social scientist, and leader of the Utilitarian reformers, the only previous edition of his works was a poorly edited and incomplete one brought out within a decade or so of his death. Eight volumes of the new *Collected Works*, five of correspondence, and three of writings on jurisprudence, appeared between 1968 and 1981, published by the Athlone Press. Further volumes in the series since then are published by Oxford University Press. The overall plan and principles of the edition are set out in the General Preface to *The Correspondence of Jeremy Bentham* vol. 1, which was the first volume of the *Collected Works* to be published.

Volumes published by Oxford University Press

Constitutional Code
Volume 1
Edited by F. Rosen and J. H. Burns   1983

Deontology, together with A Table of the Springs of Action and Article on Utilitarianism
Edited by Amnon Goldworth   1983

Chrestomathia
Edited by M. J. Smith and W. H. Burston   1983

First Principles preparatory to Constitutional Code
Edited by Philip Schofield   1989

Correspondence, volume 6: January 1798 to December 1801
Edited by J. R. Dinwiddy   1984

Correspondence, volume 7: January 1802 to December 1808
Edited by J. R. Dinwiddy   1988

Correspondence, volume 8: January 1809 to December 1816
Edited by Stephen Conway   1988

Correspondence, volume 9: January 1817 to June 1820
Edited by Stephen Conway   1989

SECURITIES AGAINST MISRULE AND OTHER CONSTITUTIONAL WRITINGS FOR TRIPOLI AND GREECE

edited by

PHILIP SCHOFIELD

CLARENDON PRESS·OXFORD

1990

Oxford University Press, Walton Street, Oxford OX2 6DP

Oxford New York Toronto
Delhi Bombay Calcutta Madras Karachi
Petaling Jaya Singapore Hong Kong Tokyo
Nairobi Dar es Salaam Cape Town
Melbourne Auckland

and associated companies in
Berlin Ibadan

Oxford is a trade mark of Oxford University Press

Published in the United States
by Oxford University Press, New York

British Library Cataloguing in Publication Data
Bentham, Jeremy, 1748–1832
Securities against misrule and other constitutional
writings for Tripoli and Greece.—(The collected works of
Jeremy Bentham).
1. Constitutional law
I. Title   II. Schofield, Philip   III. Series
342.2
ISBN 0–19–822725–6

Library of Congress Cataloging in Publication Data
Bentham, Jeremy, 1748–1832.
Securities against misrule and other constitutional writings for
Tripoli and Greece / edited by Philip Schofield.
p. cm.—(The Collected works of Jeremy Bentham)
1. Tripolitania—Constitutional law.   2. Tripolitania—Politics
and government.   3. Greece—Constitutional law.   4. Greece—Politics
and government—1821–1832. I. Schofield, Philip.   II. Title.
III. Series: Bentham, Jeremy, 1748–1832. Works. 1983.
K3165.B46   1990
342.495—dc20   90–35300
[344.9502]
ISBN 0–19–822725–6

Typeset by Joshua Associates Ltd, Oxford
Printed in Great Britain
at the Alden Press, Oxford

PREFACE

The Bentham Committee wishes to thank the Economic and Social Research Council whose generous grant allowing for the appointment of an editor and half-time Research Assistant has made possible the preparation of the present volume. The Committee is also indebted to the British Academy, the Leverhulme Trust and University College London for their continuing support.

The editor wishes to thank the following repositories for permission to quote from manuscripts in their possession: University College London Library; the British Library; the Public Record Office; General State Archives, Academy of Athens; the National Library of Greece, Athens; and the Centre for Neohellenic Research, the National Hellenic Research Foundation, Athens. Special thanks are extended to the staff of University College London Manuscripts and Rare Books Library, and in particular to Miss G. M. Furlong, for their help and assistance.

I am indebted to Professor F. Rosen, the Director and General Editor of the Bentham Project, for reading through the text and for placing the fruits of his research in Greek archives at my disposal. I am particularly grateful to Ms Claire Creffield, Dr Marilyn Morris and Miss Jane Haville, who in their capacity as Research Assistants have helped in the transcription of manuscripts, the gathering of information for the purposes of annotation and the preparation of the text on computer disk. Miss Haville has moreover read the proofs and helped to prepare the name index. Dr Cyprian Blamires has rendered invaluable assistance in the transcription of, and the gathering of information from, source material written in French. Dr Stephen Conway, Correspondence Editor, has, as always, been willing to share his considerable knowledge of Bentham's world whenever called upon to do so. Thanks are also due to Mr T. Venning for making preliminary transcriptions of many of the manuscripts; Dr P. J. Kelly for reading the proofs; and Mrs Rosamine Hayeem and Mrs Angela Hesselgren for providing general secretarial assistance.

I gratefully acknowledge the help received in the elucidation of certain references in the text from the following scholars: Dr G. R. Hawting, Professor L. J. Hume, Professor P. M. Kitromilides, Mr A. D. E. Lewis and Mr Chowdhury Mueenuddin.

P.S.

CONTENTS

SYMBOLS AND ABBREVIATIONS   xiii

EDITORIAL INTRODUCTION   xv

WRITINGS FOR TRIPOLI

ACCOUNT OF TRIPOLI   1
§ 1. Territory—population—language   3
§ 2. Chief of the State—his name—title—power—and family   4
§ 3. General Administration—its members   6
§ 4. Judicial Establishment   8
§ 5. Police in Towns: namely in some of the larger Towns   11
§ 6. Religious Establishment   12
§ 7. Public Instruction Establishment   16
§ 8. Military Land Establishment   19
§ 9. Naval Establishment   19
§ 10. Financial Establishment   20
§ 11. Relation of Tripoli to the other North African powers   21
§ 12. State of present conditions in life   21

SECURITIES AGAINST MISRULE   23
PRELIMINARY EXPLANATIONS   25
§ 1. Object of the proposed arrangements—Security against Misrule, by the sole remedy—publicity   25
§ 2. Misrule—shapes in which it is here combated   26
§ 3. Sole remedy, publicity: sole means of applying the protective power of the Public Opinion Tribunal. Publicity and notification—their mutual relations   27
§ 4. Subjects of Notification—their mutual relations. 1. Ordinances. 2. Transgressions. 3. Suffrages   29
§ 5. [I.] Operations subservient to publicity: viz. in relation to Ordinances. 1. Scription. 2. Sanctionment. 3. Registration   31
§ 6. Continuation. How, in Tripoli and elsewhere, instead of regularly sanctioned Ordinances, other matter is referred to for the purpose of judicature   32

vii

CONTENTS

§ 7. Operations necessary to adequate publicity of Ordinances
continued: 4. Multiplication of copies—its importance   36

§ 8. Continuation. Necessary instrument of multiplication as
applied to Ordinances, a printing press. Caution, as to the
throwing Scribes out of employ   37

§ 9. [Operations necessary to adequate publicity of Ordinances
continued:] 5. Distribution   38

§ 10. [Operations necessary to adequate publicity of Ordinances
continued:] 6. Public recitation   39

§ 11. II. Second subject-matter of notificative Operations—
Transgressions, viz. of men in power. Difficulties as to
the giving publicity to them—how obviated   41

§ 12. Continuation. Notificative operations applicable to such
transgressions   44

§ 13. III. Third subject-matter of notificative operations,
Suffrages: viz. of the members of the community
considered as members of the Public Opinion Tribunal.
Operations applicable to them: 1. Extraction.
2. Registration. 3. Multiplication.
4. Transmission and Diffusion or Circulation. Sole
adequate instrument, a Newspaper   44

§ 14. Extent of circulation—in the case of a Newspaper,
circumstances on which it depends:—1. Constancy.
2. Frequency. 3. Variety. 4. Cheapness. 5. Impartiality
and candour. 6. Moderation   46

§ 15. Plan for the conducting of a Newspaper at Tripoli—
Topics under which matter may be inserted   50

§ 16. Literary capital requisite antecedently to commencement   52

§ 17. How to maximize the usefulness of this instrument of
publicity and public instruction   53

§ 18. Public Opinion Tribunal—Parallel between this unofficial
[and] the official Judicatories   54

  § 1. *A Judicatory: its attributes*   54

  § 2. *Attributes belonging to this unofficial Judicatory—
  I. Members*   56

  § 3. *II. Functions or Operations of the Supreme
  Unofficial compared with those of the Official
  Judicatories*   60

  § 4. *III. Power—comparison as to*   64

CONTENTS

CONSTITUTIONAL SECURITIES OF THE TRIPOLITAN NATION: OR
SECURITIES, GIVEN BY THE SOVEREIGN, TO THE PEOPLE OF
TRIPOLI AND FEZZAN, AGAINST ABUSE OF POWER, NOW AND
FOR EVER   74

Exordium   74

The Sovereign of Tripoli to the People. Address I:
Proclamation   74
The Sovereign of Tripoli to the People. Address II:
Acknowledgement of Rights   76

Generals   79

I. Securities in favour of the Nation considered in the
aggregate   79
I. *Security against vexation on account of religion*   79
II. *Security against National Gagging: or Security for appeal
to Public Opinion and the power of the law on the conduct
of all persons whatsoever: functionaries as well as non-
functionaries*   80
III. *Security against National Defencelessness*   83
II. Securities in favour of individuals   84

Details   85

[I. Securities in detail in favour of the Nation]   85
II. *National Gagging*   85
III. *National disarmament and debilitation*   87
II. Securities in detail in favour of individuals   88

IV. *Security against secret confinement: for the protection of
the persons of individuals against oppression, by persons
in authority, without or even with the knowledge of the
Sovereign*   88
V. *Security against injurious banishment*   90
VI. *[Security] against secret and unlawful homicide*   92
[VII. *Security against Mysterious Disappearance*]   94
VIII. *Security against misuse of private writings: or Security for
the writings or other documents of individuals against
wanton or oppressive seizure, destruction, damnification
or inspection by persons in authority*   96
IX. *Security against Official depredation*   97
X. *Securities against Official Oppression at large*   99
XI. *[Security against] Extortion of personal service*   100

CONTENTS

PRELIMINARY EXPLANATIONS CONTINUED   103

§ 19. Means of obtaining the requisite Concession—probability
of success, on what it depends   103

§ 1. *Concession—what the chance in favour of it*   103
§ 2. *Means of obtainment. Precautions to be taken. Cautions
observed*   105
§ 3. *Persuasives for the Pacha's concurrence in the
concession*   109

PRELIMINARY EXPLANATIONS
Novus Ordo of 24 October 1822   113

PRELIMINARY EXPLANATIONS: OR GENERAL AND PRELIMINARY
OBSERVATIONS, SHEWING THE PLAN AND MEANS OF EXECUTION
OF THE HERE PROPOSED SYSTEM OF SECURITIES AGAINST
MISRULE   115

§ 1. Misrule, its shapes   115
§ 2. Misrule—its causes   120
§ 3. Sole remedy, Public Opinion   120
§ 4. Measure of its force, degree of notoriety   121
§ 5. Cause of influence: 1. Fear of *ultimate* obstruction   122
§ 6. 2. Fear of inferior sufferings   124
§ 7. Objection answered—irregular the judgments of Public
Opinion Tribunal   124
§ 8. Instrument of operation—Notification—Means of it—
Concession   125
§ 9. Subjects of notification   125
§ 10. Instruments of notification   125
§ 11. Notification—places and mode. Circumstances on which
its efficiency depends   126
§ 12. Institutions for notification proposed—Newspapers,
Letter-Post   129
§ 13. Recourse to penal law here necessary   132
§ 14. Collateral use of the here proposed arrangements—
matter for penal Code   134
§ 15. Slaves—can any of these securities be made to extend to
them?   134
§ 16. Concession—what the chance in favour of it   135
§ 17. Concession—chance of its answering the purpose   138

CONTENTS

LETTERS TO JOHN QUINCY ADAMS   143

JEREMY BENTHAM TO JOHN QUINCY ADAMS FOR TRIPOLI   145

HASSUNA D'GHIES, AMBASSADOR FROM THE SOVEREIGN OF
TRIPOLI, AT THE COURT OF LONDON, TO THE HONOURABLE
[JOHN] QUINCY ADAMS, SECRETARY OF STATE TO THE ANGLO-
AMERICAN UNITED STATES   153

§ 1. State of the reigning family, and of mine which is allied to
it   155
§ 2. Plan of operation, independently of any support from the
Executive of the United States   161
§ 3. Weakness of Government—Facility afforded by it   166
§ 4. Extension of the plan to the other States—its use and
facility   167
§ 5. Assistance from U.S. Why and what desired   170
§ 6. Secrecy necessary—why—means of securing it   173
§ 7. United States—their expected inducements for
concurrence   174
§ 8. Preliminary steps proposed to be taken by the U.S.
Executive in case of concurrence   177

WRITINGS FOR GREECE

GREECE: PRINCIPLES OF LEGISLATION   181

§ 1. Self-regard—its predominance universal and necessary   183
§ 2. Counter-assurance—its universality   185
§ 3. Self-sacrifice—how far exemplified   185
§ 4. Sinister sacrifice—its modes   186

BENTHAM TO GREEK LEGISLATORS   191

OBSERVATIONS BY AN ENGLISHMAN   207

I. *Apt arrangements inserted in the Spanish
Constitution, as likewise in the Grecian*   218
[II.] *In the Grecian Constitution, Articles in which features
of supposed inaptitude have been observed*   219
[III.] *Unapt arrangements inserted in the Spanish
Constitution, and not in the Grecian*   252

CONSTITUTIONAL CODE: GREECE   257

§ 1. Proper end of government, what   259
§ 2. Competent judges of what is most conducive to that end,
who: viz. all or greatest number   259

CONTENTS

§3. From contributing to the formation of that judgment and
consequent will, shall any and who be excluded? 259
§4. 1. Females 260
§5. 2. Non-Adults 260
§6. 3. Non-readers 262
§7. 4. Mahometans 263
§8. Necessary to maximization of greatest number's
happiness is maximization of the efficiency of ditto's will 264
§9. Means of maximizing efficiency of greatest number's will,
Operation by Delegates: their inducement to operate
towards the proper end 265
§10. Hence two bodies each possessed of supreme power in its
own line: viz. Supreme Constitutive and Supreme
Operative. But the Supreme Operative must be
subordinate to and dependent for its power on the
Supreme Constitutive 267
§11. Of the Supreme Operative the strictness of dependence
on the will of the Supreme Constitutive should be
maximized 268
§12. From the Supreme Operative must be detached the
Supreme Executive: remains above it, the Supreme
Legislative 268
§13. Subordinate proper ends: 1. Expence minimized 270
§14. 2. Aptitude maximized 271
§15. Rules or Maxims of Constitutional Law as to what regards
Official subordination 274

CONSTITUTIONAL CODE 277

Chapter VIII. Of the Prime Minister 279
§5. Term of Service 279
Rationale to Ch. VIII, §5 279

INDEX OF SUBJECTS 287

INDEX OF NAMES 322

SYMBOLS AND ABBREVIATIONS

Symbols

		Space left in manuscript.
[to]	Word(s) editorially supplied.
⟨. . .⟩	Word(s) torn away.
⟨so⟩	Conjectural restoration of mutilated word.
[?]	Reading doubtful.
[. . . ?]	Word(s) proved illegible.

Abbreviations

Apart from standard abbreviations the following should be noted:

Bowring	*The Works of Jeremy Bentham*, published under the superintendence of . . . John Bowring, 11 vols., Edinburgh, 1843.
UC	Bentham papers in the Library of University College London. Roman numerals refer to boxes in which the papers are placed, arabic to the leaves within each box.
BL Add. MS	British Library Additional Manuscript.
PRO FO	Public Record Office, Foreign Office Papers.
CW	This edition of *The Collected Works of Jeremy Bentham*.
MS alt.	Alternative manuscript reading, usually interlinear or marginal.

EDITORIAL INTRODUCTION

Towards the end of April 1822, having had his offer to draw up a code of law accepted by the Portuguese Cortes,[1] Bentham embarked on what was to prove the major endeavour of the last decade of his life, the drafting of *Constitutional Code*.[2] His first priority, occupying him until the end of August 1822, was to compose a fairly general essay expounding the principles of government and administration on which the code would be based.[3] But for several months thereafter, to the beginning of March 1823, Bentham turned his attention away from the code itself to the writings presented here, a series of essays in which he attempted to apply the principles of constitutional law he had been developing in the spring and summer of 1822 to the particular circumstances of Tripoli and Greece. These essays are therefore related both thematically and chronologically. Bentham himself did not publish any of this material, and only a version of 'Securities against Misrule' has appeared subsequently in print. Nevertheless much of the manuscript material on which this volume is exclusively based is in a reasonably complete condition, and each essay is, with minor exceptions, continuous and coherent within itself.

HISTORY OF THE ESSAYS

WRITINGS FOR TRIPOLI

Bentham's interest in Tripoli resulted from his contact and friendship with Hassuna D'Ghies, about thirty-one years of age, a member of a leading Tripolitan family, and carrying diplomatic credentials from the Pasha of Tripoli,[4] but who the British government refused to

---

[1] Bentham's letter offering to draw up penal, civil and constitutional codes, sent on 7 November 1821, was presented on 26 November to the Portuguese Cortes, which resolved to accept his offer. Bentham received their reply, informing him of their decision, on 22 April 1822: see Bowring, iv. 575–6 and Journal of John Flowerdew Colls, 1821–5, BL Add. MS 33,563, fo. 100. Colls (1801–78) was Bentham's amanuensis from 1816 until 1829.

[2] See *Constitutional Code*, vol. I, ed. F. Rosen and J.H. Burns, Oxford, 1983 (*CW*).

[3] See *First Principles preparatory to Constitutional Code*, ed. P. Schofield, Oxford, 1989 (*CW*).

[4] A translation made by D'Ghies of a letter from the Pasha of Tripoli to George IV (1762–1830), King of Great Britain and Ireland from 1820, dated 18 November 1821, announcing his appointment as Tripolitan Ambassador is at UC xxiv. 519. For the Karamanli dynasty, which had ruled Tripoli since 1711, see the family tree, p. xx below.

recognize in any official capacity.[1] D'Ghies had left Tripoli in about 1815[2] and, having resided for several years in France, mainly in Marseilles, had come to England in June 1821 with the hope of engaging the help of the British government in liquidating a debt, amounting to 40,000 piastres, run up between 1804 and 1810, which he claimed was owed to his father, Mohammed D'Ghies, by a former Spanish Consul to Tripoli, Don Gerardo José de Souza.[3] A treaty between Spain and Tripoli, in settlement of this and other debts, had been negotiated in 1813 by Sir William A'Court (1779–1860), later first Baron Heytesbury, British Envoy Extraordinary to the Barbary states. The government however, at the end of September or beginning of October 1822, decided that D'Ghies' claim was spurious: even if the sum demanded had ever been owed, of which there was considerable doubt, the treaty had been acknowledged by all parties as a final settlement.[4] Though there is no evidence that Bentham took any active role in these dealings, or that he even knew about the affair, D'Ghies in the meantime had become a regular visitor of Bentham.

D'Ghies appears to have procured an introduction to Bentham through James Scarlett.[5] Already familiar with Scarlett, he had dedicated his pamphlet on the abolition of negro slavery to him. Scarlett perhaps noticed the complimentary references it contained to the second Paris edition of *Traités de législation civile et pénale*,[6] and therefore encouraged D'Ghies to contact Bentham. Whatever the circumstances, Bentham and D'Ghies appear to have met for the first time at the beginning of July 1822. The earliest extant letter between

[1] See Earl Bathurst to the Pasha of Tripoli, 4 June 1822, PRO FO 8/8, fos. 25–6. Foreign relations with the Barbary states were dealt with by the Secretary of State for War and Colonies, an office held between 1812 and 1827 by Henry, third Earl Bathurst (1762–1834). It is unclear whether Bentham was aware of, or whether he chose to ignore, D'Ghies' dubious diplomatic status, since he invariably described him as the Tripolitan Ambassador.

[2] See Hassuna D'Ghies, 'A Letter, addressed to James Scarlett, Esq. M.P. and Member of The African Institution, on the Abolition of the Slave Trade. Translated from the French, By Dr. Kelly, Mathematician', London, printed 1822, p. 16n. A printed copy of this pamphlet, inscribed 'J.B.'s Copy. 1822. D'Ghies on the African Institution', is at UC xxiv. 540, and a bound autograph copy in French at UC xxiv. 539.

[3] 'Statement of the claim of The Shereef Sidi Mohammed D'Ghies Addressed to The Earl Bathurst', PRO FO 76/16, fos. 420–31. For D'Ghies' correspondence with the government on this matter see PRO FO 76/16, fos. 399–472.

[4] See in particular William A'Court to Robert Wilmot, 5 May 1822, PRO FO 76/16, fos. 386–7; A'Court to Wilmot, 18 August 1822, PRO FO 76/16, fos. 396–7; Wilmot to Hanmer Warrington, 2 October 1822, PRO FO 8/8, fos. 44–8.

[5] See Bentham to Marc René, Marquis d'Argenson (draft), 2 January 1823, BL Add. MS 33, 545, fos. 609–14. Scarlett (1769–1844), created Baron Abinger in 1835, was at this time a prominent barrister.

[6] See 'Letter on the Abolition of the Slave Trade', pp. 5, 14. *Traités de législation* was a three-volume recension of Bentham's work edited by Pierre Étienne Louis Dumont (1759–1829) and first published in Paris in 1802; the second edition appeared in 1820.

them was sent by D'Ghies on 6 July 1822: he stated that on the day following their first meeting he had received from Bentham a copy of *Codification Proposal* (which Bentham had recently published)[1] and 'the article Government'.[2] In return he was sending a map of Africa and two copies of his letter on the abolition of negro slavery, on which he asked for Bentham's comments:

comme j'ai fait usage de quelques uns de ses [i.e. Bentham's] principes dans une lettre relative à l'abolition de l'esclavage des nègres j'ai cru de mon devoir de lui en offrir deux exemplaires pour voir si l'application en est à propos ou non?[3]

Thereafter they met regularly, Bentham supplying D'Ghies with copies of numerous of his published works.[4] Bentham was captivated by the young Tripolitan. At the beginning of 1823 he informed the Marquis d'Argenson, 'Hassuna is [a] very extraordinary young man: two words will suffice to shew you to what a degree he is so: he is a disciple and adopted son of mine',[5] and told his brother, Samuel, 'You would be as jealous as a Dragon if you knew half the esteem and affection I have for this young man, of whom I have been making a study for these last 5 or 6 months. . . . Experience has given me the most entire confidence in all his facts.'[6] Indeed for several months a large part of Bentham's energies were directed towards the promotion of a scientific expedition to Tripoli and the drawing up and implementation of a scheme of constitutional reform for the country. Bentham was anxious to have his projected codes of law adopted by an established government: for instance he had been prompted to begin work on *Constitutional Code* by the favourable response from the Portuguese Cortes, and a little later he was to look to the new government in Greece to implement this code. He obviously felt that D'Ghies, through his influence in Tripoli, also presented him with just such an opportunity.

---

[1] *Codification Proposal addressed . . . to All Nations Professing Liberal Opinions*, London, 1822 (Bowring, iv. 535–94).

[2] Presumably James Mill's, which had appeared in the Supplement to the fourth edition of the *Encyclopædia Britannica*, 1820.

[3] D'Ghies to Bentham, 6 July 1822, BL Add. MS 33, 545, fos. 572–4. Bentham and D'Ghies seem to have always communicated in French, even though D'Ghies was able to write in English (see D'Ghies to Marc Antoine Jullien de Paris, 24 June 1822, BL Add. MS 15,945, fos. 235–6). D'Ghies' erratic French has, here and elsewhere, been modified.

[4] Meetings, which appear initially to have been weekly but later became less regular though at times more frequent, and other communications are recorded in Bentham's notebook, UC clxxiii. 82–94; Colls' Journal, BL Add. MS 33, 563, fos. 106–17; and at UC xxiv. 546.

[5] Bentham to d'Argenson, 2 January 1823, BL Add. MS 33, 545, fos. 609–14.

[6] Bentham to Samuel Bentham, 16 January 1823, BL Add. MS 33, 545, fos. 615–16.

Account of Tripoli

Soon after coming into contact with D'Ghies, Bentham began to interrogate him on the geographical, historical, social and political circumstances of Tripoli.[1] Bentham's concern was at first as much scientific as political[2]—he planned to send an expedition to Tripoli, with the eventual object of exploring the interior and finding a route to Timbuktu, and hoped the information he collected from D'Ghies would be of use to it. During August 1822, Bentham worked intermittently on material which he entitled 'Travellers for Tripoli'. He was far from completing 'Travellers for Tripoli', and left the manuscripts in a very disorganized state: nevertheless the intended structure of the essay is discernible in the three groups of material which survive. The first deals with the organization of the expedition, the skills and expertise which the explorers would require, and the mode of settling any disputes which might arise among them.[3] The second consists of a catechism which provides the expedition with information on local conditions. Bentham devised a series of questions, finally totalling twenty-four, to which the answers were supplied either by D'Ghies or by the travel books and journals which Bentham had available.[4] The third, which is hardly developed, contains information and advice on travel in the interior of Africa.[5]

---

[1] See the entry for 29 July 1822 in Bentham's notebook, UC clxxiii. 82.

[2] Both interests are reflected in the contents of the earliest manuscript on Tripoli, dated 3 August 1822 and headed 'Information and Projects' (UC xxiv. 546).

[3] UC xxiv. 19–22 (5 August 1822). The MSS are in the form of a letter to D'Ghies.

[4] UC xxiv. 23–7, 31–3, 38, 545 (5, 7, 26, 28–9 August, 19 September 1822). A related fragment discussing the cost of living in Tripoli is at UC cix. 242 (23 August 1822). Many of the questions are composite; question 23 has not been traced. The marginal summary sheet (UC xxiv. 37) contains a list of additional questions, dated 25 September 1822. Further lists are at UC cix. 241 (12 August 1822), xxiv. 36 (12 September 1822 and n.d. October 1822) and xxiv. 39 (20 September 1822). Other manuscript sheets headed 'Tripoli—Information', UC xxiv. 34–5 (3 September 1822), contain questions in the hand of the copyist with answers supplied by John Bowring (1792–1872), who had become acquainted with Bentham in 1820 and established himself as a favourite 'disciple'.

Bentham referred directly to the following works: E. Blaquiere, *Letters from the Mediterranean; containing a civil and political account of Sicily, Tripoly, Tunis, and Malta*, 2 vols., London, 1813; Miss Tully, *Letters written during A Ten Years' Residence at the Court of Tripoli*, 2 vols., London, 1816; John Pinkerton, *Modern Geography. A New Edition*, 2 vols., London, 1817; G.F. Lyon, *A Narrative of Travels in Northern Africa, in the years 1818, 19, and 20*, London, 1821; Paolo Della Cella, *Narrative of an Expedition from Tripoli in Barbary, to the Western frontier of Egypt, in 1817, By the Bey of Tripoli; in letters to Dr. Viviani of Genoa.... Translated from the Italian, By Anthony Aufrere, Esq.*, London, 1822. Copious notes on Lyon's text are at UC xxiv. 549, 547 (18 September 1822).

[5] UC xxiv. 28, 544, 29–30 (27 August 1822). Though in the form of a letter from D'Ghies to Bentham, these MSS are in Bentham's hand.

Bentham's own interest in the exploration of Africa reflected a much wider contemporary interest, and more specifically a desire to reach Timbuktu and trace the source of the Niger. Indeed at the time Bentham was writing, two British expeditions were operating through Tripoli—one to survey the north coast of Africa led by Frederick William Beechey (1796–1856),[1] and the other inland to Bornu led by Walter Oudney (1790–1824), Dixon Denham (1786–1828) and Hugh Clapperton (1788–1827).[2] Using Bowring as intermediary, Bentham even went so far as to approach William John Burchell (1782?–1863), who had undertaken a solitary expedition in South Africa in 1810–15,[3] to see if he would be interested in joining the projected expedition from Tripoli. Burchell declined the invitation,[4] but was happy to provide Bentham with advice on the qualifications he thought appropriate for a traveller in the Barbary states. In particular he recommended that 'before the traveller sets foot in the country' he ought to gain 'a clear notion of the manners and customs of the people among whom he is to travel . . . as far as reading will allow'.[5] It is possible that the receipt of this advice prompted Bentham to compose 'Account of Tripoli' as just such a source of information for the travellers. Much of the information he had collected for 'Travellers for Tripoli' was therefore incorporated into this new essay.

'Account of Tripoli' consists of thirty-four manuscript sheets[6] which have been neatly organized by Bentham and placed in a paper wrapper headed '1822 Octr. Account of Tripoli'. The first sheet in the sequence (UC xxiv. 61) forms a title and contents page: there are slight variations between the section titles on this contents page and those on the text sheets, which have been preferred in the present edition.[7] The bulk of the essay was written at the beginning of October 1822, but seven additional sheets were written at the end of the month and during November.[8] Four of these sheets were added to existing

---

[1] See F.W. Beechey and H.W. Beechey, *Proceedings of the Expedition to explore the Northern Coast of Africa, from Tripoly Eastward; in MDCCCXXI. and MDCCCXXII.*, London, 1828.

[2] See Dixon Denham and Hugh Clapperton, *Narrative of Travels and Discoveries in Northern and Central Africa, in the years 1822, 1823, and 1824*, London, 1826.

[3] He had just published the first volume of his *Travels in the Interior of Southern Africa*, 2 vols., London, 1822–4.

[4] Burchell to Bentham, 16 September 1822, University College London Library, MS. Ogden, 62 (2), fo. 106.

[5] Burchell to Bentham, 2 October 1822, UCL Library, MS. Ogden, 62 (2), fo. 107.

[6] UC xxiv. 61–85, 87–95. Most are headed: 'Tripoli—Account of'. UC xxiv. 86 (12 September and 3 October 1822) contains a few notes but no text. None of the sheets carry marginal summary paragraphs. For Bentham's normal working practice, and the relationship between the text, marginal summaries and marginal summary sheets, see pp. xliii–xlv below.

[7] With the exception of §12, where the text sheets do not carry a main heading.

[8] UC xxiv. 71, 73 and 80 (30 October 1822); xxiv. 72, 87 (1 November 1822); xxiv. 95 (10 November 1822); and xxiv. 94 (19 November 1822).

sections,[1] but the remaining three made up two new sections: UC xxiv. 73 formed '§4* Police in Towns', and xxiv. 94—5 formed the final section 'State of present conditions in life'. The addition of these two sections has necessitated the renumbering of the sections in the text.[2]

Since 'Account of Tripoli' contains numerous dynastic references, the following simplified Karamanli family tree may be of help in elucidating the text. Figures in brackets indicate the dates of reigns; between 1793 and 1795 the Pashalik was usurped by Ali Burghol.

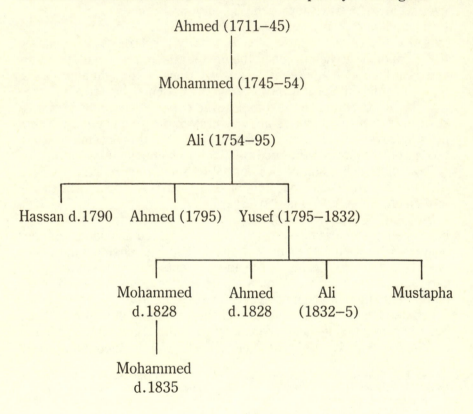

Securities against Misrule

While questioning D'Ghies about conditions in Tripoli, and drawing up plans for a scientific expedition, Bentham was also thinking about the possibility of constitutional reform. The major problem he identified

---

[1] Bentham appended UC xxiv. 71—2, 80 and 87 to §§4, 6 and 7 respectively.
[2] Bentham's §§1—4, 4*, 5—11 have been renumbered 1—12 respectively.

was the political instability resulting from the arbitrary nature of the Pasha's power and the absence of a fixed succession to the throne. He advocated the introduction of constitutional government, thereby providing some security for both the ruling family and the population as a whole. To this end he recommended the establishment of a representative assembly and of safeguards for the people against the abuse of government power, safeguards which he termed securities against misrule and which he hoped the Pasha would sanction by the issue of a constitutional charter. Bentham gave himself the task of drawing up a constitutional charter, but, as he told D'Ghies, only on condition that there existed some hope of seeing it adopted—he wanted an assurance that the Pasha would either issue such a charter on his own authority, or present it for consideration to a representative assembly which he would convoke. Otherwise he was not prepared to waste time and effort on the enterprise.[1] Consequently his interest was at first sporadic.[2] During the course of August 1822, he drew up two Addresses which he intended the Pasha to proclaim to the people: the first announced the convening of a representative assembly,[3] and the second the granting of a constitutional charter.[4] Bentham then drafted a short outline of the provisions for the projected charter.[5] However he must eventually have been convinced that his efforts would be worthwhile, for he began to work in earnest on the constitutional charter for Tripoli in the middle of September, and then devoted much of the next three months to it.[6]

'Securities against Misrule',[7] as it developed, was composed of two main parts: the first, 'Preliminary Explanations', forming a rationale to the provisions of the constitutional charter; and the second, 'Constitutional Securities', consisting of the constitutional charter itself, and introduced by the two Addresses of the sovereign. It should be

---

[1] UC xxiv. 43: see p. xxviii below.

[2] Indeed for much of August Bentham concentrated on 'Constitutional Code Rationale' (see *First Principles* (*CW*), pp. 227–331).

[3] UC xxiv. 1–8 (4–5 August 1822). A partial fair copy is at UC xxiv. 9 (28–9 January 1823) and an additional fragment at xxiv. 10 (29 January 1823). These sheets (with the exception of UC xxiv. 10) are headed 'Bey of Tripoli—Proclamation': rather than 'Bey', Bentham should have said 'Pasha' or 'Bashaw', as he did in the corrected heading to UC xxiv. 7. For the use of the titles 'Pasha' and 'Bey' see 'Account of Tripoli', §2, pp. 4–5 below.

[4] UC xxiv. 12–14 (18 August 1822). A fair copy is at UC xxiv. 15–17 (20 August 1822). For the Addresses see 'Securities against Misrule', pp. 74–8 below.

[5] UC xxiv. 313, 315–16, 324, 347 (20–1 August 1822). These MSS were incorporated into the final, substantially expanded version of the charter.

[6] Apart from the nineteen sheets written in August 1822 and the two in January 1823 mentioned above, the remainder were written between 20 September and 24 December 1822.

[7] The title 'Securities against Misrule' first appears at UC xxiv. 324 (20 August 1822): it appears in Bentham's notebook on 23 August 1822 (UC clxxiii. 84). Other MSS written on or before 20 August 1822 are usually headed 'Tripoli—Acknowledgement of Rights'.

noted that the sequence in which the material was written does not correspond with the logical order of the essay. As noted above, Bentham began with the two Addresses and a short outline of the securities in general (August 1822). He then proceeded to fill out the securities in detail and write the material for a first draft of 'Preliminary Explanations' (September–October 1822). Finally he composed the material for a second draft of 'Preliminary Explanations' (November–December 1822). There are 277 manuscript sheets of text relating to this essay,[1] and in addition twenty-one marginal summary sheets in the hand of Bentham's secretary, John Colls.[2] These correspond with the marginal summaries on seventy-three sheets of text,[3] while there are a further 142 sheets of marginalized text, but for which the marginal summary sheets either were never copied or have not survived.[4] The remaining text sheets have not been marginalized. There are also four sheets which contain plans and lists of contents.[5]

The bulk of the material for 'Securities against Misrule' was written for 'Preliminary Explanations'. Of the two drafts, the second, being Bentham's more mature consideration of the subject, has been preferred for the text, but as the first is not without interest, it is reproduced as a supplement.[6] Plans for both drafts are at UC xxiv. 191: the first is dated 24 October 1822, the second 14 November 1822, and both are headed 'Novus Ordo'.[7] On both plans, section titles are followed by a sequence of numbers which correspond to marginal paragraphs. As in the case of 'Supreme Operative',[8] Bentham would have numbered the relevant marginal paragraphs on the marginal summary sheets in one continuous sequence. By collating the marginal summary paragraphs on the marginal summary sheets with the original marginal summary paragraphs on the text sheets, it would have been possible to locate with certainty the appropriate text. Unfortunately, since none of the relevant marginal summary sheets have survived, it has not proved possible to match the text material with the corresponding marginal summary numbers, and thus with the section headings on the plan. Text has therefore

---

[1] UC xxiv. 1–10, 12–18, 96–104, 104A, 105–89, 215–377; xxxiv. 160v; xli. 179v.

[2] UC xxiv. 194–214.

[3] UC xxiv. 145–6, 234–8, 240–70, 313–44, 347–9.

[4] UC xxiv. 18, 96–7, 99, 101–4, 104A, 105, 109–13, 135–6, 142–4, 147–65, 173–5, 177–85, 189, 215–18, 220–7, 229–33, 239, 271–82, 284–312, 345–6, 350–77; xli. 179v.

[5] UC xxiv. 190–3.

[6] The MSS for the earlier draft usually carry the symbol '2°'; those for the later draft '3°'.

[7] A fair copy of the later plan, with emendations and an addition in Bentham's hand, is at UC xxiv. 193 (20 November 1822). A fair copy of other material from UC xxiv. 191, namely a small supplementary plan and an Addenda headed 'Employments for Capital whether in single or associated hands', is at UC xxiv. 192 (14 November 1822).

[8] See *First Principles* (*CW*), Editorial Introduction, p. xxx.

been allocated to the appropriate section by comparing the sense of the text with the heading, and less precisely by comparing the totals of marginal summary paragraphs on the text sheet with the marginal summary paragraph numbers on the plan.[1] By these means it has been possible to identify most of the material indicated on the respective plans.

To deal first with the earlier draft of 'Preliminary Explanations' and the plan of 24 October 1822, which divides the material into seventeen sections. The titles and section numbers used in the text are all taken from the plan. The relevant text material has been identified with the exception of that for §§ 2 and 8,[2] and part of that for §§ 1, 11 and 14–16 (these omissions seem relatively minor). Though no material has been indicated for § 17, it seems clear that Bentham went on to compose the sequence of text at UC xxiv. 350–3 (26 October 1822) with the intention of including it here. It should be noted that the manuscripts for this first draft are in an extremely confused state: this is probably because the plan of 24 October 1822 represents his second attempt to organize this material. The first attempt has partially survived in an incomplete fair copy of twenty manuscript sheets.[3] This copy was double-spaced to leave room for the insertion of a French translation, presumably for D'Ghies' benefit, but the translation appears to have been abandoned on the fourth sheet (UC xxiv. 117). The only material from this copy which has been used in the present text is the first sheet (UC xxiv. 114), which contains a title and two introductory paragraphs. Though there is no direct evidence that Bentham, when drawing up the plan of 24 October 1822, intended to use this particular sheet of manuscript, there is reason to believe that some material should precede that incorporated here into § 1. Firstly, the sense seems to require some sort of introduction; and secondly, the plan indicates the inclusion in § 1 of two sequences of text which have not been identified.

The plan of 14 November 1822 divides the material for the later draft into sixteen sections. The identification of the appropriate text

---

[1] For instance on the plan of 14 November 1822, under § 8, Bentham marked marginal paragraph summaries 48–55 for inclusion: these seem to correspond with marginal paragraph summaries 34–41 at UC xxiv. 284–6. There are however several minor discrepancies in the enumeration at various points.

[2] Some of the material indicated on the plan for use in § 8 (UC xxiv. 309–12) is also indicated for use in § 12, where it seems better placed.

[3] UC xxiv. 114–33 (26–8 September, 1–2 October 1822: UC xxiv. 127 is dated 30 October, but this may be a slip of the pen for September). These sheets form pp. 1–4, 10–16, 24–32: the remaining pages have not been traced. This material was copied from the following MSS: UC xxiv. 115–17 from xxiv. 220–1; xxiv. 118–24 from xxiv. 96–8; xxiv. 125–6 from xxiv. 102; xxiv. 127–33 from xxiv. 309–12. The original MS for UC xxiv. 114 has not been traced.

material has been relatively unproblematical, except in the case of
§§ 1 and 2. It is possible that the material which Bentham intended to
use in § 2, or even to form § 1 in place of that chosen here, is now
missing. Furthermore, no material has been indicated for inclusion in
§ 10 (i.e. § 12 in the present edition). The enumeration of the sections
in the text does not correspond exactly with that on the plan. Firstly,
there are some inconsistencies in Bentham's enumeration (two
sections are numbered 13 and two 14). Secondly, when drawing up
the plan, Bentham seems to have overlooked a sequence of manuscript: two sections have been editorially inserted in order to
incorporate this material.[1] Thirdly, all the material indicated on the
plan for inclusion in the first § 13 is also included, and seems better
placed, in the previous section: the first § 13 is thus redundant and
has been omitted from the text.[2] Therefore the sections on the plan
numbered 1–12, the second 13, and the first and second 14, are in
the text renumbered 1–8, 11–17 respectively. The titles used in the
text have in the main been taken from this plan, as modified by the
addition made by Bentham to the copy at UC xxiv. 193. However the
final two sections of the text are not mentioned on this plan as such:
the titles of § 19 and § 19 Sub§ 2 appear in a small supplementary plan
likewise dated 14 November 1822,[3] and the title of § 19 Sub§ 1
duplicates the title of § 16 on the earlier plan of 24 October 1822. The
section and sub-section titles taken from the various plans at UC xxiv.
191 are therefore as follows: §§ 1–8, 11–17, 19, and § 19 Sub §§ 1–2.
Of the remaining section titles, those for §§ 9–10 are collated from the
title to § 7 on the plan and headings on the text sheets; those for § 18,
§ 18 Sub§§ 1–4, and § 19 Sub§ 3 from the text sheets. The material for
§ 18 was composed after the plan had been drawn up, but seems
logically to follow the material incorporated in §§ 4–17. Furthermore,
it is evident that, despite being written under the heading of 'Preliminary Explanations', Bentham intended § 19 to follow 'Constitutional Securities'. He noted at the beginning of the section: '☛ N.B.
Before this must come an account of the tutelary arrangements in
detail: viz. that the offensiveness of them to the Monarch may have
been seen.'[4] The section has been placed, in accordance with
Bentham's wishes, at the end of the essay: the heading 'Preliminary
Explanations Continued' has been added for the sake of clarity.

    The second part of the essay, 'Constitutional Securities', contains

---

[1] §§ 9 and 10 in the present edition.
[2] It is entitled: 'Circumstances etc. continued. 5. Impartiality. 6. Moderation.'
[3] The material for § 19 was originally written for the first draft, but Bentham did not include it
on the plan of 24 October 1822, and afterwards decided to use it in the second draft.
[4] UC xxiv. 359 (16 October 1822).

the Addresses of the sovereign and the constitutional charter. In the first place, the charter is divided into 'Generals' and 'Details',[1] and in turn each of these is divided into those securities applicable to the nation and those applicable to individuals. Most of the titles and headings have been taken from the text sheets, but some, indicated by square brackets, have been editorially supplied for the sake of clarity and consistency. A fairly detailed summary of the contents of a large part of this material is at UC xxiv. 190 (8 October 1822), and a list of headings at UC xxiv. 194 (22 September 1822). The internal organization of the shorter sections on 'Generals' and 'Securities in detail in favour of the Nation' has been determined by Bentham's pagination and enumeration of the provisions. The lengthier section on 'Securities in detail in favour of individuals' is however less clearly organized. There are discrepancies between the various schemes of enumeration, namely between those found in the main headings and the marginal sub-headings on the text sheets, on the appropriate marginal summary sheets, and on the lists of contents. The most complete and consistent scheme, comparing it with the text sheets and the marginal summary sheets, is that listed at UC xxiv. 194, which accordingly has been adopted.[2] Moreover, Bentham inserted at the top of this list a section entitled 'Exordium'. This heading is found in the margin of the fair copy of the second Address of the sovereign of Tripoli to the people.[3] Bentham seems to have intended that the second Address should form an introduction to the provisions of the constitutional charter, and clearly the second Address should be preceded by the first. Both Addresses have therefore been placed at the beginning of 'Constitutional Securities'.

No version of 'Securities against Misrule' was published by Bentham himself, but a version did appear in Bowring's edition of Bentham's *Works*.[4] This was produced without reference either to

---

[1] For Bentham's explanation of this division see 'Securities against Misrule', p. 79n below.

[2] Bentham usually used both section numbers and Roman numerals to enumerate the headings in 'Securities in detail in favour of the Nation': as the former merely duplicate the latter, and are not used consistently in the other parts of 'Constitutional Securities', they have been suppressed. However, given that the headings in the 'Details' material often carry section numbers, and the 'Generals' material is organized into sixteen articles, it is possible that had Bentham himself printed or published the constitutional charter, he would have organized it into sections and articles, a layout resembling that eventually adopted for *Constitutional Code*.

[3] UC xxiv. 15–17.

[4] See Bowring, viii. 555–600. The title given to this version is 'Securities against Misrule, adapted to a Mahommedan State, and prepared with particular reference to Tripoli in Barbary': no such title appears in the surviving MSS. The following MSS are used in Bowring: Ch. I, §I: UC xxiv. 215–18; §II: xxiv. 219–22 (one sentence from an unidentified source has been inserted in the material from xxiv. 221); §III: xxiv. 223–30; Ch. II, §I: xxiv. 231–2, 149–54, 233; §II: xxiv. 234–9; §III: xxiv. 240–7; §IV: xxiv. 248–53; §V: xxiv. 254–70; Ch. III, §I: xxiv. 271–5; §II: xxiv. 275–82, 100, 283; §III: xxiv. 284–7; §IV: xxiv. 288–9, 99, 290; §V:

Bentham's division of the essay into 'Preliminary Explanations' and 'Constitutional Securities', to the division of the latter into 'Generals' and 'Details', or to the fact that there are two separate drafts of 'Preliminary Explanations', nor does it incorporate the Addresses from the sovereign to the people. Additionally there are more detailed problems with the text arising from mistranscription, the choice of alternative readings and the liberal addition of punctuation. Unusually for the Bowring edition, the editor is not identified. There are two pieces of evidence, neither of them very conclusive, which suggest that Bowring himself may have been responsible, or at least had some involvement. First, four sheets of text have been paginated 242–5 respectively in Bowring's hand.[1] If Bowring did edit the essay, he may have added these page numbers while preparing it for the press, though why only four sheets should bear this pagination is unclear. On the other hand, Bowring may have added them at the time, or soon after, the sheets were written. Second, a manuscript containing the two Addresses of the sovereign of Tripoli was found amongst Bowring's papers after his death, and published in his *Autobiographical Recollections*.[2] It is possible Bowring had them copied for inclusion in the *Works*, though in the end they were not used.

Letters from Jeremy Bentham and Hassuna D'Ghies to John Quincy Adams

Bentham appreciated that constitutional reform in Tripoli would depend not only on the substance of the provisions outlined in the charter, but also upon a practical plan for introducing it. This was a problem which Bentham and D'Ghies spent a great deal of time examining. Bentham's earliest hopes were of course centred on the

---

xxiv. 291–5; §VI: xxiv. 296–312 (part of a sentence from an unidentified source has been added to the beginning of the material from xxiv. 310); Ch. IV, Part I, §I: xxiv. 313–14; §II: xxiv. 315–19; §III: xxiv. 316, 320–1; Part II, §I: xxiv. 322–3; §II: xxiv. 324–8; §III: xxiv. 329–31; §IV: xxiv. 332–5; §V: xxiv. 336–8; §VI: xxiv. 339–41; §VII: xxiv. 342–6; §VIII: xxiv. 347–9; Ch. V, §I: xxiv. 350–3; §II: xxiv. 354–61; §III: xxiv. 362–73, 377, 373, 377, 374–6, 168–9 (a paragraph from an unidentified source has been added between xxiv. 376 and 168).

[1] UC xxiv. 374–7 (15 November 1822).

[2] See *Autobiographical Recollections of Sir John Bowring. With a brief memoir by Lewin B. Bowring*, London, 1877, pp. 323–6. In a short preface, Bowring recorded that D'Ghies had read *Traités de législation*, and made Arabic notes on the text. He continued: '"To what extent might reform be introduced in Tripoli," he [D'Ghies] asked, "without giving umbrage to the Holy Alliance? I want to introduce a more liberal system. It must be represented to the monarch as a guarantee for his personal safety—to the people it would recommend itself. Adopted in Tripoli, it would spread to Tunis, and so fly along the coast."'

summoning of a representative assembly, with the co-operation of the Pasha. In this event, electoral districts would need to be created and the franchise defined. Once the assembly had met, it would draw up a constitutional code, or rather adopt the one which Bentham was drafting. Bentham revealed his thoughts in a memorandum written for D'Ghies in the middle of August 1822, and headed 'J.B. à H.D'G. Avis':[1]

Fin proposée, augmentation de la félicité des habitans, par amélioration du gouvernement, de l'état de Tripoli.

Qui veut la fin, veut les moyens: ainsi dit un proverb[e] Français.

Premier des moyens nécessaires. Proclamation du Bey[2] à lire par lui au peuple dans la grande Mosquée.[3] Voilà sur quoi nous sommes déjà d'ac[c]ord.

Mais cette Proclamation sera de nul effet sans un corps de loix dont elle annonce la confection: lequel corps selon l'annonce doit commencer par le Code Constitution[n]el, Code, dont la fonction est de déterminer les classes, et par là les individus, par l'autorité desquels les autres Codes doivent être établis.

Contenu dans cette Proclamation est un engagement, de faire assembler un Corps Constituant, soit Corps représentatif de tout le peuple.

Pour avoir un pareil corps régulièrement et complettement constitué, un préliminaire indispensable seroit une division complette de tout le territoire en districts sur un plan tout-compréhensif expressément dirigé à ce même objet: y ajouté en même tems dénombrement des habitans et des habitations appartenans à chaque district: les habitans étant désignés par la mention de leurs habitations respectives, dans le cas où ils en ont de *fixes*.

De plus, ces *Districts*, il seroit apparem[m]ent nécessaire de les sous-diviser en *Sub-Districts*.

Mais cette opération demanderoit des moyens que présentement on n'a pas: et qu'on ne pourroit pas avoir peut-être que d'ici en quelques années: ainsi il faut songer à un moyen substitué pour la remplacer.

Les portions de terrain qui se rapportent aux Tribunaux de première instance ne pourroient-[elles] pas servir à marquer les Districts?

Les Mosquées hors des grandes villes au moins, ne pourroient-elles pas servir à marquer les Sub-Districts?

Une liste, telle quelle, des Districts actuels c'est ce qu'on ne peut manquer d'avoir déjà, ne fût-ce que pour faire lever les troupes, et ordonner la comparution des Milices.

Le Président du Tribunal ou à son defaut le plus ancien après lui ne

---

[1] See the draft at UC xxiv. 40–4, 46, 44–5 (14–15 August 1822). A further sequence on the topic of 'Mines' is at UC xxiv. 47–9 (14 August 1822). Several minor corrections have been made to Bentham's spelling, and accents added where appropriate.

[2] Bentham should have said 'Pasha': see p. xxi above.

[3] i.e. the first Address of the sovereign to the people which Bentham had drafted on 4–5 August 1822: see 'Securities against Misrule', pp. 74–6 below.

pourroit-il pas faire les fonctions de Président de l'Assemblée Électorale du District?

En supposant les Districts si étendus que la dépense qu'il faudroit, en tems et argent ensemble, pour se transporter au siège du Tribunal seroit trop forte, ne pourroit-on pas recueillir les suffrages dans chacune des Mosquées y comprises?

Le tout ensemble des portions de territoire soumises à l'autorité de ces mêmes Tribunaux de première instance composeroit-il le total du territoire de l'état? Si oui, voilà ce qu'il vous faut: si non, au cas que d'abord l'on s'abstient de demander des représentans aux parties du royaume non-comprises, apparemment le mal sensible ne sera pas grand: la population non représentée suivra d'abord, comme ici en Angleterre, l'impulsion donnée par les parties représentées. Voilà pour le commencement et quand l'état des choses s'y trouverait propre on pourroit remplir les lacunes.

Qualité soit condition pour être élu ne pourroit-elle pas être la possession des deux arts lit[t]éraires de première nécessité, l'art de lire, et celle d'écrire? Dans quelques années la réunion de ces mêmes talens pourroit être exigée pour constituer les qualités pour élire, c'est à dire pour rendre suffrage.

Le corps représentatif désiré, est (disons) assemblé: que doit-il faire? Ou rien du tout ou bien un Code Constitution[n]el—une Constitution par écrit. Sans doute que sans faire autre chose il pourroit, comme on a dit en Français *consentir l'impôt*. Mais ce n'est pas pour cela que vous désirez avoir un Corps représentatif: Non: c'est pour une autre chose, pour avoir laquelle, comme vous m'avez dit, vous consentiriez volontiers à augmenter l'impôt: mais s'il ne s'agissoit que de consentir l'impôt, tout ce que vous gagnerez en établissant ou convoquant cette assemblée seroit une augmentation d'impôt: et c'est ce que, si vous en avez l'envie, et que cela vous contente vous pourriez avoir à moindre fraix.

Eh bien! ce Code il n'existe pas: s'il existe jamais il faut que ce soit par nous deux. C'est précisément l'ouvrage dont je m'occupe à présent, autant qu'un tel Code pourroit être fait pour tous les pays du monde en général, sans être fait pour aucun en particulier. Mais selon le plan sur lequel je travaille, il faut pour accompaniment à ce Code un corps de *raisons*, ce qui s'appelle *un rationale*. Or ce rationale occupera peut-être dix fois l'espace du texte: et naturellement du tems à proportion. Ce que je pourrois faire pour vous en particulier c'est de construire un projet de Code, qui, pour le présent, seroit comme les Codes ordinaires dépourvu de raisons alignées.

Mais pour m'engager à un tel travail en retardant à proportion celui dont je m'occupe à présent, il me faudrait deux conditions: 1. l'assurance de vous avoir toujours à mes côtés, sans quoi tout ce que [je] pourrois faire n'aboutiroit à rien; 2. l'assurance que le projet de Code que nous aurons préparé sera présenté à l'Assemblée par le Bey, ou bien établi par sa propre autorité.

La première chose donc à faire pour vous à ce sujet est de faire une visite à Tripoli pour obtenir cette assurance.

Assuming D'Ghies was willing to go to Tripoli to seek these assurances, taking with him the scientific travellers if they had been selected, there were certain preparations which Bentham advised him to make. He should visit Hazelwood School,[1] obtain information on a new boring machine, and make translations into Arabic of certain written works:

1. Faire la traduction d'une Déclaration de Droits, s'il est à propos d'en faire donner une. But de ce manifeste, fournir des sûretés aux sujets contre l'abus du pouvoir de la part du gouvernement.
   2. Faire la traduction d'un petit écrit que l'on prépare pour fournir une idée des bases principales d'un bon Code constitution[n]el.
   3. Idem pour le Code Pénal.
   4. Idem pour le Code Civil.[2]
   5. Faire en entier ou en abrégé la traduction de ce qui se trouve sur le Panoptique, dans le premier ouvrage de Dumont.[3]
   6. Dans le même tems, le bien-aimé du Prophète tâchera de faire faire quelque[s] desseins, pour faciliter la conception de cette invention, en fait d'architecture, considérée particulièrement dans son application aux prisons.
   Un autre ouvrage qui a été proposé, c'est un recueil, ayant pour objet de présenter les principaux abus qui ont eu lieu en Angleterre et autre part, et de la manière dont ils ont été successivement abolis. Absolument pris, cet ouvrage seroit utile: mais lorsqu'on en fait comparaison, d'un côté avec la difficulté de la matière, et la quantité de tems nécessaire, et de l'autre avec d'autres ouvrages dont l'utilité est plus déterminée et plus immédiate, peut-être qu'une telle entreprise ne paroîtra pas être d'accord avec les règles de bonne économie. Pour composer un ouvrage qui soit décidément utile en ce genre, il faudroit une immense lecture d'ouvrages qui ne se trouvent qu'en Anglois, avec une connoissance profonde et détaillée de la Constitution Angloise: autrement, à chaque pas on courroit risque de donner comme réforme, ce qui n'est qu'abus, sous quelque forme déguisée. La triste vérité est que tous les vices, du plus mauvais gouvernement, sont plus profondément enracinés dans le gouvernement Anglois que dans aucun autre.

Once D'Ghies had arrived in Tripoli, he was to gather information on a whole range of subjects: on government officials and their functions, on judicial tribunals and the officials attached to them, on judicial procedure, on persons held in detention, on the Imams and their respective mosques, on the military, on hospitals and universities, on coal mines (if there were any), and on the population of the country.

---

[1] Cf. 'Securities against Misrule', § 16, p. 52 below; 'Bentham to Adams', p. 150 below.
[2] This work was possibly 'First Lines of a Proposed Code of Law for every nation compleat and rationalized', which Bentham had written in the spring of 1821. It was subsequently published, as part of *Constitutional Code*, in Bowring, ix. 8–41; the MSS are at UC xxxvi. 1–74, xxxvii. 4–70 and clx. 148–236.
[3] See *Traités de législation*, iii. 201–72.

As the months passed by, the hope that constitutional reform could be effected with the agreement of the Pasha seems to have receded, for a more aggressive plan came to be canvassed. On 23 December 1822, Bentham received a memorandum from D'Ghies outlining a scheme for armed intervention in Tripoli:[1] this seems to have arisen out of discussions between Bentham, D'Ghies and Colonel Robert Torrens (1780–1864), soldier and political economist.[2] D'Ghies proposed to raise a force of 1,000 cavalry and infantry, and a loan of £40–50,000. The force would be transported to Malta, there to await instructions from D'Ghies and Torrens who meanwhile would go to Tripoli to make preparations for an invasion. Once a landing-place had been agreed upon, the soldiers would be embarked. Some of the funds would then be used to purchase two brigs to guard the chosen seaport, a steamship to act as a courier, and three transports for use in case of emergency. Bentham responded in a sequence of manuscripts headed 'Tripoli—Enterprize',[3] in which he expressed his doubts concerning the feasibility of the plan. He was sceptical about the possibility of raising and training the soldiers in Britain, as opposed to raising officers to train indigenous troops in Tripoli. He suggested, however, linking the proposed expedition to Tripoli with the Greek struggle for independence against Turkey:

En supposant cette levée de troupes possible, pour la faciliter voici une idée qui me vient en tête. L'engagement doit porter que c'est pour une expédition secrète en faveur des Grecs, et qu'il y aura des avantages pécuniaires dont la recette dépendra du succès. Or pour la cause des Grecs il en résulteroit de l'avantage par la nature de la chose même: car par ce moyen tout secours ultérieur qui sans cela pourroit être fourni par les puissances du Nord de l'Afrique aux Turcs seroit empêché: et outre cela après la réussite on pourroit leur en fournir: et c'est ce que [je] conseillerois, ne fût-ce que pour accomplir plus décidément l'engagement, et se tenir à l'abri de toute reproche de mauvaise foi.

Dans cette supposition, agir de la sorte ne seroit que d'agir comme on a fait déjà sans empêchement et sans donner ombrage effectif à aucune des puissances Européennes: et d'après toute apparence vu la tournure que notre gouvernement a nouvellement pris au sçeu de tout le monde,[4] une telle expédition ne seroit pas vu[e] de mauvais oeil à Malte par notre

---

[1] See UC xxiv. 527–8.

[2] Bentham had introduced D'Ghies to Torrens on 20 December 1822: see Colls' Journal, BL Add. MS 33, 563, fo. 115.

[3] UC xxiv. 54–9 (23 December 1822).

[4] At the Congress of Verona (October–December 1822), Britain had distanced herself from the powers of the Holy Alliance by declaring she would not be a party to any plan to interfere in Spain: meanwhile the new Foreign Secretary, George Canning (1770–1827), had instructed the British representative, Arthur Wellesley (1769–1832), first Duke of Wellington, that Britain would not interfere in the struggle between the Turks and the Greeks.

gouvernement: au moins en supposant que l'affaire se conduit tout douce-
ment, et sans être annoncée dans les papiers publics.

Bentham also doubted whether a loan could be raised, and even if it
were, whether the proposed sum would be sufficient. He felt that the
suggested rate of return, a single payment of 50%, or even 50% per
annum, would not, in the eyes of potential investors, be enough to
justify the risk involved.

Jugez encore une fois, mon cher fils, et demandez à vous-même si avec un
plan en main aussi peu détaillée et articulée que celui que vous m'avez
encore fourni il est dans la nature de l'homme qu'il se trouveroit un seul
individu qui pour la promesse d'un million de nos *sovereigns* en donneroit un
seul?

The scheme was apparently all too vague for Bentham's liking.
Instead he began to draft a plan of his own. This took the form of a
letter from D'Ghies to John Quincy Adams,[1] with a covering letter
from Bentham himself.[2] Bentham explained that D'Ghies would in the
first instance attempt to persuade the Pasha himself to introduce constitutional reform; if this failed, D'Ghies wanted armed support from
the United States for an uprising which he would engineer within Tripoli. Once reform had been effected in Tripoli, it was hoped to extend
it to the whole of the North African coast.

Bentham drafted the covering letter to Adams between 10 and 13
January 1823,[3] and the letter from D'Ghies between 13 January and 2
February 1823. The letter from D'Ghies was not, as he was made to
say, his own; nor had Bentham merely aided him in the expression of
his sentiments.[4] It was in fact composed and corrected by Bentham,
though in places using information with which he had been supplied by
D'Ghies. There are two drafts of the letter from D'Ghies, both of
which are well-ordered and complete. Bentham composed the first
draft on 13–14, 19 and 21 January 1823,[5] and the second draft

---

[1] Adams (1767–1848), United States Secretary of State 1817–24, President 1825–9, had
been in England as Envoy Extraordinary and Minister Plenipotentiary to Great Britain from
1815 to 1817. According to *Memoirs of John Quincy Adams, comprising portions of his diary from
1795 to 1848*, ed. Charles Francis Adams, 12 vols., Philadelphia, 1874–7, iii. 511–65, he first
met Bentham on 29 April 1817, and last saw him on 8 June 1817. Cf. *The Correspondence of
Jeremy Bentham*, vol. ix, ed. S. Conway, Oxford, 1989 (*CW*), pp. 12–19.

[2] See UC xxiv. 11, 378–505, 556.

[3] UC xxiv. 378–90 (UC xxiv. 382 is dated 23 January 1823). A marginal summary sheet is at
UC xxiv. 391 (23 January 1823). A sheet of notes headed 'J.B. to Q.A. for Trip.' is at UC xxiv.
392 (n.d. January 1823): attached to this sheet is a letter from Bowring to Bentham, post-
marked 29 January 1823 but dated 30 January 1823, with information on 'Spanish Settlements in
North Africa'.

[4] See 'D'Ghies to Adams', p. 153 below.

[5] UC xxiv. 407–32, 468–9. The final two sheets were eventually incorporated into the
second draft. Marginal summary sheets are at UC xxiv. 393–6 (19, 21, 23 January 1823).

between 24 January and 2 February 1823.[1] The second draft was then copied, and the copy in turn corrected by Bentham—it contains his additions, deletions and emendations in pencil.[2] Neither the second draft nor the copy can be regarded as the definitive text. On the one hand, parts of the draft have been superseded by Bentham's later alterations to the copy; on the other hand, the copyist made mistakes in transcribing the draft—mistakes which Bentham did not correct upon reading through the copy, but of which it cannot be assumed he therefore approved—and was in the habit of adding much unnecessary and sometimes confusing punctuation. However it seems fair to assume first, that Bentham's text is more authoritative than the copyist's, and second, that Bentham's later text is more authoritative than his earlier. The text therefore has been constructed by collating Bentham's second draft with his corrections to the copy. The copy, with Bentham's alterations, has been checked against the draft. Where the copyist has mistranscribed the draft, or added punctuation which seems inappropriate or superfluous, Bentham's draft is preferred. Where Bentham has corrected the copy, the corrected version is preferred to the draft. On one occasion, the copyist has supplied a word which the sense of the draft seems to require: the addition has been retained.[3]

It seems unlikely that the letters were ever sent to Adams. D'Ghies, presumably writing after Bentham had gone to the trouble of having the letter from D'Ghies to Adams copied, told Bentham, 'puis que vous désirez savoir mon opinion maintenant à l'égard de la lettre pour l'Amérique, je crois qu['elle] n'est pas nécessaire'.[4]

As for the extension of the plan to the other Barbary states, Bentham hoped to engage the help of Mohammed ibn Hamdan Khoja (1772?–1842), a wealthy Algerian merchant and landowner, who had been the Agent of the Dey of Algiers in London.[5] Khoja had been brought to Bentham's attention as early as May 1822, as an entry in his notebook reveals:

The Consul, Khoja, from Algiers is said . . . to be a man of good information, and liberal sentiments, who deplores the state of the public mind in his own

---

[1] UC xxiv. 433–71. Marginal summary sheets are at UC xxiv. 397–406 (26, 28–30 January 1823).

[2] UC xxiv. 474–85, 487–505, 556. The copy of the introduction (UC xxiv. 503–5) was substantially altered by Bentham, and a second copy made incorporating these emendations (UC xxiv. 472–3); similarly UC xxiv. 486 is a copy of UC xxiv. 487, to which Bentham also made substantial alterations.

[3] See 'D'Ghies to Adams', §8, p. 178n below.

[4] D'Ghies to Bentham, n.d., UC xxiv. 521.

[5] See 'Bentham to Adams', pp. 150–2 below.

country, has sent his sons[1] to School in England, and talks of sending for his wife and daughters in order to civilize them. He wears a turban, but ridicules Mahommedanism—speaks English, has been 3 or 4 years in England.[2]

D'Ghies seems to have been responsible for Bentham's introduction to Khoja,[3] and though Bentham told Adams that they met twice,[4] only one meeting is recorded. This took place, with D'Ghies present, on 20 November 1822, not long before Khoja was due to return to Algiers.[5] Khoja was not informed of the plan for armed intervention in Tripoli,[6] but they did, amongst other things, encourage Khoja to send reports from Algiers which Bentham would try to insert in the English press. It appears that the only product of this arrangement was an article which D'Ghies drew up, after having received a letter from Khoja at Marseilles, on his way to Algiers.[7] This was not however the end of the collaboration between D'Ghies and Khoja. After the French invasion of Algiers in 1830, Khoja complained of the maltreatment of the natives by the French in an Arabic manuscript which was translated into French by D'Ghies, entitled *Aperçu historique et statistique sur la Régence d'Alger* and published in Paris in 1833.[8]

Before D'Ghies' departure from England, Bentham gave him some final advice on the means of establishing a constitution in Tripoli.[9] He warned D'Ghies against the machinations of lawyers, who inevitably would be responsible for implementing the new constitution. It was of great importance that the people should recognize their true interest and that government be established on the basis of the greatest happiness of the greatest number, and not the greatest happiness of

---

[1] In 'Bentham to Adams', p. 150 below, Khoja is said to have had only one son.

[2] UC clxxiii. 73. The entry is not in Bentham's hand.

[3] See 'Bentham to Adams', p. 150 below.

[4] Ibid.

[5] Bentham's notebook, UC clxxiii. 87.

[6] See 'Bentham to Adams', p. 151 below; 'D'Ghies to Adams', §8, p. 180 below.

[7] The article is at UC xxiv. 529–33 and has been endorsed by Bentham: 'From Khoja at Marseilles. 1823 Jany. 21. Written by Hassuna D'Ghies, the Tripolitan Ambassador, at the desire of, and on the ground of facts furnished by, Khoja, late Agent of the Dey of Algiers in London, for insertion in an English paper. The Algerines are tyrannized over by about 10,000 Turks. The object is, by flattering the Dey, to engage him to listen to European advice, and seek European assistance for delivering his country from that tyranny, and concurr in establishing a better form of Government. See what can [be] done in this view. This paper may serve as a *Brief* in the lawyer's sense of the word. Names must be carefully kept secret: their lives depend upon it.' The receipt of Khoja's letter to D'Ghies is recorded in Colls' Journal, BL Add. MS 33,563, fo. 117, and mentioned in 'Bentham to Adams', p. 151 below. A fragment on Algiers, in the hand of Colls but with emendations by Bentham, is at UC xxiv. 534 (31 January 1823).

[8] See Hamdan Khodja, *Le miroir: Aperçu historique et statistique sur la Régence d'Alger*, ed. A. Djeghloul, Paris, 1985.

[9] Bentham's draft letter to D'Ghies is at UC xxiv. 511–13 (26 March 1823), and postscript at UC xxiv. 514–16 (27 March 1823). A fair copy was delivered by Richard Doane, Bentham's amanuensis, to D'Ghies on 27 March 1823.

the sovereign and the lawyers. Everything depended upon improving the education of the people, especially on matters of government. To this end, as many boys as possible should be educated in the manner of Hazelwood School, the best books on legislation should be translated into Arabic and printed, and newspapers should be established. Bentham was less optimistic than D'Ghies that the Pasha would be persuaded to introduce reform: 'À peine puis-je entrevoir une très petite probabilité à ce que le grand cheval soit porté de bon gré à se mettre le mords dans la bouche.' Nevertheless the advantages which would result from reform could be pointed out to him: firstly, the security of his family against the dangers which would otherwise ensue on his death from a disputed succession; and secondly, the increase in his personal wealth which would accrue from an increase in capital, itself the consequence of the security given to property. Bentham stressed that before embarking on reform, D'Ghies would need to have a constitution already prepared. People would then know precisely what they were being called upon to support, and the leaders of the reform movement would be more effectually prevented from abusing any temporary powers they might have to exercise, in particular from replacing the previous despotism with one of their own. It seems however that D'Ghies had decided not to employ Bentham's 'Constitutional Securities' for this purpose:

J'ai emploié beaucoup de tems à composer un acte de concession de la part du Maître [i.e. the Pasha] pour faire la fonction de la Charte de Louis 18.[1] Les papiers restent, mais de l'espérance de les voir mis à profit, il [n']ly a que très peu qui reste.

He did hope that the Tripolitan reformers might adopt *Constitutional Code*:

Si vous savez où trouver une autre Constitution qui vous plaît davantage, je n'ai plus rien à dire: si non, j'en aurai une, si je suis en vie, bientôt: beaucoup plus tôt que vous ne serez en état d'en chercher une.

But even this hope proved forlorn. D'Ghies left England in May 1823,[2] more or less on the orders of the British government, who, by the time the matter of the debts owed to Mohammed D'Ghies had been concluded, had come to regard him as an undesirable, and were anxious that he should leave the country. However D'Ghies himself had run up debts, estimated at about £1,000 by Robert Wilmot, the

---

[1] The *Constitutional Charter* of 1814 granted by Louis XVIII (1755–1824), King of France from 1814.
[2] Bentham to Simon Bolivar, 4 June 1823, Archivo Histórico Nacional, Bogotá: Secretaría del Interior y de Relaciones Exteriores, Tomo 159, fo. 313.

Under Secretary of State for War and Colonies, which had to be paid before he could leave. Hanmer Warrington, the Consul in Tripoli, was therefore instructed to secure the remission of an adequate sum of money from D'Ghies' father or the Pasha to enable him to settle with his creditors.[1] This was accordingly effected,[2] and D'Ghies eventually given a passage on a packet to Malta. From Malta he was transferred to Tripoli, where he arrived on 15 June 1823.[3]

Several years later, despite all the plans and promises, Bentham had still heard nothing from D'Ghies. In a draft letter to the Pasha of Egypt, written in March 1828, Bentham reported:

Immediately after his arrival at Tripoli on his return thither he was to have written to me. Since his departure however, I have never heard either from him or of him: except his arrival in Malta in bad health. That one particular excepted, all the enquiries I have made about him (and numerous and anxious have they been) have been fruitless. I have heard in general terms that his family have fallen into misfortunes. He and I had formed [a] plan of improvement in useful knowledge and government in his country. I expended, and as it has turned out wasted, upon that endeavour more months than I can now think of without severe regret.[4]

Yet Bentham did see D'Ghies again. In 1826 D'Ghies became the Pasha's first minister, and attempted to assert Tripoli's independence against the growing influence of the European consuls, the British and French in particular. In 1829 however, the Pasha was forced to dismiss him by Warrington, who believed he was implicated in the murder of the explorer Alexander Gordon Laing (1793–1826) on his mission to discover the source of the Niger by way of Timbuktu.[5] D'Ghies returned to England in the summer of 1831 in order to clear his name,[6] contacted Bentham and sought his advice. Bentham responded, but does not himself seem to have become involved in D'Ghies' campaign.[7] D'Ghies was still in London when Bentham died

[1] Wilmot to Warrington, 2 October 1822, PRO FO 8/8, fos. 44–8.

[2] The negotiations are described in a series of letters from Warrington to Wilmot, 1 December 1822, 2 December 1822, 5 December 1822, PRO FO 76/16, fos. 326–33.

[3] Warrington to Wilmot, 15 June 1823, PRO FO 76/17, fos. 78–9.

[4] UC x. 197.

[5] The case against D'Ghies was presented in the *Quarterly Review*, vol. xlii, no. lxxxiv (March 1830), 450–75.

[6] Correspondence relating to the affair was printed in a diplomatic blue book entitled 'Papers explanatory of the circumstances under which Sidi Hassuna D'Ghies has been accused, by the Bashaw of Tripoli, of having abstracted the papers of the late Major Laing'. For the original correspondence see PRO FO 76/33.

[7] See the memorandum, in the hand of Doane but probably written at the dictation of Bentham, at BL Add. MS 33, 551, fos. 231–5, 237–8 (8 August 1831), headed 'Course recommended by me, Jeremy Bentham, to be taken by the Sherif Hassuna d'Ghies for his vindication from the aspersions alleged to have been cast upon his reputation by Mr Warrington, English Consul at Tripoli'. Presumably a fair copy was given to D'Ghies. A fragment in Bentham's hand,

in June 1832, but seems to have left the country at the beginning of September 1832. According to the editor of 'Securities against Misrule' in Bowring's edition of the *Works*, D'Ghies had recently died 'under circumstances which caused a suspicion that he was poisoned'.[1]

However, long before D'Ghies' departure in May 1823, Bentham had turned his thoughts towards Greece and its struggle for independence against Turkey.

WRITINGS FOR GREECE

Bentham's interest in Greek independence had been first aroused in August 1821 when he had met Nicolaos Piccolos (1792–1865), who had come to London to raise support for the Greek cause, and through whom he had made contact with the Greek classical scholar, Adamantios Korais (1748–1833). His interest was thus further stimulated by the arrival in London of Andreas Louriottis, dispatched to western Europe by the Greek National Assembly in order to raise a loan to further the prosecution of the war of independence. He had gone first to Madrid, where a Philhellenic Committee had been established by Bowring at the end of 1821 or beginning of 1822. There being no hope of pecuniary assistance from Spain, he had been advised to go to England where money was more plentiful. He seems to have reached London at the beginning of February 1823, and made contact with Bowring and Edward Blaquiere.[2] It is unclear when Bentham was first introduced to Louriottis,[3] but he was made aware of his presence as early as 4 February 1823,[4] and on 9 February 1823 began to draft his 'Observations' on the new Greek Constitution, which had been proclaimed at Epidauros in January 1822. They may therefore have met on or before 9 February 1823 and talked about the possibility of Bentham's writing an essay for Greece, as a result of which he had commenced work. A few days later, Louriottis wrote to

which appears to be a partial draft of a letter to D'Ghies, is at BL Add. MS 33, 551, fo. 236 (9 August 1831).

[1] Bowring, viii. 555.
[2] See Alerino Palma, *Greece Vindicated; in Two Letters*, London, 1826, pp. 6–7; Thomas Gordon, *History of the Greek Revolution*, 2 vols., London, 1832, ii. 76–8. Blaquiere (1779–c.1832), naval officer, liberal and adventurer, had been a disciple of Bentham since 1813.
[3] Bowring or Blaquiere was presumably responsible for their introduction. Their earliest recorded meeting was on 19 February 1823 (Colls' Journal, BL Add. MS 33, 563, fo. 119), but they seem to have already met by the time Bentham wrote to Samuel Parr on 17 February 1823 (see below).
[4] See Bentham's notebook, UC clxxiii. 93.

Bentham formally requesting his observations on the Greek Constitution and advice as to how the Greeks might consolidate their independence, and asking him to encourage the President of the United States, James Monroe, to support the Greek cause.[1] Since Blaquiere and Louriottis were soon to return to Greece, the former at the behest of the newly-formed London Greek Committee to prepare a report on the state of the country, and the latter to persuade the Greek government to send agents to London in order to negotiate a loan, Bentham had to work quickly. For his part, Bentham feared that the Greek rulers would try to suppress his work if it contained anything which did not suit their personal views, and had therefore demanded from Louriottis an assurance that 'fair publicity' would be accorded it. In order to secure this, he wanted to publish it himself in London in the original English, and in Greece in parallel English and modern Greek translation. He lost no time in attempting to engage Samuel Parr (1747–1825) as translator.[2] Parr however declined to make the translation,[3] and when Blaquiere, who was entrusted with the 'Observations', left London for Greece on 4 March 1823, he had only an English version to take with him. Bentham's writings on the Greek Constitution were thus concentrated into little more than a three-week period.[4] The material falls into two main groups, that written specifically for the 'Observations', and that written for a covering letter from Bentham to the Greek legislators.

Greece: Principles of Legislation as to Constitutional Law

Bentham's first thoughts were directed towards composing what appears to be a short introduction for the 'Observations', consisting of a sequence of ten manuscript sheets headed 'Greece: Constitution. J.B.'s Observations. Introductory Remarks',[5] but which he eventually decided to exclude from the essay.[6] He placed the material in a paper

[1] Louriottis to Bentham (copy), 14 February 1823, UC xii. 100.

[2] Bentham to Parr, 17 February 1823, Bowring, x. 534–6 (also printed in J. Johnstone, *The Works of Samuel Parr, LL.D.*, 8 vols., London, 1828, viii. 6–10).

[3] Parr to Bentham, 20 February 1823, Bowring, x. 536–7.

[4] The MSS are at UC xxi. 180–209, 212, 214–309 (there is an unnumbered MS between xxi. 276 and 277); cvi. 327–83; clx. 324–6. There are notes on the clauses of the Greek Constitution at UC xxi. 180 (9 February 1823), on 'Arrangements proposable' at xxi. 220 (9 February 1823), on press freedom at xxi. 271 (17 February 1823), and on 'Mahometans' at xxi. 272 (17 February 1823).

[5] UC xxi. 183, 221–9 (9–10 February 1823). Only the first sheet of this sequence (UC xxi. 221) carries marginal summary paragraphs: the corresponding marginal summary sheet has not been traced.

[6] See Bentham's note at the top of UC xxi. 221: 'Not employed but employable or consultable.'

wrapper headed '1823 Feby. etc. Greece: Principles of Legislation as to Constitutl. Law', on which he added a plan containing section titles and indicating which sheets were to be included in each section. The title of the essay and the section titles have been taken from this wrapper. By the time Bentham organized the material and drew up the plan, it seems that one sheet (UC xxi. 183) had become misplaced and was therefore not included. It has however been restored to its proper place in the text.

Jeremy Bentham to Greek Legislators

Between 21 and 25 February 1823, Bentham composed a covering letter for the 'Observations' addressed to the Greek legislators. From a total of thirty-three manuscript sheets headed 'J.B. to Greek Legislators',[1] Bentham organized twenty-three into a coherent and continuous sequence.[2] This is presumably the draft of the letter which Bentham copied himself for Blaquiere to take to Greece, and referred to in a memorandum of 4 March 1823, written on a folio sheet ruled in four columns:[3]

To the transcribed copy sent to Greece was added in J.B.'s hand, paper the same as this, a brouillon sheet in which was commenced a warning against the five sinister appetites with which the probity of the Greek Legislators would have to maintain the contest: viz. for 1. money: 2. power: 3. factitious honor and dignity: 4. vengeance: 5. ease: contrariety of interest between them and their principals noted: expence minimized the end in view on one side; ditto maximized, on the other: and that probability of appropriate aptitude was not directly but inversely as the *value* of official pay accepted.

Since this accurately describes the contents of the draft letter, and several of the manuscript sheets carry the marginal sub-heading 'Five Trials',[4] there seems little difficulty in identifying this draft with the letter actually sent with Blaquiere.

---

[1] UC xxi. 196–208, 290–309.

[2] UC xxi. 290–303, 200–8.

[3] UC xxi. 212. This sheet carries the page number 58, and thus belongs at the end of the draft of the 'Observations' at UC cvi. 327–83 (which carry the page numbers 1 to 57).

However on a wrapper enfolding UC xxi. 199–204, and dated February 1823, Bentham noted: 'Greece: J.B. to Legislators. Nothing of this matter sent in this form. Quere what parts of it employed in the matter sent to Greece 4 March 1823 through Blaquiere.' The significance of this note is unclear. It is possible that the wrapper has been misplaced, and originally referred to the MSS which Bentham wrote for his letter to the Greek legislators but finally decided to exclude.

[4] UC xxi. 200–8, 300–3.

Observations by an Englishman on a passage in Raffanel's
Histoire des événemens de la Grèce

Once Bentham had completed his covering letter, he wrote what was
to be the final draft of his 'Observations'. The essay took the form of a
comparison of the Greek and Spanish Constitutions. Its three parts, in
their original order, were as follows: first, a discussion of apt arrangements in both Constitutions; second, of unapt arrangements in the
Spanish, but not in the Greek Constitution; and third, of unapt articles
in the Greek Constitution (by far the most substantial part). Bentham
afterwards reversed the order of the second and third parts. The essay
is concluded by a short section on 'Mahometan and Jewish Natives'.
The passage to which Bentham referred in his title was a French
translation of the Greek Constitution which appeared in C.D. Raffenel
(mis-spelt 'Raffanel' by Bentham), *Histoire des événemens de la Grèce*,
published in Paris in 1822. For ease of reference, the appropriate
passage has been inserted in the text immediately below the title.[1]
The articles of the Spanish Constitution to which Bentham alluded
have been placed in editorial footnotes. They are reproduced from a
translation which was soon to appear appended to 'Preliminary Discourse, read in The Cortes at the presentation of The Projêt of the
Constitution, by the Committee of the Constitution', *The Pamphleteer*,
xxii (1823), 1–87. This was possibly the translation which Bentham
had been encouraging Bowring to undertake,[2] and to which Bentham
may have had access at this time.

The draft of the 'Observations' consists of a continuous sequence of
fifty-eight sheets of manuscript,[3] the first twenty-eight and final six of
which are in Bentham's hand,[4] and the remainder in the hands of his
amanuenses, Colls and Richard Doane,[5] with only a few corrections in
Bentham's hand.[6] These sheets, dated between 26 February and 2

---

[1] See 'Observations', pp. 209–16 below.

[2] See Bentham to Bowring, 30 September 1820, D.R. Bentham MSS; Bentham to John Cam
Hobhouse, 6 October 1820, Broughton Papers, BL Add. MS 36, 458, fos. 433–5.

[3] UC cvi. 327–83, xxi. 212. Two of these sheets contain memoranda, and no text as such:
for UC cvi. 380 (page 54) see 'Observations', p. 254n below; for UC xxi. 212 (page 58) see
p. xxxviii above and 'Observations', p. 236n below. A fair copy of UC cvi. 369–83, in the hand
of Doane, is at UC cvi. 384–94.

[4] These MSS bear a few additions and emendations in the hand of the copyist. In most
instances, these have been removed from the text and placed in editorial footnotes. However in
some cases, where the addition made by the copyist appears to be called for by the sense, it has
been retained, and an explanatory editorial footnote supplied.

[5] Doane (1805–48) had entered Bentham's service as an amanuensis in 1819, and remained
with him until 1831.

[6] Bentham added dates, headings and marginal sub-headings to some of these sheets. There
is no earlier draft of this material in Bentham's hand.

March 1823,[1] are usually headed 'Greece: J.B.'s Observations on particular Articles'. None of them carry marginal summary paragraphs. The title of the essay is taken from the first of the text sheets (UC cvi. 327). Additionally there are thirty-three sheets of manuscript, excluding those associated with 'Greece: Principles of Legislation as to Constitutional Law' and 'Constitutional Code: matter occasioned by Greece', written under the heading 'Observations', or dealing with similar themes, which Bentham did not include in the final text.[2]

Bentham was working under severe pressure of time. As a portion of the work was finished, it was copied and the copy taken to Blaquiere. He received it in three stages: on 1 March 1823, Colls took the copy of the first thirty-six pages of the draft,[3] and on 3 March 1823, Colls and Doane took the remainder in separate batches.[4] In a letter to Blaquiere, which accompanied the second portion of the 'Observations',[5] Bentham again explained that he did not want the essay printed at the order or expense of the Greek government, but at his own expense in parallel English and Greek translation.

By this means if an apt Translator can be obtained, we shall be independent of every body as to the printing and no responsibility on the score of it will attach upon the Constituted Authorities. It bears so strongly upon Monarchies in general and in particular, that it would scarcely be consistent with prudence on their part to appear to regard it with a favorable eye.

On the one hand, Bentham wanted to ensure that the Greek government did not suppress the 'Observations', but on the other hand he did not want the Greeks, by adopting or approving of it, to cause offence to the European powers. He also had some hopes of gaining help from the Muslims in Greece for D'Ghies' attempt to introduce reform in Tripoli:

In my paper of advice to the Greeks you will observe what I say in relation to the Mahomedan population of that country: supposing them treated with the gentleness there recommended they might ere long be made willing instruments for the liberation of the subjects of the Barbary Powers from the existing Despotisms. The people are every where prepared for it, as I have been satisfied by circumstances that have come to my knowledge, but of which no intimation could be given in the paper intended for publication, lest by that means the fulfilment of the prophecy should be prevented, by the

---

[1] With the exception of UC xxi. 212, which is dated 4 March 1823.
[2] UC xxi. 181–2, 184–95, 209, 234–6, 273–7, 280–9. These date from between 9 and 18 February 1823, with the exception of UC xxi. 209 (26 February 1823).
[3] i.e. UC cvi. 327–62. See Colls' Journal, BL Add. MS 33, 563, fo. 119, and Colls' note at the bottom of UC cvi. 362: 'So far took to Blaquiere March 1st. 1823.'
[4] Colls' Journal, BL Add. MS 33, 563, fo. 119.
[5] Ibid. A copy of the letter, dated 2 March 1823, is at UC xii. 103.

divulgation of it. Natural and supposed irreconcilable enemies would thus be converted into grateful and steady allies.

This mirrored the hopes he had of eventually using the projected force which D'Ghies was supposed to raise for Tripoli in aid of the Greeks.

Blaquiere and Louriottis presented Bentham's 'Observations' to the Greek Legislative Council at Tripolitza on 16 May 1823 (it is unclear whether the covering letter to the Greek legislators was ever presented).[1] Louriottis told Bentham that his essay had been received 'avec respect et reconnoissance', but unfortunately it had come too late to have any practical effect, for the National Assembly which had earlier terminated its session at Astros had not achieved any reorganization of the government.[2] Bentham was however honoured with a communication from the President of the Council, John Orlandos, expressing the thanks of the Council, and announcing, contrary to Bentham's original wishes, that the Council had ordered the translation of the 'Observations' into Greek.[3] Bentham, some months later, remarked that not only had he 'some reason to think' that the 'Observations' had been translated in Greece, but that it had also been translated in England. He was still impressed with the need to have the essay printed, 'in part for the purpose of it's serving eventually as a check upon any persons there, with whose personal interests my principles might find themselves in discordance, and who in that event would of course feel disposed to suppress it'.[4] However no translation of the 'Observations' has been traced, and in the event, neither an English nor a Greek version was printed or published.

Constitutional Code: matter occasioned by Greece

Bentham composed a further essay, consisting of a continuous sequence of twenty manuscript sheets embellished with marginal summary paragraphs,[5] on 19–20 February 1823. The relevant marginal summary sheets[6] are headed 'Constitut. Code: matter occasioned by Greece', and both these and the text sheets carry the

---

[1] Blaquiere to Bowring (copy), 16 May 1823, UC xii. 123.

[2] Louriottis to Bentham, 10/22 May 1823, Centre for Neohellenic Research, Louriottis Papers, E′ 15. In fact, some slight revisions to the Constitution had been adopted.

[3] Orlandos to Bentham, 12/24 May 1823, Bowring, iv. 580–1 (the original is at UC xii. 122, and an English translation at xii. 284). Bentham also received a testimonial from Alexander Mavrocordato, the Secretary of the Executive Senate (see Bowring, iv. 580).

[4] Bentham to Richard Rush (copy), 4 December 1823, UC xii. 161.

[5] UC xxi. 237–56. An earlier draft and related material is at UC xxi. 257–70 (11, 18, 21 February 1823).

[6] UC xxi. 214–18 (20–1 February 1823).

marginal sub-heading 'Beginning'. It is possible that this essay, like 'Greece: Principles of Legislation as to Constitutional Law', was written as an introduction to the 'Observations', but which Bentham decided to exclude. There is however another possibility. Bentham had told Parr that after completing his observations on the Greek Constitution, he intended to prepare his own *Constitutional Code* for the Greeks.[1] Bentham may have written this essay as an explanation, for the specific benefit of the Greeks, of the principles they might expect to find developed in *Constitutional Code*. The essay has been organized in accordance with the plan on the first marginal summary sheet (UC xxi. 214), which divides the essay into fourteen sections,[2] and allocates marginal summary paragraphs to each section. The relevant text has been located by collating the marginal summary paragraphs on the marginal summary sheets with the original marginal summary paragraphs on the text sheets. A further section, not included on Bentham's plan, has been added to the text. This consists of three manuscript sheets written several days later for the 'Observations',[3] but which Bentham decided to exclude from the main essay,[4] and append to the material here.[5] Later still, Bentham removed these three sheets from the Greek material and considered them for use in an early draft of *Constitutional Code*.[6]

Constitutional Code, Ch. VIII. Of the Prime Minister, §5. Term of Service

Bentham's involvement with Greece continued to be close and involved, and for several years he hoped that the new Greek government could be persuaded to adopt *Constitutional Code*.[7] When Leicester Stanhope (1784–1862), later fifth Earl of Harrington, with whom Bentham had come into contact in May 1823, offered to go to

[1] Bentham to Parr, 17 February 1823, Bowring, x. 534–6.

[2] On the plan, Bentham numbered two sections as §8: thus §§1–8, 8–13 have been renumbered 1–14 in the text. The section titles in the text are taken from the plan.

[3] UC clx. 324–6 (27 February 1823). The section title has been taken from the first text sheet.

[4] At the top of UC clx. 324, Bentham noted: '1 March. Employ not this *now*.'

[5] The relevant marginal summary sheet, UC xxi. 219 (4 March 1823), carries the same headings and is paginated in the same sequence as the other marginal summary sheets for this essay (UC xxi. 214–18).

[6] At the top of UC clx. 324, Bentham noted: '☛ Generally applicable these 3 pages.' The original heading, 'Greece: J.B.'s Observations on particular Articles', has been altered to 'Constitut. Code', and appropriate marginal sub-headings added.

[7] For a detailed account see *Constitutional Code*, vol. I (*CW*), Editorial Introduction, pp. xvi–xxxi. A few MSS were later written specifically 'For Greece': see UC clx. 322–3 (15 September 1823); xxxiv. 297–9 (27 February 1824); xxi. 210–11 (28 February 1824).

Greece as an agent of the London Greek Committee, Bentham prepared a draft of *Constitutional Code* for Stanhope to take with him. At this time Bentham envisaged that the text of *Constitutional Code* would be arranged into three parts, an enactive part followed by separate expository and rationale parts. When Stanhope left for Greece towards the end of September 1823, Bentham had not had sufficient time to complete the draft:[1] Stanhope had to be satisfied with the enactive portions of the text for Chapters I–VI, VIII–IX and for §2 of Chapter X, and the marginal summaries for the first fourteen Chapters. Two further instalments therefore were sent by post: one of 10 October 1823 included Chapters X–XII, but this never reached Stanhope in Ancona (a second copy was taken by William Parry, sent to Greece by the London Greek Committee in November 1823 to serve under Lord Byron); the other, of 14 October 1823, included a new draft of §5 of Chapter VIII, and this Stanhope duly received.[2] This section is the only part of the material Bentham sent to Greece which has been recovered. The manuscript, consisting of sixteen pages of writing paper in the hand of Colls, is in the Stanhope Papers, General State Archives, Academy of Athens. The bottoms of the pages are slightly damaged, so several gaps appear in the text, though none of more than a few words. The text is divided into a brief enactive section, consisting of five articles, and a longer rationale.

TEXT

The Manuscripts

A large proportion of the text material incorporated into this volume is in Bentham's own hand, written on single sheets of foolscap ruled with a wide margin and with a double line at the top for the date and the heading. Many of the text sheets bear numerous additions (usually interlinear, but sometimes marginal), deletions and emendations. The remainder of the text material is in the hand of Bentham's amanuensis, John Colls, with the exception of some of the manuscripts for the 'Observations' which are in the hand of Richard Doane: these sheets may have been copied from drafts in Bentham's hand or less commonly transcribed at the dictation of Bentham. Again they are usually written on single sheets of foolscap, but occasionally on

---

[1] See UC xxxvi. 284 (18 September 1823).

[2] Stanhope to Bentham, 24 October 1823, National Library of Greece, London Greek Committee Papers, vol. 10, fo. L.

double sheets, and often bear additions, deletions and emendations in Bentham's hand. Bentham's normal method of working at this time seems to have been to date the sheets and to write a sequence of several sheets of text, to read it over and make corrections, and then to write summaries of the content in the margin. The marginal summaries were written in the form of short paragraphs and numbered consecutively. These marginal summary paragraphs were then copied out onto separate sheets (marginal summary sheets) by the amanuensis. The marginal summary sheets also bear occasional additions and emendations in Bentham's hand. The marginal summary sheets are written on single sheets of foolscap ruled into four columns with a double line at the top for the date and the heading. Bentham did not add marginal summaries to all the text sheets which he wrote, while marginal summary sheets corresponding to some of the marginal summaries on the text sheets were either never made or have not survived. It should be noted that the marginal summary paragraphs were not intended for publication, unlike the marginal headings incorporated in some of the earlier works,[1] but rather seem to have been used by Bentham for purposes of reference. Additionally a few sheets containing notes, aphorisms and general principles, and others containing plans, are written on double sheets of foolscap, each sheet again being ruled into four columns.

Some of the manuscripts are found in paper wrappers on which Bentham has inscribed a descriptive heading. These headings are sometimes detailed and specific, where the number of manuscripts is small and they comprise one continuous sequence, and at other times more general, where the number of manuscripts is larger and the content more wide-ranging. These wrappers were presumably used by Bentham as a rough contents index, allowing him to find and organize his material more easily. However, some of the wrappers have been misplaced, and are therefore not always a reliable guide to the content of the material they enfold.

A few general points should be made with regard to the organization of the texts. The manuscripts for several of the essays are for the most part found in their correct order, but those for 'Securities against Misrule' and for some of the writings for Greece are in a state of confusion. In the case of 'Securities against Misrule', surviving plans have assisted in establishing the overall structure of the text, though considerable reliance has had to be placed on internal evidence. Indeed in the essays in general, the internal organization of each part or section has been ascertained by paying regard, where applicable, to

---

[1] See for instance *An Introduction to the Principles of Morals and Legislation*, ed. J.H. Burns and H.L.A. Hart, London, 1970 (*CW*).

the dating and pagination of sheets of text, the numbering of marginal summary paragraphs and of course the sense. Difficulties arise from the existence in some cases of several drafts for the same part or section, not to mention other isolated and abandoned fragments on the same theme. Usually the later draft has been preferred as representing Bentham's more mature consideration of the subject-matter in question. The location and date of any alternative draft has been indicated, where appropriate, in an editorial footnote, as has any other related manuscript which has been excluded from the text. For the manuscripts used in this edition, reference should be made to the Table of Manuscripts below.

Table of Manuscripts

WRITINGS FOR TRIPOLI

ACCOUNT OF TRIPOLI

Section	MSS (UC)	Date (1822)
Title	xxiv. 61	3 October
1	xxiv. 62–3	3 October
2	xxiv. 64–5	3 October
3	xxiv. 66–7	4 October
4	xxiv. 68–70	2–3 October
	xxiv. 71–2	30 October, 1 November
5	xxiv. 73	30 October
6	xxiv. 74–6, 78, 77, 78–9	3 October
	xxiv. 80	30 October
7	xxiv. 81–5	4 October
	xxiv. 87	1 November
8	xxiv. 88	4 October
9	xxiv. 89	4 October
10	xxiv. 90–1	3 October
11	xxiv. 92–3	4 October
12	xxiv. 94	19 November
	xxiv. 95	10 November

SECURITIES AGAINST MISRULE

Preliminary Explanations

Section		MSS (UC)	Date (1822)
Note to title		xxiv. 215–18	21 November
1		xxiv. 223, 222	10–11 October
2		xxiv. 224–6	30 October
3		xxiv. 174–5, 173	3 November
4		xxiv. 271–4	3–4 November
5		xxiv. 275–6	4, 6 November
6		xxiv. 277–82	5, 8 November
7		xxiv. 284	4 November
8		xxiv. 284–6	4 November
9		xxiv. 287	4 November
10		xxiv. 288–90	4–5 November
11		xxiv. 291–5	9 November
12		———	
13		xxiv. 296–8	9–10 November
14		xxiv. 299–304	10, 12 November
15		xxiv. 305–6	10 November
16		xxiv. 308	10 November
17		xxiv. 307	10 November
18	§1	xxiv. 234	1 December
		xxiv. 235–8	9–11 December
	§2	xxiv. 240–7	10–12 December
	§3	xxiv. 248–53	13 December
	§4	xxiv. 254–70	15–17, 20, 23 December

Constitutional Securities

	MSS (UC)	Date (1822)
Address I	xxiv. 5–8	5 August
Address II	xxiv. 12–14	18 August
Generals		
Nation I	xxiv. 313	20 August
	xxiv. 314	6 October

	MSS (UC)	*Date (1822)*
II	xxiv. 315	20 August
	xxiv. 137–41	5 October
	xxiv. 316	20 August
III	xxiv. 316	20 August
Individuals	xxiv. 322–3	5 October
Details		
Nation II	xxiv. 317–19	9–10 October
III	xxiv. 320–1	9–10 October
Individuals IV	xxiv. 324	20 August
	xxiv. 325–8	20, 22 September
V	xxiv. 329–31	23 September
VI	xxiv. 332–5	22, 24 September
VII	xxiv. 336–8	22 September
VIII	xxiv. 347	21 August
	xxiv. 348	24 September
	xxiv. 349	7 October
IX	xxiv. 342–4	24 September
	xxiv. 345–6	8 October
X	xxiv. 145–6	7–8 October
XI	xxiv. 339–41	26 September

Preliminary Explanations Continued

Section	*MSS (UC)*	*Date (1822)*
19 §1	xxiv. 359–61	16 October
§2	xxiv. 155–63	19 October
§3	xxiv. 166, 168, 167, 169	24 October

PRELIMINARY EXPLANATIONS (*Novus Ordo* of 24 October 1822)

Section	*MSS (UC)*	*Date (1822)*
Introduction	xxiv. 114	26 September
1	xxiv. 104, 104A, 103, 105	25 September
	xxiv. 227–30	25 September
2	————	

Section	MSS (UC)	Date (1822)
3	xxiv. 148–9	14–15 October
4	xxiv. 149–50	15 October
5	xxiv. 150–2	15 October
6	xxiv. 153	15 October
7	xxiv. 153–4	15 October
8	_____	
9	xxiv. 97	23 September
10	xxiv. 97	23 September
11	xxiv. 98, 102, 99	25, 28 September
12	xxiv. 309–12, 109	26, 29 September
13	xxiv. 110–13	26–7, 29 September
14	xxiv. 113	29 September
15	xxiv. 101	23 September
16	xxiv. 354–8	29–30 September
17	xxiv. 350–3	26 October

LETTERS FROM JEREMY BENTHAM AND HASSUNA D'GHIES TO JOHN QUINCY ADAMS

Jeremy Bentham to John Quincy Adams

MSS (UC)	Date (1823)
xxiv. 378–90	10–13, 23 January

Hassuna D'Ghies to John Quincy Adams

Section	Draft		Copy	
	MSS (UC)	Date (1823)	MSS (UC)	Date (1823)
Introduction	xxiv. 433–4	24 January	xxiv. 472–3	3 February
1	xxiv. 435–40	24–5 January	xxiv. 474	n.d. February
			xxiv. 556	4 February
			xxiv. 474–8	n.d. February
2	xxiv. 441–4	25–6 January	xxiv. 479–81	23 February
3	xxiv. 450–1	26 January	xxiv. 482–3	3 February
4	xxiv. 445–9	26–7 January	xxiv. 484–5, 487	n.d. February

Section	Draft		Copy	
	MSS (UC)	*Date (1823)*	*MSS (UC)*	*Date (1823)*
5	xxiv. 464	1 February	xxiv. 488–90	n.d. February
	xxiv. 465	26 January		
	xxiv. 466	29 January		
6	xxiv. 452–3	28 January	xxiv. 491	11 February
7	xxiv. 454–9	28 January, 1 February	xxiv. 492–7	11 January
8	xxiv. 467	2 February	xxiv. 498–502	n.d. February
	xxiv. 468–9	14 January		
	xxiv. 470	2 February		
	xxiv. 471	29 January		

WRITINGS FOR GREECE

GREECE: PRINCIPLES OF LEGISLATION AS TO CONSTITUTIONAL LAW

Section	*MSS (UC)*	*Date (1823)*
1	xxi. 221–3	9–10 February
2	xxi. 224	10 February
3	xxi. 225–6	10 February
4	xxi. 226, 183, 227–9	10 February

JEREMY BENTHAM TO GREEK LEGISLATORS

MSS (UC)	*Date (1823)*
xxi. 290–303	21–2, 24 February
xxi. 200–8	24–5 February

OBSERVATIONS BY AN ENGLISHMAN ON A PASSAGE IN RAFFANEL'S
Histoire des événemens de la Grèce

	MSS (UC)	*Date (1823)*
Introduction	cvi. 327–8	26 February
Part I	cvi. 329	26 February
Part II	cvi. 330–78	26–8 February, 1–2 March
Part III	cvi. 379	26 February
Mahometans	cvi. 381–3	2 March

CONSTITUTIONAL CODE: MATTER OCCASIONED BY GREECE

Section	MSS (UC)	Date (1823)
1	xxi. 237	19 February
2	xxi. 237	19 February
3	xxi. 238	19 February
4	xxi. 238	19 February
5	xxi. 239–41	19 February
6	xxi. 242	19 February
7	xxi. 243–4	19 February
8	xxi. 245	19 February
9	xxi. 246–8	19–20 February
10	xxi. 249	19 February
11	xxi. 250	19 February
12	xxi. 250–2	19 February
13	xxi. 252–3	19 February
14	xxi. 253–6	19 February
15	clx. 324–6	27 February

CONSTITUTIONAL CODE
Ch. VIII. Of the Prime Minister. § 5. Term of Service
General State Archives, Academy of Athens: Stanhope Papers K121, fo. 72

Presentation of the Text

It has been editorial policy to reflect as far as possible the manuscript sources on which the texts in this volume are exclusively based, but without the sacrifice thereby of clarity and sense. Bentham's spelling and capitalization have in most instances been retained, though editorial discretion has been exercised with regard to his punctuation, inconsistent and sparse as it often is. Punctuation marks have been adjusted and supplied where clearly indicated by the sense or required for the sake of clarity, but not in cases where this might involve a dubious interpretation of the meaning. In the case of material written in French, accents have been supplied where appropriate. The words and phrases underlined by Bentham for emphasis have been rendered in italics, as have all foreign words and phrases, some of which

1

Bentham underlined and some of which he did not. In general, standard abbreviations have been retained, though some abbreviated words have been expanded into their full form (thus 'do.' is rendered as 'ditto'). It should however be emphasized that Bentham's syntax is often very complicated and involved, and in certain passages the sense is not immediately apparent. In these cases, no attempt has been made to give any explanation of the sense, since this could give rise to the opposite danger of over-simplification and miss some nuance in the argument. Nevertheless, where there does appear to be some genuine confusion, an explanatory editorial footnote is added.

The manuscripts contain many additions, deletions and emendations, representing Bentham's later corrections to the text. The final alternative reading is usually given in the text, unless indicated otherwise by an editorial footnote. Original readings have usually not been indicated. Manuscripts which are in the hand of the copyists, John Colls and Richard Doane, are identified by an editorial footnote: these often bear additions, deletions and emendations in Bentham's hand. Where there is no text corresponding to some part of the marginal summary, the marginal summary is reproduced in an editorial footnote. These passages are taken from the original in Bentham's hand on the text sheet, and not from the copy on the marginal sheet. Square brackets in the text are reserved for editorially inserted words: if these replace a word or phrase in the manuscript, Bentham's original is given in an editorial footnote, but where these are simple additions, there is no corresponding footnote. Round brackets and braces are those supplied by Bentham. Perpendicular strokes indicate a gap or blank space in the manuscript.

Bentham had a habit of numbering with the figure '1' the first paragraph in a section, or the first point, or indeed the only point, he wished to make in a particular passage, but then failing where appropriate to continue the enumeration. This enumeration has been suppressed. In those cases where the enumeration is continued, it has of course been retained. In some instances, however, Bentham's enumeration is incomplete or inaccurate. Numbers have therefore been changed editorially to make them consistent: where this is the case, the new number is rendered in square brackets but the original manuscript reading is not noted.

Bentham's own footnotes are indicated by suprascript letters and editorial footnotes by suprascript numerals, with a separate sequence for each page of the text.

SOME ACCOUNT OF THE STATE OF TRIPOLI ON THE BARBARY COAST IN NORTH AFRICA, DERIVED FROM AN AUTHENTIC SOURCE AND COMPOSED MOSTLY OF PARTICULARS NEVER TILL NOW MADE PUBLIC IN ANY EUROPEAN LANGUAGE

§ 1. *Territory—population—language*

The territory of the State of Tripoli, according to the Maps, extends North and South from Latitude about | | Degrees | | Minutes North to Latitude about | | Degrees and | | Minutes North, and East and West from Longitude about | | Degrees | | Minutes to about | | Degrees | | Minutes.[1]

In it is included the territory of Fezzan: which has been in a state of peaceful subjection to it for between thirty and forty years:[2] extent, about one third of Tripoli proper: but population not so dense.

It is bounded on the North by the Mediterranean, on the South by the territories of various Arab Hordes, on the East by Egypt, on the West by the territory of Tunis.

The basis of the population of Tripoli proper is composed of Moors. But a large portion of it is composed of Negroes, chiefly in a state of slavery. There are in the Capital a considerable number of Jews: not many in any other part. There are also Franks of most European Nations, some in the occupation of Merchants, others in inferior occupations. There are more of the Italian than of any other language, and more of Genoese than any other Italians.

The inhabitants of Fezzan are Negroes: Religion and Government on the same footing as in Tripoli.

The population of the entire dominion is supposed to amount to about 3,000,000: of which number about | | belongs to Fezzan.[3]

---

[1] In the margin, Bentham noted at this point: '☛ Consult Lyon and Pinkerton.' According to G.F. Lyon, *A Narrative of Travels in Northern Africa, in the years 1818, 19, and 20*, London, 1821, p. 241, the southernmost town in Fezzan, Tegerry, lay at 24°4′ north latitude, while according to E. Blaquiere, *Letters from the Mediterranean; containing a civil and political account of Sicily, Tripoly, Tunis, and Malta*, 2 vols., London, 1813, ii. 3–4, the northernmost point was the island of Jerbi, at 33°25′ north latitude, and from east to west the regency extended from Port Bomba, 23°20′ east longitude, to the island of Jerbi, 11°38′ east longitude. John Pinkerton, *Modern Geography. A New Edition*, 2 vols., London, 1817, contains a description of Tripoli at ii. 731–2, but does not give the latitude and longitude of its territories.

[2] In the margin, Bentham noted at this point: '☛ Consult Lyon and Tully.' In fact Tripoli had enjoyed some degree of dominion over Fezzan since the reign of Ahmed Karamanli, Pasha of Tripoli 1711–45, who had imposed an annual tribute. According to Miss Tully, *Letters written during A Ten Years' Residence at the Court of Tripoli*, 2 vols., London, 1816, i. 29, 'The grandfather of the present King of Fezzan was, in 1714, brought prisoner to Tripoli, by Hamet the Great, grandfather of the present Bashaw' and, writing in 1783, she noted that the hereditary rulers of Fezzan, the Awlad Mohammed Sultans, were then paying tribute to the Karamanli Pashas of Tripoli. The control of Tripoli was strengthened in 1811 when the reigning Sultan, Mohammed al-Muntasir, was overthrown by Mohammed al-Mukni, who was subsequently appointed Bey of Fezzan by Yusef Karamanli (d.1838), Pasha of Tripoli 1795–1832 (see Lyon, pp. 3–4, 278 and §3, p. 7n below).

[3] According to *The Journal of Frederick Horneman's Travels, from Cairo to Mourzouk, the Capital of the Kingdom of Fezzan, in Africa. In the years 1797–8*, London, 1802, p. 69, the population of Fezzan was about 70–75,000.

3

No enumeration has ever been made: a notion prevails that any such operation stands prohibited by religion.

The capital of Tripoli proper bears the same name: population, supposed between 25,000 and 30,000. Captain Lyon reckons no more than | |. The book that bears the name of Tully reckons | |.[1]

The capital of Fezzan is Moorzuck: population supposed about 13,000: including in what may be called the Suburbs. Captain Lyon reckons no more than 2,500.[2]

§2. *Chief of the State—his name—title—power—and family*

The personal name of the Chief of the State is Yussuf Pacha Caramanali.[a] Age about 50: see Tully.[3]

His Official title is, according to the English orthography, Bashaw: for which of late the word Pacha has been employed in Newspapers. In French it has always been written Pacha. In the Arabic pronuntiation little distinction is made between the B and the P.

The title is at present altogether an improper one: Bashaw is a Turkish word: expressive of a member of a certain rank in the Military branch of the Official Establishment of the Turkish Empire.

The case is—that, till about 30 years ago, Tripoli was in a sort of subjection to Turkey. It paid Tribute to the Grand Signior: it was governed by a few Turkish Soldiers. But about that time the natives threw off the Yoke of the Turks: and the territory was altogether cleared of them.[4] The Porte, whatever was the cause of its forbearance, took no steps for recovering its dominion. The Bashaw

---

[a] From the province of Caramania.[5]

---

[1] Lyon did not give any figure for the population of the city of Tripoli, though Tully, in 1785, noted that about 3,000 persons, being about a quarter of the inhabitants, had died from a plague then raging (see *Ten Years' Residence*, i. 186). Ali Bey el Abbassi, pseud. of Domingo Badia Y Le Blich, *Travels of Ali Bey in Morocco, Tripoli, Cyprus, Egypt, Arabia, Syria, and Turkey, between the years 1803 and 1807*, 2 vols., London, 1816, estimated that the population of Tripoli in 1804 was between 12,000 and 15,000. According to Blaquiere, *Letters from the Mediterranean*, ii. 32–3, writing in 1811, the population was something under 25,000.

[2] In the margin, Bentham noted: '☛ Enquire further.' Lyon, *Travels in Northern Africa*, gave this figure for the population of Murzuk at p. 97.

[3] Yusef, third son of Ali Karamanli, Pasha 1754–95, had deposed his elder brother Ahmed, Pasha 1795, and proclaimed himself Pasha in June 1795. He remained Pasha until his abdication in 1832. According to Tully, *Ten Years' Residence*, ii. 89, he was about seventeen years of age in 1790, making him about fifty at the time Bentham was writing.

[4] In the margin, Bentham noted at this point: '☛ Refer to Tully.' Bentham seems to be conflating two separate incidents: the accession of the Karamanli dynasty in 1711 and the usurpation of 1793–5. From the mid-sixteenth century Tripoli had been nominally under the control of the Sultan of Turkey, who appointed the governors, or Pashas, by means of firman, or royal decree. In return for full powers to rule, the Pashas were required to pay an annual tribute to the Sultan's treasury, and obey his commands in relation to foreign affairs. In 1711 however

 [*See opposite page for n. 4 cont. and n. 5.*]

on the other hand, to avoid unnecessary irritation, preserved his title of Bashaw unchanged, and made not any formal declaration of independence.

As to his power, it is of course in form compleatly arbitrary. But in practice, the social sanction, under the guidance of the religious, opposes to it, as will be seen,[a] some little checks, which are not altogether without effect.

As to his family, male children regarded as capable of succeeding to him he has but two.

27 year old Ali, married to Hawe Goi: has 3 children.[1]

18 [year old][2] Mustapha, married to Khadiga D'Ghies, aged 14: married July 1822: she speaks and writes French.[3]

The official title of both is *Bey*.[4]

[a] See §|　|.[5]

the first of the Karamanli dynasty, Ahmed, seized power and murdered the Turkish Aghas or senior military officers and thereby effectively established the independence of the country (an account, which incorrectly gives the date of the overthrow of Turkish rule as 1714, is in Tully, *Ten Years' Residence*, i. 68–70). In 1793, an adventurer known as Ali Burghol, taking advantage of the divisions created by a civil war between Ali Karamanli (Pasha 1754–95) and his second son Ahmed (Pasha 1795) on the one side, and Yusef on the other, and having obtained from the Sultan a firman appointing him Pasha, seized control of Tripoli. The Karamanli family, briefly reunited, and with the aid of the Bey of Tunis, Hamuda Pasha, retook Tripoli in January 1795 and forced Ali Burghol to flee (an account is in Tully, *Ten Years' Residence*, ii. 321–88).

[5] According to tradition, the Karamanli family had come to Tripoli in 1553 when the Turkish corsairs Dragut and Sinan expelled the Knights of Malta and retook the regency for the Porte.

[1] According to Blaquiere, *Letters from the Mediterranean*, ii. 80, Ali was sixteen years old in 1811. He was in fact married to one of Hassuna D'Ghies' two sisters, whose names are given as Khadija and Fatima in 'D'Ghies to Adams', § 1, p. 157 below. (For D'Ghies' relationship with Bentham see the Editorial Introduction, pp. xv–xxxvi above.) Ali eventually succeeded when Yusef abdicated in 1832, but was deposed by the Turks in 1835, thus bringing to an end the period of Karamanli rule. [2] MS 'Y'.

[3] Khadija was the sister of D'Ghies. However in 'D'Ghies to Adams', § 1, p. 157 below, Khadija is said to be married to Ali, while Mustapha is said to be married to D'Ghies' other sister, Fatima.

[4] According to Ali Bey, *Travels*, i. 235, 'All the sons of the Pasha take the title of *Bey* . . . but when they say *The Bey* only, then they mean his eldest son, who is declared successor to the throne.' The title was also given to the governors of the provinces of Tripoli and the ruler of Fezzan.

In the text, Bentham added details of two other sons of the Pasha: 'Age of the eldest about |　|, his personal name, Mohammed Caramanali: is out of the kingdom now, is not intended to succeed: lives in the frontier country of Derna near Barca, *Cyrene* in Arab-Greece. Commanding an army he put to death 45 respectable persons without ground.

'Achmet, 30 years old, not likely to succeed—rather weak, married to his own cousin, has two children by her.'

According to Blaquiere, *Letters from the Mediterranean*, ii. 90, in 1811 Mohammed was twenty-three years old and Ahmed seventeen years old. Mohammed, Ahmed and Ali were the offspring of Yusef's white wife, Fatima (d.1813), by whom he also had two daughters; he also had six boys and five girls by his three black wives, of whom Mustapha was the eldest surviving male (see Hanmer Warrington to Earl Bathurst, 5 July 1822, PRO FO 76/16, fos. 103–6, 108).

Mohammed, having been appointed governor of Bengazi and Derna, had taken advantage of

 [*See p. 6 for n. 4 cont. and n. 5.*]

The succession is regarded as hereditary in the present family. But the order of succession as between son and son is not regarded as settled. How general a gloom is cast over the whole country by this uncertainty may be imagined. The seating of the present Bashaw on the throne was the result of a civil war between brother and brother:[1] and upon his death, unless in the mean time some effectual remedy be applied, another civil war is regarded as inevitable. When the proposition is made, that on every succeeding vacancy the eldest shall be successor, an objection is made—that, in virtue of any such education as in that situation youth[s] are likely to have, it may at any time be too probable that while in most of the children mind is in such a state of imbecillity as to be altogether incapable of holding the reins of government, in some one of them appropriate aptitude may not be so compleatly deficient.

§3. *General Administration—its members*[2]

The names Official and personal of the principal Officers of State are as follows.

1. Minister of Finance. Official name, Khaznadar: or in Algiers, Wakil al Khars.[3]

---

local discontent to lead a rebellion against Yusef. In response in 1817 the Pasha had sent an armed force against him under the command of Ahmed. Mohammed had escaped to Egypt, but had later been allowed to return to Tripoli as Bey of Derna, where he was living in 1822. (Bentham's geographical reference is confusing. Cyrene was the original capital of ancient Cyrenaica, a Greek colony founded in the middle of the seventh century BC. The city of Barca was founded about a century later in the territory of Cyrene, and gave its name to the western province of the latter's territory. The town of Derna had risen on the site of another ancient Cyrenaican city, Darnis-Zarine. At the time Bentham was writing, the eastern region of Tripoli was known as Cyrenaica, and that part of it under the control of the Bey of Bengazi as Barca. Mohammed, then, was living in the town of Derna, which in ancient times had formed part of the Greek colony of Cyrenaica.) Eventually he fled again to Egypt, where he died in 1828, thus pre-deceasing Yusef. Upon Mohammed's rebellion, Ahmed had been made 'The Bey' in his place, and therefore, contrary to Bentham's statement, would have been expected to succeed Yusef had he not also died in 1828. An account of Ahmed's expedition against Mohammed is given in Paolo Della Cella, *Narrative of an Expedition from Tripoli in Barbary, to the Western frontier of Egypt, in 1817, By the Bey of Tripoli; in letters to Dr. Viviani of Genoa. . . . Translated from the Italian, By Anthony Aufrere, Esq.*, London, 1822. The massacre of forty-five of the rebel chiefs was however carried out by Ahmed and not Mohammed (see pp. 220–8).

[5] Bentham did not go on to discuss the effects of the social sanction in 'Account of Tripoli'.

[1] Yusef had led an armed rebellion against his father, Ali Pasha, and elder brother Ahmed, in 1791–3 before the intervention of Ali Burghol had temporarily reunited the Karamanlis (see p. 5n above). Ali had abdicated in the spring of 1795 and appointed Ahmed as his successor, but in June 1795 Yusef had overthrown Ahmed and proclaimed himself Pasha.

[2] The following section is in the hand of the copyist, but bears considerable additions in Bentham's hand.

[3] In the margin, Bentham noted: 'Are these synonymous?' In both Tripoli and Algiers the

2. Commander in Chief by land. Official name, Pash-Agha. Personal name, Anno 1822, Abdallah Khangali.

3. Commander in Chief by Sea. Official name, Rais al marsa. Personal name, Anno 1822, Mustapha Gourgi.[1]

4. Minister of Justice and Religion. Official name, Cadi. Personal name, Anno 1822, Sidi Hammet Toughar.

5. Minister for Foreign Affairs. Official name, Wizir. Personal name, Anno 1822, Mohammed D'Ghies.[2]

These are all that have consideration in virtue of their Offices: if any others, it is in virtue of the personal favour they enjoy from the Pacha.[3]

The so recently incorporated Territory of Fezzan remains still the whole of it under the subordinate authority of the individual by whom it was subdued. Official name, Sultan. This is not the proper name though employed by Lyon: it is Bey. Personal name, Moukni | |. Of this personage, sundry particulars, more than are to his credit, are reported by an eye witness, Captain Lyon.[4]

In his one person, if his situation be the same as that in which he was seen and felt by Captain Lyon, he unites the Office of Finance Minister and Local Commander in Chief. That is the case with every Governor: he is likewise Collector of the Taxes.

Khaznadar was the treasurer, but in Algiers the Wakil al-Khardj was at the head of naval administration.

[1] According to Blaquiere, *Letters from the Mediterranean*, ii. 92–3, Mustapha Gurdji had been a Georgian slave who had succeeded his master, Sidi Ahmed, to this office on the latter's appointment as the Pasha's first minister in 1809.

[2] According to Lyon, *Travels in Northern Africa*, p. 8, writing in relation to 1818, Mohammed D'Ghies had retired as minister to the Pasha 'some years since on account of total blindness': this was no later than 1809 when Sidi Ahmed was appointed as the Pasha's first minister.

In the margin, Bentham noted: 'Do these ever meet together in Council? Are there any other and what persons avowedly consulted, either officially or individually?' The senior officials were consulted by the Pasha in affairs of state and local administration in the council known as the Divan. Bentham failed to mention the Kahya, who was the Pasha's counsellor and supervised the execution of the laws and ordinances of the state.

[3] In the text, Bentham noted at this point: 'Beys, four—1. of Gheryan (to the South); 2. Fezzan (South) Muslim; 3. Benghazy (East); 4. Dherna (East). They have their title for life. 'Mohammed D'Ghies has about 50 Slaves.'

Bengazi and Derna, and from 1811 Fezzan, were each governed by a Bey, or viceroy, who was an appointee of the Pasha and could be removed by him. Gharian was inhabited by Berber tribes under the leadership of their own Sheikhs: they recognized their subjection to the Pasha by the payment of tribute, and do not normally seem to have had a Bey appointed over them.

[4] Mohammed al-Mukni had obtained the post of Bey-al-nawba, collector of tribute, in Fezzan, and in 1811 had seized Fezzan by force and persuaded Yusef to appoint him Bey. (For the earlier subjection of Fezzan see §1, p. 3n above.) Lyon, *Travels in Northern Africa*, p. 3, in fact made it clear that the Sultan only enjoyed that title when within the boundaries of Fezzan, being styled as Bey when at Tripoli. For details of Mukni's treatment of Lyon and his companions see pp. 117–19, 129–30, 163–8. Yusef had removed Mukni in 1820, nominating Mustapha al-Ahmar (d.1823) in his place.

§4. *Judicial Establishment*[1]

The Judicial Establishment consists of the Minister of Justice, whose residence is in the Capital, and the Members of the several local—say provincial, Judicatories.

To some purposes, certain functionaries attached to the several mosques (places of worship) throughout the whole territory may perhaps be to be considered in this same character. Of these mention will be made in the next Section.[2]

The official name of the Minister of Justice is Cadi. To him it belongs to place, and under certain restrictions to displace, the members of the several subordinate Judicatories.

To him lies an appeal from the several subordinate Judicatories.

He exercises not any original Jurisdiction except in the capital. Thursday and Monday for causes of Appeal: for causes *de première instance*, the other days.

He hears not any cause but with open doors. This at least is what is professed.

Any cause may be brought before him alone in the first instance: if no decision in writing is required, he judges without consultation with Muftis: if a decision is required on the spot, he calls in Muftis on that same day: otherwise the cause is put off to the next solemn day, viz. Thursday or Monday.

At 12 o'clock the doors are shut and business ceases—at 1 they open again.

Five Muftis are attached to the Cadi's Judicatory: October [. . . ?] Month vacation on account of the sowing time as to Appeal causes: so in April for the harvest.

Of the abovementioned provincial and subordinate Judicatories there are 13, 14, or 15. Names of the places at which there are Judicatories are as follow:

1. Tripoli.
2. Masalati.
3. Gherian.
4. Benghazi.
5. Derna.
6. Morzuk.

---

[1] At the beginning of this section, Bentham noted: 'A Judicatory is called Al Sherrah—the place of Justice.'
Several paragraphs in this section are in the hand of the copyist.
[2] i.e. §6. Religious Establishment. Bentham later interposed the section 'Police in Towns' between the present section and that on the religious establishment.

7. Ghadames.

8. Fessatou.

9. Hoon or Houn.[1]

In each of them sits a Cadi, by whom all causes are heard, and to whom it belongs to give execution and effect to such judgment as is pronounced. To the Logical field of his Jurisdiction there are no limits. It embraces all causes, civil, penal, and religious. But to each Judicatory is attached at the same time a bench of other Magistrates, to whose opinion, antecedently to judgment pronounced, all questions of law are referred. Mufti is their official name. Each bench of Muftis has its President. His official name is | |. Number of Muftis in a Judicatory, 3, 5, or 7: five is the most ordinary number. Number in every one of these Judicatories an odd number: reason—that, on every occasion, bating accidents, there may be a majority. To the judgment, the Cadi's is the only name attached. But it is by the Muftis that the reasons of it are furnished: and without reasons the judgment would not be valid.[2]

To each Judicatory are attached three or four Secretaries or Registers to register the Decrees.

They are chosen by the Cadi from the body of Notaries.

Their Official name is *Adoil*.[3]

They are paid by the party in each instance to whom their service is beneficial. The regular fee is very small. It is commonly exceeded by the fee actually paid.

Of the pay of the several members of these several Judicatories, the source is derived partly from a landed Estate attached to it, partly from fees paid by suitors.

In the instance of some of the best paid of these Judges, the fair emolument rises as high as from 200£ to 300£ a year. An income to this amount constitutes considerable opulence. Thirty pounds a year is sufficient to enable a man to mix upon a footing of equality with the highest circles.

In Tripoli no fee is received by any Judge: neither by the Cadi nor by any Mufti. But when a question of law is put to a Mufti, it is

---

[1] Bentham did not complete the list.

[2] In the margin, Bentham noted at this point: 'Is a judgment in writing penned in every cause? If not, in what? And what becomes of it?

'Do the Muftis sign their names to their opinions?'

Under Islamic law in general, the Muftis, who were judicial experts and were consulted by the Kadi in difficult cases, did not act as a bench: though more than one could be consulted on a point of law, they gave their answers separately. Answers were given in writing and were signed.

[3] The udul (singular adl) were responsible, amongst other things, for the certification of judgements and of instruments of procedure.

customary for him to receive a present: but he has no right to demand it.

Bait al mal is the name of a functionary to whose Office it belongs to take charge of the public domain. To him a man who wishes to purchase or take on lease any part of the Crown lands addresses himself: on him it depends to recognize or dispute the title to every such property. This power of his is a source of great peculation and extortion.[1]

Personal name of him who was in that office Anno 1814, Mohammed abou Shiaib. He occupies it still for any thing known here to the contrary.[2]

According to the letter of the law and the forms observed in consequence, all the functionaries, military as well as civil, are subject to the jurisdiction of these Judicatories—the Pacha himself not excepted. If a man has a complaint against him, he is summoned to appear to answer it. He accordingly either attends, or sends somebody to attend for him.

Malthhab is the general name given to a sort of Sect among the Lawyers. There are four of these Malthhabs.

1. Hanafi was born at Koufa in the neighbourhood of Bashra. Name of the principal work according to the sect is Moktasar al Khanz. Author: Mahmoud Anassaffy.[3]

2. Shafi, born at Cairo.[4]

3. Maliki, born at Medina. Name of the principal work, Moktassar. Author's name, Khalil al Jendy.[5]

These two are the two texts that form the most accredited grounds of judicial decision. Each of them has a multitude of Commentators.

4. Hanbali: born—not recollected where.[6]

At Tripoli only the 1st. and third possess authority: the two others have authority in Arabia Felix and the neighbourhood.

---

[1] The Bayt al-Mal (literally 'the house of wealth') was in fact the 'treasury' of the Muslim state. A person wishing to purchase or lease land from the Pasha would have had to approach a functionary within the Bayt al-Mal.

[2] In the text, Bentham noted at this point: 'Note in Turkey on the death of each landed proprietor, a division takes place and the Government receives a tenth.'

[3] The Hanafi madhhab, or school of religious law, was named after Abu Hanifa (699?–767), who lived and taught at Kufa. Bentham's reference seems to be to *Kanz al-Dakaik*, a commentary in the Hanafi school, by Abul-Barakat al-Nasafi (d. 1310).

[4] The Shafi school was founded by Mohammed al-Shafi (767–820), who was born at Gaza. Cairo, however, was one of the main centres for the study and development of his teachings.

[5] The Maliki school was based on the doctrine of Malik ibn Anas, who spent most of his life at Medina where he died in 795. A basic text of Maliki law was the *Mukhtasar* of Khalil ibn Ishak, al-Djundi (d. 1374?).

[6] The Hanabila school grew up from the teaching of Ahmed ibn Hanbal (780–855), who was born at Rabi.

When it is for the entering into a Contract that the parties have need of the assistance of a Notary,[1] of course they go together: when it is for making a complaint, complainants are received singly or in numbers.

Any man may at any time go before a pair of Notaries and make his deposition, stating any matters of fact or events at his pleasure, important or trivial: the Notaries make no difficulty in receiving them.[2]

§5. *Police in Towns: namely in some of the larger Towns*[3]

In the Capital is a functionary whose Official name is Sheik al belad.

He is placed and displaceable by the Pacha.

His functions are:

1. To adjust weights and measures—to secure their conformity to the standard.

2. To take care of the Streets—i.e. of their cleanliness.

3. To settle inconsiderable differences and complaints of transgression in manufactures and handicraft trades.

4. He is the President of the Judicatory of Commerce: Members— old established Merchants and Masters of Vessels.

The Members are persons who frequent a certain Coffee-House. The number is not limited. Whether a man shall be admitted or no depends upon those who already belong to it. The Coffee-house is called Gawud: Gawut Shek al belad, Coffee-house of the Shek al belad. The Judicatory is over the Coffee-house.

Only at Tripoli is there this Commercial Jud[icatory].

His pay is not fixt.

A dishonest man may make money in this Office, but he risks his life in doing so.

---

[1] i.e. an adl.

[2] In the text, Bentham noted at this point: 'Hedaya translation occupies 4 Vols. 4to.—has he [i.e. D'Ghies] ever heard of it? It is the standard of Mahometan law in Hindostan and Persia.' The *Hedaya* of Ali ibn Abu Bakr al-Farghani al-Marghinani (d.1197), an important work in the Hanafi school, had been translated by Charles Hamilton (1753?–92): see *The Hedàya, or Guide; A Commentary on the Mussulman Laws*, 4 vols., London, 1791. It seems that on Bentham's recommendation, D'Ghies looked over a copy of the translation: see D'Ghies to Bentham, n.d., UC xxiv. 522.

[3] Bentham only discussed the police in the capital.

§6. *Religious Establishment*[1]

Of the Chief of the Religious Establishment, the official name is | |.[2]

The personal name of the functionary now in Office is | |.

In Tripoli, as in every other country in which the established religion is Mahometanism, the Edifices in which religious service is performed are called Mosques. Number of Mosques in the whole territory, Fezzan included, about 3,000. The several districts in each of which a Mosque is situated may be considered as so many sub-districts, with reference to the several districts belonging to the respective Judicatories.

Of the whole territory of the State there is not any part that is not included in the field of authority belonging to some Mosque, and thereby belonging to some Judicatory. In the language of Christian Religion and English Law there are therefore no Extra-parochial places. With as much etymological propriety as in the case of a Christian Church, the field of authority of a Mosque may be stiled a Parish.

Attached to each Mosque is a Minister of Religious Worship: one and no more. His official name is Iman.

Under the Iman are certain functionaries who are known by several names: viz. 1. Mazeen: 2. Mouwakit: 3. Mouathen: 4. Kaim: 5. Mosammen:[3] and between twenty and thirty others.

In the absence of the Iman, the eldest of these Assistants takes his place.

Names by which the field of the authority of the Iman is designated—or as we say the Parish—are: 1. Homa. 2. Hara.[4]

They are chosen by the Parishioners.

These Electors choose one another: i.e. each vacancy is filled up by those who are already in office.

The Iman is elected by the Parishioners as above: and must be confirmed by the Cadi he belongs to. But in the case of an alledged improper Election, Appeal goes to the Cadi of the Capital.

---

[1] This and the following section are in the hand of the copyist, but bear considerable additions and emendations in Bentham's hand.

[2] Possibly Bentham had in mind the Mufti, to whom Blaquiere, *Letters from the Mediterranean*, ii. 88, referred as 'at the head of the Maraboot order; not unlike, componere magnis, our Archbishop of Canterbury'.

[3] The muadhdhin (i.e. both the 'Mazeen' and the 'Mouathen'), or crier, summoned the people to divine service; the muwaqqit, or timekeeper, was a special crier who, during the fast of Ramadan, announced the last hour at which the dawn meal could be taken; kaiyim, or superintendent, was a vague title covering a variety of duties, but probably referred to the secretary of the Mosque; the remaining functionary has not been identified.

[4] A hara was a quarter or a ward of a town.

12

Attached to every Mosque are moreover two Notaries. Such, in the language of Rome-bred law, is the appellation by which, in the compass of a single word, a general conception of their functions may be best conveyed. In the language of English law they may be termed Conveyancers: it being understood that in those same functions, as in those of the French *Notaire*, is included the conveyancing part of the business of the English sort of professional lawyer who used to be called an Attorney, but who, that name having been so much worn by obloquy, has tried to make [his][1] escape out of it, and within these few years is affronted if spoken of or to out of Court or Office by any other name than Solicitor.

Of these official persons, the function consists in drawing up the several written instruments, private as well as public, to which such a degree of importance is attached as causes them to be committed to writing.

In particular, conveyances and contracts having for their subject-matter property or condition in life.

Another service in which their skill is occasionally employed, is that of drawing up what, in the language of the French Edition of Rome-bred law, is stiled a *procès-verbal*. For preventing the deperition of a lot of evidence that may eventually become necessary on the occasion of a suit not yet in existence, or not yet ripe for the receipt of Evidence, provision for instance is made by the Ministry of these functionaries. Witnesses are in this way examined *in perpetuam rei memoriam*:[2] and, how incredible soever it may appear to Lord Eldon,[3] without the assistance of a suit in Chancery, or that side of the Court of Exchequer which calls its proceedings Equity.[4]

In Tripoli, as well as elsewhere under Mahomet, for want of those distinction[s] the light of which has been shed on the subject by English Equity, the care of preserving necessary evidence from deperition has not been confined to Equity: whatsoever may be meant by a word the import of which has so much more of sweetness in it than it has of clearness.

Having experienced, for example, an act of forcible depredation or oppression in any other shape at the hands of a man whose power and influence is such as to leave no hope of redress, or of any thing better than ruin in case of known complaint, while that power or influence

---

[1] MS 'its'.

[2] i.e. to perpetuate the memory of the thing.

[3] John Scott (1751–1838), created Baron Eldon 1799 and Earl of Eldon 1821, Lord Chancellor 1801–6, 1807–27.

[4] Courts of equity allowed the depositions of dead witnesses to be presented as evidence.

continues, to take [his]¹ chance for better days, the sufferer may repair to one of these Notaries. The Notary, after hearing the narrative, and administering on his part such interrogatories as to him seem proper and necessary to the giving to it the clearness, correctness and comprehensiveness requisite for the purpose, committs the whole to writing.

Instances have happened in which a Document of this kind has been drawn up in the character of an Instrument of eventual redress for injury, inflicted by the reigning Sovereign. Thrones are every where vacated by death, and in that country they have been in a remarkable degree exposed and apt to be vacated by other causes.

Good, it may be said, good perhaps in some such extraordinary cases, but what shall we say of it in ordinary ones? Should we not call it mere *ex-parte* evidence? In this way, whether it be in penal cases or in civil cases, but more particularly in civil cases, might not evidence be manufactured in a most untrustworthy and deceptious shape, and give effect to the most nefarious designs? Yes certainly, if it were regarded as conclusive, which however there seems to be little danger of its being on any occasion in any place. Yes, but too probably, if in Tripoli the Examination were conducted in a no more apt manner than in a London Examiner's office under the auspices of English Equity. In a more unapt manner it could not be conducted even at Paris or Constantinople. At Tripoli, it is conducted in a different, and therefore in a more apt, manner.ᵃ

Assessors on these occasions to the Notary are—Witnesses, 40 in number, chosen it is said out of the men of best repute in the parish. At the worst, they could not be chosen upon a worse principle than an English Jury, taken with choice under the pretence of chance by an English Master of the Crown Office, dependent on the Minister by a revocable Sinecure, as well as on another dependent creature of the

---

ᵃ If on the side which is in the right the only piece of Evidence—that Evidence being at the same time indispensable, and if credited conclusive, perishes, this deperition has the prevalence of wrong for its certain consequence. By no observation which it is in the power of the most transcendent wisdom to make can the prevalence of wrong be prevented. No evil approaching to this in magnitude has place in the case where admission is given to such *ex-parte* evidence, as above, even on the supposition of the non-application of any of those securities which, where right has really the preference over wrong, might so effectually be employed. Of Evidence in this shape the weakness is undeniable. But it is at once so obvious, and so capable of being presented with effect in exaggerated colours by those whose interest it is, that the danger is much greater of its being taken for less than it is worth, than of its being taken for more than it is worth.

---

¹ MS 'its'.

Monarch, in the shape of a Chief Justice, against whose corruption they are to afford security:[1] or a French Jury, creatures of the official creature to whose corruptions they are to oppose a check.[2]

So far from being appointed by the Monarch or by any person under his influence, if any member of this Mahometan Jury (for to the purposes in question with less impropriety [than][3] to a jury of the purest Church of England Christians chosen as above might the appellative be applied) were known to be a functionary of any cast in the service of the Monarch, it would be a cause of nullity: and so universally is this understood that, into any such company, no such creature of the Monarch has ever been known to venture to intrude himself.

Punishment[4] of a Notary convicted of malversation in his Office. His beard is compleatly shaved, he is mounted on an Ass, his head to the Ass's tail, and for three days together is conducted all round the town, and in the Bazars and other public places.

Of a Notary the Official name is Adil, or say Adala.

A man can not be [admitted][5] a Notary without a certificate in favour of his aptitude signed by at least 40 individuals, householders in his parish.

For every business that requires the intervention of a Notary, there must be two Notaries. This is the law under the most recent of the 4 most accredited Codes. The use is to afford the better rampart against despotism. No Sovereign dares maltreat a Notary for any thing done in the exercise of his Office.

A man who regards himself as injured in any of his rights by the oppression of the reigning Sovereign may make his appearance before two Notaries and tell his story. The Notaries, by their signatures, attest his signature. Furnished with this document he keeps it till the death or departure of the Sovereign affords him a chance of relief.

On the occasion of these depositions the Notaries have fees: they are not fixed.

---

[1] The striking of special juries on the crown side in the Court of King's Bench was carried out under the supervision of the Master of the Crown Office, an office usually held by the King's Coroner and Attorney, who was appointed for life by letters patent under the Great Seal. For a fuller discussion of the striking of special juries in the Courts of King's Bench, Common Pleas and the Exchequer see *The Elements of the Art of Packing, as applied to Special Juries, particularly in cases of Libel Law*, London, 1821, Ch. IV, pp. 26–43 (Bowring, v. 76–84).

[2] Under the *Code d'Instruction Criminelle* of 1808 (see Titre II, Ch. 5, 381–91), the jury list in each *département* was drawn up by the Prefect, who was himself appointed by the Minister of the Interior.

[3] MS 'and'.

[4] The remainder of this section was added at a later date by Bentham, and includes some repetition.

[5] MS 'omitted'.

A man who gets together two Notaries to make a complaint may have the doors closed or open and the audience public at his choice.

§7. *Public Instruction Establishment*

In Tripoli proper there are two seats and sources of public Instruction, both of them on the same plan: one at a place called Tajaoura: the other at a place called Zanzour: both of them in Tripoli proper. They serve likewise for Fezzan: since the Incorporation, students from that province having been admitted. They have both of them for their principal object, the qualifying the students for the several situations in the Judicial and Religious Establishments as abovementioned.

Of these seats of instruction, Tajaoura is the principal, judging at least from the habitual number of the Students. This number is between four and five hundred. This at least was the number about 8 years ago.

The situation of Tajaoura is on or near the Sea Coast. Distance from the Capital about 30 miles to the West of it.[1]

Zanzour is likewise on or near the Sea Coast. Distance from the Capital: about the same distance or somewhat less to the East. Habitual number of Students: between 300 and 400. The plan of instruction pursued being in both these seats of Learning much the same, one account will serve for both, except in so far as differences are mentioned.

Whatsoever in the way of Literature is taught any where is taught there. The Elementary Arts of Reading and Writing, as well as every thing that bears the name of Science, [are taught there].

The following are the branches of art and science which are there professed to be taught: the order in which they are taught is that in which they are here mentioned.

1. Grammar, including reading and writing.

2. Rhetoric.

3. Logic, taken it is believed from Aristotle.

4. Law: that is to say, the principles which the decisions of the Judicatories take for their ground.

5. Mathematics: namely what is called pure Mathematics: algebra included: and the *calcul différentiel et intégral*, otherwise Fluxions: with little or no application to practice: the principles probably taken from Translations of the Greek Mathematicians.

---

[1] In the margin, Bentham noted: 'According to Della Sella, p. 8, but ten miles.' Della Cella, *Expedition from Tripoli*, p. 8, stated that 'the plain of Tagiura' was 'above twelve miles' from Tripoli. In fact, Tajaoura lay about twelve miles to the east of Tripoli, and Zanzour about the same distance to the west.

6. The Koran.

7. Of the commentaries on the Koran, such as are most esteemed, and referred to as authorities, in this country.

Each of these Seminaries is governed by one Chief. His official name is Shekh.

They are appointed by | |.

At Tajaoura, the situation of Shekh has for some generations been in one family—the family of Nahas.

Under the Shekh are Teachers | | in number: for each branch of instruction, one.

The Official name of this Functionary is Moudarris.

Among them, there is no gradation of rank. They are distinguished by number: the first, the second, etc.

The pay of these Functionaries is derived wholly or principally from an Estate in land allotted to the purpose in former days by the piety of individuals.

Altogether, the annual emolument attached to the Office of Shekh may be estimated at about[1]—nothing in money: but the land attached to the University furnishes him with a comfortable subsistence.

That of a Moudarris is provided for in the same way.

The Moudarrises are placed and displaceable by the Shekh.[2]

The Students pay nothing. They are boarded as well as lodged.

Whether an applicant shall be admitted depends on the Chief. Few applications are refused. Sole punishment, expulsion.

Age generally, 18 to 20.

They come from Schools.

Students are not lodged in any common edifice as in Oxford, Cambridge and Trinity College. They find Lodging and Board as they can in separate Houses and Families, as in Edinburgh and the other Scotch Universities.

Lodging and Board are both of them matters of great simplicity in Tripoli compared with what they are in England. Neither Bedsteads nor Chairs are there in use any more than in any other Mahometan country. The cold not being for any length of time considerable enough to cause artificial warmth to be regarded as [matter][3] of necessity, no such things as chimnies or Fire-places are to be seen any where. If, on any occasion, recourse is had to artificial warmth,

---

[1] The remainder of the sentence seems to have been added subsequently by Bentham.

[2] In the margin, the copyist has written, 'Any instance of a Shekh or Moudarris being displaced? or otherwise punished? or promoted?' to which Bentham has responded in the text: 'No instance does he [i.e. D'Ghies] recollect of any such removal.'

[3] MS 'matters'.

17

the only source employed is charcoal enclosed in a portable receptacle.

In Russia, you may be entertained with magnificence in a spacious gentleman's House in which no such utensil as with us is placed under beds is provided for the guest. This considered, that Utensils of this sort should be in plenty at a Tripolitan University will hardly be expected.

The use of fermented liquors being interdicted by religion, it will be seen to what a degree of simplicity the article of beverage is [reduced].[1]

The article of nourishment in a solid form, though not quite so little diversified as the article of liquid nourishment, will naturally in a Tripolitan University be upon a footing of great simplicity in comparison of what it is on in an English one.

The age at which a Student is entered at one of these Tripolitan Schools or Universities, whichever they are to be called, is commonly from 18 years to 20 years.

The time during which his residence continues is from three to four years: or if remarkably slow, sometimes more.

Times of vacation are from Thursday afternoons to Saturday mornings—the Friday being their Sunday. Holiday times 4 in a year, a week each.

The degrees are constituted by the authors read. The order in which these authors shall be read is determined by the custom: no skipping from an author of lower degree to one of two degrees higher without passing through the intermediate one.

To the lectures read by the Professors, not only the Students belonging to the Universities but every body else is freely admitted.[2]

Of the Schools.

In every Parish there are Schools one or more according to the population. *Maktab* is the name of a School of this sort.[3]

Official name: the [. . . ?] Mooatheb—Teacher of Civilization. He is paid by the Scholar. Every Thursday the Scholar brings his present—more or less considerable according to the circumstances of his family.

---

[1] MS 'produced'.

[2] The following note is in the margin in the hand of the copyist: 'In what manner is the completion of the Education and aptitude with reference to functions established? Examinations public or private? Continual or only final? Certificate? Mode of administering Instruction? Other seats of Instruction for Reading and Writing? Any students not designed for functions?' A fragment in Bentham's hand containing similar questions is at UC xxiv. 86 (12 September and 3 October 1822).

[3] The maktab was the school in which children were taught to recite the Koran.

No such School exists but by the bounty of some individual who builds it for this purpose.

The same motive by which a man is induced to establish a foundation of this sort engages him, within the sphere of his observation, to look out for those parts of the country in which, in respect of the proportion between the actual population and the distance of the nearest Mosques, the demand for a foundation of this sort is most urgent.[1]

§8. *Military Land Establishment*

1. Commander in Chief. Official name, as above noticed (§3), | |. Personal name, Anno 1822 | |.[2]

2. Commander in Chief of Cavalry. Official name, Bash Agha. Personal name, Anno 1822 | |.

3. Commanders of Legions, number | |. Name of a Legion, Orta. Official name of the Commander, Agha. Number of Troops in an Orta, from 3,000 to 4,000.

4. Colonel or Captain. Official name, Bayrizdar. Number of Men under his command, 100. Number of these officers, Anno 1822, | |. So of the Bash Agha's, Anno 1822, | |.

5. Serjeant or Corporal. Official name, Shawioh. Number of men under his command, 10.[3]

§9. *Naval Establishment*

[1.] Official title of the Commander in chief, Capitana. Personal name of the present Capitana, Morad Rais. He is a Scotchman by birth: he is a Renegade: his original name unknown.[4] He has no fixt pay.

Artillery they have from Europe: in Algiers there is a foundary.

2. Next to the Capitana is the Patrone.

---

[1] In the text, Bentham noted at this point: '☛ Observe to Hassuna the utility of Maps and a system of Statistics for this purpose. This would interest the religious in the advancement of Statistical Science.'

[2] See §3, p. 7 above, where Bentham gives the official title of the commander in chief as Pash Agha, a title he also gives to the commander in chief of cavalry below.

[3] The following note is in the margin in the hand of the copyist: 'Quere—Number of Troops, and where distributed? How many Household troops?' Ali Bey, *Travels*, p. 236, states that the Pasha's guard consisted of 300 Turks and 100 Mamelukes on horseback.

[4] Murad Rais, whose original name was Peter Lyle, had been mate of the packet boat *Hampden* which had brought Simon Lucas, the new British Consul General, to Tripoli in 1793. In order to avoid a court martial for theft, he had slipped away from the ship and declared his conversion to Islam.

19

3. Next to him, Reale. Each of these, one after the other, while at sea has the power of life and death. Not while on land—on land the power belongs to the ordinary Judicatories.

4. Official name of every Commander of a Vessel, Rais. Commanders of merchant vessels have the same title.

§ 10. *Financial Establishment*[1]

At the head of the Financial Department there is one chief: his official name is *Khazmadar*.[2] The personal name of the present functionary is | |.

In each Judicial District he has a Deputy. The Financial Districts coincide exactly with the Judicial Districts.

In certain stations, either the quantity of the business, or the distance from the place where the Deputy has his residence, has given occasion to the appointment of Sub-Deputies. The fields of authority of these several Sub-Deputies constitute of course so many sub-Districts, to any of which it may happen to include several of the abovementioned parishes.[3]

Unhappily, between the fund allotted to the maintenance of Government, and the fund allotted to the personal expences of the Sovereign and his family, no line of separation has ever yet been drawn. In English, there is no Civil List; or, in other words, the revenue of Government is all of it Civil List. The personal expence of the Sovereign is of course a maximum: the portion allotted to the service of the universal interest, a minimum.

This evil, however, is not altogether destitute of palliatives. The expence of the Judicatory is provided for, as above, by funds of its own: mostly by what, in the language of excellent Church, may be called Church lands.

The Universities, such as they are, are, as has been seen, in the same fortunate case. Piety, in the Mahometan edition of it, has made the same provision in both cases. In the Pagan edition, it was thus in ancient Greece. Xenophon, so he himself informs us, found better security in a tenancy at will under Excellent Church at Delphi, than he could have found in a fee simple any where.[4]

---

[1] This and the following section are in the hand of the copyist.

[2] MS alt. 'Wakil al Khars'. Bentham seems to have been confused with regard to the title of this official: see § 3, pp. 6–7n above.

[3] The following note is in the margin in the hand of the copyist: 'The tribute being collected in kind how does any part find its way in money into the Bashaw's Treasury?'

[4] See *Anabasis*, III. v. 5–13. Xenophon's estate was however at Scillus, near Olympia, and was in fact dedicated to the goddess Diana.

Another palliative is the absence of all National Debt. No written promise which the Sovereign could give on any account, in any shape, would go for anything, any where.

§ 11. *Relation of Tripoli to the other North African powers*

Tripoli is at present, and for a considerable time past has been, in a state of perfect amity with all its neighbours. Meaning always its neighbours of the same religion, living under a sort of regular government: Egypt to the East, Tunis, Algiers and Morocco to the West.

With its nearest neighbour to the west, viz. Tunis, as being its nearest neighbour, it is in a more particularly close state of amicable and frequent intercourse. From the Capital of Tripoli to the Capital of Tunis, the distance is by land ten days' journey, twenty miles being reckoned as an ordinary day's journey: by sea, commonly about 3 days'.

Compared with that of Tripoli, the condition of Tunis in respect of Government has its advantages and disadvantages.[1]

§ 12. *State of present conditions in life*

Of land sold upon a valuation, the ordinary price is ten years' purchase.

Land is frequently sold by auction: in that case the range is from 7 to 15 years' purchase.

Whether a man shall be deemed of *age* or no—*majeur*—depends not absolutely on his age but on a certificate which he must obtain. Two persons are requisite to give validity to it: 1. the Iman of the Mosque to which he belongs: 2. a person of reputation belonging to that same Mosque. Twenty or twenty-one is generally speaking the age at which he is presented for such certificate. The man of reputation is chosen by the relations. This certificate being shewn to the Cadi of the Judicatory, upon him it depends to give validity to the instrument which puts the young man in possession of his property.

Marriage of a boy may have place at the earliest age if the relatives of the girl consent. According to Hanafi, a male child can not be forced by his father to marry: but according to Maliki he may.

---

[1] The section appears to have been abandoned at this point.

According to Hanafi, no parent can force his female child to marry at any age.[1]

According to Hanafi, a girl before she is married is examined by a Notary *tête à tête*, neither father nor mother being present, that her freedom may be the better secured. According to law she may even marry without consent of father or mother: though access being a matter of difficulty, this is an occurrence that does not often happen.

---

[1] In the text, Bentham noted at this point: 'N.B. D'Ghies is of this Sect, the Sect of Hanafi, and is perfectly acquainted with the work. But he rather thinks that according to *Maliki*, a girl may be forced to marry till she is thirteen years old: after which, if she remains unmarried, she can not be forced.' In general, Maliki law was more strict in this regard than Hanafi law, though the rules of both were rather more complex than Bentham suggested.

SECURITIES AGAINST MISRULE[a]

[a] Generally speaking, legislative arrangements that have been established or been endeavoured to be established for the security of the governed against the governors have for their expectations of success trusted to force actually in hand: if not to force in a state of independence, as in the Anglo-American United States,[1] at any rate to force in a state of resistance, as in England in the Petition of Right under Charles the first, and in the Bill of Rights, passed on the occasion of the transference of the Crown from James the 2d. to William the third: and in France, the *Declaration des Droits de l'Homme* issued by the earliest of the successive National Assemblies.[2]

This sort of title has in itself a radical defect: it presents no conception of the object which it has in view: the object which it really has in view is—no other than that which is here expressed—the affording to the governed security against misrule—i.e. bad government at the hands of their governors. Nothing can be clearer than the meaning given to the word *security*: nothing, for the present purpose at least, can be clearer than the meaning given to the word *bad government*—or as their signification stands expressed by a single word—*misrule*.

If in place of the words *securities* and *misrule*, you employ such a word as *right*, a cloud, and *that* of a black hue, envelops the whole field. The attitude you take is restless, hostile, and menacing. You shew that you are in discontent, but you shew no clear grounds for your discontent. What you give intimation of is—though even to this no explicit expression is given—that some rights of yours have by somebody or other been violated, and that a determination has been formed by you not to sit still and see them violated any longer. But these rights the violation of which is thus declared, from what source is it that they are derived? To any such word as *right* no clear conception can ever be attached, but through the medium of a law, or something to which the force of law is given: from a really existing law comes a real right: from a merely imagined law nothing can come more substantial than a correspondently imagined right. Lay out of the case the idea of a *law*, and all you get by the use of the word *right* is a sound to dispute about. I say I have a right: I say you have no such right. Men may keep talking on at that rate till they [are] exhausted with vociferation and rage, and when they have done be no nearer to the coming to a mutual conception and agreement than they were before.

On the other hand, if no demand for security against misrule can have place until—and except in so far as—some law is violated, no such security can possibly be

<hr />

[1] An allusion to the War of Independence 1776–83 fought by the American colonies against the Crown of Great Britain.

[2] The Petition of Right was presented by Parliament to Charles I (1600–49), King of England, Scotland and Ireland from 1625, who gave his assent to it on 7 June 1628. The Bill of Rights, based on the Declaration of Rights submitted for acceptance to William and Mary, and outlining the terms on which they were to be offered the throne following the removal of James II (1633–1701), King of England, Scotland and Ireland from 1685 to 1688, received the Royal assent, as 'An act for declaring the rights and liberties of the subject, and settling the succession of the crown' (1 William and Mary, sess.2, c.2), on 16 December 1689. The Declaration of the Rights of Man and the Citizen was adopted by the French National Assembly on 26 August 1789, and with slight modifications incorporated into the French Constitution of 1791.

obtained in the case in which it is most needed: for the case in which it is most needed is that in which, the laws being altogether at the command of the rulers—the very work of their hands, no violation of law can be needed for the accomplishment of the misrule: on the contrary, the more frequent and extensive the violations of the law are, the more extensive is the mitigation thus given to the evil for the production of which they were established.

By the phrase Securities against Misrule, all this perplexity is avoided.

But the great advantage of it with reference to practice is—that it is employable, and with equally undisputable aptitude, in every state of the society: whatsoever is the condition of the governed under or in relation to the governors. 1. It may be employed by a sovereign representative body on the occasion of the establishment of the constitution of the State: 2. it may be employed not only under a Monarchy, but under a Monarchy altogether absolute, unless in so far as by the very arrangements in question a limit or at least a sort of bridle to his authority is regarded as being applied.

On this latter account it is, that—in one event at least—i.e. upon the supposition that the form of government continues unchanged, it will be found, to the exclusion of every other sort of phrase, capable of being applied to the purpose.

For the subjects to say to the Sovereign—'This or this is our right—say or do what you will'—is as much as to say—'You are no longer Sovereign'. For the Sovereign to be made to say—'You have such or such a right as against me'—or, 'I have not such or such a right as against you', is as much as to say—'I am no longer your Sovereign'.

On the occasion of the here-proposed arrangements, the course taken is—to put them in such a form that, with the government still in the state of an absolute Monarchy, they may possess whatsoever chance of acceptance can in the nature of the case be possessed by arrangements of the same or equally effectual import, aiming at the same object: but if, even in so unfavorable a state of things, a paper in this form may possess a chance of answering its wished for purpose, in proportion as the state of things is more and more favorable, its aptitude will be still less and less exposed to doubt.

That, otherwise than by fear of evil, a Sovereign can be brought to consent knowingly to tie up his own hands is generally speaking too much to expect. But what without such fear he may perhaps consent to do, with less reluctance at least, is to tie up in the way in question the hands of his Agents: in which case matters may be so managed, as that without knowing it he may thus be made to throw obstacles in the way of his own steps in so far as they proceed in a sinister direction.

PRELIMINARY EXPLANATIONS

§ 1. *Object of the proposed arrangements—Security against Misrule,
by the sole remedy—publicity*

The here proposed system of arrangements has for its object, as the
title imports, the applying, to such of the evils as are most apt to be
produced by the immediate agency of the Monarch or those in authority under him, such remedies as present the least unpromising chance
of obtaining the application of them at his hands.

One word—*misrule*—will serve for conveying a general conception
of the disease: another word—*publicity*, for conveying the like conception of the remedy:—the only remedy (it will be seen) which,
without a change in the form of the government, the nature of the
disease admitts of.

Thus much for a general conception. But under both heads some
explanations present themselves as necessary: necessary in the first
place for rendering the ideas clear and determinate: in the next place,
for shewing that it is to this one *recipe, publicity*, that relief, in every
shape in which the nature of the disease admitts of, is referable. Some
observations will follow in the view of shewing in what ways application may be made of it to most advantage: also some others, having
for their object the shewing what the chance is that the remedy will be
found obtainable.

Whatsoever may be the chance which the here proposed remedy
affords of being productive of the desired effects, the smal[l]ness of it
affords not any ground of objection to it: for under a Monarchy, such
being the nature of the case as not to admitt of any other, the option
is—this or none. The great difficulty is in obtaining the concessions.
Should that point be accomplished, its efficacy to no inconsiderable
degree need not be despaired of. True it is—abundant indeed are the
instances which history affords of concessions having the same
object. None in which the engagements taken by those concessions
have not been grossly and continually violated. Still however there
seems sufficient reason to think, that without this safeguard, weak as
it was, the instances of oppression would have been still [more]
numerous and afflictive. The Charters, in which the concessions were
expressed, afforded a determinate denomination and standard of
reference for the several grievances, a rallying point for sufferers with
their complaints. If even in these shapes the paper when employed in

25

the character of a breast plate of defence against the Monarchical sword was not altogether destitute of efficacy, still less need its efficiency be despaired of in the present case—for in none of these instances had any such care been applied to the making the most of the only possible remedy as will here be visible in the system of arrangements here proposed.

§ 2. *Misrule—shapes in which it is here combated*[1]

First as to the shapes in which the evil is capable of presenting itself.

1. Shape 1. Sufferers all determinate: the individuals all determinate and assignable. Examples: *Homicide, Confinement, Banishment*. In the aggregate of this suffering consists the evil of the first order: for distinction sake it may be called *purely* private.

2. Shape 2. Sufferers, altogether undeterminate. Examples: Waste of public money: Act of engaging in an unnecessary war. In this case the evil may be called purely public.

3. Shape 3. Immediate sufferers determinate, but the greater part of the evil composed of the sufferings of individuals altogether undeterminate. Examples: 1. *Political gagging*: i.e. obstructing in any way the communication between mind and mind for the melioration of the common lot on any subject of discourse: more especially on a political subject. 2. *National debilitation*—weakening the means of defence and security in the hands of the people against injury at whatsoever other hands, those of the rulers themselves not excepted. In this case the evil may be said to be *mixt*; or public through the medium of private: through the sides of one individual the public is wounded—that is to say all other individuals are: as well those who do not feel the wound as those who do.

Under the general name of *vexation* may be included every political evil, in so far as the consideration of it is confined to the sufferings of determinate and assignable individuals: namely the individual persons who are the immediate sufferers by the individual mischievous act in question.

Oppression is *vexation*, in so far as the hand of power is considered as occupied in the production of it. Thus, if inflicted without sufficient warrant, i.e. without being necessary to the preserving the community from evil of still superior magnitude, *homicide, confinement*, and *banishment*, are, if produced by a hand not armed with legal power, acts of *vexation* simply: if by a hand armed with legal power—if for

---

[1] Fragments with the marginal sub-heading 'Misrule—shapes' are at UC xxxiv. 160v (10 October 1822), xli. 179v (28 October 1822) and xxiv. 176 (26 November 1822).

example by the hand of the Sovereign, acts of *oppressive vexation*, or in one word *oppression*.

In oppression by the hand of rulers, two stages are discernible, and require to be distinguished. By oppression in its *first* stage, the disease is produced as above. By oppression in the second and last stage, the remedy is excluded or endeavoured to be excluded.

By the same act, whereby oppression in this its last stage is exercised, oppression in the first stage may also be exercised: it is so in most instances in those several cases in which the evil has been spoken of as being of a mixt, or public and a private, nature: the afflicting hand wounding the public through the sides of individuals. Examples: 1. *Political gagging*; 2. *National debilitation*, as above.

In so far as the suffering, by loss or otherwise, to the party vexed and oppressed is attended with profit to the oppressor or other vexer, or any one whom it is his design thereby to favour, *oppression* has the effect of *depredation*.[a]

§3. *Sole remedy, publicity: sole means of applying the protective power of the Public Opinion Tribunal. Publicity and notification—their mutual relations*[1]

So much for the disease. Now as to the remedy. A single word, *publicity*, has been employed for the designation of it. For this same purpose another expression—*Public Opinion*—might have been employed: employed and without impropriety, though, with reference

---

[a] Note that, in so far as all future evil is out of the question, the loss to sufferers being supposed the same, the evil produced by depredation is less than that produced by barren vexation by destruction and otherwise: for in the case of depredation, though the enjoyment produced is less than the suffering, still to set against the suffering there is the enjoyment.

But, when the future is taken into the account—the future, pregnant with the danger and the alarm—then it is that the evil from depredation may be seen to be greater than from barren vexation: the inducement that excites men to the productive injury being so much more extensive and constant, as well as commonly stronger in its operation, than that which excites them to the barren one.

Thus it is in the case where a community is plundered by its rulers by the support given to an unnecessary war: suppose two such wars, and the sums extorted for the purpose of the war the same in both, the one in which depredation to the greatest amount has had place is thus far the least mischievous. If during the course of the war a million of money is paid for gunpowder to the makers, better it is for the community that the half of it be put in the shape of profit into the pocket of the makers, than that

---

[1] A further draft on the subject of publicity and the public opinion tribunal is at UC xxiv. 231–3, 177–85 (26, 28–9 November 1822). Other fragments are at UC xxiv. 135 (2 October 1822) and xxiv. 186–8 (24 December 1822).

to the other expression, not synonymous nor any thing like it. Of what nature the relation between them is—will be seen presently.

Employing on this occasion the denomination *Public Opinion*, it will be necessary to go further and add the word *Tribunal*: the Tribunal of Public Opinion we must say—or for shortness the Public Opinion Tribunal. True it is that thus to speak is in some sort to use the language of fiction. But the fiction is not of the sort of those of which deception is the object and the effect. It will be seen to be the work of necessity, interwoven with the texture of all language, and not having deception either for its object or its effect. The groundwork it will be seen is composed of truth: from fiction all that it borrows is a sort of covering necessary to fit it for use.

If we consider the whole number of the members of the political community in question as constituting the entire body, the functionaries of government, all ranks together, will be the agents of that body, placed by the suffrages of the rest under a representative democracy, placed by birth or narrow election under every other form of government: and in both cases, all those by whom any cognizance is taken of public affairs may be considered as constituting the Tribunal of Public Opinion, a sort of Committee of the whole body formed in the manner of a Committee of the English House of Commons in the case where, at the institution of the Committee, it is ordered that every Member of the House who chooses to attend, attends accordingly and has a voice.

Only in so far as these individuals the whole aggregate of them are considered as constituting but one body—and that body acting with the formalities of a Judge—is there any thing of fiction in the representation here made: for as to effects—effects produced by the action of this body, or at any rate by the anticipation of it, nothing can be more real or more perfectly out of dispute.

Regarding then this body in the character of a workman, operating on the minds of public functionaries, *publicity* may be stated as the characteristic and indispensable instrument of this workman: an instrument no less indispensable and characteristic than the *turninglathe* is of the sort of workman called a *turner*. It is by publicity that the Public Opinion Tribunal does whatsoever it does: any further than employment is given to his instrument, the workman can not do any thing.

Intimately and inseparably connected with the import of the word

the whole be converted into gas, producing or not producing the destruction which it was intended to produce.

Only to aid conception are the above suppositions put: for, how far they are from being ever exemplified is sufficiently manifest.

publicity are the words notify—to notify, notification. By the word *notification* action in a certain shape and the effect or result of that same act are indiscriminately designated. Such is the poverty and thus such the confusedness of language, at any rate of our principal Rome-sprung languages. Publicity has for its synonym notification in the case where it is employed to designate the effect. Take any matter or supposed matter of fact at pleasure, the degree of its publicity is as the number of the persons to whom notification of it has been made, into whose minds the knowledge of it has found entrance: the knowledge, or at any rate the conception in question whatsoever it may be.

The general nature of the remedy being thus explained, further matter will be brought to view under the heads following.[1]

§4. *Subjects of Notification—their mutual relations. 1. Ordinances. 2. Transgressions. 3. Suffrages*

Subjects of or for publicity and thence for notification:

1. Ordinances: 2. Transgressions, or say violations of those same ordinances: 3. Suffrages: opinions formed by the several Members of the Public Opinion Tribunal, on the subject of those same transgressions as compared with those same ordinances.

Transgression supposes something transgressed; in the instance here in question, that something is something having or designed to have the authority of law.

1. In the first place come the several *ordinances*, of which misrule, in each of the several shapes against which a security is by this system endeavoured to be provided, will have been a transgression: ordinances: or supposed rules having the effect of ordinances: ordinances inhibitive of vexation and oppression in all its several shapes. If at the time of giving establishment to security in these several shapes, ordinances adapted to the purpose are already in existence, it is well: if not, fresh ordinances for the purpose must on this occasion be provided.

2. In the next place come whatsoever instances of transgression happen to take place. If none, so much the better: the ordinances have in the compleatest manner possible fulfilled their purpose. If within the time in question any transgressions have had place, the number of them being given, the nearer the number by which notification and publicity have been received to the total of the number that have had place, the better.

[1] In the text, Bentham noted at this point, '☞ Here add the list as soon as settled', presumably a list of the titles of §§4–17, which deal with the topic of publicity.

3. *Suffrages*. Understand by suffrages, the opinions produced in the minds of the several Members of this same tribunal by the cognizance of the several transgressions. The degree of publicity, as applied to persons taking cognizance of the several transgressions, will be as the number of these suffrages.

Note that in the number of the members of this same tribunal is included the number of all those on whose obedience [depends][1] as well the effect of the several general ordinances by which vexation is prohibited, as also of any particular acts or particular ordinances in consequence of which any acts of vexation and oppression are exercised in violation and transgression of those same general and salutary ordinances. Power on the one part is constituted by and is greater or less in proportion to obedience on the other. It is in the direct ratio of the obedience, and in the inverse ratio of resistance. But the greater the number of the members of the whole community to whom the existence of an act of oppression has been made known, the greater is the number of those by whom, on the occasion of an endeavour to exercise other acts of a similar nature, supposing the past act notified to them, not only may obedience be withholden, but resistance opposed.

Rule. Abstraction made of the several degrees of influence possessed—influence of understanding on understanding and influence of will on will included, the actual power of the Public Opinion Tribunal will be as the number of the suffrages actually declared in the minds of the several members: its power, as supposed by other persons, and in particular the head functionary and other functionaries to whose transgressions it is the object of this Security to oppose a check, will be as the number of the suffrages which they expect to find formed.

This influence with its several possible degrees it may seem may be laid out of the account altogether, for of the persons on whom by possibility it is capable of being exercised, the only persons here in question are the members of the political community in question—considered in their character of members of the Public Opinion Tribunal belonging to it. Thus accordingly, when considered in a general point of view, for the most part does the matter stand. One point however there remains in relation to which the sort of influence in question is capable of having a distinct operation. The suffrages suppose of all the members of this tribunal take the same direction: they being all of them pronounced in condemnation of the oppressive act in

---

[1] The addition is suggested by the marginal summary: 'Note, among these members are all persons on whose obedience depends the effect of the vexation-prohibiting ordinances, and of ordinances violating ordinances and acts.'

question. Thus far, as between suffrage and suffrage, it makes no difference which was the result of a self-formed opinion, which of them the result of an opinion derived from the influence exercised on the mind in question by that of some other member, exercised whether on will or on understanding, or on both together. But, though, by the supposition, the direction in which the suffrages act is the same, and the ultimate number of them, by what cause so ever produced, is the number in question, yet the degrees of energy with which, upon occasion, they may respectively be disposed to act in conformity to those same suffrages may be to any amount different: and in each case this degree of energy may be greater or less according to the nature and energy of the influence received.

Note that to simplify the conception, the direction taken by the suffrages in question is on this occasion supposed to be, in the instance of every one of them, the same. But as by the supposition the subject of these suffrages is in every instance some act of oppression, exercised by the Sovereign on individuals, there is nothing in this supposition that seems likely to be in any very considerable degree wide of the truth.[1]

§5. *[I.]*[2] *Operations subservient to publicity: viz. in relation to Ordinances. 1. Scription. 2. Sanctionment. 3. Registration*

So much for the several subject-matters to which the act of notification may have need to apply itself. Now as to the several successive operations the performance of which may be necessary to the production of the effect.

These preparatory operations will be in a considerable proportion varied according to the nature of the subject-matter: according as it comes under one or another of the three above-mentioned denominations: namely ordinances, transgressions, or suffrages.

I. First as to Ordinances.

First let the appropriate and requisite ordinances be supposed already in existence, and possessed of binding force.

If, so far as regards the purpose here in question, they are already present to every mind capable of taking cognizance of the matter, it is well. Unfortunately there is not any where on the surface of the globe any country in which this sort of omnipresence or any thing like it has place: not even in that country, the Anglo-American United States, in

---

[1] There is no text corresponding to the following marginal summary, which belongs here: 'The suffrages here meant are not the external but internal: it is by internal that action of the same person is influenced: by the external alone action of other persons. Only in respect of their effect on action are their suffrages, i.e. opinions, worth regarding.'   [2] MS '*II*'.

31

which the productions of the printing press are most extensively diffused: much less in Northern Africa, where even the instrument itself has never yet been in use.

Necessary to the existence of an Ordinance in a binding state are three distinguishable operations: namely scription, sanctionment and registration.

1. Scription. By this understand the act of composing and committing to writing the matter in question.

2. Sanctionment. By this understand the investing it with binding force, by some person or persons generally recognized as being possessed of the correspondent power.

3. Registration, or say recordation. By this understand the depositing and keeping in some appropriate receptacle, the individual instrument to which the act of sanctionment has been applied. But for this, the correctness and even genuineness of all copies, written or printed, might stand exposed to doubt and dispute.

Minute and useless will the distinctions thus brought to view be apt at first sight to appear. Upon a second view, nothing it will be seen can be farther from being so. No where will that country be seen, in which, throughout a vast and indeterminate portion of the field of action and legislation, an operation so essential as sanctionment will not be seen wanting to that matter to which is given nevertheless the name and binding force of law.

§6. *Continuation. How, in Tripoli and elsewhere, instead of regularly sanctioned Ordinances, other matter is referred to for the purpose of judicature*

Thus far, Ordinances, appropriate and adequate to the exigency, have been supposed to be already in existence. If so it be well. But suppose the state of things to be in the contrary case? what is then to be done?

Case 1. In relation to the matter in question, no Ordinance of the above description in existence. But on the occasion of judicial decisions, the standard of reference composed of anterior decisions, or inferences deduced from them.

In the European Governments, with the exception of the small extent to which a general Codification has had place, such is the state of the rule of action, under the dominion of what is called Common Law or unwritten law. On most parts of the field of law a quantity of matter has been written—written by men not invested nor so much as pretending to be invested with legislative authority: and out of this huge and shapeless mass of writing the Judge on each occasion makes choice of such portions as appear to him best adapted to his purpose: to the purpose which is most agreable to him, whatever it may happen to be. In this state of things, singularly unfortunate, if not unskilful, must that Judge be who, out of so rich a treasury, fails on any occasion to find that which is most agreable to his wishes whatsoever they may happen to be: to his wishes, guided as they can not but be by what at the moment he looks upon as being his interest.

In the countries in question, if I understand the matter right, none of those memorials have been collected, which in England over so large a portion of the field of thought and action stand [in] the place of law. I mean that sort of matter which is composed of statements of cases by which judicial decision has been called for—the particular decision pronounced in each case, and the general positions which have been brought forward by the Judge in support and justification of his particular decision, or such general positions as in the way of inference have been deduced from it by mere volunteer dissertators not invested with any such authority as that of a Judge.

Case 2. The standard referred to in Judicial decisions, composed—of inferences drawn not from former decisions, but from an original standard of antient date.

In the countries in question the standard of reference is it seems of this second sort. There stands the Coran, the work of Mahomet, the universally acknowledged standard of opinion and practice in all matters of religion as well as law. But for a great portion of those particular cases [to] which the occurrences of life are continually giving birth, in this book the matter, being for the most part of a nature extremely general, is not susceptible of an application particular enough to serve as an adequately determinate guide. Influenced by this observation, different persons without concert with each other have at various times set themselves to work to fill up the vacuities, all of them agreeing in the homage paid to the general positions discoverable in the sacred text, but differing from one another in no inconsiderable degree in respect of the inferences drawn from them—the particular positions of which, as being included within them, application has been made. With reference to the sacred text, these works of inferior authority stand in the relation of Commentaries.

Throughout the dominion of the Coran, four of these Commentaries have obtained the preeminence over all the others.[1] Such is the degree of that preeminence as to have given rise as it were to two classes of Commentaries: Commentaries of the first order and Commentaries of

---

[1] For the four major schools of religious law, the Hanafi, Shafi, Maliki and Hanabila, see 'Account of Tripoli', §4, p. 10 above.

the second order—those of the second order being not exclusively at least Commentaries on the sacred text, but Commentaries upon those of the first order: Commentaries on Commentaries. Commentators of the first order, four, as above: Commentaries of the second order, not so few as seven hundred.

Though[1] clear of confusion from that source of which indication has been given as above in the case of the European, and especially the English, Books of Reports and Treatises deduced from them, the Eastern system fails not however to labour under very obvious, and such as can not but be very grievous, imperfections.

In the first place, no one of them having in a direct way taken for its object of pursuit the greatest happiness of the greatest number, none can unless by accident have made any clearly defined provision for such arrangements of detail as are to be found deducible from it.

In the next place, in spinning out the thread of inference they have all of them taken on various occasions courses more or less different.

From all these diversities, to an extent more or less considerable, two evil consequences can not but have taken place. So indeterminate in this or that case is the bearing of some or all of these previous Commentaries upon that case, that the Judge, be his probity ever so pure, finds more or less difficulty in determining in what manner he shall make application of them to the case. The other consequence is—that amidst such a diversity, the Judge, in so far as the union of disposition and opportunity produces on his part an inclination to corruption, seldom finds any difficulty in gratifying it.[2]

With[3] regard to aptitude of phraseology—aptitude of phraseology on the part of the rule of action, thence security and sense of security on the part of the members of the community, thus much may with confidence be asserted with reference to the most apt Codes of European law, namely that in respect of determinateness of designation as well as aptitude with relation to the only proper end of legislation, the greatest happiness of the greatest number, they are in a deplorable degree deficient. Continuing to apply the words which custom has applied on the several occasions, on each occasion the assumption they proceed upon is that of the word in question the

[1] The corresponding marginal summary paragraph is headed: 'I. Disadvantages of these Commentaries or inferential standards of reference compared with modern sanctioned Ordinances.'

[2] There is no text corresponding to the following marginal summary, which belongs here: 'II. Disadvantages as compared with Books of Reports and Treatises grounded on them. Reports bring to view actual particular cases presenting demand for legislation: Commentaries as above, not.'

[3] The corresponding marginal summary paragraph is headed: 'III. Disadvantages of even the best-penned European Codes of Ordinances.'

import is adequately determinate, and scarcely perhaps in a single instance is that assumption true.

If such is the case in the instance of these Codes of law, the authors of which during the penning of [them][1] kept before them all along a determinate object of pursuit, namely the greatest happiness of somebody—the greatest happiness of the Monarch whose power was employed in giving birth to them and binding force—still more assuredly must it be the case in the instance of which the rule of action has from time to time been spun out in the way of inference from a work which, whatsoever may have been the talent employed in the writing of it, was and is of a mixt character, having something of religion in it, something of law, with here and there a passage of history, springing in the whole texture of it out of the occurrences of the day, and that day a very remote one with reference to present days, the state of society being at the same time in a great variety of particulars widely different from what it is at present: widely different, and amongst other points of difference, far less diversified.[2]

Be the exigency however ever so pressing—be the demand for new and precise definition of leading terms ever so urgent, every thing can not be done at once. With the stock of these terms—whatsoever may be the contents of it—with this stock of instruments, in the penning of the proposed Securities in question, must the scribe content himself, putting them to use in the best manner he is able.

In the character of a guide to Judges, in so far as their intentions are honest, the necessity of a collection of Ordinances has thus far been brought to view—of Ordinances in the form of Ordinances—of an all-comprehensive collection covering the whole field of legislation and putting an exclusion upon every standard of reference that is not in that exclusively apposite and adequate guide.

But if even to the Judge, to that functionary to whose function it belongs to decide upon the conduct of the members of the community at large—pronouncing those decisions which never can be pronounced without producing suffering in some shape or other, from the lowest to the highest degree, to a party or parties on one side or the other, how much more necessary must it not be to an individual in the situation of one who every day of his life is exposed to the danger of

---

[1] MS 'it'.

[2] The marginal summary differs slightly from the text at this point: 'Still more persuasively operative must those imperfections be where of no one has the greatest happiness been distinctly aimed: not even that of the ruling one or few with whose happiness that of the many will every where be more or less connected: his happiness being more or less dependent on theirs. So likewise as to indeterminateness of the diction, in particular that which regards the designation of the several sorts of acts to which, under the notion of their being pernicious to the community or disagreable to rulers, punishment is attached.'

becoming party to a suit for want of access to a document which would enable him by anticipation to preserve himself from the sufferings which otherwise can not but await him at the hand of the Judge.

If necessary to the right termination of these afflictive processes called causes or suits at law, how much more strictly necessary are they[1] not to the prevention of them? Without any such forewarning guides and timely instructive guides, a termination in some way or other these courses of suffering can not but receive: but by no other means than these sources of timely information can they be anticipated and prevented.

§7. *Operations necessary to adequate publicity of Ordinances continued: 4. Multiplication of copies—its importance*

4. Multiplication. So much as to scription, sanctionment and registration. Now as to multiplication.

In the country in question, written discourse, though not printed discourse, being in use, of whatsoever ordinances are in force as such, copies one or more can not but be in existence somewhere. In the Metropolis of the country of course. In the seat of the principal Judicatory of the country of course. In the case here in question, the first operation therefore that requires to be performed is—multiplication. For this purpose the newly invented instrument called the lithographic press seems for a first beginning preferable to the ordinary printing press: not that there is any reason why either should put an exclusion upon the other.

The advantages which at the outset it presents itself as in possession of are the following:

1. It is by much the cheaper.

2. It requires for the production of the effect, a much less numerous association of different arts and thus of different artists.

3. Being with difficulty distinguishable from ordinary manuscript, the use of it will be less alarming than that of the printing press to the artists who at present are employed in the transcription of manuscript works.

---

[1] i.e. collections of Ordinances.

§8. *Continuation. Necessary instrument of multiplication as applied to Ordinances, a printing press. Caution, as to the throwing Scribes out of employ*

On the occasion of this as of every other mode employable for the abridgment of human labour, an effect which can never be too scrupulously attended to, and which at the same time has been almost universally turned aside from, is its effect on the interest—on the very means of subsistence—of the operative hands whose subsistence is derived from the practice of the art in its antecedent state. In various countries of Europe—in England more perhaps than in any other, prodigious is the mass of evil that has been produced by this neglect.

First branch of the evil, distress of the laboring hands whom the introduction of the new art causes to be dismissed, and thence deprives of the means of subsistence. Second branch of that same evil, suffering in the shape of pecuniary loss and other shapes, experienced by those who, thinking to profit by the new art, dismiss in a proportion more or less considerable the hands whom they were wont to occupy in the exercise of the old established one: suffering, namely that produced by the hostility of those who find themselves thus deprived of the means of subsistence—hostility exercised under the notion of its being an exercise of retributive justice.

To the one great master manufacturer, the sufferings of these his discarded servants, to how many hundred so ever they may amount, have generally speaking been of little or no importance. But to no one of all these human beings, strange as it may be in his eyes, is it a matter of no importance. To each of these discarded servants, the difference between comfortable subsistence and death or scanty subsistence from the Parish fund is in reality of much greater importance than is to the Capitalist the difference between the old established rate of profit to which he has been accustomed, and the new and encreased rate of profit to which he aspires.

The law relative to this subject being uniformly the expression of the will either [of] himself or [of] men belonging to a class still more insensible than he is to the miseries of men less fortunate than themselves, the act by which he deprives them of the whole of their subsistence is never treated on the footing of a crime or even of an offence: but on the other hand any act whereby the men who by him have each of them been deprived of the whole of their subsistence shall endeavour to retaliate by depriving him of ever so small a part of his vast opulence is treated on the footing of a crime,

37

and deep is the turpitude imputed to those who have defiled themselves with it.

As to this depravity, whatsoever may be the amount of it, one thing is undeniable, namely that he to whose loss it is manifested, under the circumstance of neglect in question, is the author of it, and has himself to thank for it.

In his own eyes, as also in those of his superiors on whom the state of the laws depends, the heart of the man of opulence is no less full of virtue than his purse of money. To himself the difference in the article of profit is no object. But the public, the sole object of his regard, the public is enriched by it. The discarded laborers—a mean and groveling race, who care nothing about the public, experience nothing but what they deserve.

In the instance here in question, happily the evil here in question, if so it be that it requires any care for the exclusion of it, requires no such care as in the case ante-mentioned. Supposing the Securities in question granted, the copies, the production of which will be necessitated, will furnish of themselves a fresh demand, for which no adequate means of supply can at the time when the demand commences be in existence.

Meantime whatsoever be the improved mode of multiplication employed—lithographic press or ordinary press—care should be taken that the employment given to it should not be such as to throw out of employment any of the existing scribes, except in so far as other employment not less advantageous is found for them. Measures should at the same time be taken to prevent the influx of fresh hands into their business. If notification of the stoppage of the demand for their art be not sufficient, even prohibition might be employed: prohibition absolute, or unless by licence.

§9. *[Operations necessary to adequate publicity of Ordinances continued:] 5. Distribution*

Next to the operation of multiplying the copies of these literary instruments of national security against misrule comes the exposure of the copies to unlimited dissemination. Next to *multiplication* comes *distribution*. Distribution is either gratuitous, or for a price, for example in the way of public sale.

Of copies to a limited amount the distribution might, it is true, be gratuitous. But on such terms the demand might be indefinite: for to no man, able or not able to read the characters on it, would a quantity of paper be without its use. Exposure to sale presents itself therefore as an indispensible mode. But the price demanded should not at any rate be to any the least amount greater than what will suffice to cover the expence. If it were insufficient, it might be so much the better: on the side of economy all that is essential is that it be not so small, as that for purposes other than that of reading it should be worth a man's while to purchase it.

Obvious and unanswerable is the reason why, so it does but prevent mere waste application to purposes other than those intended, the price can not be too small. The efficiency—the usefulness—of these securities will be as the number of the minds by which cognizance of them is taken. On this ultimate security depends the efficiency of whatever else can be designated by that name. For the benefit of this security, no expence that can be incurred by [the distribution of] a number of copies equal to that of the individuals able to read them can be too great.

§ 10. *[Operations necessary to adequate publicity of Ordinances continued:] 6. Public recitation*

As far as it goes, compared with simple Exposure to sale, this operation presents several advantages.

1. By this means, conception of the master document in question may be conveyed to minds in vast multitudes to which by the other, in a word by any other, means it would not be possible to convey it.

2. It is not necessarily attended with any expence.

3. It is susceptible of any additaments applied to it in the view of rendering it the more impressive: of these presently.

On the other hand the signs by means of which the conception is conveyed or endeavoured to be conveyed to the minds in question being of the supremely fugitive and evanescent kind, their existence ceasing as soon as it has commenced, deplorably inadequate will this mode of communication necessarily be in comparison of that which operates by signs susceptible of indefinite permanency. [Not] even for the single instant in which the communication has place can the conception derived be reasonably expected to equal that which has place in the other case in any of the qualities requisite: namely either in clearness, correctness or comprehensiveness: much less at any instant separated from that first instant by any considerable interval of time.

Now as to impressiveness. This quality is capable of being raised above the ordinary level by any one of the following circumstances:

1. The rank of the person by whom the recitation is performed.

2. Any extraordinary degree of aptitude on his part in respect of the properties desirable on the part of a public reader or speaker: for example clearness of pronunciation, strength and agreableness of voice, propriety of intonation with reference to the sense.

3. The place at which the recitation is made.

4. Any circumstance of ceremony with which it may be thought advisable to accompany the operation.

The discourse in question being drawn up and agreed on, the Sovereign, for example, in the principal Mosque, stationed in an elevated station, in which he may be seen by the whole Assembly, takes the paper in hand, and reads it in a voice suited to his convenience. When read he touches it with his seal, with the seal by which his acts as Sovereign are in use to be authenticated, he touches it with his seal, and that instant a signal being given, notification is conveyed to the greatest distance by the firing of artillery and musquetry and the sounding of drums, and trumpets, or whatever loud instruments of music are in use.

After this, for the more effectual information of the surrounding audience, the best reader in all points taken together as above that can be found reads the paper over again, and the notifying sounds as above are repeated. The ceremony might be preceded and followed by a procession from the Palace of the Sovereign to the Mosque and back again.

In those Monarchies of Europe which are called Constitutional—in those and in those which have elsewhere sprung from them—it has been customary for the Monarch to open and close the Legislative Assembly by a speech from the throne—a speech of which though not so much as supposed to have been the penner, he is himself the recitator. But of all these several speeches one general character may be given. For the most part they contain nothing but vague generalities: they contain no enactments: they contain no specific engagements. They are not intended to give expression [to] any specific engagements: indeed the manifest and scarcely dissembled object is to avoid binding the royal speaker to any thing, to keep his hands as free as possible. If on any occasion they amount to any thing, it is when the object of them is [to] notify, though in the most general terms, the assent of the Monarch to a new Constitutional Code or to any particular law to which a preeminent degree of importance is attached, or to propose in the most general terms possible a subject for deliberation and eventual enactment.

In the case of Tripoli, should the consent of the Sovereign to the proposed system of Securities be obtained, the design if I understand aright is—to endeavour to prevail upon him to recite with his own lips not merely a form of words expressive of his assent, but the whole contents of the discourse, unless the length of it should be such as presents an unsurmountable obstacle to the physical exertion necessary.

For this purpose the example of the Sovereigns of the West, as above, might perhaps contribute more or less to the surmounting of any reluctance of which the novelty of the proposal may have been productive in his mind.

§ 11. *II. Second subject-matter of notificative Operations— Transgressions, viz. of men in power. Difficulties as to the giving publicity to them—how obviated*

II. Second class of matters to which publicity requires to be given, *transgressions*.

By transgressions understand, as above, instances in which, the tutelary ordinances having been established as above, acts of oppression as above characterized happen notwithstanding to have place.

Unfortunately in this second instance, the placing the matter in question in broad day-light is not altogether so safe nor therefore so easy as in the former instance.

To an operation of this description the nature of the case will be seen opposing three obvious opponents: namely fear, indolence and poverty. It remains for inquiry what can be done towards the surmounting of these several obstacles.

Obstacle 1, fear. To observe where this passion attaches, we have but to observe the parties whose conjunct labours are necessary to the production of this result.

These are—1. the person or persons from whom in each instance the information should come: 2. the person or persons [by]¹ whom it should be received. Furnisher of the information any person may be: a receiver of it is as such a sort of public functionary: understand if so it be that he does what is requisite to the giving publicity to it, as he must do sooner or later, or he might as well not receive it.

In comparison of that which is opposed by fear, the force of all other obstacles put together is inconsiderable.

Fear is the expectation of eventual evil—evil at the hands of all those to whom publicity in relation to the event in question may come to be disagreable. Against all such fear the most effectual of all securities is *concealment*: concealment of every person by whom any

---

¹ MS 'from'.

thing has been contributed to the publicity of the obnoxious state of things.

Known it is necessary they should be—known to the functionary by whom the information is received or extracted, were it only for the sake of eventual responsibility in case of disturbance given to the peace of the community, or of individuals at least, by false accounts. To one functionary or perhaps one set of functionaries it is necessary that for this purpose every person contributing to the furnishing of the information should be adequately known: known to the purpose of being eventually forthcoming to the purpose of being subjected to punishment in case of mendacity or unjustifiable temerity. But to no other person is it necessary that he should be known.

Next come the several persons by whom any part is borne towards the giving permanence and appropriate publicity to the information when received. At one stage or other some one person at least there must be—naturally persons more than one, whose agency in the business can not be kept concealed: concealed that is to say from those from whose power vengeance will naturally be to be apprehended. But when once any one person is known as having borne a part in it, the greater the number of the persons thus known to have done so, the better: the greater their number, the higher their situation, meaning their official situation—and the more dispersed their several situations, meaning their local situations: for the higher their official situations and the greater the number of the persons occupying those several situations, the more dangerous will it be for the oppressor to endeavour to extend to them his oppressing hand: the higher and more numerous, the more dangerous: and the more dispersed, the more difficult.

Suppose for example by one such functionary or set of functionaries information of an act of oppression received and committed to writing: if their situation is that of a set of functionaries constituting a Judicatory of the higher order, then suppose a copy sent to every Judicatory in the dominion, and by the joint authority of them all made public at one and the same time: made public, by whatsoever means of publicity happen to be at their command. Here the security against vengeance from the oppressor is at its maximum: unless it should be deemed advisable that from this branch of the authority of the state communication be also made to the military.[1]

---

[1] The following fragment on this theme is at UC xxiv. 172 (2 November 1822): 'If in the event of an act of oppression exercised by the Sovereign, and a deposition stating the transaction, made before a pair of Notaries attached to a Mosque, or before the Cadi of a Judicatory, copies were sent to all the several other Judicatories, might not a representation in which the whole body or a considerable part of it concurred be presented to the Sovereign, and rendered

[Obstacle 2, indolence.] A case may be supposed, in which whether fear have place or no, indolence may oppose a bar more or less powerful to communication. Suppose the oppressed party alive and in condition to act, indolence is not in his instance very likely to have place: for affording the requisite excitement, the desire of compensation and vengeance will generally speaking be sufficient. But to him, even though living, it may happen that the injury is not for some time known: and in the case in which the oppression—the injury—is at its maximum, this is the case where adequate excitement is most apt to be wanting: this is the case in which by the oppressive act the life of the victim has been made a sacrifice. In this case whether any connection of his disposed to come forward and seek redress be in existence will be matter of accident. In one case, and that not a very uncommon one, the non-existence of any such person will be an occurrence altogether natural. A dead body, say at the dawn of day, the dead body of a man, is found lying in a high road or some other such public place, and for some time nobody knowing whose it is, by no connection of his is the catastrophe known or suspected.

In a case of this sort the object is to obtain information from the person to whose senses the spectacle has happened to present itself in the first instance. In this, for surmounting the resisting force of indolence, three active forces present themselves—appeal to social affection by a standing authoritative and appropriate discourse, punishment in the case of non-performance, reward in the case of performance, of this public service. Of these instruments, whether one or more or all may with most propriety be employed will depend upon circumstances: circumstances too particular to lay claim to a place here.

Obstacle 3, poverty: understand relative poverty—inability to defray the expence, whatsoever it may be. Of the operations necessarily preparatory to the ultimate publication above brought to view, an indefinite number may, any or all of them, be unavoidably attended with an indefinite amount of expence. 1. Collecting from places in indefinite number, each of them indefinitely distant, persons capable

publickly notorious all over the Capital and elsewhere with very little danger to the individuals concurring in it? If no more than a single Iman or no more than a single Cadi were to present to the Sovereign a representation of this sort, he might be tempted to render the troublesome man shorter by the head. But under any Pacha that ever sat or any Pacha that is ever likely to sit on the throne, is it likely that the whole body of these functionaries to whom the attachment of the people it seems is so strong, the whole body or any considerable part of it, would be apprehensive of such a fate?

'Be this as it may, what seems evident enough is—that the greater the number were of these respected functionaries that joined in a representation of this sort, the less the cause they would have to apprehend destruction or oppression at the despot's hands.'

of serving in the character of reporting, or say deposing, witnesses. 2. Committing to writing the result of their respective depositions. 3. Transmitting from judicatory to judicatory, from office to office, copies of the written instrument to which the statement of the case was first consigned.

That provision might in some way or other be made for them, the case required that these several sources of expence should be brought to view. In what particular way such provision may most conveniently [be] made will depend upon local circumstances, such as lie not within the cognizance of him by whom these particulars are offered to view.

Note here, that as well upon those who are likely to be most willing as upon those who are likely to be most unwilling, should the tone of whatever ordinances are issued for promoting publication be as forcibly imperative as possible. The more irresistible in appearance the coercive process, the greater will be the security given to him in whose breast any desire to cooperate towards the beneficial effect in question has place: against the wrath of the offended and denounced oppressor he has coercion to plead [for] his excuse.

§ 12. *Continuation. Notificative operations applicable to such transgressions*[1]

§ 13. *III. Third subject-matter of notificative operations, Suffrages: viz. of the members of the community considered as members of the Public Opinion Tribunal. Operations applicable to them: 1. Extraction. 2. Registration. 3. Multiplication. 4. Transmission and Diffusion or Circulation. Sole adequate instrument, a Newspaper*

III. Suffrages.

To the subject-matter thus denominated, of the abovementioned operations those which apply will be seen to be the following: viz. 1. Extraction. 2. Registration. 3. Multiplication. 4. Transmission, or say Diffusion.

For all these several operations, one and the same article presents itself as the effectual and the only effectual instrument. This instrument is no other than a *Newspaper*: multitude of instruments of

[1] No MSS for this section have been indicated on the plan at UC xxiv. 191 (14 November 1822), and none appear to have been written.

the same sort employed by so many different sets of hands, and multitude of copies of each, as great as possible.

In this instrument may be seen not only an appropriate organ of the Public Opinion Tribunal, but the only constantly acting visible one.

In this the same Tribunal, it is by the Newspaper Editor that in each case the motion in which the decision originates is made: and thus much of the matter is no fiction but the exact truth. Thereupon come the suffrages—suffrages given by those members of the community, being at the same time readers of the Newspaper or in converse with those that are, to whom it happens to take cognizance of the matter. These being from the nature of the business incapable of being collected, the number of them must in each case be left to inference and conjecture. Mean time one thing requires to be remarked, namely that in the instance of each person it is by the real opinion and the real and inward affection—not the opinion and affection declared and avowed, that the salutary effect, the check applied to misrule, is produced: for it is by opinion and affection really entertained, and not by the opinion and affection professed to be entertained by a man, that his action in the shape in question is produced.

Newspapers suppose two: taking different sides of the question in each case: one suppose the side of the suffering people; the other the side of an oppressing Sovereign and his misrule: the case is rendered more complicated; but [not] the nature of it. Motions the tenor of them in every instance visible and permanent: outward suffrages, expressed or not expressed, i.e. with or without tenor—but in both cases, invisible and evanescent. Of these suffrages, some are on the side of one of the motions, others on that of the other.

Greater is the efficiency of this one sort of written instrument than that of all other written instruments put together. On this or that question, pamphlets and books—works small and great—may be written in any number, each of them of any bulk in use. But by no one of them is any regular cognizance taken of the several occurrences as they take place: for by any publication suppose any such regularity and constancy of attention kept up, it becomes the very thing here in question—a Newspaper.

In a Representative Government, at any rate in a Representative Democracy, with the exception of the function of the principal Minister, greater is the importance [of] the function of this unofficial functionary than of any official one: more important, that is to say particularly to the great purpose here in question—that of making application of the power of the Public Opinion Tribunal in by far the most beneficial and the highest character of a check upon misrule. By the Prime Minister impulse is given to the machinery of the political sanction: by the Editor of the prime popular Newspaper, to that of the social sanction. Of this superiority the causes are: 1. the greater the number of the suffrages which, on each occasion, [take for their ground] the motions made by this representative of the people,[1] the motions made by this unofficial compared with those made by any official representative, but 2. more particularly the constancy and continuity of action which has place in this case—sources of influence in respect of which no official representative, limited as his motions and discourses are to particular and scattered seasons and scattered points of time, can hold comparison.

§ 14. *Extent of circulation—in the case of a Newspaper, circumstances on which it depends:—1. Constancy. 2. Frequency. 3. Variety. 4. Cheapness. 5. Impartiality and candour. 6. Moderation*

The aptitude of the Newspaper in question as measured by the greatest happiness of the greatest number being given, its usefulness will be as the extent to which the diffusion of it has place: in other words as the number of the minds to which it finds its way.

The circumstances on which the degree of this extent depends, in particular at the outset of the sort of institution in question, are: 1. the constancy, 2. the frequency, of its publication: 3. its mixture with matters of a nature more universally interesting: 4. its cheapness—the smallness of the price: 5. the impartiality of its procedure in respect of the admission or rejection of articles: 6. the moderation of its language: i.e. its purity from expressions of vague and ungrounded vituperation and laudation of men and measures.[2]

Of these several qualities the three first are at once the most essential, and the most easy to secure to it, as being more compleatly independent of the mental qualities, moral and intellectual, of individuals.

1. As to constancy. This quality is of all others the easiest to secure. The interest created and kept up by it can not but be in the closest degree dependent upon the assurance with which on the occasion of each paper a reader looks forward to a regular succession of the like entertainment provided by the same hand. So invariably is this property possessed by this species of discourse wherever it has

---

[1] MS '1. the greater the number of the suffrages by which, on each occasion, the motions made by this representative of the people are taken for their ground'.

[2] In the margin, Bentham added a further circumstance: 'the quantity of talent in all shapes employed in the composition of it'.

place, that the absence of it, not being presented by experience, is not easily presented to view by imagination.

2. Next in the order of importance comes the article of frequency. The number of readers being given, the greater the frequency of its appearance, the greater the degree of diffusion: nor, in the instance of the aliment thus administered to the mind, is the appetite slackened by the frequency of its application, as in the case of the aliment administered to the bodily frame:[1] on the contrary it is rather kept alive and invigorated: the meal of each day operating as an excitement to look out for that of the next day following.

3. Variety. Admixture of this sort with matters of other sorts the most [general][2] and this in the greatest variety possible. What gives this property an essential claim to notice is—1. that besides the degree in which the degree of diffusion depends upon it, the degree of frequency with which it can appear is to such a degree dependent on it, and 2. that it is so little dependent upon the talent employed in the conducting of it.

Suppose for example six sorts of matter each of them interesting to one class of readers, no one sort interesting to classes more than one: by this means you have six times as many readers and regular purchasers as if there were no more sorts of matter in it than one. Each class stands assured of having something in which he takes an interest: as it is on no other terms that he can get any thing, no one of them is debarred from the purchase of his own sixth by the consideration that more than that sixth is not obtainable.

Where this variety of matter is kept up, in respect of attractiveness no imaginable literary composition can by possibility enter into competition with them, nor in particular with reference to the uses here in question. From the physical association, the contiguity of the material and visible signs, an association is insensibly formed between the ideas of which they are respectively the representatives. Taking up the Newspaper, each person is upon the look-out for the matter of that sort in which he takes a more particular interest. But while he is upon the look-out for that, matter of all other sorts is continually offering itself to his eyes. Little by little, the strangeness and repulsiveness of each wears away, each in some degree or other becomes more and more familiar to him: and even supposing that matters in which he takes no interest at all are regularly passed over without a glance, still of those in which he takes some interest, the interest is in this way, little by little, encreased.

[1] In the margin, Bentham added at this point: 'it being understood that the frequency is not greater than once in four and twenty hours'.

[2] MS 'generally'.

In what abundance, by the mere circumstance of their being among the contents of his newspaper, a man is led to the reading of articles for which he would not ever have looked in any publication exclusively appropriated to the reception of them, is a circumstance which can scarcely have escaped any person's experience.[1]

5. Impartiality—its uses. Wheresoever Newspapers have place, so will parties: and wherever there are parties, all minor divisions naturally coalesce under one all-comprehensive division, the assailants and the supporters of the party which has the power of the country in its hands. If there be any tolerable degree of freedom, a newspaper can scarcely have place for any length of time but rival newspaper[s], one or more, will start up likewise. Be the number of newspapers ever so great or ever so small, great would be the advantage in respect of extent of custom, if the Editor could prevail upon himself to keep up an impartial course between the two parties: to give equal admission to attacks and to defences. Obvious altogether is the advantage which the course thus prescribed by justice would secure to him: readers of all parties would be invited—no reader of any party would be repelled. Number of readers in each party suppose equal, on this impartial plan the number would be the double of that which it is on the ordinary partial plan.

But for securing to the instrument of instruction this at once most respectable and most difficult endowment, and this without prejudice to the currency of it, what would be the most eligible course? Not to omitt controversial matter on both sides, but to admitt it on both sides: by the omission of this stimulating matter the publication would be rendered [insipid]:[2] by the reciprocal and double insertion, it will be rendered doubly excitative and attractive.

On the part of a Newspaper Editor, nothing is more easy than to profess impartiality; few things more difficult [than] to maintain it. But if in the highest degree utility depends upon impartiality, upon actual impartiality, in a not much inferior degree does it depend upon the reputation of impartiality—upon the proportion between the number of those of its readers in whose eyes it is impartial and the number of those in [whose eyes][3] it fails in respect of a quality so highly desirable: and unhappily it may be in ever so high a degree actually impartial, and yet, and even from that very cause, be partial in the eyes of both.[4]

---

[1] Bentham did not consider the fourth point, 'Cheapness'.

[2] The addition is suggested by the marginal summary: 'Effect of the exclusive mode, insipidity'.

[3] MS 'which'.

[4] Bentham seems to contradict himself by maintaining that a newspaper may appear partial to a group of readers to whom the same newspaper appears impartial. His point was that the

For keeping up impartiality without diminution of pugnancy, the most effectual course, supposing extent of sale sufficient, would be for the proprietor of the Newspaper to employ two Editors, one whose affections were on the one side, the other whose affections were on the opposite side: the number of days in the year allotted to each being the same. There should not however be any regular course of alternation: in particular the most obvious course, each conducting the paper every other day, should not be employed. Why not? the answer is—lest in that case there should be a correspondent alternation and division among the customers: one set buying the paper on the government day and not on the opposition day: the other on the opposition day and not on the government day. Not that the greater part of the readers would thus content themselves with no more than half of the aggregate stock of facts: but still some there would be, and antecedently to experience it would not be possible to say in what number. As to any endeavour to conceal this part of the arrangement, it would neither be practicable nor desirable. To exclude fraud and injustice and to secure harmony, some arrangements of detail would be necessary—nor does the framing such as should be adequate present to view a task of any considerable difficulty.

6. Moderation, or say Good temper.

Unhappily for securing this quality, important as it is—there is no such simple and effectual recipe as hath been shewn to have place in the case of impartiality.

Of moderation the simplest and clearest description, as far as it goes, that can be given is—the avoiding to employ for the giving expression to disapprobation, whether of men or modes of action, any words or phrases of vague and violent vituperation that express aversion and displeasure, without any precise[?] designation of the cause of it.

Of every violation of the line of moderation, various and serious are apt to be the evil consequences:

1. By the disgust which it can not but provoke, it tends to repel readers in a number altogether unascertainable and unlimited: and among them not only those who are decide[d]ly attached to the party whose sensibility is thus wounded, but others who are neutral, indifferent or undecided.

2. By the hostility thus manifeste[d], correspondent hostility on the opposite side can not but be provoked.

newspaper, despite its actual impartiality, might appear partial to readers of both parties. See the corresponding marginal summary: 'Of impartiality, profession easy; practice difficult: nor from actual follows reputed ditto, but reputed partiality in the eyes of both.'

3. Among the consequences of such hostility, prosecutive attacks in the field of judicature will, with more or less frequency, have place.

§ 15. *Plan for the conducting of a Newspaper at Tripoli—Topics under which matter may be inserted*

[Sorts of articles] by which an interest more or less extensive can not fail to be excited [are]:

[1.] an indication[1] of things offered for purchase or hire:

[2.] prices of goods of various sorts at various places:

[3.] probabilities in respect of future encrease and diminution of price.

[4.] In particular, descriptions of the Slaves as they arrive from time to time for sale. To attract attention, to every such advertisement might be prefixed the image of a Negro—as in the Newspapers of the United States.

So likewise the images of other sorts of articles on sale.

[5.] Accidents. At all times by occurrences of this sort more or less of interest can scarcely fail to be excited in most breasts. The greater the interest taken, the greater the encouragement and assistance afforded to the sympathetic affection upon an extensive scale: that affection upon the strength of which morality and felicity so essentially depend.

[6.] Offences. Of matter under this head the usefulness is of prime importance with reference to the particular design here in question. Of the misdeeds of various sorts from time to time committed, few in comparison at the utmost will be those committed by the orders of the Sovereign, or which it is matter of pleasure or advantage to him to see committed. For the greater part they will be of that class by which, while no profit in any shape is produced to men in power as such, suffering is produced to individuals, and through individuals danger and alarm to the community at large—thereby to the members of government in their quality of members of the community at large. This being the case, to the publication of misdeeds in general no aversion will be excited in their minds, no objection will have place in their eyes. But the habit of inserting and reading accounts of misdeeds of all shapes being once established, mention of misdeeds committed by or agreable to men in power will find their [way][2] in along with the rest, will flow in along with the crowd, will slide in unobserved by the

---

[1] MS '1. One sort of article by which an interest more or less extensive can not fail to be excited is—an indication'.

[2] MS 'away'.

50

editor, or at least as if unobserved. And thus the way will be paved for the general admission of misdeeds by the commission of which the interest of the man in power is served, or imagined by him to be served.

7. Proceedings of Judicatories: especially that of the Cadi in the Metropolis: being that by the proceedings of which the greatest interest will naturally be excited.

8. Deaths. Number of, in the Metropolis and other principal towns: according to a periodical enumeration, if obtainable.

In the case of those of remarkable persons, their names given, with any particulars that can be collected of their characters.

9. Births. Those of persons of the male sex may be ascertained by the acts of circumcision: of which a register, if not actually kept, might it is supposed without much difficulty be caused to be kept by the Imans and Notaries of the several Mosques.

10. The like occurrences in the domains of the neighbouring States.

11. Parallels between the particulars indicative of the state of society and manners as between the State in question and other Mahometan States on the one part, and Christian States in general or in particular on the other: viz.

1. Points on which the advantage appears to be on the side of Mahometan States.

2. Points on which the advantage appears to be on the side of the Christian States.

In all these cases, constant standard of reference, greatest happiness of greatest number.

12. Indication of physical inconveniences; with or without hints respecting the most eligible means of remedy.

To each class of articles as above there might be a use in prefixing the denomination of it in a separate line and larger type: as thus—

Accidents

Offences

Deaths

By this means, 1. a reader would be directed instantaneously to the class, whatever it were, in which it happened to him to take an interest: 2. the attention would by this perpetually-recurring excitement be kept awake: 3. by these exemplifications, the minds of readers would be familiarized with the practice and general conception of commodious arrangement.

§ 16. *Literary capital requisite antecedently to commencement*

Particulars of the mass of literary capital to be provided antecedently to the commencement of the publication of a work of this sort.

Antecedently to the setting up of any such Newspapers, it would be highly advisable to have a stock more or less common of Newspapers to serve as sources by which heads of information would be brought to view, and might be selected. Of all newspapers the English are by far the most instructive: next to them, those of the Anglo-American United States. In comparison of these, the French are worth but little: the newspapers of all other nations put together, nothing at all. A public document which it is hoped will accompany this paper will serve to shew the prodigious number of articles of this sort that are every year published in England. Also the common revenue derived from them:[1] always remembered that this is among the worst of all sources of revenue: more especially so would it be, in any country in which Newspapers were set up for the first time. The reason is that to an extent more or less considerable every tax operates as a prohibition: a prohibition applied to the sort of article taxed: and in the instance in question, though a bounty would not be necessary nor therefore useful, a bounty would be less mischievous than a prohibition.

Suppose a dozen boys receiving at the School in question their education,[2] the most useful and thus the highest occupation which the best head among them could be put to would be that of conducting a Newspaper on his return to his own country. The Master might choose for this purpose the most promising and he might be trained to it, even at the School itself before his return.

Antecedently to the setting up as above, a stock of matter should be prepared and kept in readiness: trying various topics for the purpose of observing and learning which of them excited the strongest interest. As the publication went on various articles—advertisements in particular—would of course be sent in by those whose tastes were pleased or their interests as it seemed to them served. As this miscellaneous and more highly interesting matter by degrees came in, the

---

[1] According to 'Stamps issued for Newspapers', ordered to be printed by the House of Commons 2 May 1822, *House of Commons Accounts and Papers 1822*, xxi. 381–4, there were 24,779,786 stamps issued in 1821, yielding a revenue of £412,996.

[2] Bentham had encouraged D'Ghies to write to his father recommending him to send twelve boys to Hazelwood School, which had been founded at Edgbaston, Birmingham, in 1819 by Thomas Wright Hill and his sons Arthur, Rowland and Matthew Davenport Hill: see 'Bentham to Adams', p. 150 below.

less interesting matter belonging to the original stock would give way to it. It is of the utmost consequence—that on no appointed day whatsoever any failure of the appearance of the paper should take place: and by the preparatory stock in question all such failure might effectually be prevented.

§ 17. *How to maximize the usefulness of this instrument of publicity and public instruction*

A degree of diffusion sufficient for continuance being supposed already to be established, now then comes the question concerning the general usefulness of it, by what means it may be raised to the highest pitch.

In the first place as to the only right and proper end of social action—the greatest happiness of the greatest number—this all-comprehensive and all-important principle, though not on every occasion held up to view in its own name, should on every occasion be inwardly kept in view: and even by name the greater the number of the occasions on which, without exciting alarm and disgust, it can be brought to view, the better: for by it a standard is held up—the only legitimate standard—by which the mischievousness of misdeeds can be proved, and the degree of it measured and indicated.

Every occasion should be embraced of making application of the greatest happiness principle to the individual occurrences of the day, shewing: 1. how morality and happiness depend upon the notoriety of the rule of action referred to by the judicatories: 2. importance of the greatest degree of equality consistent with security in the case of the external instruments of felicity in all their shapes—in particular, power and the matter of wealth in all its shapes: 3. shewing how compensation to all sufferers by a misdeed in any shape ought to take place of barren punishment, because the burthen of affording compensation operates as punishment as far as it goes: [4.] how punishment should be adapted to misdoing, that by allotting to the more mischievous misdeed the more severe punishment those who can not refrain from misdoing altogether may be induced to committ the less mischievous in preference to the more mischievous, etc. etc.

53

§ 18. *Public Opinion Tribunal—Parallel between this unofficial [and] the official Judicatories*[1]

Sub§ 1. A Judicatory: its attributes

The more closely the nature of the Public Opinion Tribunal is looked into, the more clear and strong will be the conception of its efficiency and consequently its existence.

When announced it will be apt to present itself as nothing more than the offspring of imagination and language:—a purely fictitious and verbal entity. The cause and reason of this is—that on no occasion are the several members of it seen sitting all together in their official and judicial capacity, or so much as capable of sitting and taking part in the business at the same time and in the same edifice or inclosure, or when at a distance maintaining any thing like a regular course of correspondence.

It wears therefore the colour of fictitiousness. But it possesses the substance of reality. This will be rendered manifest in proportion as observation is taken of the operations by the performance of which the ordinary sort of judicatories commonly so called—those in the instance of which no one would think of contesting the denomination, are characterized.

To a judicatory, as such, belong certain functions: these functions are exercised by the performance of correspondent operations.

To every judicatory as such belongs a certain mass of *power*: namely the power necessary to the performance of those same operations.

To the will of the several members of every judicatory applies moreover a certain *ruling interest*: in the exercise of this power they will of course be guided by the direction in which their will is acted upon by this same ruling interest.

To the head of ruling interest belongs that of *pay*: for as much as the ruling interest by which they are respectively actuated depends of course in a great degree on their pay, if pay they have: [on][2] the manner in which it is connected with their continuance in their situations and the line of conduct therein maintained by them.

As to the Operations called functions, they may be thus enumerated:

1. Receiving claims and accusations: claims referring to what is

---

[1] Abandoned fragments relating to topics discussed in this section are at UC xxiv. 189 (n.d. December 1822) and xxiv. 239 (10 December 1822).
[2] MS 'of'.

called the civil branch, i.e. the non-penal branch, of judicature; accusations, to the penal.

2. Receiving oppositions and defences: oppositions, to claims; defences, against accusations.

3. Receiving, compelling, collecting, and storing evidence: viz. in support of the oppositions as well as claims, of defences as well as accusations.

4. Hearing or reading arguments, or say reasons, of parties or advocates or both.

5. Forming on each occasion an opinion, or say a judgment, with a correspondent will.

6. Giving expression to such judgment and will.

7. Giving execution and effect to such judgment and will.

Amongst different judicatories, it is evident, may these functions in various ways be distributed. But to the attainment of the ends of justice the exercise of them all is necessary—it is necessary that [by] some persons or other, in some way or other, they should be all performed.

Inserted in some way or other in the string of these essential operations may be other incidental ones, such as citations, applications for delay, and so forth. But it will be found that these belong, and that there are no others that do belong, to the catalogue of essential ones.

As to the word *power*, before it can serve to bring to view in any clear and distinct form the attributes comprehended under it, certain particulars serving as sources of division will require to be brought to view, namely: 1. the several fields over which it exercises itself: 2. the means of efficiency: means by the use of which it gives to itself execution and effect.

1. As to *fields* of exercise. To the power of every efficient official judicatory belong two distinguishable fields:—the local: which may also be termed its territorial, topographical or geographical field: the logical, termed also the metaphysical. In the logical may moreover be distinguished: 1. the corporeal subjects comprehended in it, namely the persons and things; 2. the incorporeal subjects, namely the sorts of suits, causes, or *demands* of which cognizance is taken, i.e. of claims and accusations.

[2.] As to means of efficiency, they are its means of operating with effect, with relation to whatever be the end proposed, on its above-mentioned subjects, namely on persons, and on immovable portions of territory [and] moveable things: on things by means operating on body alone, namely physical force; on persons, by those same means with the addition of forces operating on mind, namely prospect of punishment—i.e. of eventual evil in any shape, and the prospect of reward, [good][1] in any shape: matter of evil, applied as punishment, matter of good, applied as reward or otherwise: viz. as capital.[2]

On the aggregate amplitude of these its several fields and means of efficiency depends the aggregate amplitude, or say the magnitude, of the mass of power belonging to any official judicatory: in the same elements will be found the measure of the power of the Public Opinion Tribunal.

As to *ruling interest*, it is a topic that will be apt to present itself as more new than agreable when applied to any official judicatory: it does not however the less indisputably belong to it, as well as to the Public Opinion Tribunal: and in this one of its attributes will this all-comprehensive though unofficial judicatory be seen to possess its strongest title to regard. The interest of the Public Opinion Tribunal, that is to say of the aggregate number of its members, the interest can never be in discordance with the interest of the aggregate number of the members of the political state or community in question: whereas whether we take the aggregate interest of the whole number of official tribunals or their several particular and distinct interests, that is to say the aggregate of the interests of the several members, it can never be in compleat accordance with the abovementioned universal interest.

Such is the identity on the part of the real net interest: and in so far as correctly understood and capable of being pursued, it is the real net interest that in every individual and in every aggregate of individuals will on each occasion be the actual ruling interest.

Sub§2. Attributes belonging to this unofficial Judicatory—I. Members
To every official judicatory, the above several attributes will be allowed to appertain without dispute. No less truly will they be seen to belong to this unofficial judicatory.

First as to its Members. On this first point will be seen to lie the greatest, or rather the only, difficulty. In this front part of the picture reality wears somewhat the air of fiction. Of the object designated by the appellation of Public Opinion Tribunal, familiar as the expression is, the existence will be apt to be suspected of being no other than figurative and merely nominal. On the other hand the name of it is not more perfectly familiar than the existence of its power is universally recognized. As to the particular instances of its manifestation, they will not be left to rest on so uncertain a support as that of un-scrutinized usage: in proper place some of them will here be brought

---

[1] MS 'evil'.
[2] In the text, Bentham noted at this point: 'Quere.'

to view: and of an object the power of which is admitted, a proposition which should deny the existence would be a self-contradictory one. Even in regard to Members the only difficulty lies in the determination of the individuals to whom on the several particular occasions the appellation can without impropriety be applied: but even as to this point, the uncertainty may not unfrequently be seen shared in by official Judicatories.

Be this as it may, a function supposes a functionary: at the least one functionary: an operation, an operator. Ere any account can be rendered of the operations of the unofficial Judicatory, some individual or individuals must be brought to view as and for so many Members of this judicatory, members by whom the several operations are performed.

At the head of them as being the most conspicuous, and as exercising the function in question in a manner the most conspicuous, sits the Editor of a Newspaper [in a State][1] in which the press howsoever legally manacled otherwise is, to the purpose of being capable of affording an example of this sort of judicature, practically free. Say for example an English Newspaper. An Anglo-American United States Newspaper is to this purpose legally as well as practically free, but, it being in Europe less known, the English Newspaper will be the more convenient object of reference.

But, of the unofficial judicatory, an English Newspaper Editor is but one member amongst millions. To shew in what way he is so it will be necessary to shew in what relation this one individual stands to the millions: in a word of what different classes and ranks, to so many different purposes, this judicatory taken in its totality is composed: to shew the constitution of the whole judicatory.

Take any political community—the British empire for example. Of the aggregate of all the persons belonging to it, rulers and subjects taken together, will the Public Opinion Tribunal be composed. Not only the inhabitants of the two Islands but the inhabitants of the several distant dependencies in the once four quarters, now five great portions, of the globe must to this as to other purposes be considered as included. But not to speak of those who do not take a part in the consideration of subject-matters of the nature in question, a large proportion of the number, to wit children below a certain age, is composed of those who by physical infirmity are rendered absolutely incapable of taking such part. Distinction 1st.: those members who

---

[1] The addition is suggested by the marginal summary: 'First, as most conspicuously existing, and extensively and constantly operating, Newspaper Editor: viz. in a State, for example England, where, howsoever legally manacled, to a certain degree he is in practice free.'

belong to the Tribunal in respect of interest and future practice only, and those who belong to it in respect of present practice.

Not excluded from this judicatory are, as such, any persons of the female sex. From the exercise of a share in the Constitutive power by means of votes in the election of the possessors of the supreme operative power or a share in it, they the gentler half of the species stand as yet excluded by tyranny and prejudice. But from a share in the power of this judicatory of judicatories, not even the united force of tyranny and prejudice ever have altogether excluded them any where, much less will henceforward ever exclude them.

In those who belong to it in respect of present practice may again be distinguished [four][1] classes: viz. 1. those who are merely speaking members: 2. those who are not only speaking but also reading members: 3. those who are not only speaking and reading, but also writing members: 4. those who are not only speaking, reading and writing, but also printing and publishing members.

The class of merely speaking members forms the basis of the several others: it can not any where at any time be extinguished. If it could be extinguished, European governments are not wanting in which it would most assuredly be extinguished, at least be endeavoured to be extinguished. For example by cutting tongues out it might be extinguished, and would of course be extinguished. But tongues and the use of them are indispensable to the performance of that labour without which the stock of the external instruments of felicity, by means of which the felicity of the ruling one and the sub-ruling few is reaped, could not be brought into existence. By any such extinction as this the interest of these same rulers would, in their conception of it, be not served but disserved. Accordingly no such extinction has ever yet been endeavoured at, or seems at all likely ever to be endeavoured at. Not so by the general extinction of those other classes, saving and excepting such a portion of them respectively as under the direction of the supreme ruler may be necessary to be employed in the production and preparation of these same useful instruments, and securing him in the undisturbed possession of them, and in the application of them by him and for him to their respectively appropriate purposes.

So long as human beings come in presence of each other it is impossible generally speaking to prevent their conversing with each other: and so long as they converse with each other on any subject it is not possible to prevent them from conversing occasionally upon political subjects. In the interior of a palace, even without the trouble

---

[1] MS 'three'.

of cutting their tongues out, men may be converted into mutes: accordingly in palaces in which the art and science of legitimate-rule has been carried to perfection, a transformation of this sort is known to have been accomplished. But in places other than palaces, for preventing conversation from taking any such dangerous direction, no means does the nature of the case afford but the employment of spies: but here occurr divers difficulties: spies adequate to this purpose would require to be no less numerous than soldiers, and to be even more highly paid, and how well soever paid, among them, no one can say in how large a proportion, might be those who seeing it necessary to put a deceit would prefer putting it upon the universal enemy to putting it upon their respective friends. Moreover the more strict and efficient the system of discipline employed in the extinction of the several classes of publishers, writers and readers, the more apt would this policy be to become the subject of frequent not to say constant conversation among the classes of speakers whom in conclusion it would never be possible to extinguish.

If all the several members of the political community in question be considered every one of them as being so many members of the Public Opinion Tribunal, those who are physically speaking not incapable of acting as such may be considered as composing a standing Committee of the whole body, invested with the powers of the whole.

That which however would be no less simple in conception, and would be more exactly conformable to strict truth, would be—to consider the whole aggregate of those who are physically speaking not incapable of taking a part in the consideration of public affairs as composing and constituting the entire judicatory: invested with the power in trust for themselves and the several other members of the community at large.

These then constituting the entire body, a standing Committee of that same body will be the aggregate composed of all those who at any given point of time do actually concur in taking cognizance of the affairs in question or any part of them, and they whether in the way of publication, writing, reading or oral converse: and of this General Committee may be conceived as constituted so many Sub-Committees as there are aggregates of individuals who on any occasion in any place take actual cognizance of this or that operation of a political nature, to whatsoever part of the field of government it appertains.

Of these several Sub-Committees the several authors by whom respectively a literary work of any kind, bearing in any way upon any part of the field of government, is published may be considered as so many Presiding, or say Leading, Members, or in one word *Presidents*: and a political Newspaper Editor, being the only one in constant activity, is as it were among the Presidents of these same Presidents: King of these Kings; Lord of these Lords;[1] real and not sham representatives of all who buy and of all who read with sympathy their respective publications, the products of their respective labours.

Among the infinity of Sub-Committees of the Public Opinion Tribunal as above indicated, three as being the most efficient ones [are] required to be distinguished. These are:

1. The Sub-Committees of General Superintendence. President, a Newspaper Editor: other Members, his customers and readers, and in particular his correspondents. These last belong to the catalogue of Leading Members.

2. The Sub-Committees of Judicature, or say Justice. Members, the several individuals who, being present in the several Judicatories during the dispatch of the several businesses, take interest in what is going forward, in such sort as to form an opinion of approbation or disapprobation in relation to any part of it.

3. Sub-Committees of Religion. Members, the persons present at the several Sermons or other discourses held on the subject of religion by the several officiating Priests: also those by whom the several works on that subject are read or heard in places other than those which are appropriated to this sort of occupation.

In one and the same number of an English Newspaper may commonly be seen the united fruit of the labours of a number of these Sub-Committees.

Thus much may, it is hoped, suffice, for the purpose of illustration, and for the giving to our conceptions on the subject such degree of clearness as the nature of the case admitts.

Sub§3. II. Functions or Operations of the Supreme Unofficial compared with those of the Official Judicatories

The several operations included in this part of the business of one English Newspaper being thus taken as and for a specimen or sample of the functions of a Sub-Committee of the Public Opinion Tribunal, let us see in what way the mode in which these several functions are there performed by it agrees with, and in what way it differs from, the mode in which those same functions are most commonly performed in and by an Official Judicatory.

To the present purpose they may be enumerated as follows:[2]

1. Receiving claims and accusations.

2. Receiving oppositions and defences.[3]

---

[1] See I Timothy 6: 15.

[2] This list of functions differs slightly from that given in Sub§1, pp. 54–5 above.

[3] The remainder of this list and the following two paragraphs are in the hand of the copyist, but bear additions, deletions and emendations in Bentham's hand.

3. Receiving, compelling, collecting and storing evidence.

4. Receiving and hearing or reading arguments of parties litigant or advocates.

5. Forming opinions or judgments on ditto: with correspondent *will*.

6. Giving expression to such judgments and will.

7. Giving impression to such expression.

8. Giving diffusion to such impression.

9. Giving execution and effect to such judgment[s] and will.

Distinct in themselves are all these several operations: and in and by the ordinary Judicatories, who have the time of other men as well as their own time at their disposal, as well as the channels of communication at command, they are performed at different times and in regular succession, as above displayed.

In and by the Public Opinion Tribunal, a Member of it not having, generally speaking, either any channel of communication or the time of any other person at his command, these several operations can not respectively be performed but as occasion offers; and when occasion does offer, it must be made the most of, and the several operations, all of them, or as many as can to advantage be performed, be performed at once.

Follow, under the above several heads, a few observations, having for their object the bringing to view the principal points of agreement and difference between the one sort of judicatory and the other.

1. Receiving *accusations*. Note that, in the case of a *claim*, conception not being quite so simple, it may for the purpose of the present exemplification be put aside. In the Newspaper in question an allegation is made of misdoing in a certain shape as having had place on the part of a certain functionary or set of functionaries: the accuser, whether the Editor himself or a correspondent, makes to this purpose no difference. Here the function of receiving accusations stands exemplified.

2. Receiving defences. Of the exemplification made of the exercise of this function, indication will be made presently.

3. On this same occasion, a correspondent makes mention perhaps of this or that particular as having fallen within his own knowledge: for the security of Editor and Printer the name though not signed, having or not having been privately communicated. Here the function of reception of evidence and, at the same time, that of the impression of it, and that of the diffusion of it, stand exemplified.

At the same time, whether directly by means of appropriate and direct questions, or at any rate indirectly and virtually, by means of apposite allegations as above, the party accused is called upon either to confess the act thus indicated with its inculpative circumstances, and at the same time thus directly or virtually to confess the culpability of it, or to deny the act or some essential inculpative circumstance or circumstances belonging to it, or admitting what is above to argue in justification of the act.

The next day or the next but one suppose, the party thus called argues in justification of the act; but at the same time either directly avows the having done it or by his silence or the turn given to his argument virtually admitts it. Here the function of compelling evidence stands exemplified.

On the former day, intimation is moreover given of certain other persons as having been percipient witnesses of the act or this or that inculpative circumstance belonging to it, and as being thereby rendered capable, if so disposed, of rendering themselves in relation thereto reporting, narrating, or say deposing, witnesses. Here a commencement of the function of collecting evidence stands exemplified.

Purchasers, in number more or less considerable, being in the habit of filing and preserving the numbers of the Newspaper in question as they come out, here the function of keeping in store, in a word of *storing*, the stock of evidence in question stands exemplified.

4. With the evidence thus received, compelled, collected and kept in store, [is][1] commonly at the same time mixt up and thus received and kept in store, in some proportion or other, matter on both sides bearing the character of argument: argument having for [its] object the bringing to view either the probability or improbability of the alledged act or of the alledged inculpative circumstances, or the impropriety or propriety of it, or both together: each party, by or with the argument he delivers, directly or virtually calling for counter-argument on the other side. Here then the function of receiving arguments at the hands of parties litigant or their advocates, or both, stands exemplified. The function of reading or hearing this mass of argument together with the correspondent mass of evidence is in this case left to the purchasers and other readers or hearers of the News-paper, each one exercising it for himself or this or that associate of his.

5. and 6. Having received from his correspondent the above-mentioned letter and thereupon the several other masses of evidence and argument above-mentioned, the Editor in the course of the controversy forms and declares some opinion, or say judgment, of his own, provisional or definitive, in favour of the accusing or the defend-

[1] MS 'are'.

ing side. Here the function of forming and that of giving expression to such opinion and judgment stand exemplified.

The judgment suppose is a judgment declaring conviction, and passing sentence of condemnation on the party so accused. But in such judgment and sentence of condemnation is included an opinion that by the party thus condemned a disreputable act has been committed, an act whereby he will be depressed in the estimation of other members of this same unofficial judicatory in an indeterminable and incalculable number: in consequence of which depression he will in the natural course of things be deprived in some sort and proportion or other of their good offices, and upon occasion even be exposed in some sort or proportion to positive ill offices at their hands: and in such judgment is naturally at least, if not necessarily and virtually, included the declaration of a will, or say a desire, that such should be the result.

By this President and leading member of this Sub-Committee of the Public Opinion Tribunal by which cognizance is taken of this affair— by him, not to speak of others who agree with him, expression is given to the judgment so formed. But by others in an incalculable number by whom no judgment is expressed, a judgment on the subject—the like judgment suppose—is in mere conscience formed. But the judgment being formed, though no expression is ever given to it, a correspondent will, as above, is naturally formed, a correspondent will, from whence result substraction of good offices, and performance of ill offices, as above.

7. and 8. From the Newspaper Editor the aggregate of this mixt mass of evidence and argument together with the accompanying preliminary matter as above, and the expression given to the judgment and will as above, receives of course impression and diffusion in the way of his business. Here then the several functions of giving impression and diffusion to the judgment and will in question, and to the expression given to them, stand exemplified.[1]

9. In ways and by members of this same unofficial judicatory in a number altogether out of the reach not only of general perception but of calculation, execution and effect will naturally, and as it were of course, be given to the judgment in question, namely by the consequent will, and ill offices—positive and negative—as above. Here

---

[1] In the text, Bentham noted at this point: '☞ Here state the superior utility and efficiency as compared with practice of Ordinary Judicatories.' He expanded on this theme in the marginal summary: '7 and 8. Giving impression, multiplication and diffusion to the above. This is done in the ordinary and constant course of his [i.e. the Newspaper Editor's] business. By him done constantly and compleatly. By Ordinary only casually: and rather permitted by them than done. By many not permitted.'

then the function of giving effect and execution to the opinion, or say the judgment, in question stands exemplified.

From a review of the above several functions or operations may be formed a deduction of no small practical moment. This is the prodigious importance of the profession and functions of this President and leading member of so many Sub-Committees of this not the less supreme and all-embracing because unofficial judicatory: the importance in an absolute and more particularly in a comparative point of view: comparison had with all other members of all other and whatsoever classes, as abovementioned.

Next to him in the order of importance comes the author of works belonging to this or that department in the field of politics—of that vast field the whole of which lies [within][1] his domain and is every day coming under the survey of this all-embracing superintendent.

Sub§4. III. Power—comparison as to[2]
[I.] Means of efficiency and effect—among the constituent elements of political power, this, though in the above list of them it occupies the last place,[3] is the first to be looked to: this being the essential one, without a clear conception of which no clear conception of any of the others can be formed.[4]

Of the means of execution and effect the aggregate efficiency will be composed of:

1. the number of persons disposed to concurr in contributing to the effect;

2. the internal force, physical and mental, of each;

3. the quantity of external physical force at the command of each, i.e. of the sorts of things capable of giving encrease to human physical force such as arms, ammunition, etc.;

4. their facility for operating in concert; the smallness of all opposing forces;

5. the magnitude of the evil to which the possessor of the power has the physical faculty of subjecting the individuals subject to it in case of non-compliance and disobedience;

---

[1] MS 'with'.

[2] In the text, Bentham noted at this point: '☞ Quere whether to insert this?'

[3] See Sub§1, pp. 55–6 above.

[4] In the text, Bentham noted at this point: 'Are not the elements of political power considered in some part of Constitutl. Code 1822 and Letters to Toreno?—if so they must be consulted. Modes of Subordination certainly are.' For such a discussion see 'Economy as applied to Office', Ch. 1, §§4–6 and Ch. 4, in *First Principles preparatory to Constitutional Code*, ed. P. Schofield, Oxford, 1989 (*CW*), pp. 6–12, 30–9. A similar discussion does not however appear in *Letters to Count Toreno on The proposed Penal Code, delivered in by The Legislation Committee of The Spanish Cortes, April 25th, 1821*, London, 1822 (Bowring, viii. 487–554).

6. in the case of a rival possessor of power, [the comparative magnitude of the evil to which the possessor of power,]¹ as compared with the magnitude of the evil to which such rival, is able to subject the common subject or subordinate.

Compare now under these several heads the condition of the unofficial Judicatory with official ones, considered separately or in the aggregate.

1. In respect of the number of persons disposed, in the character of agents, to concurr in giving execution and effect to the opinions, judgments and wills in question.

In this particular the advantage which this unofficial judicatory possesses when compared with that of the official judicatories—all of them put together—is at first mention manifest. Of those by whom on any occasion the judgment and will in question has been and remains formed, and those whom it finds disposed to concurr in giving execution and effect to it, some with more energy, others with less, the number is exactly the same: it is the aggregate of all the individual members of the whole community.

2. In the same case is the aggregate amount of internal force, physical and mental.

3. So likewise of that portion of the aggregate means of execution which is composed of objects belonging to the class of things: for to the aggregate of the individuals abovementioned as belonging on this occasion to the class of *persons* appertains the aggregate of the individual objects belonging to the class of things.²

4.³ So likewise as to the *magnitude of the evil*—to which, in quality of possessors of the power, that is to say of the abovementioned elementary ingredients of it, the members of the judicatory in question have the physical faculty of subjecting those at whose charge the execution and effect in question are to be given to the power in question in case of non-compliance and disobedience. For in this magnitude is comprehended without any exception or limitation the aggregate amount of all the evil in what shape so ever it is in the power of man to subject man.

---

¹ MS 'the comparative magnitude of the evil to which in the case of a rival possessor of power'. The emended text follows the sense of the marginal summary: 'In case of competition between power-holder and power-holder, superiority of the evil the one can inflict on the common subject in comparison of what the other can.'

² In the marginal summary, Bentham added a qualification to the second and third points, namely 'saving *scission*'.

³ Bentham did not consider the fourth point in the preceding list here, where he deals with the points in which the unofficial judicatory was strong in comparison with official judicatories, but further on where considering the points in which it was comparatively weak (see pp. 67–73 below). The enumeration of the final two points is therefore not consistent with the above list.

5. So likewise, in case of rivality, as to the magnitude of the evil to which the members of this unofficial judicatory and the members of the several official judicatories its rivals are able separately or collectively to produce at the charge of any individual or individuals considered in the character of their common subjects.

II. Personal branch of the corporeal field of the jurisdiction of a judicatory.

Under the head of *Members* has been brought to view the all-comprehensiveness of this branch of the power [of the] unofficial judicatory compared with that of any official judicatory or judicatories.[1] Not only sharers in this power but contributors to its magnitude, because so many ready executioners of its will, are the members of this unofficial judicatory, every one of them. Under that same head has also been brought to view the faculty which in each political community this unofficial judicatory has of receiving reinforcements to an unlimited amount from the members of the like judicatories in the several other political communities having place on the surface of the globe.[2]

Compare this element of its power with the correspondent element of the most powerful official judicatory in the same political state: the power of the official judicatory will be still the inferior: no such faculty has it of receiving reinforcements to an unlimited amount from other states.

Correspondent to the extent in respect of the number of the individuals of whose force the force of this aggregate is composed, is the extent of the number of those on whom the force is capable of being exerted. As on the one hand all enter into the composition of the public force; so on the other hand all behold all in a state of subjection to this same public force.

III. Real branch of the corporeal field of the jurisdiction of a judicatory.[3]

[IV.] Incorporeal field of jurisdiction of a judicatory—extent of the classes of suits or causes appertaining to it, i.e. of the *rights* on which claims may be grounded, and the *wrongs* on which accusations may be grounded.

In the case of the official judicatories, the rights which their field of jurisdiction embraces are those only in which, proceeding under the system of procedure pursued by them, more good than evil with refer-

---

[1] See Sub§2, pp. 56–60 above.

[2] Bentham did not raise this point in Sub§2 above, but see *Constitutional Code*, vol. I, ed. F. Rosen and J.H. Burns, Oxford, 1983 (*CW*), Ch. V, §4, Art. 2, p. 35.

[3] There is no text corresponding to the following marginal summary, which belongs here: 'Correspondent in extent to its power over persons as above, is its ditto over things belonging to ditto persons.'

ence to the interests they are employed to give support may, it is supposed, be produced by their interference: and so in the case of accusations. By the unofficial Judicatory cognizance is taken not only of these same rights and wrongs—claims and accusations, but also of all others in which the interests of the community in respect of the several individuals included in it, in the opinion of the several members of the standing Committee of the Judicatory and of its several Sub-Committees as above, are concerned.

Thus much as to the points in which this unofficial Judicatory is superior to the Official Judicatories. Now as to those in which it lies under a disadvantage.

1. In the first place, taken in its totality, it labours under a division—a constant and universally established division—in respect of interest: two parties, constituting so many sections—the democratical and the aristocratical, are destined in all communities and at all times to have place in it. The interest of the few, the extra-opulent and thereby, even if by no other means, the powerful few, being in a state of constant opposition to that of the many—that of the consuming class which produces nothing to that of the producing class which produces more than it consumes—hence it is that whatever power is in the hands of the aristocratical class over and above that which is in the hands of the same number of those of the democratical class constitutes a sort of disease, with which the body politic taken in its totality is afflicted.[1]

By the original structure of its constitution this body is destined to labour under two distinguishable diseases, having for their cause or causes the inward existence of two intestine sets of enemies: one set composed of the ultra-indigent class of malefactors, who, being as such weak and powerless and objects of general disgust, are thereby exposed to punishment: the other composed of the ultra-opulent who, being as such powerful and objects of general respect, stand thereby exempted and preserved from punishment. Of both depredation is the characteristic occupation: by the ultra-indigent it acts ever upon a small scale, by the ultra-opulent upon the largest scale.

Intestine depredators of [both classes][2] being innate accompaniments of the constitution of every political community, they exist, nor

---

[1] In the margin, Bentham noted at this point: '☞ Consult Thomson on Medicine for the nomenclature.' See Alexander Thomson, *The Physician; or, Domestic Medical Friend*, 2nd edn., London, 1807, p. 98: 'Worms are chiefly of four kinds: the large round worm; the very small maw-worm, or ascarides, resembling bits of thread; the short, flat worm, or cucurbitina; and the jointed, called the tape-worm, or tænia, which is sometimes many yards long.'

[2] MS 'this class'. The emendation follows the sense of the marginal summary: 'Both depredators being innate in every government, they are so even in the purest representative democracy: sole government founded on greatest happiness principle.'

can they ever cease to exist, in a representative democracy even though constituted in the purest form possible: in that form they may be kept under in such sort as not to be productive of any considerable mischief: but they can not consistently with the security of the whole ever be altogether extirpated. Thus stands the matter in the only sort of government which has for its object the greatest happiness of the greatest number: for as to all others they have for their object the greatest happiness of the smaller number, at the expence of that of the greater.

In a Monarchy at the head of the highest prædatory class is stationed the arch-depredator—the Monarch: a parasite in whose one maw, for the small chance of giving encrease to the felicity of that one being, the sustenances of thousands and ten thousands of others whose claims are as good as his is consumed.

The analogy between this innate disease of the body politic and one of the diseases which in the body natural, though frequent, is but casual can not have escaped the observing eye: in the class of malefactors so called and treated as such may be seen the minute ascarides by which the lowest parts of the intestinal canal are occupied and infested: in the higher parts in the aristocrats may be seen the *teretes*, the smooth and polished sort as the name imports: in the Monarch, the solitary worm, in French *le ver solitaire*, no constitution being equal to the endurance of more than one, the extraction of which is at once so difficult, so perilous, and yet so necessary. An emblem is not a proof; accordingly neither is it here meant for such. But if furnished by the nature of the case and happily chosen, it will contribute clearness and strength to the conception, and for this purpose alone is it on this occasion brought to view.

Happily the disease, such as it is, is in a particular degree the disease of infancy: sooner or later, the body politic, if not killed by it, outgrows it. Every addition made to the number of readers, is an addition made to the number of persons capable of reading books on political subjects, and in that character becoming Members o. Sub-Committees of this unofficial Judicatory: through these means it makes an addition to the number of persons by whom discourses on that subject in public, or at the worst in private, may [be] heard from the lips of the fraternity of readers, and in that character constituting an addition to the number of Sub-Committee men as above. Every addition made to the number of persons becoming inhabitants of *towns*, in contradistinction to the being inhabitants of the country, separated from one another by distances more or less considerable, becomes an addition to the number of readers of politics as above, or at the least to the number of hearers of political discourse.

Every addition thus made to the number of the persons habituated or disposed to the constituting themselves members of these un-official Committees is an addition made to the number of those capable of taking cognizance and likely to take cognizance of any appeal made to this tribunal by any members of the government—by any of the official functionaries when disagreeing among themselves. By every such disagreement an addition is therefore naturally made to the power of this judicatory—of the only political body the interest of which is not in discordance but in accordance with, as being the same thing with, the interest of the greatest number of the members of the political community in question whatever it be: for by every publica-tion on the subject of the disagreement whatever it be—even by every verbal discourse held [between] man and man among the people at large on that same subject—an appeal of this sort is made. Accord-ingly by every such disagreement, so as the subject-matter and the particulars of it do but transpire, a service is rendered to the public interest, to the greatest happiness of the greatest number. No such service naturally is commonly intended: but how far so ever from being intended, it is not the less rendered.

Of such disagreement the causes are happily not a few:

1. In a Monarchy, a disputed succession is liable to have place.

2. A minority—the non-age of the Monarch.

3. The manifest mental debility of the Monarch, whether from old age, permanent bodily ill-health, or mental derangement. Extra-ordinary it must be, and undisguisably so, to constitute any thing that can be regarded as a particular and casual cause—for as to intellectual inferiority, comparison had with the ordinary level, it is among the necessary results of the situation itself.

4. Between any two branches of the Monarch's family, any dis-agreement in which the Monarch takes or is thought to take a part.

[5.] Disagreement amongst the members of an administration, or as between the members of an existing administration and the other men of opulence and rank who are habitually collected within the field of the Sovereign's observation.

[6.] A disagreement between the Monarch in possession and the Monarch in expectancy—between the reigning Monarch on the throne and the next Monarch in expectancy.

In a mixt Monarchy, the existence of disagreement between the component parts of it is of the very essence of the species. True it is that another property belonging to the essence of the species is the having a bond of union, a sinister interest in which they share, a sinister interest acting in constant opposition to the interest and greatest happiness of the greatest number: and by this unity of interest the government may for a length of time more or less considerable be kept from dissolution.

Not less true is it that in a government of this species not less constantly causes of disagreement have place.

If between the power of the Monarch and whatsoever other power there is by which his is kept in check the limits are not sufficiently defined, thereupon comes contention between the one power and the other.

So if between two powers subordinate to that of the Monarch, if so it be that the Monarch takes a part on the one side or the other, which is what can scarcely fail to happen.

By a certain degree of prudence, disagreement from any one of the above [two][1] causes may be kept from breaking out.

One cause however there remains which is of the essence of the species, and which can not by any human prudence be at any time compleatly shut out. This is the competition for power as between party and party in the class of statesmen.

The matter of good in the shape of the matter of corruption is suppose even the whole of it in the hands of the Monarch or at his disposal. Still be it ever so vast, and be his desire of satisfying every body ever so ardent, to give satisfaction to that desire is at all times plainly impossible. So far from decreasing as the quantity at his disposal and accordingly disposed of encreases, the aggregate amount of the appetite encreases in that same ratio: the more of it there is to be had, the greater is the number of those each of whom beholds for himself a probability of obtaining a share of it.

Thus then between the party by whom this mass is shared, including those who by their means are in constant expectation of succeeding to shares in it on the one hand, and the party to whom neither in possession nor in expectancy is any share in view, strife constant and interminable has place. Constantly is the excluded party occupied in forcing itself in. For doing so it has no means but that of preferring against the party in possession accusations, matter for which never has been, nor in such a form of government ever can by any possibility be, wanting. But for the receipt of any such accusation, there exists but one possible judicatory, and that is the Public Opinion Tribunal.

Difficult however is the course which at all times has to be taken by the corruptionist in expectancy. Otherwise than by appeal to the power of the unofficial judicatory, in no way can he do any thing

---

[1] MS 'three'.

considerable towards the forwarding of any of his wishes. But to carry on any such appeal is to act as accuser either of the functionaries who act under the form of government, or of the form of government itself, or both. As to the pointing of the accusation against the individuals their rivals—if that were all, in this it is not in the nature of things that there should be any thing that is not perfectly agreable to them: what is thus aimed at is all profit, no loss. But under such a government the utmost mischief that is ever done beyond that which the government itself affords a warrant for, in comparison of that which is done with a warrant from the form of government, and that a sufficient one, is very inconsiderable. Depredation, and with it oppression in every other imaginable shape, may be carried on to any pitch, and yet nothing done in which condemnation in any shape is passed by either the letter or the spirit of the law or the usage of government in or under it. Meantime that same burthen, at all times and with ever-encreasing force, will be pressing on the shoulders of the people, and these men being by their hapless condition condemned to keep up the profession of being friends to the people, no sooner is any particular instance of misrule in either of these shapes brought to view than all eyes are turned [to them],[1] in expectation of [their][2] taking up the accusing part.

In a word, the misrule exercised having all of it the form of the government for its cause, it is not possible that the connection between the effect and the cause can escape all eyes.

2. Second point of disadvantage—comparative incapacity of acting in concert.

Of this disadvantage there are two sorts of causes: the one natural, the other factitious.

Of the natural causes, the radical and principal one is *local distance*. It presses of course with particular weight on the situation of the inhabitants of the country, as compared and contrasted with that of the inhabitants of towns: in both cases its pressure is in the inverse ratio of the density of the population: and as between town and town in the inverse ratio of the number of inhabitants in each.

Of this cause the efficiency is capable of being counteracted and diminished by every circumstance by which either facility is given to the means of communication, or a counteradvantage afforded by means of profit, in a pecuniary or any other shape, from frequent intercourse. By water carriage for example, whether by sea or inland

---

[1] MS 'by him'. The reference here is to 'these men', i.e. the corruptionists in expectancy: Bentham seems inadvertently to have used the singular instead of the plural.

[2] MS 'his'.

navigation, the facility is afforded: by mutual demand in the way of trade the counteradvantage is afforded.

Of this same disadvantage the factitious causes are those which are produced by prohibitions and restrictions imposed by governments.

In every government but a democracy the interest of the ruling few being in a state of opposition to the general interest, the consequence is that, in every government but that one, the class of functionaries beholds in the Public Opinion Tribunal not a support, but an adverse power: a power capable of becoming superior to its own—capable not only of opposing limits to it but even in case of necessity of extinguishing it, and commonly the only one that is so: the only one without exception, on the supposition that the political state in question sees nothing of this sort to fear from any foreign State or States.

Hence consequently with the supreme operative body of every state but that one it is a constant object to throw in the way of such communication so far as applied to political purposes—i.e. so far as applied to the formation of Sub-Committees of the unofficial judicatory in question, every obstruction possible.

To this endeavour it finds two natural counterforces and difficulties: the odium inseparably attendant on it; and the obstructions thrown in the way of communications for the purpose of such transactions as are regarded as being serviceable to its interests, and as such approved of.

As to the odium, in intensity and extent it will be exactly in the ratio of the degree in which the attributes of moral and intellectual aptitude have place in the community. By no government which is not an enemy—an uncontrovertible enemy—to the rest of the community, can any such endeavour be ever or any where employed: by every such endeavour an avowal is made of such enmity, consequently of its own inaptitude, and consequently of its being the interest of all who are subject to it to put it down with all possible speed and by whatsoever means promise to be at the same time the most efficient and, in respect of evil in all shapes, least expensive: an avowal not in words it is true, but in deeds: in deeds by which, of the state of the agent's mind, on every occasion evidence is afforded to such a degree conclusive, that evidence the most probative that in the nature of the case can be given by words alone shrinks into insignificance: and in truth amounts to nothing at all when opposed to the abovementioned practical evidence.

The other impediment consists in the difficulty of preventing or obstructing communication for this unacceptable purpose without preventing or obstructing it in its application to others that are regarded by the government as serviceable to its interest or even necessary to its existence.

Take for instance the English Government with its tax upon Newspapers: amount of the tax, Anno 1801, £2.., 000: Ditto Anno 1821, £4.., 000.[1] In any coolly reflecting mind, no doubt can have place that were it not for these counter-considerations all newspapers, the Editor of which acts in the character of leading Member of a Sub-Committee of the Public Opinion Tribunal, would long ago have been extinguished. The odium, had that been all, the government for so great an advantage would have been content to subject itself to: but the odium with the loss of little less than £500,000 a year added to it,[2] and at a period of so much financial pressure and difficulty, would have been decidedly more than could be afforded to be paid even for so mighty and decisive an advantage.[3]

---

[1] According to 'Stamps issued for Newspapers', *House of Commons Accounts and Papers 1822*, xxi. 381–4, the revenue derived from this source in 1801 had been £234,571, and in 1821 £412,996.

[2] In the margin, Bentham noted at this point, 'the immensity of the mass of the matter of corruption affording so many [. . . ?] for sharers in it and supporters under it', but it is unclear where this phrase should be placed.

[3] In the text, Bentham noted at this point: '☞ Add the gratification to individuals even of the most servile party—corruptionists in expectancy and even corruptionists in possession—from the entertainment, particularly the scandal part of it.'

CONSTITUTIONAL SECURITIES OF THE TRIPOLITAN NATION: OR SECURITIES, GIVEN BY THE SOVEREIGN, TO THE PEOPLE OF TRIPOLI AND FEZZAN, AGAINST ABUSE OF POWER, NOW AND FOR EVER

EXORDIUM

The Sovereign of Tripoli to the People. Address I: Proclamation[1]

People! Beloved People! People! whom God hath committed to my care! harken now to my voice, it shall be a sound of sweetness in your ears.

Opening on a former day (for so did God ordain) the Book of life, I read in it this sentence. 'Ruler! act not of thy own will purely: that which is of moment, do it not but with advice of wise and honest Counsellors.'[2]

No sooner had I read these words, than it seemed as if a film had fallen from my eyes. I looked up: and lo! all the errors of my past life stood, as it were in array, before me. I trembled. I should have sunk under the sight, had not the same divine words, which thus brought to my eyes the evil, brought with them, and left in my heart, the remedy.

On a sudden, it seemed to me as if the Prophet were looking down upon me: and that—not with hand, as when he delivered to our forefathers the book of truth[3]—not with hand, but with tongue and lips, he spake to me these words.

'My Son! Adore God, and listen to his Prophet. Thou hast erred; I will set thee right: thou hast been severe; I will make thee gracious: thou hast been selfish; I will make thee generous: thou hast been

---

[1] A draft of this Address is at UC xxiv. 1–4 (4–5 August 1822) and a partial fair copy at xxiv. 9 (28–9 January 1823). The text is in the hand of the copyist but bears additions, deletions and emendations in Bentham's hand.

[2] The Koran does not contain these words as such, but cf. sura iii, verse 159 and sura xlii, verse 38, where the ruler is invoked to take counsel in matters of administration.

[3] According to the orthodox view, Mohammed was not himself responsible for the transcription of the Koran, as Bentham suggests; his revelations, which were delivered orally, were memorized or written down by his followers and only after his death collected together to form the Koran.

weak in mind; I will make thee wise: thou hast been in peril; I will make thee safe: thou hast been weak in power; I will make thee strong: thy power would end with thy life; I will continue it even to the end of time. The power of those that shall come after thee shall thus be bounded. But thy own power shall receive encrease. Yea, verily it shall receive encrease. For, that obedience which those who went before thee were wont to receive from fear, *that*, yea and more also, shalt thou receive: receive, from admiration, love, and gratitude. Do that which I command thee, the whole multitude of the faithful throughout the earth shall look up to thee: they shall envy thee, until they imitate thee: all generations to come shall bless thee: they shall bless thee, even as a second Prophet, from whose word they will have received a new being, a being, compared with which the state of all who went before thee was a state of affliction, fear, and darkness.

'Ruler! thou takest upon thee to provide for the *wants* of thy people, and thou knowest not what they are: thou callest upon them to obey thy *will*, and they know not what it is.

'My Son! thou shalt call the *people* around thee, and thus shalt thou *then* know their wants. Thou shalt call around thee *men chosen* by the people, and, when thou hast heard their counsel, thou shalt profit by it. Thou shalt cause thy will to be written in a *book*, and wheresoever the book of *my* law is kept, the book of *thy* law shall be heard.

'Thou shalt divide thy dominion into districts, and from each district thou shalt call unto thee a wise man—the man whom the people shall have chosen.

'In each district thou shalt place a *Judge*. At his right hand shall lie the book of *my* word: at his left hand shall lie the book of *thy* word, and of the words of those, concerning whom it is written on the Table of brass, that in all ages they shall come after thee.[1] The seat of the Judge shall be on high; it shall be in the presence of the people. Under him shall sit at all times two men, three men, or, as the case may require, some greater number, taken by lot among the fathers or sons of families. Without these men he shall do nothing. On each occasion he shall pass such decision as, in his own judgment, shall be according to the law, and according to the facts that have come before him: but, whatsoever these men shall see good to say, shall, in the first place, have been heard.

'Thus doing, thou shalt be loved, as Sovereign was never before loved: for never before did people receive from Sovereign such gifts as thy people will thus have received from thee.

---

[1] Presumably an allusion to the 'preserved' or 'well-guarded' tablet, mentioned in the Koran at sura lxxxv, verse 22, in which all events, past and future, have been recorded.

'Thus doing, thou shalt be safe—safe against adversaries from within, even as before thee no Sovereign was ever safe: for, that safety which other Sovereigns seek in vain from fear, thou wilt have received from love.

'Thus doing, thou wilt be safe—safe against adversaries from without, even as before thee no Sovereign was ever safe: for, seeing thy people clinging to *thee*, while their subjects flee from *them*, they will see, that, instead of assailing thee, those whom they would lead or send against thee, would cast themselves at thy feet, and sue to be received into the number of thy subjects.

'The yearly growing wealth, which God hath committed to thee as Sovereign, thou shalt divide into two parts. The one thou shalt continue to receive for the subsistence of thee and thy family; this thou shalt not of thyself encrease. The other shall be diminished or encreased, as necessity calls: and the receipt as well as disposal thereof shall be according to that, which thou, after hearing the wise men from the people, shalt have ordained.'[1]

People! I know not as yet, whether what it seemed to me that I then saw and heard was the truth, or whether it was but an illusion and a dream. When the men of your choice shall stand before me, we will pray with one voice to the Almighty: his will shall put aside all clouds, and make the truth manifest to all hearts.

The Sovereign of Tripoli to the People. Address II: Acknowledgement of Rights[2]

People! beloved People! I address myself to you a second time.

I have begun: I continue: I will persevere. I will persevere, until, in so far as depends upon the understanding and the will which God has given to me, the edifice of your felicity shall have been completed.

---

[1] Bentham may have intended to insert the following passage from UC xxiv. 10 (29 January 1823) at this point: '"When by the blessing of God the fruit of their labours has encreased, then, by the like same blessing may thy share of it receive encrease. That fruit can not encrease till their assurance of having it at their disposal shall have encreased. That assurance can never be encreased, so long as without any consent of theirs it can be taken at any time out of their hands."'

[2] A fair copy of this Address is at UC xxiv. 15–17 (20 August 1822). A related fragment is at UC xxiv. 18 (7 October 1822).

The following explanation, headed 'Reconnaissance de Droits', which Bentham wrote for D'Ghies' benefit, is at UC xxiv. 50–1, 53, 52 (18 August 1822): 'I. *Reconnaissance*—raison pour employer ce mot.

'Le projet de manifeste ayant pour but la sûreté du peuple contre les abus de pouvoir de la part du Souverain—on propose de le désigner par quelque titre ambigu et capable de recevoir l'une ou l'autre de deux interprétations sérieusement différentes en effet: savoir, 1. la récognition des droits en question comme déjà existant d'eux-mêmes et n'ayant besoin de l'acte du Souverain

Opening a second time that book which is the perennial fountain of the sublimest wisdom, I have read in it these words. 'Sovereigns! Ye are but Shepherds of men: the people are your flock: for them are you at all times responsible to God.' Thus saith the Prophet.[1] But

pour les confier: 2. la concession de la part du Souverain, mais provisionellement seulement, le Souverain et ses successeurs étant censé se réserver le pouvoir de révoquer, quand bon lui semble, ce que par ces présentes il accord[e].

'Si les droits étaient décidément regardés comme déjà existans sans lui et indépendamment de sa volonté, le danger est qu'il n'y auroit pas moyen de l'engager volontairement à signer l'écrit en question: la répugnance étant universelle nonseulement de sa part mais aussi de la part de la majorité, pour ne pas dire la totalité, de ceux auquels il aura communiqué l'affaire.

'Si ces mêmes droits étoient décidément regardés comme étant originairement dépendant de sa volonté, le danger est s'il lui arrivoit de les révoquer en tout ou en partie, ou, ce qui reviendroit au même, de les enfreindre de même sans les révoquer, les sujets seroi[en]t disposés à souffrir la révocation sans réclamation, et sans la regarder comme une injustice.

'II. En cas d'adoption, moyens de publication pour le présent et pour toujours.

'1. Déposer aux Archives avec formalité l'original signé de la main du Souverain: c.-à-d. le papier même qu'il est supposé avoir lu dans la grande Mosquée.

'2. Ne seroit-il pas convenable de le faire écrire en grandes lettres d'or, et sur un fonds noir pour plus de relief?

'3. Envoyer un exemplaire à chaque Tribunal pour y être toujours suspendu en grandes lettres, le tout sur une seule et même surface de façon à en être constamment vu le tout ensemble par tous les assistans. Comme le nombre de ces tribunaux ne passe pas 15 ou environ, ne pourroient-ils tous ces exemplaires recevoir la signature du Souverain?

'4. Envoyer de même un exemplaire à chaque Mosquée pour y être de même en tout tems devant les yeux de toute la congrégation.

'Le motif ostensible et même un des motifs véritables seroit pour donner une étendue correspondante à la gloire du Souverain et à la reconnaissance et l'amour du peuple.

'Un motif non prononcé et plus important seroit de lier la volonté du Souverain et de ses successeurs en déterminant les sujets partout de ne pas viser la révocation ou l'infraction des concessions sans faire leur possible pour l'empêcher.

'Moyens de parvenir.

'1. Commencer par envoyer au Chef de chaque Tribunal séparément un exemplaire du papier proposé pour sonder son opinion. Dans le cas de chaque Tribunal seroit-il mieux de l'adresser au Chef seulement, en lui recommandant le secret, ou au Chef officiellement pour être communiqué à tous les Membres du Tribunal à la fois?

'2. Supposant réponse favorable de la part du plus grand nombre des Tribunaux, et peu favorable de la part des autres. Que faire? Pourroit-on les faire s'assembler dans la Capitale? et avant l'assemblement, conviendroit-il de faire connoître aux répugnans que la majorité est contr'eux?

'Quelle seroit l'autorité à laquelle il conviendroit de commencer pour sonder les esprits? 1. Le Souverain même? 2. Parmi les personnes qui l'entourent, celles censées avoir la plus grande part à sa confiance? 3. Les membres des Tribunaux comme ci-dessus?

'N'est-il pas vrai que le motif principal sur lequel on compte, ou au moins un motif, est son besoin d'argent? Si cela est, qui sont les personnes que l'on regarde comme capable[s] d'induire les autres sujets à fournir la contribution qu'on se proposeroit de donner? Ces personnes ne seroi[en]t-il[s] pas celles desquelles on s'assureroit d'abord? en suite de quoi, leur consentement supposé, il faudroit être d'accord sur la somme que l'on proposeroit de lui offrir.

'Si on commençait de cette manière, ne seroit-ce pas un moyen d'éviter tout soupçon de la part du Souverain? Étant le premier objet dans l'ordre du tems, l'affaire de subvenir à ses besoins auroit la mine d'avoir été regardée comme l[e] premier dans l'ordre de l'importance: et l'obtention de la Reconnaissance de Droits ne paraîtroit qu'un moyen du second ordre employé pour faciliter l'obtention de l'objet principal.'

[1] The Koran does not contain these words, but similar sentiments are expressed in a saying of Mohammed narrated by both al-Bukhari and Muslim: see *Mishcàt-ul-Másábíh or A Collection*

responsible in respect of what? in respect to what unless it be their happiness.

But if any one man ought to be happy, then why not every other? And if every man, then why any one man more than any other? If all then could be made equally happy, so much the better. If all my beloved subjects could be made equally happy—every one of them as happy as the happiest—Oh! how would my happiness be encreased! This however is what the nature of man forbids. In the scale of happiness the plunderer and the plundered, the oppressor and the oppressed, ought not to be placed on the same degree. The rich man and the poor man can not be placed upon exactly the same degree. For if men in general, rich and poor together, could not keep what they got, none would labour, and all would die. All therefore can not be kept in a state of equal happiness: the will of God as shewn by the nature of man forbids it. And thus it is that, from any thing that I could do for my subjects, it were in vain for me to hope any thing more or better than the greatest happiness of the greatest number: in that I behold the boundary of my hopes.

Meditating on these things, I acknowledge, and do hereby declare—that the greatest happiness of the greatest number of the members of the community whatsoever it be, is to the ruler or rulers of that same community as such the only right and proper end in view and object of pursuit: the only right and proper measure of the goodness or badness of all their actions.

People! Beloved People! God hath given me the power over you. I hold it even as every one of you holdeth the hands of which he is possessed. God hath given me power over you: but it is only for your happiness that he has given it to me. Behold therefore now the use which I make of it. Receive now from my hands the benefits which, in obedience to God and his prophet, freely and of my own motion I give. I give them to remain to you and your posterity throughout all ages. It will be for you and your posterity to secure them to yourselves as against any who shall attempt (which God forbid!) to take them from you.

These benefits are the rights and securities which I hereby acknowledge to be yours: the securities against misrule: securities against abuse of power on the part of the Sovereign or those in authority under him. Doing what I do, I do it without fear of error, seeing that in so doing I take nothing for myself, and that it is to you my beloved people that I am giving whatsoever it is that I give.

of the Most Authentic Traditions, regarding the Actions and Sayings of Múhammad, trans. A.N. Matthews, 2 vols., Calcutta, 1809–10, ii. 211–12.

GENERALS[1]

I. Securities in favour of the Nation considered in the aggregate

I. Security against vexation on account of religion

Article 1. Every person is at liberty to perform divine worship after his own manner. For this purpose any persons without exception may assemble together in private or in public.

Counter-Security. Provided[2] that it be in a chamber enclosed and covered, and that the eyes of the True Believer be not annoyed by public ceremonies or processions, with religion for their cause or pretext, or his ears by the sound of bells or other noises. Provided also that by no religion shall any justifying cause be made for causing suffering in any shape to any individual, in respect of his person, property, reputation, or condition in life.

Article 2. Every person is at liberty to write and publish whatsoever

---

[1] The following fragment, at UC xxiv. 136, 147 (9 October 1822), explains the division of the securities into 'Generals' and 'Details' and the scope of the securities: 'The proposed legislative provisions, proposed in the character of means of Security, or in one word Securities against evil in the shapes in question, are divided into two classes. In the first are placed those which are conceived in general terms: in the other those provisions of detail which have for their object the giving execution and effect to those which are in general terms. Without the particular ones, the correspondent general ones would be in a great degree, if not altogether, inefficacious: without the general ones, the design of the particular ones might not be universally and clearly understood.

'Be the subject what it may—be the persons in question who they may, in vain would rules imposing or endeavouring to impose obligations on those persons be laid down if from non-fulfilment no penal consequence were to follow. Hence it is that from beginning to end provisions of a penal cast—belonging as such to the penal branch of law—could not fail to be interspersed.

'Of the evils producible in the condition of individuals by the action of individuals, not one is there which directly or indirectly is not producible in them by the action of the Sovereign who ever he may be. But in this boundless aggregate there will be some which are not in use nor much in danger of being produced by hands so situated. Are these then to be left without remedy? No certainly. But for these together with all other evils that are regarded as such, remedies, such as they are, are applied by those arrangements in the framing of which the hands of individuals only, and not those of the Sovereign or any person whom he is disposed to give authority, licence or impunity, are [regarded as] the peccant hands. Calumnies for example, or personal injuries, or injuries to marital or paternal rights, are not in the natural course of things in a way to be inflicted by the hands or by the order of persons so situated. The reason why these subjects have not been taken in hand is that to those cases the particular remedies here provid[ed] are either needless or inapposite.

'Another class of evils which do not belong to the case in hand are those which consist in depredation or waste in the case where the subjects of these misdeeds belong not to the stock of individuals but to that stock which is at the hands of government, of the persons by which the powers of government are exercised.

'The reason why these cases are left untouched is—that in these cases remedies of a different kind are necessary and those which are here provided would have little or no application.'

[2] This sentence is in the hand of the copyist, but bears emendations in Bentham's hand.

he pleases on the subject of religion, even although the truth or the goodness of the only true religion be impeached thereby. By the True Believer that which is adverse to the only true religion will either not be read at all, or read with the merited contempt.

Counter-Security. Provided that no writing or imitative figure, containing matter thus adverse to the only true religion, be exposed any where to view in such manner as to be offensive to the eyes of the True Believer as he passes. For any such exposure every person is responsible to the purpose of punishment.

Article 3. Every person is at liberty to speak what he pleases on the subject of religion, even although the truth or the goodness of the only true religion be impeached thereby. By the True Believer that which is adverse to the only true religion will either not be heard at all, or heard with the merited contempt.

Counter-Security. Provided that no discourse, whereby either the truth or the goodness of the only true religion is impeached, be uttered in any public place in such manner as to be offensive to the ears of the True Believer as he passes: or in the presence and to the displeasure of any True Believer in any private place. The utterance of any such discourse in the hearing of the True Believer is an injury to him, and as such may be punished according to law.

II.[1] *Security against National Gagging: or Security for appeal to Public Opinion and the power of the law on the conduct of all persons whatsoever: functionaries as well as non-functionaries*

Article 4.[2] Every man is at liberty to express, as well by visible as by audible signs, and in any way and to any extent to make public, whatsoever in his judgment it will be contributory to the greatest happiness of the greatest number [for men][3] to be informed of: and this, although disapprobation be thereby expressed towards persons in authority, whether on account of the general tenor of their conduct, or on account of their conduct on this or that occasion in particular.

Counter-Security. Provided always, that, for any injury thereby done to the reputation of any individual by false imputations, every person concerned in the doing of such injury is responsible to the purpose of reparation and punishment at the suit, and for the benefit, of any individual or individuals injured: and that, for any thing which

---

[1] This heading and the following two paragraphs are in the hand of the copyist, but bear emendations in Bentham's hand. The original draft is at UC xxiv. 18 (20 August 1822).

[2] The enumeration of the articles is continued in the marginal summary, though not in the text.

[3] The addition is suggested by the marginal summary: 'By signs visible or audible any man may express and in any way and to any extent make public whatsoever it is in his eyes conducive to greatest happiness that men be informed of.'

being so expressed has for its object the exciting men to the commission of this or that particular offence, any man shall be responsible, as above, according to the nature of such offence.

Article 5. If, on account of any indication given of supposed delinquency in any shape on the part of any person, non-functionary or functionary, a person be proceeded against at law as for injury to reputation, proof of the delinquency so indicated shall be received as a cause of justification: and, for the making of such proof, the testimony of that same individual on whom the delinquency is charged may be extracted in the same manner as that of any other person.[a]

[a] On this subject, namely the interdiction of the party defamed in an action for defamation, a general error and confusion of ideas has place at all times in the English mind.

If the discovery of the facts of the case be the object, nothing can be more absurd than the exclusion put upon the testimony of the individual who it is certain knows more of them than any other individual whatsoever, and by whom in case of delinquency every possible endeavour has commonly been used to keep them from the knowledge of every individual who on the occasion in question was not in confederacy with him.

Impunity is thus secured to every delinquent to the proof of whose delinquency the extraction of his own testimony is necessary.

Nothing can be more absurd than the use so commonly made on this occasion of the words tenderness, humanity, and so forth. If on the score of tenderness, humanity or whatever else be the word, there were any good reason to inhibit the extraction of the evidence of a party accused, there would be much better reason on this same score for inhibiting the extraction of the testimony of every other person whatsoever. For what other person can there be of whom it is so sure that he will avoid doing injury by his testimony to the person in question, as this same person himself will?

The accident of a man's delinquency being known or not known to persons other than himself can not have any thing to do with any claim which on the score of tenderness, humanity, or whatever be the word, a man can have for remission or mitigation of punishment. It has nothing to do with any of the circumstances by which the turpitude of delinquency is encreased or lessened: nor with any of those other circumstances by which a reasonable demand for remission or diminution of punishment is created.

Absurd and mischievous as it is, the rule by which such extraction stands inhibited appears to have had its origin in one which is plainly and undeniably a reasonable one. The words of it are in Latin. For this language being a generally unintelligible one was accordingly a favorite one to English lawyers. The words of it were in Latin: *Nemo tenetur accusare seipsum*: No man is bound to accuse himself.

Of the religious tyranny established by Queen Elizabeth[1] one feature was the authorizing the Inquisitorial Judicatory created under the name of High Commission Court to force a man to appear before the Judge or Judges and make answer to questions calling upon [him][2] to state what his opinions were on all points whatsoever at their choice. But to hold on this or that point this or that opinion was at that same

---

[1] Elizabeth I (1533–1603), Queen of England and Ireland from 1558.
[2] MS 'them'.

time an outrageously punishable, and in some instances a mortally punishable, offence.

In this way the same tyrant who inflicted the punishment, gave birth to the offence, for the purpose of giving [herself][1] a pretext, and such was the effect of the law made on the occasion in justification for the infliction of the punishment.[2] Thus was the [. . . ?] victim placed between two fires: a real one if what he said were true: an imaginary one, but, being in imagination eternal, not less terrible for being imaginary, if in what he said there were any thing that were false.

Even in this case the application of the word accuse was improper and an abuse of words. To accuse is one thing: to give testimony is another: a man may make accusation without giving testimony: a man may give testimony without making accusation. To accuse is to call upon the Judge, expressing a desire that in the case in question he will inflict punishment on the party who is the object of the accusation.

The thief who being apprehended on suspicion of what he has done, and accordingly on being asked what he chooses to say on the subject, chooses to answer to this or that effect in the hope of saving himself from being provisionally sent to a prison— this malefactor or any other malefactor—is it really his desire to undergo the punishment? Thus palpable are the absurdities into which rational beings may be led by following one another without reflection, like sheep or geese.

Vast in an incalculable degree is the evil produced by this absurdity on English practice. Immense is the addition it makes to the rigour of the penal system: immense again is the addition it clearly makes to the mass of criminality: for the greater the rigour of the punishment, the greater on the part of a humane people the reluctance to contribute to the execution of it.

Two classes of men have contributed to the establishment of this error: namely, 1. Lawyers, in virtue of that interest by the pursuit of which their endeavours have in all countries and at all times been engaged in the maximization of the aggregate number of delinquencies in every punishable shape: 2. delinquents themselves.

Under all governments, without any exception other than that of the Anglo-American United States, and under the English Government in particular, among delinquents have at various times been numbered those members of the country that have deserved best of it, and to a great extent been thought to do so—understand those by whom opposition has been made to those by whom the powers of government have been exercised, accompanied in some instances with the endeavour to substitute to the bad government in which they lived some other form in a greater degree contributory to greatest happiness. Till the Anglo-American Government made its appearance, no system of law having really had for its object the greatest happiness of the greatest number, nor any other object than the greatest happiness of the governors and those who shared with them in a community of particular and sinister interest, at all times the security of governors against [the governed][3] was the main object of the system of laws, at no time the securing of the governed from depredation and oppression at the hands of the governors. At all times it has therefore been the interest of the greatest number that the laws made for the support of rule should have as little strength and efficacy as possible.

This being the case it is better, or to speak more properly less bad, for the

---

[1] MS 'himself'. Presumably Bentham meant to refer to Elizabeth I.

[2] Apparently an allusion to the Act of Supremacy of 1559 (1 Eliz. I, c.1), in consequence of which the High Court of Commission was established on a statutory basis and empowered to investigate and proceed against 'heresies, errors, schisms, abuses, offences, contempts and enormities'.

[3] MS 'government'.

Article 6.[1] All persons are at liberty at all times, and in any number, to hold converse with one another, on all subjects in general, and on the subject of the conduct of persons in authority in particular: and on the means of rectifying whatever may be amiss either in the conduct of rulers or in the form of the government: to hold converse, namely as well in the way of correspondence at a distance, as in presence: and, if at a distance, and thence through the intervention of others, as well by written as by oral discourse.

Counter-Security. Provided always, that if, for the prevention of evil to person or property, it shall at any time be thought good, by the proper authority, for limited times to prevent or inhibit persons at large from coming together, in numbers greater than are capable of hearing from beginning to end the discourse of the same speaker at the same time, especially if in the night time, or with arms about their persons, in any such case that which shall be so done by them to this purpose, shall not be considered as done in breach of this article.

III. Security against National Defencelessness

Article 7. All persons are at liberty to keep arms of all sorts: to wit, either in their own habitations, or elsewhere at their choice: also to exercise themselves, and cause themselves to be trained, in the use of arms, whether it be separately or in any numbers.

Also, singly, or in companies in any number, to carry arms about them for their own defence.

Counter-Security. Provided always, that if, for guarding against a

---

people—it is in the greater degree contributory to the greatest happiness of the greatest number, that this rule of law, absurd and mischievous as it is, should be observed in every application made of it, than that it should cease to be observed in every application made of it. Why? Only because such is the depravity [of] the constitutional branch of the penal law, or say the penal branch of the constitutional law, that more good is done by the enfeeblement of this branch than evil by the enfeeblement of every other.

In those circumstances that which would be best to be done is sufficiently obvious. Leave the rule in existence in so far as it applies to this class of offences, abolish it in its application to all others.

Mean time the propriety of this course is not more indisputable, than is the certainty of its not being pursued. For to pursue it would be to confess that the political part of the penal system is what it is—a system of tyranny: a confession of which assuredly no reasonable expectation can be entertained.

A better course still and only positively good one would be to abolish the whole of this branch of the penal system. But if the less bad course is impossible, the only good one is one impossibility mounted upon another.

---

[1] This and the following article are in the hand of the copyist, but bear additions, deletions and emendations in Bentham's hand.

temporary oppression of the greater number by sudden insurrection of the smaller number under favour of surprize, it shall at any time be thought good by the proper authority to inhibit such assemblages from having place otherwise than after due notice, neither shall any such inhibition, nor any necessary measures taken for giving effect to it, be considered as amounting to a breach of this article.

So, if to prevent slaughter, spoliation or oppression of individuals by individuals, it shall seem good to the proper authority to inhibit the carrying of offensive arms in this or that particular place, or by this or that particular person or set of persons, or on this or that particular occasion, or during this or that particular time, or to inhibit all persons from carrying any offensive arms in a concealed manner at any time.

II. Securities in favour of individuals

Article 8. No one shall against his will, or as the case may be against the will of those under whose guardianship he is placed, be arrested, imprisoned or otherwise confined, except for the purposes, and on the occasions, and in the manner determined and declared by law.

Article 9. No person shall against his will, or as the case may be against the will of those under whose guardianship he is placed, be sent or kept out of the dominions of the state or any part thereof, except for the purposes, and on the occasions, and in the manner determined and declared by law.

Article 10. No person shall be put to death but for the purposes and on the occasions determined and declared by law.

Article 11. No person shall be mutilated, disabled, bruised, wounded or otherwise made to suffer in any part of his body, except for the purposes, and on the occasions, and in the manner determined and declared by law.

Article 12. Of no man shall any personal service in any shape be exacted, except for the purposes, and on the occasions, and in the manner determined and declared by law.

Article 13. On no man's property shall any infringement be made, except for the purposes, on the occasions, and in the manner determined and declared by law.

Article 14. On the security of no man's private writings shall any infringement be made, except for the purposes, on the occasions, and in the manner determined and declared by law.

Article 15. Of the security of a man's private writings it may be an infringement if, against his will declared or reasonably presumable, they be placed or kept out of his custody, within or without the dominions of the State, or destroyed, or in any way damaged, or inspected, or seized for whatsoever of these or any other purposes it be.

Article 16. If, for giving execution and effect to the law, it becomes necessary, in virtue of any exception mentioned in Articles [8, 9, 10, 11, 12, 13, 14] or [15] to make infringement on the security of body or goods, no such infringement shall be made beyond what such necessity requires. For any injury in either shape, all persons therein concerned, functionaries or not functionaries, shall be deemed trespassers: and as such responsible in respect of burthen of compensation and punishment in the same manner as wrongdoers at large.

DETAILS

[I. Securities in detail in favour of the Nation]

II. National Gagging[1]

Every act having for its object the production of the effect thus denominated belongs as above to the list of injurious acts. Every person who has knowingly any part in the production of it is accordingly punishable by the obligation of making reparation, with or without punishment in other shape, according to the shape in which the injurious act has shewn itself.

The *right* of which the offence thus denominated is the infringement is the right of exercising influence in the choice of the whole number of those members of the community by whom a public function in any shape is exercised, and of declaring an opinion on their conduct as well as that of every other individual in whose good conduct all members without exception have an interest: the right of censorship: including the right of receiving and writing unlimited information relative to all grounds on which, to be just, the exercise of that function requires a man to be possessed of: in a word, the possessing on each occasion, in a manner adequately correct and extensive, the proper grounds of censorship.

Liberty of communicating by word of mouth, to as many as chosen, information in any shape in which it is regarded by the individual in question as contributory to greatest happiness.

Right recognized. Giving *expression* and *publicity* to all facts and observations of which, in the judgment of the individual in question,

---

[1] Under the heading of 'Details', Bentham does not appear to have considered the topic 'I. Religious Persecution'.

the conception promises to be contributory to the greatest happiness of the greatest number: whether the tendency of the correspondent information be to raise or lower this or that person in the scale of public opinion.

Correspondent acts of power prohibited as being violations of these rights, and thereby placed upon the footing of punishable offences, punishable in the same manner as they would be if exercised by individuals not invested with any such power:

1. Punishing, or contributing or endeavouring to contribute to the punishing, of any person for the having given utterance to any such discourse, to any discourse to the effect in question, when expressed by audible signs.

2. Punishing etc. any person for giving expression to ditto discourse by visible signs: that is to say in characters written or printed. Issuing any order for such punishment.

3. Punishing any person for transferring to another for a time or in perpetuity, either gratis or for a price, any paper or other substance on which such signs stand visible. Issuing any order for such seizure. Giving or being concerned in giving execution to any such order.

4. Seizing, detaining, destroying or deteriorating any paper or other substratum on which signs expressive of a discourse in question are marked. Issuing or contributing to the [issuing of][1] any order for such seizure, detention, destruction or deterioration. Giving or contributing to give execution to any such order.

5. Obstructing by force, intimidation or deceit the approach, entrance or continuance of persons in any number to, into or in any place in which they have separately any right to station themselves. Obstructing them while in the act of making reciprocal communication of such their information and the opinions and wishes suggested by it.

6. Seizing the body of any person so occupied, thereby infringing upon his liberty of locomotion. Corresponding offence: Injurious Confinement.

7. Seizing any paper, writing, printed book or other visible instrument of discourse having for its object the inviting two or more persons to assemble for any such purpose as above. Corresponding offence: Violation of private secrets, of written instruments of communication between man and man.

8. Consequence in respect of eventual acts of corporal injuriation, homicide included.

In case of any bodily contest between persons occupied in the exercise of any of the above rights and other persons, functionaries or

---

[1] The addition is suggested by the marginal summary: 'Issuing or contributing to issuing, or execution, of order for seizing etc.'

non-functionaries, occupied in any such endeavour as that of disturbing such exercise, any wound or other suffering unavoidably produced by the lawful exercisers in the way of self-defence, or any supporters of theirs, is lawful and unpunishable: but if occasioned by the disturbers on the bodies of the exercisers, unlawful and punishable: punishable in the same manner and degree as if no such pretence had been set up.

[9.] On the occasion of every such contest, all persons are warranted in giving their corporal assistance to the exercisers. No person is warranted in giving assistance to the obstructors.

10. So in regard to damage done to property on the occasion of any such bodily contest: damage unavoidably done by the exercisers or their assistants to property of the obstructors is lawful and unpunishable: damage done by the obstructors or their assistants is unlawful and punishable.

III. National disarmament and debilitation
Every act having for its object the production of the effect thus denominated stands as above in the list of injurious acts.

Correspondent rights violated are:

1. Right of putting and keeping one's self in a state of aptitude in the character of member of the armed force of the community.

2. Right of exercising one's self and being exercised in the use of arms.

Correspondent exercises of power prohibited, rendered unlawful and as such punishable as being acts of violation with reference to the above rights: punishable as if exercised by persons not invested with power.

1. Punishing any person for having been occupied in being so trained or in training any other person.

2. Punishing any person for repairing for the purpose of being trained to any place in which for any other purpose he had a right to station himself.

3. Punishing any person for giving invitation in any shape to others, oral or graphical, to engage in any such exercise or to meet others for the purpose of such exercise.

4. Obstructing, or contributing to obstruct, the meeting of persons in any number for this purpose.

5. Obstructing them as above in the commencement or continuance of the sort of operation here in question.[1]

---

[1] There is no text corresponding to the following marginal summary, which belongs here:
'Annoying any person on account of his having been engaged in such exercise.
'Modes of obstruction: 1. Force. 2. Intimidation. 3. Deception. 4. Corruption.'

II. Securities in detail in favour of individuals

IV. Security against secret confinement: for the protection of the persons of individuals against oppression, by persons in authority, without or even with the knowledge of the Sovereign

1. Whensoever, on the alledged ground of justice, the person of any man is put under confinement, information thereof shall be given in the most public manner to the end that all persons taking an interest in his welfare may have it in their power to take lawful measures for securing him against injustice.

2. To this end, the name and situation of every habitation designed by authority to be used as [a place]¹ of confinement, whether on the score of delinquency or insanity, shall be entered in an appropriate register, one exemplar whereof shall be kept in the metropolis in the Office of the Chief Judicatory; and of this exemplar a copy shall be kept at the Office of every other Judicatory.

3. On the commitment of an individual to any such place of confinement, entry of such commitment shall be made on a register to be therein kept for that purpose, mentioning the name by which, in his own declaration or otherwise, such individual is distinguished; the person or persons by whose hands he has been brought; the person by whose authority he has been brought; the time for which he is so committed: and the evidence on which such commitment has been grounded: a sufficient description by name and otherwise of every person on whose testimony the commitment has had place being added, as also the cause for which he has been committed.

4. Within | | hours after the commitment of the prisoner, a copy of such entry shall be pasted up over the door of the Judicatory, in such characters and situation as shall be legible to all passengers.

5. If at any time by some special necessity the commitment of the prisoner to the appropriate prison be rendered impracticable or improper, any other building, public or private, may for the time be employed for the purpose, care being taken that the vexation thereby occasioned, as well to the occupant of such building as to the prisoner, be as little as possible, and that at the expence of the prisoner, if found guilty, or at the expence of the public, if there be fund sufficient, compensation be made to the occupant for the vexation: for which reason also, that building which for this purpose may be employed with least vexation, compensated or uncompensated, to the occupant be in each case preferred.

---

¹ MS 'places'.

6. Causes for which, instead of the ordinary appropriate prison, an extraordinary prison as above may be employed are as follows:

1. The ordinary prison by its fullness rendered incapable of holding the prisoner without danger to health or safe custody.

2.—or by want of repair.

3.—or by unhealthiness produced for example by contagious disease.

4.—or rendered by distance inaccessible without halting for repose.

5.—or by hostility on the part of enemies, foreign or domestic.

6.—or by danger of forcible rescue.

7. If in any such occasional prison a prisoner be detained more than {24} hours, over the door thereof shall be fixt up a paper of notice such as that prescribed by Article | |[1] in the case of an ordinary prison: and for the framing or attestation thereof the assistance of some Iman be invoked: that of the nearest Mosque in preference.

8. Of the commitment of a person to any such extraordinary prison the bringer shall make known the fact together with the cause by which, as supposed, it was rendered necessary, and whether such notice as should have been fixt up as above was fixt up, and if not, why not.

9. The bringer shall make known to such Keeper of the ordinary prison or such Judge, as the case may be,[2] the fact of such detention at the extraordinary prison, together with the causes and circumstances of it: if he omitts so to do, the detention shall, for and during the time of it, be deemed injurious.

10. Every person who knowingly and wilfully has been contributory to the injurious imprisonment of any person shall himself suffer imprisonment for a length of time equal to that during which the imprisonment had place: and shall moreover, to the extent of his means, be compelled to furnish, or contribute to the furnishing, compensation in a pecuniary shape for the injury.

[11.] Any person by whom it shall be known or suspected that in a certain building a certain person is kept in confinement may repair to the Keeper and require to be informed by him whether such person be actually under his custody. If being so interrogated the Keeper refuses or forbears to make answer, or makes a false answer, the Keeper, being thereof convicted, shall suffer condign punishment: and if at the time of the interrogation the person in question was actually in his

---

[1] See the fourth point above.

[2] According to the marginal summary, the bringer 'shall give earliest possible notice of commitment and its cause' both to the 'Keeper of the ordinary prison' and to the 'President of the Judicatory in whose district the extra prison is'.

custody, shall be punished as having been guilty of injurious imprisonment.[1]

[12.] To the interrogation whether the person in question be at that very time in the custody of such Keeper may be added the interrogation whether at any and what time he had been in such custody: and if yes, in what manner and by what means he ceased to be so.

[13.] For prevention of vexation and impertinent inquiries, the Keeper, before he makes reply to any such interrogation as above, may require the applicant to make himself known to the purpose of eventual responsibility.[2]

[14.] Any person may repair to the Judicatory of the District in which such place of confinement is situated, and there require of the Judges that the person so under confinement may be produced before them, and at a public audience, inquiry made into the cause of such confinement: which inquiry made, the person shall be remanded, or set at liberty, or otherwise dealt with as the case may require.

What is here said of a prison shall be understood of any other place in which, whether according or not according to law, the person in question is under confinement.

[15.] If to avoid his being produced to the Judicatory, as above, a prisoner is shifted from place to place, all persons concerned in such shifting, and conscious of its having that for its purpose, are responsible as for injurious imprisonment.

V. Security against injurious banishment

Injurious banishment is where, without or otherwise than according to lawful sentence of a judicatory, a subject of the State is, to his vexation, by force, unlawful commination or deceit, sent or kept out of the territory of the State or any part thereof.

If out of the whole territory of the State, the banishment is external; if out of this or that particular part, internal.

The commination is unlawful, if the means employed be a threat of vexation by unlawful means, or even of lawful prosecution for other cause than injury done to the individual by whom the comminatory intimation is conveyed or to some other individual on whose behalf he is entitled to prosecute.[3]

---

[1] In the marginal summary, Bentham added: 'if no [i.e. if the prisoner was not in his custody], Keeper falsely answering or not answering, punishable at discretion'.

[2] The marginal summary is more detailed than the text here: 'For responsibility, applicant, on requisition by Keeper, is bound to make known to Keeper his name, condition in life, and abode. On his silence or false answer, Keeper still bound to answer, but the inquirer punishable as for vexation.'

[3] In the text, Bentham noted with relation to this paragraph: '☞ Quere whether to insert this?'

Of every sentence of banishment, external or internal, pronounced by a subordinate Judicatory, notice shall, by the earliest opportunity, be sent to the Office of the Head Judge: nor shall the sentence be executed, until confirmed by his signature: nor then executed, until thirty days after the sentence has been read in the Chamber of audience.

Every person who knowingly and wilfully has been contributory to the injurious external banishment of any person shall suffer imprisonment for a length of time equal to that during which such banishment shall have had place: and shall moreover, to the extent of his means, be compelled to contribute to the furnishing compensation in a pecuniary shape for the injury.

Observations on the subject of measures of prevention against injurious and secret banishment.

For security against secret and injurious banishment two obvious measures of the preventive kind present themselves. One is—prohibiting egress without a passport; the other is—prohibiting egress without previous entry of the fact in an Official Register book.

It may perhaps be too much to say that in no state of things either of these means ought to be employed: but what may be said with truth is—that generally speaking the evil of the remedy will be found preponderant over the good. The state of things will be an extraordinary one if for one instance in which the egress is involuntary there will not be hundreds, not to say thousands, in which it is voluntary. Say for argument's sake, one thousand. Here then, in the hope of saving from the greater vexation a single person, a thousand are subjected to the lesser. But in the case where a passport is rendered necessary, neither in its length nor therefore in its aggregate amount has the vexation any certain limit. Power without limitation over every one who has need of the passport is thus given to the functionary or functionaries, whoever they be, whose signature or signatures are necessary to the giving validity to it: and thus for the hope of saving one from injurious banishment, a thousand are exposed to arbitrary confinement, confinement not the less vexatious for not being against law.

In the case where simple registration is all that is required, the power of granting or refusing the passport not being given in a direct way, the danger of abuse may seem as if materially lessened, if not removed. It is not however by a great deal so effectually lessened in reality, as in appearance: for still, so long as the minute in question remains unmade, the confinement is as effectual as if the case had been that of a passport that had been delayed.

For argument sake, the security thus afforded has hitherto been

91

supposed entire. This however it can not be in any case: and the more uncertain the effect of it is, the less the utility, absolutely considered, and thence comparatively with reference to the vexation produced by it. This efficacy will depend upon the nature of the communications with other countries, and the efficacy of the means actually employed for keeping persons and things in this way in a state of confinement. True it is, that exportation performed upon the person of another against his will will not in general be so easy to a man as if performed upon his own person, or upon an equal mass of inanimate things.

VI. [Security] against secret and unlawful homicide

On the death of every person, notice thereof shall forthwith be given to the Iman of the Parish within which the death took place. If it was in any habitation, by the Occupier thereof, or some other person in whose presence the death took place: if not in any dwelling or the ground belonging to a house and occupied therewith, as for example on a journey, then by some one or more of any persons who were present: if found dead, then by some person by whom the body was so found.

In every case in which it appears that in the production of the death of any individual human agency has in any shape borne a part, every person to whose mind or senses appearances tending to give probability to such an incident have presented themselves is expected and required to give to his conception in relation thereunto whatsoever publicity it may be in his power to produce.

To this end, after making inspection of the dead body, if it be in his power, with his own eyes, let him repair to the nearest Mosque with all possible dispatch, and communicate to the Iman such observations as he has made: to the end that this servant of God may take cognizance of the facts, and in case of criminal agency on the part of any individual, do whatsoever may be in his power towards the discovery and punishment of every criminal so concerned.

Having received such communication, let the Iman with all practicable diligence repair to the spot on which the body lies, and there make examination of the state of the body and make inquiry in relation to the matter at the hands of all persons by whom appropriate information is offered, or at whose hands it seems capable of being obtained. Of whatsoever he thus sees and hears he shall make a minute, authenticating by the name of the witness the purport and as near as may be the words of every person so examined—causing such party interrogated to authenticate with his name, if able, such his testimony, after having first read it over, that so the correctness of the minute so made may be established.

In taking such examination let the servant of God proceed as follows:

1. Except as excepted, let every thing done by him on this occasion be done as publickly as possible.

2. If in regard to this or that person, he sees reason to suspect that on seeing what passes, he may give information thereof to some person or persons contributory to the death for the purpose of enabling them to escape, he may have reason to keep secret from such person any thing that tends to point suspicion upon the person so suspected, until measures have been taken for his arrestation.

3. Let him in the name of God and his Prophet, adjure all believers so interrogated to declare the truth, the whole truth and nothing but the truth, in relation to the matter in hand, and that as well spontaneously as in answer to all such interrogatives as he shall have put to them.

4. In case of refusal to give information, or to make answer to this or that question, let him take note thereof: but if any allegations in justification of such refusal be made, let him make mention also of such allegations.

5. So, if any means be used to evade giving such information.

6. So, if after promise to give it, such promise be not fulfilled.

[7.] Of the discourse of every individual at whose hands testimony is required as above, let him take account in writing, noting as correctly as possible the very words of every thing that is said:

[8.] questions as well as answers.

9. So, demeanour.[1]

10. In the case of each individual so interrogated, at the end of what is written in relation to him, let him read over to him what has been written: in every instance where intimation has been given by the witness that the account so given of him [is][2] in this or that particular incorrect, and that it ought to have been so and so, let him make addition accordingly. But let him not on this account obliterate any thing that has been written: for any contradictions which have place between any subsequent part of a man's testimony and any antecedent part may help to make known the truth.

11. At the end of the account thus given of each person's testimony, let him cause the witness, if able, to write his own name in confirmation thereof: if unable, then let the servant of God write the name, and cause the witness in confirmation thereof to take the pen in hand and make a mark:

---

[1] This point is not included in the text, but is taken from the marginal summary.
[2] MS 'are'.

12. and to this mark let him add, in his own hand or the hands of the respective persons, the names of the persons who saw the mark made, or of a competent number of them, choosing such whose ulterior testimony may upon occasion be resorted to with least inconvenience in every shape.

13. If, by any person present, a desire be expressed that a question to this or that purport be put to any other person in relation to this same business, let the servant of God, if in his judgment such question be not irrelevant, include the same accordingly in the number of the questions. If, regarding the same as improper, he declines putting it to the witness, still if by him by whom it is propounded, or by any other person present, it be desired that entry be made of such request and refusal, so be it.

14. Of the names of all persons present during the examination of each witness, let entry in like manner be made: unless the number should be so great that such entry would occupy too much time. In such case the number may be limited to twelve: insert those by whom a desire to have entry of their names has been expressed [in preference] to those by whom no such desire has been expressed—nor let refusal be made to any by whom such desire has been expressed until the number of 24 has been completed. If by any person complaint be made of partiality in the choice, let note be made of such complaint, the servant of God following his own judgment notwithstanding.

[VII. Security against Mysterious Disappearance]

In case of the unexpected disappearance of any person, if it be known or suspected that he is secretly kept in confinement any where or has been secretly put to death or by force or fraud sent out of the country, application being made on his behalf to the Cadi or to any inferior judicatory, entry shall thereof be made in the Register Book of such judicatory: means shall be employed for the recordation and notification of the fact, to the end that if unlawfully confined he may be liberated or otherwise dealt with, if unlawfully transported he may be brought back, or if unlawfully put to death measures may be taken for the punishment of all persons thereto contributory.

Such application being made, the Judge shall hear and make entry thereof in an appropriate Register Book of the Judicatory, and shall do whatsoever shall be in his power towards the causing notification to be made thereof throughout the dominions of the State.[1]

---

[1] The marginal summary is more detailed than the text here: 'Of such application with the alledged grounds of it, let entry be made, including examination of all apt witnesses suggested by applicant or Judge. Name of the application—information of mysterious disappearance—name of the written discourse containing the evidence—record of mysterious disappearance etc.'

On the occasion of any such application, the Judge shall immediately deliver to him, or suffer him to take, or cause to be taken, a copy thereof signed by the said Judge: copies in any number being taken of such copy, the Judge shall without delay cause examination thereof to be made, and as soon as they have respectively been found or made correct shall in like manner authenticate them by his signature, to the end that by the applicant transmission thereof be made to all such judicatories and Mosques as the applicant shall be desirous of sending them to: whereupon immediately upon the receipt of each such copy, the Iman of the Mosque shall make publication thereof by reading the contents to the faithful in full congregation assembled.

In every judicatory in the office of which any such copy has been received, the presiding Judge shall cause it to be kept in the archives, having first made notification thereof in the promptest and at the same time in the most public manner that the circumstances of time and place admitt of.

Attached to such *record of disappearance* shall be an invitation to all persons having knowledge of any facts, tending to the discovery of the authors of the injury, or if the party be alive to the causing it to cease, to repair to any judicatory or to any Mosque at their choice, there to testify what they know: which done, the President of the Judicatory or the Iman of the Mosque shall upon their responsibility use such means as their situation admitts of to the forwarding to the proper Judicatory the information so obtained.[1]

The petition on which a record of disappearance is grounded must be signed by some one person, namely to the end that in case of its being presented through malice, or otherwise without justification or sufficient excuse, the person presenting it may be responsible to the purpose of pecuniary compensation, with or without ulterior punishment, for the vexation so produced.

Such petition may be signed by persons in any number:[2] and in such case, such signatures may be in lines one under another, or in lines forming the rays of a circle. The use of this radial form is to save the individual principally concerned from being more exposed than the rest to vindictive treatment at the hands of any functionary or other person in whose breast the application might excite displeasure.

In so far as applicants are unable to defray the expence of copies

---

[1] There is no text corresponding to the following marginal summary, which belongs here: 'On receiving such record, power to Judicatory or Iman to compell attendance of all apt witnesses.'

[2] In the marginal summary, Bentham added: 'Of each the name and description sufficient for responsibility must be given: else no record made.'

and transmission, let the Judicatory defray such expence out of any such means as it has in its power.

VIII. Security against misuse of private writings: or Security for the writings or other documents of individuals against wanton or oppressive seizure, destruction, damnification or inspection by persons in authority

No writing, against the will, known or reasonably presumable, of the owner, shall be carried or kept out of his custody or power, or be seized, destroyed, damaged or inspected by order of any person in authority, nor otherwise than in pursuance of the order of some judicatory: of an appropriate judicial functionary.

Such order may be either subsequently to the definitive sentence pronounced in a suit or cause, and for the purpose of giving effect to such sentence, or antecedently to such sentence, and for the purpose of furnishing due grounds for it in the shape of evidence.

In case of any such misuse, every person concerned in the infliction of the injury shall be responsible to the purpose of pecuniary compensation, with or without ulterior punishment, as the case may require.[a]

If by any illegal means writings be obtained contributory to the proof of any offence, the illegality of the means shall not have the effect of exempting the possessor from the punishment adapted to the offence: but in the liquidation of the punishment, any evil suffered by him in consequence of the inspection thus obtained of any other writings shall be considered.

So in the case where as between two parties who are in a state of dispute, with relation to a certain right, a writing having for its tendency the giving effect to the claim of one of the parties, and which as such, the other ought to produce or to have produced, has been obtained by illegal means.

If by legal means employed for the purpose of obtaining evidence of this or that act of delinquency, or of the correspondent non-delinquency, or in support of this or that particular right, [are obtained][1] writings or other documents capable of serving as evidence respecting any other supposed offence or right, the evidence thus obtained may be employed accordingly. But if in this way possession

---

[a] Note that the evil produced by such injurious inspection is capable of wearing any shape in which evil to any person or persons is capable of having place: in his person, in his reputation, in his property, in his condition in life—in any of these ways an individual is liable to be made a sufferer from such a cause.

---

[1] MS 'If by legal means employed is obtained for the purpose of obtaining evidence . . . particular right'.

or inspection has been obtained of writings or other documents by the disclosure of which evil in any shape has been produced to any person without service rendered to justice in any shape as above, for such evil all parties concerned in the production of it shall be responsible to the purpose of reparation, or punishment, or both, as the case may require.

If for the purpose of producing serious evil by disclosure of writings or other documents, evidence not applicable to any other than a trivial offence or a trivial right be obtained, though it be by legal means, all persons knowingly concerned in such inspection or divulgation shall be responsible to the purpose of reparation or punishment or both. But from the punishment deduction may be made proportioned to any such good as shall be deemed to have been produced by the production of such evidence.[a]

IX. Security against Official depredation

Official depredation may have place at the expence of an individual, or at the expence of government: that is to say at the expence of the whole community at whose expence the money employed in the service of government is collected.

Official depredation at the expence of government belongs not to this purpose.

Official depredation has place in so far as any public functionary avails himself of the power or influence possessed by him by means of his office to obtain from any person money, money's worth or beneficial service in any shape, not having a right thereto by law.

The instrument wherewith [this][1] misdeed is committed may be either force, intimidation or deceit.

Intimidation may be exercised by producing either the fear of some eventual positive evil, or by the fear of failing to obtain the matter of good which the functionary had no right to prevent the individual from receiving.

Injunction of secrecy is evidence of official depredation. If on the occasion of the valuable thing or service received, intimation is by the functionary conveyed to the individual that it is the wish of the functionary that the transaction should be kept concealed from any

---

[a] Example. For the purpose of causing a person to be disinherited or otherwise made to suffer by an over-severe or tyrannical father, husband or master, an enemy obtains by legal means, in company with documents applicable to the purpose of a trivial offence or right, others which by means of some exasperation produce the evil effect intended as above.

---

[1] MS illegible.

person, such declared wish affords a presumption of official depredation: and such presumption, if the fact of the having given intimation of such a wish is credited, shall be regarded [as] conclusive.

If, on account of any service or supposed service, rendered or supposed to have been rendered, or to be about to be rendered, to an individual by a public functionary by reason or in respect of his official situation, gift or service in any shape other than what is appointed and allowed by law be received by him, or to his use, or to any person specially connected with him by any tie of self-regarding interest or sympathy, intimidation or corruption shall be presumed to have been exercised by such functionary: intimidation, namely by apprehension lest evil in some shape in which it ought not to be inflicted by him on the individual be so inflicted, or lest good in some shape in which it ought to be rendered to the individual by the functionary without such gift or service should not be rendered by him accordingly: corruption, in the view of obtaining of the functionary, at the expence of the public service, the matter of good in some shape in which it ought not to be so rendered to him.

In case of intimidation the gift or the equivalent for the service may be recovered of the functionary, or his heirs at any time within | | years.

So in case of corruption, it may be recovered for the use of the public treasury.

If by any public functionary gift or service not due to the Sovereign by law be received or required of any individual on pretence that it is for the Sovereign's use or by command of the Sovereign, the intimation by which it is asserted or supposed that the Sovereign issued any such command, or would receive any such gift or service if presented, shall be deemed a calumny, and every person wilfully contributing to the conveying such intimation shall be punished as the authors of such calumny.

If on any such occasion any writing to any such effect be produced purporting to be authenticated by the signature of the Sovereign, the same shall be regarded as a forged instrument and the persons concerned in the exhibition thereof shall be punished as for forgery.

Provided always that if the Sovereign be pleased to repair to the judicatory and in the face of the bystanders declare that the signature was really his signature, in such case it shall be acknowledged as such, and all due obedience shall ensue.

Every functionary by whom, on account of any branch of the public service, money or money's worth or the loan thereof is required at the hands of any individual shall, on receiving that which is required or any part of it, deliver to the person of whom it has been received an appropriate instrument in writing acknowledging such receipt. This instrument may be termed an acknowledgment of receipt, or in one word a receipt.

If no such instrument be so delivered, the act of receipt shall be deemed an act of *official depredation*, or say in one word *extortion*.

Of every such receipt two copies shall be made. One of them shall be delivered to the requisitionist[1] as above.[2] On it shall be written:

1. Name of the Place in or at which the requisition is made. District, Town if any, and Parish.

2. Time at which the requisition is made.

3. The branch of the public service for which the requisition is made: for example the financial, the judicial, or the military.

4. Official name of the functionary by whom the requisition is made.

5. Personal name of the functionary by whom the requisition is made.

6. Name of the individual on whom the requisition is made.

7. The subject-matter of the requisition so made.

8. The time on or before which it is expected that the article so required shall be delivered.

9. The place at which it is expected that the thing in requisition shall be delivered.

10. If the thing in requisition be delivered accordingly, mention of such delivery.

11. If no such delivery has place, mention of the non-delivery with the cause of it as alledged by or on the part of the requisitionist.

If lawful such requisition will be either specially or generally manifested.

By specially manifested, understand manifested by a requisition made to the particular requisitionist in question.

By generally manifested, understand manifested to all such persons as come within the description thereupon given, as for example all the persons in a certain district, or all the persons of a certain class whose ordinary abode is within that same district.

X. Securities against Official Oppression at large[3]

Oppression is vexation by means of power.

By an act of vexation, understand every act by which a person is made to suffer in any one or more of man's six vulnerable points.

---

[1] By 'requisitionist' Bentham meant the person on whom the requisition was made, rather than the person who made the requisition.

[2] In the marginal summary, Bentham added: 'Duplicate of receipt with requisitionist's signature kept at the Office or by the functionary receiving.'

[3] A further draft on this topic, which Bentham finally considered inappropriate for use here, is at UC xxiv. 142–4 (7–8 October 1822).

These are:
1. Mind.
2. Body.
3. Reputation.
4. Property.
5. Power.
6. Condition in life.[a]

To misrule in this mode apply the several provisions which on the subject of Official Depredation apply to the several heads following: namely,

Art. 3. Instruments incorporeal.
Art. 4. Modes of intimidation.
Art. 5. 6. Presumptive evidence.
Art. 7. Reparation of the injury.
Art. 8. 9. [10.] Sole case in which Sovereign's consent is credible.[1]

For the mode of examination and recordation in this case, see the general provision under that head.[2]

XI. *[Security against] Extortion of personal service*[b]

By no person, functionary or non-functionary, shall personal service in any shape be exacted of any individual on account of government, without giving him in writing a sufficient acknowledgement thereof.

[a] As of enjoyment, so of sufferance, mind is the sole immediate seat. In this one vulnerable point is included (it may therefore be observed) all these others. But either through one or more of these five distinguishable points, considered as so many channels, may the sensation be produced, or in an immediate way, without passing through any one of them. The word mind has on this occasion been found necessary in the character of a receptacle for giving lodgement to various modes of vexation not produced through any one of these other vulnerable points.

Vexation is produced in the case where property is the vulnerable point on which the oppression bears. But in this case it stands designated by the more particular name of *depredation* or *spoliation*.

Remain for vexation, and oppression in the narrowest sense, the cases in which it is in mind immediately, or through body, reputation, power, or condition in life, that the vexation is produced.

[b] Extortion of service may be considered as depredation: viz. to the amount of the profit derived from it on the one hand, and the loss or other sufferance produced by it

---

[1] This enumeration corresponds closely to that of the marginal summary paragraphs in 'IX. Security against Official depredation', pp. 97–9 above. Bentham seems to have intended to organize the material on depredation, and possibly the whole of the 'Details' section, into distinct articles: see the Editorial Introduction, p. xxvii above.

[2] On the plan at UC xxiv. 190 (8 October 1822), under the heading 'Procedure or Collection of Evidence', Bentham listed the following points: '1. Publicity saving special cause for secrecy. 2. Means of securing deposition and verity of ditto. 3. Minutation—mode of. 4. Power of interrogation to Bystanders. 5. Attestation by bystanders.' For a discussion of these topics see 'VI. [Security] against secret and unlawful homicide', pp. 92–4 above.

In such acknowledgement shall be contained the particulars following—namely:

1. The name of the person at whose hands the service was required.

2. The proper name and official name of the functionary by whom the service was required.

3. The particular nature of the service.

4. The nature of the exigency: i.e. of the demand or need which on the public account there was for the performance of such service.

5. The time: that is to say the year, month, day and hour at which the service was first required.

6. The time during which the service was required to be continued.

7. The willingness or unwillingness of the individual to render the service so required.

8. In case of unwillingness, the reasons, if any, alledged by him, why the service ought not at all, or ought not at that time, to be exacted of him.

9. The due performance, imperfect performance, or non-performance of the service so required.

10. Collateral damage, if any, inevitably sustained by the requisitionist by the performance of the service.

Of such act of acknowledgement, let two copies be taken: one to be delivered to the individual, the other kept by the functionary.

On each of them let the individual signify his assent or dissent to the several statements, attesting the same by his name or his mark: his name, if he be unable to write it, being written by, or by order of, the functionary.

The nature of the service and the fact of the exaction of it being thus recorded, it will then be to be compensated for on account of government, or left uncompensated, according to the nature of the case.

Let the act of acknowledgment, as to all particulars antecedent to the performance of the service, be made out and signed antecedently to such performance, or not till afterwards, according to the nature of the exigence: that is to say according as this testimony can or can not be given beforehand without prejudice to the service.

Examples of cases in which it may probably not be capable of being given without prejudice to the service:

1. Prevention, stoppage or diminution of damage by any physical calamity such as that occasioned by fire or inundation.

---

on the other. In so far as to the individual in question labour is a source of profit, forced labour is loss to an amount equal to the profit which in the time so employed by him might have been gained.

2. Prevention, stoppage or diminution of damage to body or goods by delinquency in any shape: such as killing, wounding or beating, forcible depredation, destruction or damnification of goods by internal evil-doers.

3. Prevention, stoppage or diminution of damage in the like shapes by foreign enemies.

Where the nature of the service is such as to require that it be exacted of individuals in an indeterminate number at the same time, no such act of acknowledgment need be given.

But in this case let a general statement of the matter be committed to writing by the proper functionary, and deposited either at the Mosque or the Judicatory within the District of which the matter happened, or both as the case may require.

If so it be that by the magnitude of hazard to body or goods, or by the success or energy of his exertions, it has happened to this or that individual to signalize himself in an eminent degree, let note thereof be taken and a duly attested copy thereof be delivered to him. In this case, if the degree of merit so manifested be sufficient, let an entry be made in an appropriate Register to be kept in every Mosque and in every Judicatory. It may be stiled, The Register of Merit: or the Register of extraordinarily meritorious public service.

PRELIMINARY EXPLANATIONS
CONTINUED

§ 19. *Means of obtaining the requisite Concession—probability of success, on what it depends*

Sub§ 1. Concession—what the chance in favour of it

Such are the securities proposed[1]—proposed as presenting the fairest promise in every point of view: natural consequences if conceded, and probability of concession taken together. Unfortunately whatsoever may be the chance of such concession, blindness on the part of the Sovereign to these its beneficial consequences is (it will be seen) a condition little less than indispensable to the existence of so felicitous a state of things. Only in proportion as it[2] applies a restrictive check to the doing of his will, only in proportion to the extent in which it operates in this direction, can it be productive of any of those salutary effects for the purpose of which it is proposed. But the general idea of any effectual opposition to his own will, in whatsoever direction operating, is an idea to which in a mind so situated a quantity of pain is attached greater than can be outweighed by the consideration of any particular pleasure which he may [be] capable of deriving from the contemplation of any particular good effects in which the creatures subject to his power must receive a share before he receives his, their share being at the same time if taken in the aggregate much greater than his. His situation is as to this matter that of the infant with his physic. Some years must have passed over its head before any such remote, contingent and imperfectly conceived event as the cessation of the suffering he is enduring from the disease can form of itself an adequate inducement to be voluntarily instrumental in afflicting himself with the pain so certainly and immediately attached to the intro-susception of the nauseous dose.

The chance of the requisite concession is not equally minute in all imaginable cases. To obtain security against vexation in all its shapes, and at all times, and as against all persons, but more particularly against all such as have it most completely in their power to give birth to it, is the object of these arrangements: more particularly against

---

[1] For the placing of this section after 'Constitutional Securities' see the Editorial Introduction, p. xxiv above.
[2] i.e. 'any such arrangement', as per marginal summary.

vexation at the hands of the Sovereign and those in authority under him: vexation for the gratification of their respective appetites and passions.

The classes of persons at whose hands it is most to be apprehended are thus distinguishable: 1. the Sovereign himself: 2. the Sovereign's favourites: 3. the several functionaries under him considered as being on any such occasions apt to be employed as his and their instruments for his and their personal gratification: 4. these same functionaries considered as being in a condition to employ their power in the production of vexation and oppression for their own gratification and supposed advantage.

To vexation of this latter description, so far as confined to this latter purpose, the Sovereign will not naturally entertain any considerable aversion: what may be the sufferings of the people taken at large will, on this occasion as on every other, be to a mind so situated of itself a matter of indifference: against any sentiment of sympathy of which they may be the object, may be set that portion of sympathy which has for its object the enjoyments of a select set of men who being in a more especial manner in his service—the whole of whose time is regarded as being employed in his service, belong to him by a nearer and closer tie than the members of the community at large, remote as they are from his sight and his cognizance. If in this case there be any thing by which the scale can be turned in favour of the people, it must be a species of fear—fear of the evil that by possibility may be turned toward even his own hand by the consideration of the connection that has place between himself and these creatures of his will—the oppressors whose power of continuing the oppression a word from him would suffice to terminate.

If then according to his calculation any odium produced by the divulgation of instances of oppression will on every occasion take them and them alone for its object—if it will not rise higher—if it will not rise so high as to reach either his own person or those of his more especial favorites—in such case no very urgent inducement may be necessary to obtain his consent. In Tripoli, as in England, if at any time he can set the people at rest by this sacrifice of a set of instruments in which no special favorite is contained, a comparatively small inducement—a comparatively slight degree of apprehension—may suffice. Turning out this set, and taking in a different one, he may, through their instrumentality, go on in the same track, beginning only a new score. Dismissing a set of Tories, as a gamester tosses on the floor an unlucky set of cards, he may go on playing the same game with a pack of Whigs.

Sub§2. Means of obtainment. Precautions to be taken. Cautions observed
On the part of the Monarch the probability of his concurrence in arrangements directed to this end will be in the direct ratio of the relative inoffensiveness of the proposed arrangements, and in the inverse ratio of his proneness to take offence.

By the first of these considerations the problem is of course suggested—how to render the arrangements in form as well as substance as little offensive as they can be consistently with the accomplishment of the end or purpose. The cautions that present themselves as being suggested by this object are as follows, viz.

1. Be the vexations and oppressions what they may, bring not to view so long as it can be avoided any such supposition as that of their being practiced by command or so much as with the knowledge of the Sovereign. Present them as liable to be practiced by functionaries or opulent individuals at large, by functionaries as necessary to their official connections: by men of opulence as necessary to their opulence. But neither should any such precise designation as this [be made] without necessity: by words indicative of human beings in general these will be included as well as all others. If in any case there be necessity or use in giving any such particular designation, it will be to prevent any such supposition as that, by the consideration of the moral excellence supposed to be naturally attached to such high dignity, the intention of including them in the compass of the arrangement was not present to the mind of the legislator: or else to obviate any such apprehension on the part of the injured, lest the Judge, for want of words of sufficient force to compell him, should decline making application of the penal part of the law in the case of an oppressor of sufficient power to be formidable to the Judge.

2. Avoid as much as may [be] the appearing to proceed upon any such supposition as that of there being any thing amiss in the conduct of the Monarch.

3. If therefore the case be such that without something done towards it by some functionary the act of vexation in question can not have been committed, let the supposition be that it has been in pursuit of his own individual or some other particular sinister end that it has been practiced by the functionary and not in the view of benefit in any shape to the Monarch.

4. Even if from the nature of the case it appears plain that by the subordinate functionary in question no particular benefit can have been accrued, no effect beneficial to any person other than the Monarch produced, still it will not be necessary to suppose that either the will or the knowledge of the Monarch had any part in it. On the part of the subordinate functionary the inducement may have been

overzeal in the service of the Monarch: or the desire of affording to himself a gratification from the vexation produced in the breast of some individual regarded by him with the eyes of an enemy.

5. If the case be such as that without special concurrence on the part of the Monarch himself the vexation can not have been practiced, as where his signature is attached to a mandate in execution of which it has been practiced, in this case the supposition proceeded upon must be that of his having been deceived by this or that functionary by means of false representations concerning matters of fact. For in the elevated situation in which a Monarch stands, this is a mode of deception from which the most consummate wisdom can not in every case preserve a man from being misled. Be the man who he may, in regard to whatsoever matters of fact have not been present to his own senses, if inference from other facts will not suffice, his conception must have for its ground reports made by others.

6. If the case admitts not of any other supposition than that the Monarch has been misled, let the supposition implied be that it has been by false statements as to matters of fact, than by unwise judgments and advice. The being misled by false statements is a misfortune from which no degree of wisdom can always preserve any human being: on the part of a person thus misled no error in judgment, no intellectual weakness in any shape, is implied in the supposition. Not so in the case of being misled by bad advice. Intellectual weakness in some shape or other is in this case necessarily implied. The opinion of another man is looked to by him as a ground for the opinion on which he is to act. Why looked to? unless it be because he is not only incompetent to form an opinion of his own for the guidance of his own conduct, but so clearly so, as to be himself conscious of his own incompetence. Thus in the first place, by the consciousness of the weakness of his own judgment, he is in a manner compelled to borrow a judgment from another man: in the next place, when this judgment is lent to him, though by the supposition it is an erroneous one, his judgment has not enabled him to see in it what it is, to discern the real character of it.

7. If the nature of the case be such as not to admitt of any such supposition as that on the part of the Monarch either misinformation or bad advice from others had any part in the business, if at the same time a document purporting to be with his signature has been employed in the production of the vexation, as in the case of a signed mandate to tear a female from the arms of a father or a husband and bring her to his bed, the only avowable supposition remaining is that his signature has been forged, or by mistake attached to a wrong instrument. If in any public manner, for example in a judicatory or a

council of any sort, he comes forward and avows it, in such case there is no other alternative but submission or open disobedience. Example: French *Lit de Justice*.[1]

Note well the period at which these suppositions require to be brought and kept in view. It is the period of the framing of the arrangements—the period when the Monarch's consent to them is to be endeavoured to be obtained: final cause to lessen as much as possible his apprehension of seeing his desires restrained, or his misdeeds exposed. But supposing his sanction once obtained, the stronger the restraint, and the more entire and extensive the exposure, so much the better, unless a danger should appear of his being to such a degree irritated by the restraint or the exposure as openly to infringe or even abrogate the securities.

Remains for [consideration] the quantity in the inverse ratio of which the probability of concession will in this case encrease: the degree of proneness on the part of the Monarch to take offence in such sort as to refuse his concurrence.

This will depend partly upon external, partly upon internal circumstances: upon the situation of his affairs, and upon the state of his mind, general and particular, by whom in the case in question the situation in question is occupied.

External circumstances favorable to such a result may be thus expressed: 1. on the part of the Sovereign an extraordinary demand for money, or 2. personal service to a great extent, say in a military capacity, coupled with the persuasion of the inability to obtain it by any other coercive methods: in a word by any other means than the free consent of the individuals at whose hands it is looked for.[2]

As to frame of mind, so far as depends upon the condition thus designated, the following are the psychological causes by any one of which, supposing the quality adequate, the effects may be produced:

1. Timidity—fear of popular resentment in case of non-compliance.

2. Facility of yielding to advice, coupled with the favorable accident of having for advisers men who themselves have, by whatever causes, been disposed to give advice to the effect in question.[3]

---

[1] Under the ancient monarchy in France, Royal decrees had to be registered by the Paris *Parlement* before they came into force. If the *Parlement* remained opposed to a particular decree, the King could impose his will by means of a *Lit de Justice*, whereby he appeared ceremonially at *Parlement* in order personally to supervise the registration.

[2] There is no text corresponding to the following marginal summary, which belongs here: 'Cause of demand: 1. Personal expenditure. 2. Defensive war. 3. Offensive ditto for depredation or conquest.'

[3] In the text, Bentham noted at this point: 'Add 3. Love of reputation. 4. Sympathy for the people.' In the marginal summary, he added the following points: '3. Sensibility to the love of reputation. 4. Sensibility to the love of power thus exercisible in a new way. 5. Sensibility to the happiness of his subjects.'

[6.] Prospect of extending his reputation, his influence, and eventually his dominion, over the neighbouring nations.

As to persons in a situation to act as advisers, on the part of each individual so situated, concurrence or non-concurrence will depend upon the preponderance as between [the] degree of force with which his will is operated upon by the restraining inducements on the one part and the impelling inducements on the other.

To the list of restraining inducements belong the following.

1. In so far as the securities in question are productive of the effect aimed at, loss of the share which he might otherwise have expected in the benefit of any vexation or oppression practiced for the advancement of his own interests or the gratification of his own desires.

2. The like in respect of any person or persons connected with him by any special tie of self-regarding interest or sympathetic interest.

3. Fear of resentment as being producible in the breast of the Monarch by the observation of the part taken by him in the promotion of the innovation in question. If on the part of the Master, upon the balance there be any real reluctance in regard to the coming in to the proposal, it is not his actually coming into it that will have the effect of doing away any resentment he may have conceived towards those by whom in his view of the matter support has been given to it.

In the situation of the advisers in question, impelling motives with reference to the measure in question may be as follows:

1. to 6.[1] Considerations of a social nature in the same shapes as those above indicated in the case of the Monarch.

7. Sense of insecurity under the form of government as it exists.

In this inducement lies the main hope of concurrence at the hands of men so situated. This inducement applies to all ranks, the highest not excepted: it applies to them in all circumstances with reference to prosperity.

It applies to all the vulnerable points for the protection of which the tutelary arrangements in question are required.

Neither for life nor for liberty, for neither of those possessions, against resentment, fear, concupiscence or erroneous conception in the breast of the Sovereign, can any permanent security be possessed by any one individual in the community in the present state of the government.

In respect of property all men labour under insecurity, not merely in that shape in which it involves danger and alarm in respect of what they have already, but in that shape likewise in which by the sense of it they are prevented from making all those additions to it to which a

---

[1] The enumeration follows that in the marginal summary.

feeling of security such as is enjoyed even in the worst-governed European nations is sufficient to give birth.

In the present state of insecurity, no man who has capital to any considerable amount can make application of it to any source of profit, the reaping of which supposes and requires the assurance of reaping the fruits of the disbursement for an indefinite length of time.

Sub§3. Persuasives for the Pacha's concurrence in the concession[1]
1. On the event of his death, danger to his whole family from dispute among his sons as to the succession to the Sovereignty.
2. Danger to the whole nation from a Civil war produced by that dispute.

No possible means of security against these dangers but a meeting of persons chosen by the people to ratify beforehand the choice he shall have made.

If he can not endure to see a successor thus fixed upon for fear of his making a party in opposition to him, may not the choice be made by a secret instrument of declaration sealed up and not opened till his death?

Or, if made public in the first instance, might not a power of revocation be annexed to it?

As to the choice of the future sovereign, those who concurr in the measure should be previously agreed among themselves. This done, they may make him believe that the choice depends absolutely upon his will and pleasure, if whenever he speaks to any one of them upon the subject he finds them all speaking in favour of the same person: it being presumed that having so strong an interest in the goodness of the choice, they will find no difficulty in assigning the reasons for it.

3. Supposing a Representative body were established, Tripoli would exhibit the first example of a Mahometan country in which undertakings, for private or public benefit, requiring the permanent employment of capital to a considerable amount will have been set on foot. Example[s]:
1. Manufactories of articles suitable to the local wants and means of supply.
2. Means of communication—such as roads, canals, bridges, improvements in the facilities for communication afforded by rivers: source of profit, money in the shape of tolls.

---

[1] A further but apparently incomplete draft of this topic, headed 'The Sovereign's inducements to concurrence' and dated 14–15 November 1822, is at UC xxiv. 362–77 (the final five sheets are in the hand of the copyist).

3. Reservoirs for the preservation of a supply of water in extraordinarily dry seasons: for example by wells dug in apt places, and water raised from them by horse power or a steam engine.

4. Embankment of rivers in their course for the purpose of irrigation, or for giving motion to mills.

5. Erection of a prison on the Panopticon plan for deriving profit from the labour of prisoners.

6. Digging of mines: extraction of useful mineral substances of various kinds from the bowels of the earth, when by the use of boring machines, directed by Geological observations, their existence has been discovered. To conduct it with advantange an enterprize of this sort commonly requires large advances in the shape of capital.

But to this end all claim to the absolute ownership of mines on the part of the Sovereign in grounds belonging to individuals must be solemnly given up. By such surrender he might profit to an indefinite amount, and would not lose any thing. For the effect of such claim is neither more nor less than of an interdiction prohibiting the working of any such mines. It would remain for consideration whether any profit could be derived to the Sovereign from a tax upon the produce of such mines.

4. In such a state of things, individual foreigners would by degrees be found who would venture to embark their capitals in enterprizes of such descriptions as the above.

5. Loans might even be obtained by Government for the establishment of any such public works as might be too great for the purses of individuals. This advantage will receive considerable facility from the extraordinary accumulation of capital that has taken place of late years in the European nations, and the diminution in the rate of annual profit in return for the use of it.

6. The Pacha's revenue consists in the whole or in great part in a tax on the produce of the soil. Such produce can never receive any considerable encrease, but from a proportionate encrease in the quantity of labour and money laid out upon it in the shape of capital: and the quantity of capital can never receive any considerable encrease but from a correspondent encrease in the degree of general security: and the degree of general security can never receive any considerable encrease but from a correspondent change in the constitution. Where in respect of person and property every man's lot depends upon the momentarily changeable and never assuredly cognoscible will of a single individual, no human being in the country can with reason regard himself as safe, and least of all the Sovereign. By keeping every human being in the country in a state of perpetual insecurity, danger and alarm, he converts every man into a natural enemy

110

and keeps himself in the character of an enemy to them, exposed to hostile retribution at their hands.

7. Supposing the system established, his nation, and above all he as the head of it, will be illustrious among, and even above, all the Sovereigns of Europe and the other parts of the Christian world. In every one of these instances without exception, whatever portion of power has been given up—whatever change has been made for the better in the condition of the people in the character of subjects, it has been the work of necessity, not of free will on the part of the Monarch. By the supposition, the change is not only on his part altogether voluntary, but it is his own work. By the supposition, there will be no difficulty in making it known that it is so: all the circumstances by which it is [transacted][1] will be conveyed to England, and blazoned forth in the English Newspapers: from whence they will find their way into those of the Anglo-American United States, and in the mean time to the liberal French Newspapers, if with any tolerable hope of safety they can be published there.

8. Coupled with this intelligence would be that of the encouragement given to the useful arts and sciences of modern European invention by the translations made of works of that class into Arabic and the lectures read in the Tripolitan Universities.[2]

These circumstances taken together would constitute as it were a *pump for capital*: a pump by the force of which capital would be drawn into Tripoli from all countries in which it overflows.

9. By curiosity, and the desire to see the country in which such moral wonders had been wrought, Travellers from other countries, but from England in greater numbers than from all others put together, would be drawn to Tripoli, and as none of them would go thither but with money in their pockets, here may be seen another channel through which capital will flow into it.

---

[1] MS 'transmitted'.

[2] Bentham and D'Ghies had discussed the feasibility of sending a scientific expedition to Tripoli (see the Editorial Introduction, pp. xviii–xix above), the members of which, it was hoped, would read a course of lectures and demonstrate equipment in the schools at Tajaoura and Zanzour (see UC xxiv. 23, 26, 38).

PRELIMINARY EXPLANATIONS

NOVUS ORDO OF 24 OCTOBER 1822

PRELIMINARY EXPLANATIONS: OR GENERAL AND PRELIMINARY OBSERVATIONS, SHEWING THE PLAN AND MEANS OF EXECUTION OF THE HERE PROPOSED SYSTEM OF SECURITIES AGAINST MISRULE[1]

Misrule is the general and all-comprehensive denomination by which the evil against which it is the endeavour of the here proposed arrangements to apply a remedy may be designated: not, however, to misrule in every shape is it in the nature or in the hope of it to apply: at least in a direct and immediate way. Not to misrule in any of those shapes in which it bears upon the members of the community in an undistinguished mass: not for example to lavish expenditure, or to unnecessary and therefore unjust war. To those cases alone has it any direct and immediate application in which the evil comes home to the feelings of particular and those determinate, and in each case assignable, individuals.

Before any thing is presented in the character of a remedy, the natural order of the design requires that the several shapes in which the disorder is liable to shew itself be brought to view.

§1. *Misrule, its shapes*[2]

Of Misrule the evil effects may all of them, when considered as brought home to individuals, be comprized under the import [of] one and the same word, namely *vexation*. Vexation when considered as having men in power for its authors receives the name of oppression. In so far as benefit in any shape to the oppressor, or any persons

---

[1] The title and first two paragraphs are taken from the first sheet of an incomplete copy of 'Preliminary Explanations' which has been double-spaced in order for a French translation to be inserted (UC xxiv. 114–33). The French translation extends to UC xxiv. 117, at which point it appears to have been abandoned. Bentham has made one emendation—the translation of 'Misrule', the first word of the first paragraph, being changed from 'Mal-administration' to 'Mauvais Gouvernement'. For further details concerning this copy see the Editorial Introduction, p. xxiii above.

Abandoned drafts of the introduction to 'Preliminary Explanations' are at UC xxiv. 164–5 (originally dated 20–1 September 1822) and xxiv. 219 (26 November 1822).

[2] A fragment on this theme is at UC xxiv. 220–1 (27 September 1822).

whom he is disposed to favour by it, is considered as among the results of it, it has the effect of *depredation*. Without any determinate power possessed or conferred by public functionaries as such, a wealthy man, in proportion to the amount of his wealth, has the means of oppression, and to a certain degree unavoidably, in his hands.

As to depredation, though in respect of the suffering it may be considered as included under the denomination of oppression, yet for several reasons depredation requires a distinct consideration. In any shape other than that of depredation, inducement to practice oppression presents itself but occasionally: and the individuals against whom it is directed are only such particular individuals against whom a particular sentiment of displeasure has happened to be produced in the breast of the man in power. But the inducement to depredation has place at all times and against all persons: vengeance is not incapable, rapacity is altogether incapable, of being satiated.

Till the government of the Anglo-American United States came into existence, depredation for the benefit of the ruling few has been the chief object of all government, the only object coming into competition with it being the security of these rulers themselves: in the first place against resistance and vengeance on the part of their plundered subjects, in the next place against foreign powers in respect of their endeavours to take the plunder for themselves. Of such depredation—an evil continually on the encrease, natural and almost unavoidable effects have every where been discontent with a tendency more or less strenuous to self-liberation. From such tendency on the one part has come on the other encrease of oppression, partly for self-preservation, partly for vengeance: at the same time for the expence of such self-preservation, ulterior depredation: and thus has come on the everlasting *repetend*.[1]

The evil against which the demand [for security][2] presents itself in the first instance is oppression itself in all the several forms of which it is susceptible: the next evil is that which consists in the absence of the means of relief against or under the first.

These means of relief are, on the part of the people, 1. knowledge of the facts, circumstances and living instruments of the oppression in every instance: 2. faculty of communicating with each other, by

[1] The following fragment is pinned to the text sheet at this point: 'Be they what they may, from the Sovereign, if from any thing, will they [i.e. the securities] have been derived: from his free and voluntary act: from the free and continued operation of his will. On the existence of such will on his part will the whole system be altogether dependent for its existence. On what foundation the hope of such concurrence rests is a subject that will be brought to view at the close of these explanations.'

[2] MS 'The evil for security against which the demand'.

speech and writing, in presence and at any distance, for the purpose of conjunct application for redress, and in case of necessity, conjunct resistance: and ultimately, on the supposition that an effectual demand for resistance has place, the faculty of applying arms and military discipline to that purpose.

Vexation as applied to individuals, vexation in all its shapes, [is][1] particular: as applied to the suppression of the above-mentioned means of relief it is all-comprehensive in its application. Suppression of the peaceful means of relief above spoken of may be termed in one word *silencing*: suppression of the forcible means, disarmament.[a]

On the present occasion, only in so far as men in power in general—and more particularly the Sovereign, as the chief of them and master of all of them, are concerned in the production of it, does vexation in any shape present itself as the evil to which the remedy is required to apply itself. Against vexation in all its shapes, in so far as liable to be inflicted by individuals as individuals, provision must on the present occasion be supposed already made by the existing laws. But against vexation in so far as practiced by the possessors [of] power against those over whom their power is exercised, the absence of every thing that applies to them with efficacy in the shape of law cannot but be as universally recognized as it is felt. The vexation therefore against which alone provision is on the present occasion to be endeavoured to be made is that which by the possessors of power is liable to be inflicted on those over whom the power is exercised. In so far as openly and avowedly practiced, vexation for [. . . ?] is plainly without the reach of remedy. But against vexation in so far as secretly practiced—either the act or the actor or both being unknown, the government whatever it be may perhaps be not determinately unwilling to suffer provision to be made. 'Against vexation by others, vexation from which we ourselves derive no gratification, we

---

[a] In respect of the means of relief, felicitous is the state of Tripoli when compared with European countries in general and England in particular. In England such means of relief have place but against law. By law all has been done that can be done towards depriving the people of all knowledge of the instances in which official oppression and official depredation are practiced, of the means of communication for the purpose of obtaining redress, and of the means of resistance by the possession of arms and the practice of military exercises: whatsoever means of relief the people remain undeprived of, it is to the weakness of the government they are altogether indebted for it. That which the people of Tripoli have need of is the building up of the social edifice: and happily good materials for it are not wanting: that which the people of England have need of is the pulling down of the edifice still in existence: an edifice which, in the state into which it has fallen, is a mere den of thieves.

---

[1] MS 'are'.

ourselves (they may say to themselves) can have no objection to see remedy provided: to all such vexation secrecy, if not essentially necessary, [is][1] at least useful—but to us it is not necessary. Without fear of resistance, much more without fear of punishment, in this way as in all other ways we can do as we please: therefore against vexation in these ways let the remedy [be] provided: it will contribute to the satisfaction and thence to the quiet, to the patience and obsequiousness of those who are under us.' To this effect may the rulers whoever they are be conceived as addressing themselves.

But if, thus addressing themselves, they think that by means of the provision thus made against vexation in a secret state no impediment to the production of vexation by themselves or for their gratification will be opposed, they will be deceived. Whatsoever may be the means by which vexation when produced by individuals, and therefore naturally with all practicable secrecy, is provided against or endeavoured to be prevented or made to cease, by these same means will vexation produced, with or without endeavours at secrecy, by men in power be made known—whatever may be their deformity, made known to the people, to a greater or less extent, according to the means of publicity employed for the purpose: and thus will the only check which in the nature of things [can] be applied to the supreme power of government, be accordingly applied to it.

The way may now perhaps be found sufficiently prepared for a list of the several shapes in which the evil—oppression—is liable to operate. The provision of detail by which the remedy is endeavoured to be applied will follow under these several heads when the nature and use of the remedy have been explained. Meantime, by a short distinction the nature of them will in some instances be rendered the more distinctly visible. Oppression may accordingly be distinguished into *primary* and *persevering*: into that which is in its original state, and that which is in a more matured and rooted state: in the one case it may be stiled simple oppression; in the other case *ultra-oppression*.

I. Modes of Oppression against which security is here endeavoured to be provided are as follows—

1. Vexation on the account of religion: or say *Religious persecution*. N.B. In this particular case, what may happen is—that the Sovereign, if from oppression on this account he does not himself derive any particular gratification, may be content to deprive his successors of it: while by his own act he stands deprived of the power only because he

----

[1] MS 'or'.

118

has no desire to make use of it, they will by the same act stand deprived of it even though they should have the desire to make use of it. In this case therefore a direct promise of non-exercise, or even a direct appropriate abdication, may, not without hope, under favorable circumstances be sued for at his hands.

2. Secret Confinement, viz. of the person of an individual: confinement, namely within the walls of a prison, or within any other less narrow space.

3. Secret Banishment: i.e. by forcible exportation, or in any other way exclusion, of an individual from the whole of the dominion of the state in question, or from this or that part of it.

4. Secret Homicide.[a]

5. Mysterious disappearance: namely disappearance of an individual from a cause as yet unknown: it may be any of the above three—confinement, banishment, or death.

6. Official depredation: i.e. Vexation by ditto.[b]

7. Extortion of personal service.[c]

II. Modes of Ultra-Oppression.

8. Obstruction of intellectual communication.[d]

---

[a] Against vexation in these three shapes provision is of course already made in the existing system of law whatever it may be, and, the vexatious act being made punishable, secrecy is of course an accompaniment endeavoured to be given to it. But when hands by which the injury is inflicted are of the number of those which are armed with power, that power extends to the giving to the whole operation a degree of secrecy beyond any which could be given to it by ordinary and powerless hands: and for the maintenance of secrecy, even where power is irresistible, the avoidance of odium affords commonly an adequate inducement. By the arrangements proposed under these heads secrecy will be found combated by instruments of elucidation of which none are every where in use and of which some are not any where as yet in use.

[b] If exercised by the Sovereign himself, the nature of the case admitts not of a remedy. But if exercised by this or that functionary subordinate to him, a not impossible event is—that this or that other functionary equally subordinate to him, for example a judicial functionary or set of functionaries, shall hold themselves warranted in the supposition that, being unjust, the Sovereign has no participation in it:—in declaring this supposition, and proceeding upon it accordingly: that is to say unless and untill compelled by irresistible tokens to know, that the Sovereign himself is the person, or of the number of the persons, from whose will the vexation has emanated.

[c] This article is necessary to compleat the description of depredation: the subject-matter of wealth is composed either of things or of the services performed by persons.

[d] To this head belong all measures of suppression or restraint applied to public discussion, or to the use of the pen or the press, on the subject of political measures and men: or to communication on those subjects in the way of epistolary correspondence or personal intercourse by persons in any numbers.

9. National Enfeeblement.[a]

10. Violation of private documents.[b]

§2. *Misrule—its causes*[1]

§3. *Sole remedy, Public Opinion*[2]

On the part of the oppressive hand, the mode of operation is in both stages much the same to the greatest part of the extent. On body and goods it operates when the vexation is inflicted, on body and goods it

[a] To this head belong all measures of suppression or restraint applied to the practice of openly carrying arms, offensive and defensive, or that of being trained in the use of them in conjunction with other men in any numbers.

Say *openly*: for of arms secretly worn, the only purpose is individual assassination. It is not by daggers that the defensive force of a people against misrule can be augmented. For defence against malefactors, no use can there be in any such concealment. As to the case of a whole people kept in an oppressed state by an irresistible military force, foreign or domestic, it is here noticed, but this is not a place for the consideration of it.

[b] To this head belongs what is sometimes designated by the inadequate expression of *seizure of papers*. This mode of oppression has for its subject such letters, memorandums, and other visible and tangible instruments of discourse, by the communication of which, to persons other than those for whose eyes they were intended, vexation in any one of an infinitely diversifiable variety of ways is liable to be produced. So far as the only effect as well as object of the invasion is the furnishing evidence of a misdeed committed or meditated, the vexation, whatsoever might be the shape or the amount of it, could not with propriety be spoken of by the appellation of *oppression*: nor yet, where between individual and individual, of the portion of visibly expressed discourse thus dealt with, no other use is made other than the causing it to be subjected to inspection for a judicial purpose in the character, or for the discovery, of evidence: of evidence tending to give validity or invalidity to this or that *claim* of *right*.

But, by vexation committed in this shape by public functionaries, if without limitation or controul, oppression to an indefinite amount is capable of being practiced. On the occasion, or on pretence, of a search for evidence of a misdeed in this or that shape, committed or not committed, writings of all sorts, and in any numbers, might be destroyed, damaged, carried off or inspected: inspected, and the contents divulgated: commercial credit might be ruined, enmities excited, peace and reputation of families destroyed, and so forth. On pretence of search for evidence alledged to be in the possession of the person in question, papers, or other objects not found in his possession, might by the authors of a pretended search be inserted among such as were found in it: the friendly deceit practiced by Joseph upon the effects of his brethren might in this way be practiced for a hostile and homicidal purpose.[3]

---

[1] The MSS for this section have not been identified.

[2] An earlier draft on this topic is at UC xxiv. 96, followed by fragments attached to xxiv. 103 (22 September 1822).

[3] See Genesis 42: 35.

operates when the means of information and cooperation for redress are cut off.

In one stage as well as in the other whatsoever relief the nature of the case—that is the nature of the government—admitts of, there is but one source from which it can come. This source is the force of what is called public opinion: the only force which is not included in the force of government: the only force therefore from which the force of government when operating in a sinister direction can experience any the least impediment to its course.

It is by a sort of imaginary tribunal that the force of public opinion must be spoken of as bringing itself into action: to enable it so to do, publicity must be considered as a sort of torch the light of which is kept cast upon the road [which] leads from the spot where the oppression is acted to the seat of that same fictitious judicatory, with a branch going off to the throne of the Sovereign.

The fiction is of the number of those innoxious and necessary ones which in the state of imperfection to which language stands for ever condemned are necessary to the giving communication of ideas from mind to mind.

What there is of reality in the case is this. The persons considered as members of this tribunal are an indeterminate portion of the whole number of those of whom the community in question is composed. Those by whom actual cognizance is taken of the matter in question in the first instance may be considered as a Committee: those who in consequence of the opinions expressed by this same Committee, but without taking actual and particular cognizance of the circumstances of the case, join with them at different times in the same opinions, affections, wishes, designs and endeavours, constitute the body at large of which the smaller body above-mentioned is the Committee. Of the members of this larger body, the number may be of any magnitude not exceeding the sum total of the adequately adult members of the community.

§4. *Measure of its force, degree of notoriety*

The greater the suffering produced by any act of oppression, the greater, provided it has been made known to them, is the number of the individuals who, in the character of members of this Committee, are likely to take cognizance of the affair in the first instance. The greater the number of these members of this Committee who, having joined in the cognizance thus taken, pass condemnation on the deed, the greater the number of those other members who on the authority of their report take cognizance not of the affair at large but of the conduct of the actors, whoever they may be, in the act of oppression, so far forth as to concurr in the opinion, the judgment, the sentence of condemnation, passed upon those oppressive agents in consideration of such their oppressive acts.

The greater the number of those who concurr and join in the provisional sentence, the greater the number of those who are likely to concurr and join in the definitive sentence.

§5. *Cause of influence: 1. Fear of ultimate obstruction*

As to the sentence, whatsoever may be the intermediate gradations of punishment, the ultimate punishment which it is in the power of this tribunal to inflict on the oppressors, whosoever they may be, consists in the withdrawing from them altogether that obedience to the extent of which that of their power is correspondent and commensurate. This substraction of obedience—suppose it universal, the corresponding power is by the very supposition at an end.

This same substraction is, according to the description thus given of it, a mere negative act. But to the production of the effect aimed at by it, positive acts directed to the same end may in any number and variety come to be exercised.

The extinction of the life of the oppressor in chief for example may be the punishment indicated by the sentence. Executioners, any number of the members associated for the purpose, or even this or that single one of them.

By the adherents of the oppressor the corresponding sentence with the execution given to it will of course be objected to on the ground of irregularity. But to set against this word irregularity some other will be found by the concurrers in and approvers of the sentence.

In England for example, if the King were among the individuals upon whom this supposed sentence had been passed, and execution given to it accordingly, a natural and constitutional objection would be—that to render it regular and constitutional [an] Act called an Act of Attainder was necessary: an Act of Attainder passed like every other Act of Parliament by the joint consent and concurrence of the King's Most Excellent Majesty, as well as that of the Lords and Commons of Great Britain and Ireland, almost all of them in some way or other in a state of dependence on his good pleasure: and that his Majesty not having been pleased to give such his consent to any such Act, the sentence so passed and executed was thereby null and void.

By any regular tribunal composed of Judges placed by his said most

Excellent Majesty this objection would be held valid: and on the individual by whom the sentence in question had so been executed on the body of his said Majesty, a sentence including amongst other things the extinction of the life of the irregularly commissioned executioner would accordingly be executed. On the other hand by the member or members of the irregularly constituted tribunal of public opinion by whose authority the sentence of extinction on the Monarch had so been executed, [this objection] would as surely be overruled.

On the part of this as any other malefactor, it would have been perfectly regular for him to have given his assent to the sentence passed upon himself. But though perfectly regular it is by no means usual—it is so far from being so, that if any such assent were waited for it may be stated as a matter of certainty that neither to the purpose of extinction of life nor to the purpose of any the slightest restriction would any bar be opposed in any case to the utmost quantity of suffering which it would be physically speaking in the power of a supreme ruler to inflict on the individuals subject to his power, in the legal sense of that same imposing appellative.

In this strain for example thought and acted the Members of that Section of the Public Opinion Tribunal by whose warrant, under the denomination of a warrant by the Members of the High Court of Justice, the life of Charles the first of England was extinguished at Westminster in the Year [1649].[1]

This is what the power and decisions of the Tribunal of Public Opinion must lead to and in case of necessity give existence to, or it amounts to nothing: and, under a Monarchy for example, the sufferings of the people are at their height as well in respect of extent as well as of intensity and duration, and particular Slaveholders, if in the community in question such they are, are with reference to the universal Slaveholder placed in the same condition and relation as their several gangs of slaves are in relation to their respective owners. Not that in this case the several particular Slaveholders would any of them have any ground of complaint against the Monarch on the score of justice, but that their stock of sufferings would in this state of things experience very considerable augmentation seems not much exposed to doubt: their sufferings, and in proportion to their number, the sufferings of the whole community of which they are members.

---

[1] MS '1648'. On 6 January 1649, the Rump of the House of Commons, on their sole authority, passed an ordinance creating a High Court of Justice to try Charles I. He was subsequently sentenced to death as a tyrant and a traitor, and executed on 30 January 1649.

§6. *2. Fear of inferior sufferings*

Of this sort among the punishments which it belongs to the power of the Tribunal of Public Opinion to inflict is that which stands highest in the scale. But beneath it stand others in number and variety indefinite—among them, all obstructions to the exaction of taxes the produce of which is to [be] placed at the disposal of the Sovereign: all obstructions capable of being opposed to the execution of the judgments of the several regularly constituted judicatories: all modes of annoyance by which, in retribution for the demonstrations of hatred and contempt received, demonstrations of correspondent hatred and contempt are rendered: invectives said and sung: invectives written and posted up: of whatsoever liberty is left to the citizens, to the members of the community at large, by the laws and practice of the government, use made to the purpose of opposing and as far as may be frustrating those same laws and that same practice.

§7. *Objection answered—irregular the judgments of Public Opinion Tribunal*

All this while be the quantity of suffering ever so enormous, all this while so long as regularity and nothing else is looked to, all this while to the acts of government by which all this misery is produced, on the score of regularity at least, nothing can be [excepted][1]—of whatsoever is done by the supreme authority of the State, or by any subordinate authority by its order or with its allowance, in how great a degree so ever productive of human suffering and destructive of human happiness, regularity is an inseparable quality and accompaniment: irregularity, of whatsoever is done by the Tribunal of Public Opinion in opposition to any thing which is done by the constituted authorities: irregular it is in whatsoever degree it has the effect of diminishing the quantity of suffering produced by the regular tribunals, and in that or any other way productive of addition to the net amount of human happiness. In so far then as by the acting members of this irregular judicature their own interest is rightly understood, the option is throughout between regularity and happiness. By those by whom regularity is preferred to happiness, this same irregular tribunal will be hated and in so far as fear permits despised, and every thing done that can be done to diminish and if possible annihilate its force.

[1] MS 'expected'.

Those who desire to see any check whatsoever to the power of the government under which they live, or limit to their sufferings under it, must look for such check and limit to the power of the Public Opinion Tribunal, irregular and, to the degree in which it has been seen, fictitious: to this place of refuge or to none: for no other has the nature of things afforded: to this tribunal they must on every occasion make appeal: to the power of this tribunal they must on every occasion give what contribution it is in their power to give: for do what they can, never can they give to it too much power: never can they even give to it enough: never can they give to it so much as to the greatest happiness of the greatest number it would be conducive that it should have.

§8. *Instrument of operation—Notification—Means of it—Concession*[1]

§9. *Subjects of notification*

As to the appropriate subjects of notification, indication of them has already in a considerable degree been given by the denominations by which oppression in its various shapes has above been designated. Modes of vexation corresponding to those several shapes: acts whereby it has been produced: persons bearing part in this or that way in those several acts: causes of justification, if any, whereby the vexation in whatsoever shape or degree produced is shewn not to have been accompanied with the circumstances necessary to bring it under the name of oppression: such for instance as shew that in the case in question it has been no other than that which was necessary for the furtherance of justice—and so in regard to circumstances of aggravation or extenuation.[2] Thus much as to the subjects requiring notification.

§10. *Instruments of notification*

Now as to the instruments or means applied or applicable to this purpose. These will be either persons, things, or operations: persons, the functionaries, or others, by whom the evidence probative of the facts in question shall be collected and expressed by permanent signs: things, the signs so made and employed: operations, the acts by

---

[1] The MSS for this section have not been identified.
[2] i.e. causes of justification whereby the vexation is shown to have been accompanied with circumstances of aggravation or extenuation.

which the evidence is collected and the signs by which it is designated brought into existence, preserved, and conveyed to their respective destinations. As to persons, only in so far as functionaries to whom this service already belongs, or can be committed, are in existence, or can be brought into existence, and in so far as they are in existence, only in proportion to their appropriate aptitude in all its several branches, can that which it is here endeavoured to bring about be actually accomplished—that security be actually established: only in proportion as apt tools have place can work in this any more than in any other shape be accomplished. In the present case such alone as he found in existence, such alone are the tools which the workman—the penner of the here proposed arrangements—could find to work with. For no deficiency either in respect of existence, or in respect of appropriate aptitude in that quarter, can justice regard him as responsible.

On the occasion of such of them as apply to the case of homicide, it seemed necessary to give some proposed *Instructions*: instructions respecting the manner of collecting, authenticating, and preserving the evidence. The head to which this portion of the matter appertains is (it will be seen) that of *Judicial Procedure*.[1]

§11. *Notification—places and mode. Circumstances on which its efficiency depends*

Of whatever *knowledge* comes to be conveyed by the here proposed system of notification, the effect produced will for its *intensity*, at the first instance of its being in each instance conveyed, depend upon the degree of *impressiveness* of the means employed for the conveyance of it: for its *duration*, on the permanence of the *signs* employed in the designation of it.

Supposing a Charter, or Act of recognition,[2] establishing the

---

[1] See 'VI. [Security] against secret and unlawful homicide', pp. 92–4 above.

[2] The following discussion of the relative merits of a charter and a contract is at UC xxiv. 100, 283 (28 September 1822): 'It may be matter for consideration whether to this fundamental and all-important commencement of rational government, the form of a Charter or the form of a Contract shall be given.

'If obtainable, the form of a Contract will unquestionably be the more beneficial: whatsoever securities are afforded will thus be fixt upon the firmer basis. The case of a Charter remains always more or less exposed to one cause of failure: being the free and sole act of the Sovereign, whatsoever is granted by him on any one day may be taken back by him on any other: when he granted it, it was on the supposition that no bad consequences would result from it: but that supposition being disproved, necessity compels him to revoke it. To this effect are the words which at any time may just as easily be uttered as any others of the same length and number:

Securities in question, or some of them, acceded to by the Sovereign, — the *subjects* of *notification* will be of two sorts: namely—1. The Charter itself, by which the Securities are conceded: 2. the several occurrences by which as above the demand for the application of them comes from time to time to be produced; in other words, the several instances in which the several modes of vexation, which it is the object of the Charter to prevent, have notwithstanding, with or without the concurrence of men in power, had place: in a word, the several infractions or supposable infractions of the Charter so conceded.

In regard to impressiveness, only in the case of this original instrument of national security does any particular importance seem to attach to it: as to the several occurrences, to which application of it may come to be made, they will operate each of them for itself.

As to the places for notification, they will be, in the first instance,

---

and, wheresoever and by whomsoever in the situation in question uttered, no want of voices to echo them need ever be feared.

'So much for Charters. Charters the people in question can not have been much used to. Contracts—compacts—all people are more or less used to: more or less in the use and expectation of seeing them kept: and, at any rate, of regarding the infraction of them as an act of injustice, and a reasonable cause of displeasure and discontent: a reasonable cause for endeavour to obtain remedy.

'In the case of a Charter, if it be regarded as really obligatory, there is but one party on whom any obligation attaches: in the case of a Contract, there are two parties: the people forming one of them. If then the Contract form be the form employed, consistency would seem to require that on the occasion of the solemnity from which it appears to derive its sanction there should be something done by and on the part of the people: —thanks to the Sovereign for his entering into his part in it—thanks with acclamations: thanks [to] the Sovereign—to God—to the Prophet—to every body—nothing of this sort need be grudged. But on their part, if any thing, what more can be done with safety and advantage? Promise to obey him and all his descendants to the end of time? this would be too much: too much even although on the part of those potentates the condition of their performing their part of the Contract were attached to the promise on the part of the people. For—what if another form of government should come to be regarded as in a greater degree contributory to the greatest happiness of the greatest number? Promise to obey his descendants so long as the Contract were on their part kept inviolate, and so long as Monarchy continued to be the form of government? This is exactly what seems desirable: but unfortunately, the more desirable on the one part, the less likely to be acceded to on the other.

'In the case of England, the Whig Monarchists who brought about the Revolution in the time of James 2d. saw the advantage attached as above to the Contract form; and in their arguments, employed it accordingly. Their contract however—the *Original* contract they called it—[was] a mere fiction: and of its being a mere fiction an evil consequence was—that, on each occasion the terms of it remaining to be feigned, they made them whatsoever seemed to them most advantageous to their own particular interests. But, in the case here in question, there would be no fiction, and there being two contracting parties to this contract, the terms of it might, by mutual consent of both parties, be changed at any time. So long as the terms were kept by the Monarch, the people would not be likely to feel much inclination to change: but, supposing them at any time infringed by him, it would be for them to make themselves amends, and provide for that purpose whatsoever security seemed to them most efficient: for example the change from the mixt Monarchy to a Representative Democracy: and for the bringing about such change, the Constitution here in question would prepare them, by giving them power in every shape.'

the seat of supreme and universally extensive authority: thenceforward, the several seats of local and subordinate authority: say the Judicatories and the Mosques.

As to the person by whom the reading should be performed, the principal in each instance, if his voice be suitable, is obviously the person most desirable. But, where his voice is not suitable, or he can not be induced to perform the part in his own person, then some subordinate, whose voice and manner is most suitable, may be employed: the principal being present and uttering, according to his physical ability, signs of consent. Possibly even two readings, one of them performed by each one of the two different sorts of persons, might be found eligible: the one, by the principal, for authentication, the other by the subordinate, that the number of those by whom it is actually heard, and heard at the same time, may be as great as possible.

For permanence, the reading might be periodically repeated: say, annually on some particular day in the year on which already some public solemnities are performed. But, for some few years, namely until the institution is regarded as sufficiently established, it might be desirable the solemnity should be repeated with greater frequency: say, once in every quarter of the year.

To secure performance, information might be required to be given thereof to the Cadi from every Judicatory: also, to each Judicatory from the several Mosques within the territory belonging to it: thence afterwards within a certain time from each Judicatory, reporting in one list the Mosques from which a report of performance has been received, and in another those from which no such document has been received, mention being made of the cause of the omission in each instance, in so far as known or supposed.

In the case of the Charter, for the impressiveness of the notification made of its existence, suppose in the Metropolis a procession, of the persons chief in authority and consideration, at the place at which the notification is to be performed: a procession setting out from some remarkable spot which will be to be determined, and terminating in the edifice, whether Judicatory or Mosque, at which the reading is to take place. If the Sovereign himself can be induced to go in this manner from his Palace to the Judicatory of the Cadi, so much the better.

After the reading has been performed, any such declarations of censure on all infractors may be added as the forms of the religion and the usages of the country will admitt of.[a]

---

[a] In England, when concession was made by King John and afterwards by his son Henry the third, copies were ordered to be deposited in certain Monasteries: also

§ 12. *Institutions for notification proposed—Newspapers, Letter-Post*

The power of public opinion being the only check that can be applied to the power of arbitrary government, and the efficiency of that tutelary power depending as above upon the number of the persons to whom on each occasion the appropriate information is notified, the great misfortune is—that in the country in question the means of notification are so narrow: in that country free Newspapers—the matchless instruments of notification—even Newspapers of every kind—being as yet altogether wanting. Production of the statements, multiplication, conveyance—all these operations are necessary: production and multiplication are ensured by Newspapers: conveyance, by the Letter-Post. In the country in question, of the possible sources of notification for the purpose in question, the two Universities, the 14 Judicatories and the 3,000 Mosques compose at present the whole catalogue. In this state of penury, every thing that can be done must therefore be done to employ to the greatest advantage and extent possible those sole existing resources: and by every addition that can be made to the number of them, benefit will be produced—not in this shape only, but in an infinite variety of other shapes.

Supposing the here-proposed Securities established, the number of the written instruments brought into existence—instruments written in the Judicatories and the Mosques, would, were it from this cause alone, receive very considerable encrease. There would be the originals, and there would be the copies taken for transmission. For the originals, no means of multiplication would be of

---

public maledictions to be pronounced at certain times against all infractors. These means of publicity and impressiveness proved lamentably insufficient, as the numerous recorded infractions and renewals of these *Charters* (such was the name given to the written instruments) abundantly demonstrate.[1] But the means of publicity and permanence which then had place in England were as nothing compared with those which at present have place in Tripoli: not to speak of the ulterior ones which it might be made to have. Besides that there was no printing press, [and] the arts of reading and writing were not to the amount of a tenth or a twentieth part, or more, so extensively in use.

---

[1] Magna Carta was first issued by John (1167?–1216), King of England from 1199, in 1215, but was reissued in slightly modified forms in 1216 and 1217. It attained its final form when it was reissued in 1225 on the majority of Henry III (1207–72), King of England from 1216. Copies seem to have been sent to each county, where they were deposited in the cathedral church, or where none existed in a monastery. In 1253 sentence of excommunication was denounced against those who attempted to infringe it or alter its clauses. It was confirmed some thirty-seven times down to the reign of Henry V (1387–1422), King of England from 1413.

any use. But, for the copies taken for transmission in the Universities and Judicatories printing presses would be indispensable: one allotted to this purpose, in each of the Universities, and in each of the Judicatories.

To the Iman in his Mosque no such expensive apparatus would be necessary: he having on each occasion but one place to correspond with—namely the Judicatory within the jurisdiction of which his Mosque is situated: unless by accident a particular demand should arise for his transmitting copies of the document in question to Judicatories more than one.

All this while, copies are of no use, but in proportion as they are conveyed to their respective destinations. Between any two places in the dominion in question, is there any such establishment as a Post for Letters?—a Messenger or chain of Messengers travelling at stated intervals between the one and the other? Between the Capital for example and the two Universities, or one, and which of them? The first thing to be done in this way would be to establish a system of communication of this kind between the office of the *Cadi* at the Capital, and the several judicatories. Next to that would be the establishing the like between each Judicatory and the several Mosques within its territorial field of jurisdiction, Messengers, one or more, going the Circuit among the Mosques.

In time, pay received for letters sent by individuals to individuals might lessen the expence to government. As the number of persons who read and write receives encrease so will the receipts of every such Post Establishment. But at no time should these receipts be made a source of revenue. A tax on the intercourse between man and man, being a prohibition on all who can not afford to pay the tax, cripples social intercourse, cripples it for all sorts of purposes, and nips all improvement in the bud.

Of this proposed system of communication the direct as being the most important object is—personal security: and in particular security against oppression by the hands of rulers. But a system of communication, if once established for this major purpose, will apply itself of itself to all minor purposes. It will contribute to the efficiency of the judicial power as applied to its more obvious and more ordinary purposes. It will contribute to the security of individuals as against injury by individuals.

It will contribute to the encrease of commerce: in regard to each article, making known to each possessor of a surplus beyond his own use where those individuals are to be found who to the desire of possessing the article add the means of paying for it. Whether, for the mere chance of finding individuals in sufficient number able and willing to make use of it for merely commercial purposes, it would be worth while to establish a system of communication in the first instance would be matter of uncertainty, calling for calculation: but, on the supposition that it would be worth while to establish it for the sake of security alone, any the least chance of its being contributory to the encrease of commerce, that is to say to the encrease of opulence, can not but operate as an additional probable benefit, and as an additional inducement.

Meantime, in the early state of the establishment, by whom shall the expence—whatsoever may be the amount of it—be defrayed?—A question this, which, where any advance is proposed to be made in the track of civilization, is unhappily obtruding itself at every step. As to the Sovereign, the funds of the State, which are all of them his funds, are never sufficient for so much as his own personal expences: never sufficient, as yet, nor in the nature of the case under such a form of government ever likely to be.

Soldiers in a certain number—say 8,000—are at present kept up. If of these a certain number were regularly employed as letter carriers, they would not be the less fit for service in the character of soldiers. They would even be the more fit. By thus changing their situation these Messengers would, each of them, become every day better and better acquainted with the country, and in that way as well as others be by so much the fitter for service in their character of soldiers. A slow conveyance, so it were but regular and constant—a slow conveyance extending over a large portion of the territory, might be preferable to a more expeditious one extending over a less portion of territory. For quick conveyance horses, mules or dromedaries would be necessary: but by this means the expence would perhaps be doubled. In certain districts Camels might be necessary for the carriage of the water necessary for subsistence: but this would be only in certain districts.

The greater the number of the persons to whom these occurrences and documents, in which all are, in one way or other, interested, and the acts of government in particular, were thus made known, the greater would at the same time be the controuling power of the people, and the stronger the sense of it in the breasts of their rulers: the stronger their apprehension of eventual discontent on the part of the people—that salutary apprehension by which to a greater or less degree they could not but be restrained from at least such acts of misrule by which a sense of injury can not fail to be kindled in the breasts of individuals: in the first place from positive acts of oppression; and by degrees, in proportion as popular vigilance gathered strength from exercise, restrained even from negligence, in so far as manifested by the omission to do what ought to have been done towards the prevention of all such positively oppressive acts.

§ 13. *Recourse to penal law here necessary*

So much as to misrule, considered as applying its galling pressure to the feelings of assignable individuals. To the cases in which it applies to the members of the community no otherwise than in an aggregate mass, the remedy here in question has not (so at the outset it has been confessed) any direct and immediate application. In an indirect and unimmediate, however, yet by no means inefficient way, the operation of it, supposing it but established, can not fail to have this additional salutary effect. It is indeed for the security of individuals in their separate capacity only that the bit applied to the mouth of absolute power has been constructed. But let it be but once lodged in the mouth, this bit may be applied, or rather will naturally and of course apply itself, on those more extensive occasions, on which the evil finds the whole mass of the community involved in it: as for instance, to war for conquest or depredation or vengeance: to war for robbing states of land, or individuals of moveable goods or personal liberty: for of all war and thence of all such war, depredation and forced service, in a military and other shapes, are among the immediate accompaniments: vexations, the individual sufferers by which are, as the plague spreads, but too clearly ascertained by deplorable experiences.

Regarded in its immediate and principal point of view, the task of providing security for individuals against oppression—against vexation by the hand of rulers—belongs exclusively to constitutional law. But no sooner are any arrangements proposed in any such view, than it will be seen to contain of necessity matter belonging at the same time to two other branches of law: to the penal branch, as also to judicial procedure, in so far as occupied in the giving execution and effect to the portion, whatsoever it may be, of penal law, the assistance of which it will be necessary to call in. This intercommunity is altogether unavoidable. To what branch so ever applied, legislative arrangements can not be made but compliance with them must, at the hands of all persons concerned, be called for: and to call for compliance would be idle unless inducements, and those adequate ones, were at the same time furnished: nor on any occasion can any set of inducements be adequate unless those which are of a penal complexion be of the number. But in vain would such penal inducements be provided, unless in some way or other a description of the several sorts of non-compliance, on the occasion of which the penalties will attach, be furnished. In so far as in this or that instance this description is furnished by the law in its existing state, it is well: a simple reference will suffice. But, in so far as no such description is already in existence (as must be the case at the first creation of every offence) a fresh description will require to be given: so likewise in every case in which, though a form of words which may be considered as a description of the offence [exists], if either in respect of clearness, correctness, or comprehensiveness, any deficiency be found in it.

So again as to judicial procedure. In so far as the forms already in use are adequate to the purpose of giving execution and effect to the several proposed arrangements, it is well. But if in any instance they are otherwise than adequate, new ones must be provided, or the security which it is desired should be possessed can not be afforded: whatsoever be the necessary means, he who determinately desires the attainment of the end, can not but desire the employment of those or other adequate means.

By these observations a sufficient apology, or rather a justification, will, it is hoped, be found afforded, not only for several definition and penal enactment, but even for some *institution*, which in the country in question may not improbably present a face of novelty. Among institutions for example, not only the celebrated one so uncharacteristically expressed in English by the two Latin words *Habeas Corpus* (*have the body*), but the one known in England by the name of the *Coroner's Inquest*.[1] Of the *Habeas Corpus* the use is—to afford a remedy against clandestine or pertinacious imprisonment or confinement of the person: a remedy, terminative or preventive, as the case may be. Of the Coroner's Inquest the use is to throw the light of notoriety upon every such death as shall afford grounds for suspecting that the hand of man has in the production of it borne an improper part. But of the three distinguishable causes by any of which the disappearance of a human being, where it has had injury for its cause, may alike have been produced, death and confinement are but two. The other is banishment. For ascertaining by which of them all such disappearance, where it has place, has been produced, no course of procedure is (it is believed) to be found in any system of law as yet known. To this deficiency an attempt to furnish a supply will here be found under the head of *Mysterious Disappearance*.[2]

Lastly, in regard to judicial procedure: and in particular that most essential branch of it which regards the collection of evidence. In vain

---

[1] A fragment dealing with Habeas Corpus and the Coroner's Inquest is at UC xxiv. 170–1 (2 November 1822).

[2] See 'VII. Security against Mysterious Disappearance', pp. 94–6 above.

would any arrangements for the prevention of injurious confinement, injurious banishment or injurious homicide, or for the termination of injurious confinement and injurious banishment (not to mention any other injuries) be established, unless, on each occasion, the means of ascertaining by sufficient evidence the facts thus respectively denominated were in existence. In so far as they are in existence, it is well. But, in the country in question, not to speak of other countries, it seems but too probable that no such adequate means are in existence. Hence the attempt that will be seen towards the furnishing them, or at any rate the endeavour to make some contribution towards a result so universally desirable.[1]

§ 14. *Collateral use of the here proposed arrangements—matter for penal Code*

Such are the arrangements which have presented themselves as being indispensably necessary to the particular purpose here in hand, namely the affording security to individuals against injurious vexation, in the several shapes in question, by the hands of rulers. Should they be found at the same time applicable, and in no less degree, to the affording security against these same injuries at the hands of individuals, and thus a more effectual one than has as yet been provided in those same instances by any existing Code, here will be an additional benefit. This incidental benefit will be seen to be the more valuable when it is observed that, supposing the provision to fail, in a greater or less degree, to be effectual against the injury in a case where it is by the hands of rulers that it has been, or would otherwise have been, inflicted, it may still be more or less effectual in the case where it is by the hands of individuals that it has been, or would have been, inflicted: understand of such individuals to whom, in the prosecution of their evil designs, the rulers of the country do not take upon themselves to give support.

§ 15. *Slaves—can any of these securities be made to extend to them?*[2]

In the country in question one deplorable and deplorably extensive case—the case of slavery—has been seen alone presenting a par-

---

[1] See 'IV. Security against secret confinement', 'V. Security against injurious banishment' and 'VI. [Security] against secret and unlawful homicide', pp. 88–94 above.

[2] An abandoned fragment carrying the marginal sub-heading 'Slaves—how affected' is at UC xxiv. 106–8 (26 September, 2 October and n.d. October 1822).

ticular demand for attention. For, though in the here proposed arrangements it is not on any occasion mentioned, it has not, on any occasion, been overlooked. Not knowing what chance there may be that assistance would be given to any endeavours towards the placing this part of the population of the country upon a footing in any respect superior to that of the brute creation, I must leave it to those to whom it belongs to determine what, if any thing, can be attempted in this view with any prospect of success.

Neither on the subject of confinement nor on that of banishment, in so far as the vexation has the Master for its author, does there seem to be any immediate hope of remedy. Not so, on the subject of homicide. Suppose the body of a person recently dead found lying any where, it can not always be known whether his condition was that of a freeman or a slave: and if in the case of a person in this unfortunate condition the legal sanction gives impunity to the master where the death has him for its author, it will not be thus indulgent to any other person: nor will the social sanction in all future time shew the same indulgence to oppression in this its most aggravated shape as it does at present.

§ 16. *Concession—what the chance in favour of it*

The question concerning the probability of consent on the part of the Sovereign was brought to view at the outset. It has never been out of remembrance. Unfortunately, having as they have for their object the applying limits to his power, the greater the efficacy which the several proposed arrangements would have on the supposition of his consent, the less sanguine the hope of its being obtained can not but be. As to this point, such as they are, they must take their chance. That hopes have place that to the purposes here in question he may be brought to bestow upon the people a benefit so transcendent and so unexampled is a *datum* without which the work could not have been undertaken.

In form and manner, the object has been to render what is done as little offensive to the feelings of man in the situation in question as the nature of the case can admitt of their being. Of misdeeds and misdoers, a description, in the several cases, is given:[1] if so it be that it is his will and pleasure to give himself a title to that appellative, there is

---

[1] The following passage appears in the margin at this point, but its relation to the text is unclear: 'that if for the gratification of a desire, real or supposed on the part of the Sovereign, vexation in any shape shall at any time be inflicted, the fact with all the circumstances shall be made as extensively known as possible'.

no help for it: but, to him, personally and individually, it is not on any occasion applied.

If to stop the course of justice be his will and pleasure, so it must be: all that could be done is—so to order matters, that the security thus endeavoured to be afforded can not in any case be taken away without its being known to the people that it has been and in what manner it has been taken away.

Not only so, but matters are so ordered, as that, unless in so far as special injunctions of secrecy have been communicated, whatsoever has place is, by the general means of notoriety, whatever they are, that have been provided, read and made notorious: to wit according to the degree of notoriety, whatever it be, which by those same universally-applying means has been established.

But in all internal concerns at least—not to speak of international ones—secrecy [in] the acts of constituted authorities, or in the circumstances in which they have been performed, affords a presumption, and indeed, with the exception of certain cases to a comparatively small extent, which may without difficulty be distinguished and declared, amounts to a confession, of guilt: of moral and political guilt: a confession—that the promotion of some sinister interest and not the universal interest is the object of what is done. A confession of this sort neither the Sovereign himself nor any subordinate of his will very willingly be seen to make.

A bit of some sort or other and that an effectual one the courser must have in his mouth, or nothing at all can be done. The object is to render it so soft and smooth that, as far as possible, it shall be imperceptible. Accordingly whatsoever be the obstacle, on no occasion is it to the person of the Sovereign that it is opposed: not to him, either by name or description, but to the persons concerned in the vexatious practice whosoever it may be: and the practice being not only vexatious, but with reference to determinate individuals plainly injurious, that the Sovereign should in his own person be an actor in the injury can scarcely in decency, and therefore need not by the penner of the proposed arrangement, be supposed. The injurious act being brought to light, whatsoever censure attaches upon it will attach, at any rate in the first instance, upon the instruments whom he employs. On them he will see it attaching: and on them he will without much chagrin or resentment as towards any body, so long as it is not seen by him to come home to himself, see it attach. For its not doing so, he will naturally be led to trust to the splendor that environs him, and to the delusion and awe which it inspires.

To a certain degree what he thus reckons upon may have place. But in the mean time, of a fund of discontent in breasts of individuals not known to him, and therefore not exposed to punishment, symptoms will continually be breaking out. By the obscurity which encompasses the source, danger, in the eyes of him on whom it impends, far from being diminished is magnified: and thus it may be, that upon the whole he will find his situation rendered more comfortable by the abstaining from the injury than by indulging himself in it. Compared with a set of provisions bearing in express terms upon the person of the Sovereign, opposition in this mode will be analogous to that which in mechanics is opposed by friction compared with that produced by an opposing bar.

Accustomed to contemplate all objects in a general point of view, the draughtsman will have some advantage over the Sovereign who in his situation is not accustomed to the labour of regarding them in any other than a particular point of view.

By the legislative draughtsman the objects that belong to the occasion will be seen, all of them, in a general point of view—the vexations which, whether in the shape of depredation or in that of simple vexation, a man in the situation of the Sovereign can not fail upon occasion to conceive the desire of practicing: the instruments and other favorites, whom, whether on their personal accounts respectively, or in virtue of their common relation to him, as being part and parcel of his property, he will feel disposed to let into a participation of these his privileges, in some instances beforehand, and in the way of previous permission and licence, in all instances in the way of impunity in the event of any endeavours used to call them to account: so, on the other side, the resentment which by any endeavour or so much as a disposition on the part of the persons injured to obtain remedy or so much as relief can scarce fail to be kindled in a breast so situated.

To the eyes of the Sovereign himself no such extensive views will naturally be present. When the means for securing general notoriety to his proceeding are proposed to him, if so it be that there exists no particular act of depredation or vexation in any shape that he has conceived the desire to committ, he will not be forward to suppose that there will be any such in future: he will not be forward to impute to himself a disposition which even in his own instance were it harboured [he][1] could not regard as altogether free from blame: if so it be that no individual instrument or favorite, to whom in respect of any particular instance of depredation or oppression it would be agreable to him to afford licence or impunity, happens to be at the moment in his eye, it will not be agreable to him to look backward to past instances of any

---

[1] MS 'by'.

such undue favour, or forward to future contingent ones: if so it be that there exists no particular individual against whom by the audacity of his endeavours to obtain remedy or relief his resentment has been kindled, he will not find much satisfaction in any such supposition as that of his being angry without just and sufficient cause.

Not that in his situation advisers, to whose situation reflections of a general nature are more necessary, are likely to be wanting—advisers by whom representation will be made of the danger with which improvement in any shape, and particularly in the shape here in question, can not but be pregnant: nor therefore does there seem any ground for hope that without some special and particularly strong impulse [and] favorable concurrence of circumstances a concession so unexampled and naturally so revolting to ruling pride will be submitted to. But be it what it may, this chance is the only peaceable one: and such being the case, no argument against the taking it can be derived from the exility of it.

§17. *Concession—chance of its answering the purpose*

In the first instance, all that to this effect can be done by the Sovereign—all that can be asked for at his hands, is resolvable into one thing—promises. Towards the fulfilment of these promises, all that can be made to have place in the event of a violation of the promises in question, whatever they are, is—the notoriety of the several acts by which such violation shall have been effected.

Every thing that he can do on his part amounts, I say, to the giving of a promise, nothing more. If for example he grants a representative assembly—what he thereby does by such grant amounts to a promise to suffer the deputies to be elected, and to meet, according to forms of their own choosing, or forms recommended by him, as the case may be.[1] If on the occasion of such invitation or permission, he adds a declaration or assurance that in the event of their meeting he will not thenceforward give or endeavour to give execution and effects to any laws to which their consent has not been given, whether antecedently to their receiving his sanction, or not till afterwards, here again is another promise or set of promises.

If what is obtained of him consists in the obtaining of edicts interdicting the exercise of every act by which in certain ways therein

---

[1] There is no text corresponding to the following marginal summary, which belongs here: 'Permitting or ordaining such assembly amounts to nothing if it does not amount to a promise to suffer it to meet—to give expression to its desires and opinions; and to pay more or less regard to such desires and opinions, when made known.'

mentioned men are made to suffer in their persons or their property by whomsoever such acts may have been exercised, in this again is comprized a promise not only to abstain from such acts himself, but to punish without exception all persons by whom they shall so have been executed.

As a security, and that a necessary one, for the performance of this primary class of promises, comes a sort of secondary class of promises having for their subject-matter, in the event of every violation of these promises, the giving existence, execution and effect to a set of mandates and permissions having for their object the giving to every such infraction notoriety to every degree of extent possible.

If notwithstanding these promises, explicit and implied together— promises engaging not to give any such prædatory or otherwise oppressive orders, orders to that effect are given by him—here again is another instance of violation of promise on his part. If, notwithstanding the correspondent order to the Citizens of all classes not to exercise any such acts of violation, acts of that sort being exercised, he omitts to give any requisite orders for appropriate prosecution and eventual punishment—if to any exertions made by the injured parties or others for the purpose of instituting and continuing such prosecution until judgment be pronounce[d], and if condemnatory executed, he, by himself or others, opposes obstruction in an immediate and declared or unimmediate and undeclared way, obstruction to any endeavours used for the purpose of bringing about such punishment—here again is another violation of a promise, in one word another instance of perfidy on his part.

Still in all these cases every thing that is done by any person other than the Sovereign himself consists in an appeal made to Public Opinion: of every thing that is thus done or endeavoured at the success depends upon the spirit, the intelligence, the vigilance, the alertness, the intrepidity, the energy, the perseverance, of those of whose opinions Public Opinion is composed.

As every thing depends upon Public Opinion, so every thing depends upon *notoriety*. Notoriety in the first place of all ordinances by which the security in question is professed to be given;—notoriety in the next place of all acts, should any such have place, whereby the promise necessarily implied in every such ordinance is violated. Not that, be the instances of violation ever so frequent, it will follow from such frequency that the ordinances in question have been altogether without effect: much less that in their own nature they are inefficient and nugatory. Of the instances in which the promise is violated, in few will the violation escape being brought to light: of those in which it is observed, all evidence is suppressed by the very nature of the case.

The use of them may be exemplified in the instance of the ordinance whereby assistance given to a person engaged in the commission of this or that act of oppression is declared to be criminal and as such punishable, resistance to it lawful and not punishable. Antecedently to this concession, every person by whom any such act of oppression was observed would regard it as lawful and be without hope of seeing punishment applied [to] any person concerned in it. Suppose on the other hand the concession and the virtual promise contained in it made, every one would in the first instance, and unless taught to the contrary by experience, entertain the expectation and hope of seeing it observed: and in pursuance of such hope, individuals might rise up with one accord and concurr in opposing effectual resistance: individuals into whose conceptions, but for such ordinance, no idea but that of unreserved obedience, active or at least passive, would have ever entered.

This view of things—this hope—this persuasion of the usefulness of monarchical promise, how flagrantly so ever violated, is confirmed by all history—by the history of all nations in which they have been made.

In England for example, take the instance of Magna Charta and the Bill of Rights—Magna Charta in the thirteenth Century of the Christian æra, the Bill of Rights towards the close of the 17th.[1] Abundant and flagrant have been the violations of both these charters of promise. Yet it is to them that the English [are] indebted for every Security against Misrule—for every abstention from Misrule—by which their condition is distinguished to its advantage from that of the inhabitants of the Continent of Europe.

So France. Take for instance the Charter which the conquering despots forced the people to receive at the hands of the reigning Monarch.[2] The security miserably inadequate: the principle on which it is grounded, a security for, not against, misrule: like cattle upon the will of the proprietor, the lot of all the members of the Community declared dependent upon the arbitrary will of a single one of them: that one who by his situation is rendered in every intelligible sense of the word the worst of all of them. On every occasion he would be warranted in sacrificing the interest of these thirty millions of his fellow countrymen to his own single interest or caprice: yet such is his benevolence, cases are mentioned by him in which he promises so far to lay a restraint on his desires as to forbear from making this sinister sacrifice. Each moment he would be warranted in taking all they have:

---

[1] For Magna Carta see p. 129n above; for the Bill of Rights see p. 23n above.

[2] On the restoration of the French monarchy in 1814, Louis XVIII (1755–1824), King of France from 1814, issued the *Constitutional Charter* as a concession and grant of the Crown.

yet such is his generosity, of the fruits of each man's labour there is a part which in so far as it may happen to this promise to be kept, [he leaves to him].[1] Even of this scandalous promise, insulting and enormously inadequate as it is, the violations are incessant. Still however under this so inadequately bridled mixt Monarchy the lot of the people is much less disastrous than under the despotism by which the Revolution was produced.

[1] The addition is suggested by the marginal summary: 'His is all they have: yet, such his benevolence, he leaves them a part.'

LETTERS FROM JEREMY BENTHAM AND HASSUNA D'GHIES TO JOHN QUINCY ADAMS

JEREMY BENTHAM TO JOHN QUINCY ADAMS[1] FOR TRIPOLI

Dear Sir,

The Barbary powers are a constant plague to you. I am not although without hopes of seeing you finally rid of it. Either in the present or the *paulo-post* future time, you behold in them, one and all, trouble some enemies: I am not altogether without hopes of seeing you obtain them among your grateful disciples and constant friends. Half an hour's reading, if you can spare time for it, will I hope suffice to remove from the idea the imputation of extravagance. My apology is short: what you have here from an obliged friend you could not have from any body else.

First hear my alledged facts, as if from a lawyer speaking from his brief: I will then present to you, such as it is, my evidence.

Throughout the whole of the Barbary Coast from Tripoli to Tunis both inclusive, there has existed, for no inconsiderable length of time, a most urgent longing for emancipation from the yoke of despotism: a perception more or less correct of the comparative degree of security under even the worst European Governments, and a [longing][2] ardour to share of [it]. At the same time, as against any attack on the part of the people, there is and always has been what in medical language may be termed an extraordinary prostration of strength: on the part of the people, all who can afford and choose to have arms have arms: for our Six Acts do not extend to Barbary:[3] and as to disarming them, it is what the fiercest despot has never thought of. As to the despots themselves, altogether wonderful is the debility of their means.

Of the four Barbary powers, Tripoli would be the country for the Revolution to take its commencement in. In that country, there exists not any regularly trained or paid armed force whatever. Not so much as a body-guard in the condition of a standing army has the Sovereign of that state. His domestics like any one else's, some in a state of declared slavery, some in a state which by comparison is called

---

[1] For Bentham's relationship with John Quincy Adams (1767–1848), United States Secretary of State 1817–24, President 1825–9, see the Editorial Introduction, p. xxxin above.

[2] MS 'lodging'.

[3] The so-called Six Acts were passed by Parliament in 1819 in the wake of the Peterloo massacre in order to suppress radical agitation. Of these, one prevented the training of persons in the use of arms (60 Geo. I and 1 Geo. IV, c.1), and another authorized magistrates to seize arms if they believed they might be used to disturb the public peace (60 Geo. III and 1 Geo. IV, c.2).

freedom, are armed, but each in his own way. As to pay, sometimes they have pay, and sometimes they have [none]: now and then they are gorged, much more frequently they are half-starved.[1]

As to money, neither in this nor in any other Mahometan country would any written engagement, whatsoever were the sum mentioned in it, find any man, Mahometan, Jew or Christian, who would risk the value of a *cent* in the purchase of it. Meantime the despotism continues because no man, with a hundred others to stick by him, has ever been found to stand up and propose any thing better.

Could they but rely on their chief and on each other, the hundred men with whom our Henry 7th. commenced his standing army, or even the fifty men with whom Pisistratus set up his tyranny,[2] would suffice for establishing a popular constitution, supposing a constitution of that description ready made; a constitution tolerably well adjusted to the state of habits and opinions, drawn up and ready to be produced.

It is here I should mention my authority for all this. The principal one is Hassuna D'Ghies—thus it is he writes his name in an European language and character, Ambassador from the Sovereign of Tripoli to this Court, and as such recognized by our Foreign Office.[3] It is by his desire that I write this: he will give his attestation to that effect by his signature.

His age is about one and thirty: the eight last years of it he has passed in different countries of Europe, principally in France, the Netherlands and England: about a twelvemonth or thereabouts in this country in the quality abovementioned. His father | | D'Ghies is and for | | years has been Secretary of State for Foreign Affairs to the Sovereign.[4] The Sovereign, though all dependence on the Ottoman Porte has for many years been at an end, is still designated by the appellation of Pacha, or as in English we say Bashaw. He has three and no more than three legitimate sons: the eldest | | is a monster of

---

[1] There is no text corresponding to the following marginal summary, which belongs here: 'Sole armed force, Collectors of the revenue. Of these, for the whole country, six or seven thousand.'

[2] The original establishment of the Yeomen of the Guard, instituted in 1485 by Henry VII (1457–1509), King of England from 1485, was probably fifty men. Though the number had varied in subsequent reigns, from 1669 it had been settled at one hundred men plus officers. Peisistratus made himself tyrant of Athens in 561 or 560BC after having persuaded the Athenian assembly to grant him a body-guard of fifty men for his protection.

[3] A translation made by D'Ghies of a letter from Yusef Pasha of Tripoli to George IV (1762–1830), King of Great Britain and Ireland from 1820, dated 18 November 1821, announcing his appointment as Tripolitan Ambassador is at UC xxiv. 519. He was not however recognized in any official capacity by the British government (see Earl Bathurst to the Pasha of Tripoli, 4 June 1822, PRO FO 8/8, fos. 25–6).

[4] For Mohammed D'Ghies see 'Account of Tripoli', §3, p. 7 above: he had apparently retired from office no later than 1809.

cruelty, who, for his cruelty having been by an armed force sent by his father thrown out of the country, lives in a state of dependence and contempt somewhere in Egypt where he took refuge. The two next are married to the two only legitimate daughters of the above-mentioned Secretary, father to the Ambassador.[1] The Secretary before he [was] placed in this his situation had for seven years been making his observations in different countries of Europe: hence the idea of giving to this the eldest of his four sons the same advantage: and what profit has been made from it, you will when this letter closes be in some measure enabled to judge.

His country—and in particular his family and the Bashaw's own family—are as matters stand under the constant terrors of a disputed succession, whenever the reigning Bashaw's death takes place—with the expelled monster for one of the competitors, by whom all the others with their adherents might, in case of his success, be made to expire in every variety of torture. Against any such catastrophe the notoriety of his character among the people at large is it is true a considerable security, but not an adequate security: for not to speak of the ignorance and prejudices of the people, who might possibly be wrought upon by some device or other to come over to him, there is the half-dependent half-independent Bashaw of Egypt (the next country to the East),[2] of whose situation the taking up the monster and employing him as an instrument for subjugating the country would be but a natural result.

In Tunis a disputed succession, a contest for the throne, is not attended with consequence so disastrous to the people: the country is under the dominion of a few hundred Turks, who are recruited from Turkey: they fight it out among themselves: the body of the people take no part in the quarrel, but submitt patiently to the prevailing party whichever it be.

Under these circumstances, there will be nothing absolutely incredible in the supposition of a disposition on the part even of the despot himself to barter power for security.

Having been no less than 8 years absent from the country, the plan of procedure must necessarily be subject to modification from the view taken of the state of things upon his arrival [at] the proposed scene of action.

1. To propose in general terms to the Bashaw himself a

---

[1] For the Karamanli family see 'Account of Tripoli', §2, pp. 4–6 above. The three 'legitimate' sons were presumably those Yusef Pasha had by his white wife, Fatima, namely Mohammed (the monster), Ahmed and Ali, though Bentham may have had in mind Mohammed, Ali and Mustapha, since the latter two were married to D'Ghies' sisters.

[2] Mehemet Ali (1769–1849), Pasha of Egypt 1805–48.

147

Representative system on the plan of virtual universality, secrecy, equality and annuality of suffrage—the Bashaw's personal means to be limited and fixt, the official means determined by the representatives of the people: and in case of his concurrence, the appropriate operation will be his convening the people to the principal Mosque, and reading to them a speech which from the instructions given me I have drawn up.[1]

2. Supposing his consent not obtainable by private conferences betwixt himself and Hassuna, the plan to be proposed to his two sons for them to try to prevail on their father to give his concurrence on their account.[2]

3. Failing this measure, then to propose the thing to some of the most leading men in the country, one by one, that in the case of the concurrence of a sufficient number they may go, separately or in a body, and employ their endeavours to persuade him.

4. Should even this fail, as a last resource to repair to a tribe of men who inhabit a mountainous part of the country at no great distance from the capital, say from 60 to 80 miles, and who have been in a fluctuating state betwixt dependence and independence:[3] and to endeavour to engage them to set up for the above purpose the standard of insurrection, to which any of those who have without success operated in any of the former ways may repair, and try what can be done by intimidation with an armed force. In this case he reckons with confidence on support from the great body of the people.

So far as regards Tripoli alone, he has very little doubt of success: nor for so limited an object would it have occurred to him to take any such extraordinary measures for obtaining support and assistance *ab extra*. But he is a Citizen of the world, a man of unbounded benevolence, beginning with those linked with him by the ties of religious opinion, as such a passionate admirer of good government— which is as [much] as to say of the only good government as yet established and tried—that of the Anglo-American United States.

His wish would therefore be to give communication of the same blessing to all those countries which have such intense need of it, travelling in the first place west as far as Morocco, and in case of success then eastward. On the part of the body of the people, as well as the most enlightened and influential classes, he reckons[?] on receiving the like concurrence as in Tripoli.[4]

---

[1] Presumably the Addresses in 'Securities against Misrule', pp. 74–8 above.

[2] Presumably Ahmed and Ali, though possibly Ali and Mustapha.

[3] i.e. the Berber tribes of the Gharian Mountains.

[4] There is no text corresponding to the following marginal summary, which belongs here: 'Uses of U.S. assistance: giving 1. certainty: 2. promptitude: 3. extent. Extent, besides the advantage to the other nations, would give permanency to Tripoli.'

With the state of minds as well as external circumstances in Tunis, Algiers and Morocco, Hassuna is well acquainted. His father, you will bear in mind, has for many years conducted the business of his own country with these several countries. He himself has several times been a visitor at Tunis, and has been in correspondence with the leading men there.

1. *Tunis* is under the dominion of a few hundred Turks who share with the despot the plunder of the country, and keep up their numbers by recruits from Turkey—the people being—partly by ignorance of any better state of things, partly by the absence of all prospect of relief, kept at all times in a state of passive obedience.

2. Algiers. It is in this one of the Barbary States that despotism has its firmest root. The power of the country is shared among not fewer than 10,000 Turks who, according to an established process, keep up their numbers by volunteers from different parts of the Turkish Empire. A curious circumstance is—that in contradistinction to all the other powers of North Africa, the Sovereignty of this country, under all the mutations that have taken place with regard to the individual possessors, has been in a state of constant affluence. Credit, pecuniary credit—it has none: and this cause of comparative weakness it shares, as above, with all Mahometan countries. But in the coffers of the Sovereign are treasures that have remained there since the time of the Saracens.[1]

Neither in Tripoli, in Tunis, in Algiers, nor [in][2] Morocco, is the deplorable insecurity in which they live, the value of security against misrule, or the existence of it, in different proportions, in the several parts of Christendom, unknown to the body of the people. With respect to this matter, how scanty soever in detail, so efficient is the state of knowledge as to generals, that a popular representative government, if established in any one, would spread over every other as a matter of course. But to this purpose a body of men, regularly trained, disciplined and paid in the European manner, would be an indispensable requisite. This would be needful to serve as a basis or centre of union, a *point d'appui*, a moving fortress, to which volunteers might come in and attach themselves. With the interests and affections of the people in their favour, and no [opposing] force whatever of the same trustworthy description, small indeed is the number that would be sufficient. The smaller the number, the easier the obtaining it and keeping it up in each of the States, from whatever source or sources obtained, home or foreign.[3]

---

[1] Algiers was seized by the Turkish corsairs, Arudj and Khayr al-Din, the so-called Barbarossa brothers, in 1516, and became subject to the Porte in 1519.   [2] MS 'to'.
[3] The remainder of the letter is in the hand of the copyist, but bears a few corrections by

Now as to Algiers. In relation to that country, in addition to the general information furnished by Hassuna, I am in possession of some particular information furnished by an intelligent native Mohammed Ben Hamdan Khoja.[1] After a stay of 3 or 4 years in this country, he has within these few weeks returned to Algiers: possessing in a high degree the confidence of his Sovereign, and being as I think I see reason to believe in an eminent degree deserving of it, he has made large purchases in this country, in various articles, chiefly I believe military stores: amongst other things, a first rate mechanician of my acquaintance has made for him and dispatched to Algiers a system of machinery having for its object the removal of obstructions such as sandbanks in the port of Algiers. It has not been however from that Mechanician but from Hassuna that I have made acquaintance with this Algerine: I regret much it had not been made earlier. Had I been as fully apprized of the character of the man as I am now, I should have taken the earliest opportunity of adding an acquaintance with this man with that of Hassuna. He has had with him his only son, a youth of about 18 who, for 3 years, he has been keeping at a Boarding School at Brixton, a few miles from London, at the enormous expence of 208£ or guineas per annum for board, lodging and instruction alone: a sum that would suffice for the complete maintenance of half-a-dozen men in any of those countries, in a condition enabling them to live in the highest company. To my no small regret unexpected circumstances concurred in preventing my making acquaintance with the young man before his departure. I understand that he has made such good profit of such instruction as was to be had at that school as to be able, both in speech and writing, to pass for an Englishman. Before his departure, the father at my suggestion wrote to his Sovereign, recommending to him to send hither to Hill's School at Hazlewood near Birmingham a dozen boys.[2] At that school they will receive an incomparably better instruction at about a third of the expence. I saw the father but twice, but by what he had heard about me from Hassuna, he was induced to ask of me as a favor, permission to send to me from time to time articles for insertion in our English Newspapers. He himself, though a prime scholar, Hassuna tells me, in Arabic, and though he speaks English as well as French with some fluency, cannot write or even read in either. In his correspondence with me it must therefore be the son that holds the pen. He takes with

---

Bentham. There is some confusion in the order of the letter: Bentham went on to discuss Algiers again, but did not consider Morocco at all.

[1] For Bentham's relationship with Khoja see the Editorial Introduction, pp. xxxii–xxxiii above.
[2] For Bentham's connection with the Hills and his encouragement of the school see *Chrestomathia*, ed. M.J. Smith and W.H. Burston, Oxford, 1983 (*CW*), pp. xvii–xix.

him either a printing or lithographic press and means to propose to the Dey the setting up of a periodical Newspaper, as frequently recurring as may be, but daily or even every other day is too frequent a recurrence I fear in the first instance. I observed the fire lighted up in his countenance as often as the word Liberty occurred. The present Dey[1] I understand is a quiet, inoffensive, well-meaning sort of man: his spirits somewhat broken and kept low, by the image of the cruel treatment he experienced at the hands of his immediate predecessor.[2] While in that situation he received sympathy and relief from the generosity of this man: and this is the source of the confidence. The Dey whom the English Government made war upon and bombarded was not the immediate predecessor of the present Dey, but the one next before him.[3] Upon Hassuna's taking up some work of mine and giving to [Khoja][4] an extempore translation in Arabic, the translator observed, as he spoke, the tears flowing into the hearer's eyes. They are to keep up a regular correspondence in a sort of cypher which they have settled, but the plan for Constitutional Reform etc. has not been communicated to the Algerine. I gave to the Algerine as many of my works in English as I could scrape together: I asked him whether he knew of any person in Algiers who would be able to read them. The answer was no body at present except his son. Since his departure Hassuna has received a letter from him from France, I think: it was from Marseilles at the eve of his sailing for Algiers. He desired to be remembered to me and spoke of me in terms of great affection.[5] Though the plan has not yet been communicated to him, Hassuna makes no doubt of most ardent concurrence on his part should circumstances ever be ripe for communication of it to Algiers. He had with him here 2 companions of his own country whom I did not see. I believe they were neither more nor less than his clerks. He is a man of about six and forty, the husband of one wife, for whom, as well as for this son, I understand him to have the tenderest affection. I endeavoured to persuade him to let his son stay here one year longer that he might during that time have the benefit of the superior instruction administered at that school: instruction of the importance of which, in a moral and political view, he was duly sensible. He said he

---

[1] Husain III, Dey of Algiers 1818–30.

[2] Ali V Khoja, Dey of Algiers 1817–18.

[3] Umar, Dey of Algiers 1815–17. Algiers was bombarded on 27 August 1816 by a combined English and Dutch fleet under the command of Edward Pellew (1757–1833), created Baron Exmouth 1814 and Viscount Exmouth 1816, with the aim of securing the abolition of Christian slavery.

[4] MS 'Cauja'.

[5] The letter from Khoja was received by D'Ghies on 20 January 1823: see the Editorial Introduction, p. xxxiii above.

certainly should but for the uneasiness his wife is continually expressing at the thoughts of so long a separation from her son, but if he
could bring her to consent, he would, after a year's stay there, send
him hither again. The Mechanician above al[l]uded to spoke of him as
a man of perfect probity in all his dealings. His father he told me was a
Turk, but he himself was born in Algiers. His zeal for the service of his
Master, or rather perhaps of his country, had at different times, led
him to make purchases without authority, offering each time to stand
the loss if the purchases should not be approved: they were approved
in every instance and this circumstance I embrace as a favorable omen
with relation to the recommendation given to send the 12 boys.

A propos of boys: some time ago Hassuna wrote to his father at
Tripoli recommending the same measure for the same number: a
recommendation which of course he would not have hazarded
with[out] reasonable expectation of seeing it adopted.[1]

---

[1] The letter appears to have been abandoned at this point.

HASSUNA D'GHIES, AMBASSADOR FROM THE SOVEREIGN OF TRIPOLI, AT THE COURT OF LONDON, TO THE HONOURABLE [JOHN] QUINCY ADAMS, SECRETARY OF STATE TO THE ANGLO-AMERICAN UNITED STATES

Sir,

Warranted by the character, public and private, of the person I am addressing, in writing what you see I am placing my life in your hands. In some parts, as you will see, it has my correction in my own hand-writing:[1] and in every other part my approbation. Though in your language I could not have worded it exactly as you see it, it contains not a word the import of which is not understood and of course approved by me.

Yes, Sir, my life is in your hands. For, an acknowledgment I must begin with is—that, though on this very occasion the personal welfare of my Sovereign and his family is among the prime objects of my solicitude, and though I do not by any means despair even of *his* concurrence in the plan you will see, it will be plain enough to you that it could not have been written with his knowledge. As to the concealment thus made, you will soon see whether it has not for its justification, a necessity of the most imperious kind. I say *justification*, for it wants no *excuse*.

Surprize, naturally enough, but in a situation such as yours, whatever be the ultimate result, something considerably different from dissatisfaction, will (I can not but flatter myself) be at least the immediate sensation produced in a mind like yours by an address from such a quarter with such an object, as you will see. From acceptance, if given to the proposal which it serves to convey, you will have to judge, whether amongst other benefits one which has been, and I see reason to believe still is, amongst the objects of national desire may not result from it to Your United States.

Now Sir, as to the nature of the necessity: of the necessity in both its branches—private as well as public.

What I have to state to you is a political *disorder* of a most violent nature, and a *remedy* which I am about to endeavour to apply to it:

[1] The surviving MSS do not bear any corrections in D'Ghies' hand.

153

what I have to solicit at your hands, is your assistance towards the application of that same remedy.

In this disorder you will see the necessity just alluded to. It has two branches, public and private: branches in themselves distinguishable, but so intertwined as to be inseparable: and, the material thing is— that the same remedy applies to both: nor are they, either of them, susceptible of any other.

The root of the private disorder is in the public one: in that state of universal insecurity which, as you so well know, is the necessary fruit and accompaniment of a government such as ours.

Out of this universal and constantly existing evil grows at this particular time a particular and most horrible danger: a danger of a domestic, and in that way of a comparatively private nature: but magnified into a public and universal danger by the situation of the family:—a danger of civil war, and at the conclusion of it that of the country's falling into the power of a monster more atrociously cruel and mischievous than is perhaps to be seen in any page of history:—a monster to whose already experienced and notorious appetite for carnage, and delight in the spectacle of human tortures, the rest of the reigning family, together with my own in connection with it, would be among the earliest and surest victims.

On each vacancy, a Mahometan throne, I need not inform you, is, among the brothers of the last Sovereign, the object of a general scramble. Of the sons of the reigning Sovereign of Tripoli, this monster, Mahomet Caramalli, is the eldest: some traits of him you will see presently.

Now, Sir, as to the remedy: and opposite as it is to the existing Constitution, I look without doubt to your agreeing with me, that it is the only possible one. It is neither more nor less than a Constitution—a Constitution as near as may be to that of your United States. Sir, in looking up to this great edifice of your's, arduous as it is, neither my imagination, nor yet my judgment, can stop at Tripoli. Established in any one of the four Barbary States, the change would travel on in an assured course over all the others. Believe me, Sir, even with us, feelings and opinions—in a word the *times*—are ripe for it, much more so than you would naturally imagine. Yes, Sir, we are all of us ready for a Washington.[1] Perhaps you may be able and willing to send us one. I can not be he: but I hope to be able to prepare the way before him: I shall endeavour at it if I have life.

Thus much in generals. Now as to details. What I have to submitt to

---

[1] An allusion to George Washington (1732–99), Commander in Chief of the Continental forces 1775–83, President of the United States 1789–97.

154

your consideration in this way, you will find ranged under the following heads:[1]

§ 1. Inducements of greatest urgency together with facilities for the proposed enterprize. State of the reigning family and of my own in connection with it.

§ 2. Plan of operation, on the supposition of no foreign assistance.

§ 3. Weakness of the Government—facilities afforded by it.

§ 4. Extension of the felicitous change to Tunis, Algiers and Morocco—its use and facility.

§ 5. Assistance from the United States, why and what desired.

§ 6. Secrecy why necessary—thence cooperation prior to all communication to Congress.[2]

§ 7. United States—their expected inducements for concurrence.

§ 8. Immediate preliminary measures proposed in case of concurrence.

§ 1. *State of the reigning family, and of mine which is allied to it*

The name of the reigning Sovereign is Yussuf Pacha Caramanli. Caramanli means from the province of Caramania. It is the proper name of the family.

His authority, as you have probably understood from such of your functionaries as have been on the spot, is altogether independent of every other. The Turkish title of *Bashaw*, as you write it in English, *Pacha* in other European languages, imports indeed subordination to the Porte. But for about | | years past no such subordination has had place, neither tribute nor any other token of subjection having been either paid or claimed.[3]

His power is, as almost every where else where Mahometanism is the religion of the State, monarchical and without any distinct limit: but, in practice, as well as theory, it is somewhat tempered and softened by the influence exercised by that body in which, in that as in every other Mahometan country, the judicial and ecclesiastical functions are united.

The reigning Sovereign is about 50 years of age. About | | years ago, he seated and settled himself on the throne, in the manner so

---

[1] There are differences in wording between the headings listed below and those which appear in the text.

[2] This and the following heading have been transposed to make them consistent with the order in the text.

[3] The first of the Karamanli dynasty, Ahmed, seized power and expelled the Turk in 1711. Since then, Tripoli had effectively been independent of the Porte except for the brief intervention of Ali Burghol in 1793–5 (see 'Account of Tripoli', § 2, pp. 4–5n above).

usual in Mahometan States, by what you would call the murder of his brother.[1] He is however by no means of a sanguinary or harsh disposition: and his temper has been rather softened than hardened by age. His greatest imperfection is profusion in expenditure: and by this weakness he is kept in a state of perpetual indigence, and his subjects—so at least it appears to them—in a state of proportionable insecurity in respect of property, not to say in respect of life.

He has four legitimate male children:

1. Mohammed Bey, aged { }.
2. Achmet Bey, aged about 30.
3. Ali Bey, aged about 27.
4. Mustapha Bey, aged about 18.[2]

The title of Bey, which may be rendered Prince, is shared with the reigning family by four others.[3]

In ours as in other Mahometan nations, the order of succession is not regarded as fixt. Hence, on every vacancy of a throne, the incidental confusions produced by fratricide and civil war are liable to be added to the habitual insecurity and universal indigence perpetuated by despotism.

1. The eldest son, *Mahomet*, is generally regarded as excluded from all probability of succeeding by his notorious and matchless cruelty, as well as rebellion against his father.[a] For | | years he has been a fugitive in Egypt. He is unmarried.[4]

[a] Instances of the cruelty of Mahomet Caramalli, eldest son of the Bashaw of Tripoli, Ao. 1817. From Della Scalas 'Narrative of an Expedition from Tripoli to the Western frontier of Egypt: translated by Aufrere'. London. 8vo.[5]

p.4 to 6. 'Among all the monsters generated by Africa, which by the ancients was denominated the country of monsters, the first place is due to Mhamet Karamalli, eldest son of the present Pacha of Tripoli; of intellect the most obtuse and impenetrable; of mind the most grovelling and unenlightened; and of disposition the most brutal; unbridled in the gratification of the most atrocious passions, there is no cruelty with which he is not stained, no violence which he has not committed; and one of his choicest pleasures was to watch the convulsive motions, comparative

---

[1] Yusef had in fact murdered his eldest brother Hassan in 1790 (see the account in Tully, *Ten Years' Residence*, ii. 101–9), but had succeeded to the throne in 1795 after deposing his surviving elder brother, Ahmed.

[2] For further details see 'Account of Tripoli', §2, p. 5 above.

[3] For the use of the title of Bey see 'Account of Tripoli', §3, p. 7n above.

[4] For the expedition against Mohammed, led by Ahmed and not Ali as Bentham states below, see 'Account of Tripoli', §2, pp. 5–6n above. Mohammed was in fact married to the daughter of his deposed uncle Ahmed, and had three sons, the eldest of whom, Mohammed, committed suicide in 1835 after failing in his attempt to seize the throne on the abdication of Yusef.

[5] Paolo Della Cella, *Narrative of an Expedition from Tripoli in Barbary, to the Western frontier of Egypt, in 1817, By the Bey of Tripoli; in letters to Dr. Viviani of Genoa.... Translated from the Italian, By Anthony Aufrere, Esq.*, London, 1822. The text here is reproduced from the original work, rather than from the copy made for Bentham (UC xxiv. 556).

2. The second son, *Achmet*, is weak in mind: and that to such a degree, as to be likewise regarded as debarred from all probability of succession.

3. The third son, *Ali Bey*, is regarded as competent to receive the succession. Anno 1817 he commanded the little irregular army, by the terror of which, without bloodshed, his eldest brother, deserted by all his followers, was expelled. He has these { } years been married to one of my two sisters, Khadija D'Ghies. By her he has { } sons.[1]

4. The fourth son, *Mustapha Bey*, is also regarded as competent to receive the succession. In the course of the last year he was married to my other sister, Fatima D'Ghies.

Now, as to my own family.

My father, Mohammed D'Ghies, has now for these | | years, namely since the year 181., with some intervals, been Secretary of State for foreign affairs.[2]

He is about | | years of age.

sufferings, and dying agonies of some of his slaves, to whom he occasionally caused graduated doses of arsenic to be administered. This savage having been employed by his father, at the head of a small army, to reduce to obedience a tribe of Bedouins who had infested the shores of the gulph, ravaged the adjoining districts, and (*proh nefas!*) refused to pay the customary tribute, he so fully executed the commission, that not a single one of the whole tribe remained alive.

'Upon his return to Tripoli, elated with the success of his sanguinary expedition, and accustomed to the most implicit and blind obedience to his orders; he no longer treated his father with respect, but in one of his many sallies of passion struck at him with a poniard, which was fortunately warded off by a female slave. Instead of punishing him as he deserved, and depriving him of the means of further aggression, his father sent him out as governor of the provinces of Bengasi and Derna, upon the eastern frontier of his territories, inhabited by a powerful tribe of Bedouins, called Zoasi, long ill affected towards the Pacha, and frequently breaking out into open rebellion. But no sooner was the new governor arrived at Bengasi, than the Pacha found that in his son he had given a chieftain to the malcontents; and the rebellion spreading rapidly throughout those provinces, the Pacha judged it expedient to dispatch a considerable body of troops, under the command of his second son, Bey Ahmet, in order to check the progress of the insurrection, and punish the treacherous conduct of the rebellious son. . . .'

p.179 to 180. 'At Derna we had speaking proofs of the cruelties committed by the rebellious Bey previous to his retreat; for the ground in the fort was stained with the blood of those whom the monster, at the moment of marching, had sacrificed to his passion and suspicions. The first victims were his female slaves, who were slaughtered because he did not choose that others should possess what had once belonged to him, and because he thought they would retard his flight.'

---

[1] In 'Account of Tripoli', §2, p. 5 above, Bentham says that Ali had three children, but that Mustapha was married to Khadija.

[2] Mohammed D'Ghies had apparently retired from office no later than 1809: see 'Account of Tripoli', §3, p. 7n above.

He has four sons.

1. His eldest son, myself Hassuna D'Ghies, | | years of age: born Anno | |.[1]

2. His second son, Mohammed D'Ghies, | | years of age: born Anno | |.

3. His third son, | | D'Ghies, | | years of age: born | |.

4. His fourth son, | | D'Ghies, between 13 and 14 years of age: born Anno | |.

Daughters, the two abovementioned.

About seven years of his life, my father passed in visiting and making his observations in several countries in Europe. He was at that time the only man of distinction in Tripoli, perhaps the only man of any class in that State or any other of North Africa, who was ever in possession of any such advantage: except in so far as here and there a short diplomatic mission to some particular Court may have made exception.

By his experience of the benefit derivable from such a source of intellectual culture, he was led to communicate it to me his eldest son. I had been bred to that part of the official Establishment by which, under the religion of Mahomet, the functions of religion and those of Judicature are united. For qualifying men for those offices, we have, besides ordinary Schools, two Seminaries which may be termed Universities: one of them, Tanjiura, about 12 miles to the west of Tripoli; the other, Zanzour, about the same distance to the East.[2] In the Mahometan Universities in general, the subjects of study, in addition to the Coran and Grammar as applied to that subject, are Mathematics, Logic and Rhetoric: Mathematics little applied to practice: all three derived from translations made of old from the Greek. Of no branch either of Natural History or Natural Philosophy is any cognizance taken. At Tanjiura our family has an estate. From between 3 and 4 years, namely from 18.. to 18.., I studied at Tanjiura. To Zanzour likewise I made occasional visits, receiving instruction from the Professors there. In the month of | | 181., I left Tripoli and landed at Marseilles in my way to Paris. I passed my time in France, till the 8th. of March 1821: on which day I set out for Brussels on a tour through the Netherlands. In that country I continued till the { } of June 1821, on which day I arrived in London with the character of Ambassador from the Sovereign of Tripoli to the King of Great Britain. At Paris I endeavoured to fill up in some sort the deficiencies left in my education by our Universities. In France my acquaintance was extensive: it included many men of eminence in different lines. I had once a confer-

---

[1] Hassuna was in his early thirties at this time.
[2] Tajaoura was in fact to the east of Tripoli, and Zanzour to the west.

ence of some length with the King.[1] In England my acquaintance has
been still more extensive. By a friend of Romilly,[2] Mr. Scarlet, who,
as you must know, is at the head of the profession of the law in England,[3] it was recommended to me to make acquaintance if possible
with Mr. Bentham. I tried: and at length on the | | of June 1822, I
succeeded. It is by him and him alone that I have been led to look to
the United States as affording the only example of a government in
which the greatest happiness of the greatest number is the object
really pursued: by him, I have been encouraged and supported in the
great wish which with so much ardour I have for many years entertained—the wish of contributing to impart the blessings of good government to the oppressed and suffering country in which I drew my
first breath.

For a purpose such as that in question the state of the other
countries of North Africa is pretty sufficiently known to me. Before I
left my own, my father's situation in it enabled me to obtain a conception more or less ample and correct on that head in relation to every
one of them, not to speak of the less civilized countries of the interior
to the South. *Tunis* I had visited, and formed acquaintance there with
the leading characters. In regard to *Algiers*, in addition to what I
possessed at that period, I have very recently obtained much and
valuable information from *Hamdan ben Othman Khoja*—a most intelligent and worthy man who is high in the confidence of the Dey. For
more than three years he has been in London making considerable
purchases. I have been on terms of intimacy with him. A few weeks
ago he returned to Algiers by way of Paris and Marseilles. With him,
at his request, I have entered into a confidential correspondence, having for its object the impressing the inhabitants of North Africa with
the persuasion that good government, as near as may be approaching
to that of the United States, would be the effectual, and the only
possible, means of relief from that state of insecurity, and consequent
penury, of the miseries of which they are so universally and acutely
sensible. At our request, Mr. Bentham has consented to endeavour to
procure in this view insertion for articles which Khoja requested
permission to send him from time to time in the most liberal and best
conducted of the London Newspapers. Unfortunately, Khoja, though
a man of learning in the Mahometan stile, and though in conversation
he expresses himself, with more or less facility, in English as well as

[1] Louis XVIII.

[2] Sir Samuel Romilly (1757–1818), Solicitor General 1806–7, had known Bentham since
1784, and had remained on close terms until his death.

[3] James Scarlett (1769–1844), created Baron Abinger 1835, Attorney General 1827–8,
1829–30 and Lord Chief Baron of the Exchequer 1834–44, was at this time a prominent
barrister.

French, is not able to read in either language. But he takes with him a son of his, aged eighteen, who for these three last years had been at a Boarding School near London, and is said to have made such a proficiency in English as to be capable of passing for an Englishman.

In Egypt, my Father and I have confidential correspondents: one of them, *Ibrahim Pacha*:—a man well known to the Officers of the English Army that served in Egypt: he having been the means of their getting possession of Alexandria.[1] He resides there in the character of Ambassador from our Sovereign to the Pacha of Egypt, a character we obtained for him for his greater security.

Between the two families—the Bashaw's and mine—there has had place at all times the most uninterrupted harmony. In my father—such has been his kindness to his children—I have never ceased to behold an object of the tenderest affection as well as of filial reverence: to him I stand indebted for my liberation from those prejudices, by the weight of which, with so few exceptions, my countrymen are still so unhappily depressed. A want of energy, the result of the state of his eyes (for he is nearly blind), added to age, would render it a useless source of anxiety to him were I to apply to him for assistance in any such enterprize as that in question.

Under this excellent father, my Brothers, notwithstanding so long a separation, have all along been in the habit of listening to my advice. By the Bashaw himself I have always been kindly treated: and experience has led me to flatter myself, that on the most trying occasions no advice of mine to him would be altogether without influence. You may judge of it by the speech which you will see, and which I should not have given myself the trouble of preparing for him without some hopes of seeing it adopted:[2] as also by my recommendation to him, in a late letter, to set up a periodical work, with a printing press.[3] I flatter myself with the like persuasion in relation to the only two of his four sons who, to any purpose of government, can be considered on the footing of active citizens;[4] and, to this effect, their friendship for my brothers as well as their love for their wives, my sisters, afford additional grounds for hope.

In the year 1804, I had the pleasure of seeing Captain Bainbridge of

---

[1] Ibrahim Pasha Kataraghasi of Aleppo commanded a contingent of ashraf in the army led by the Grand Vizier, Kur Yusuf Diya-al-Din Pasha, which cooperated with the British in their campaign against the French in Egypt in 1801. Ibrahim was detached to take Damietta, which fell on 14 May, and then rejoined the Grand Vizier for the march on Cairo, which capitulated on 27 June. The Grand Vizier however remained at Cairo, while the British, aided by a separate Turkish force under Hussein Capitan Pasha, went on to attack Alexandria, which they entered on 2 September.

[2] Presumably the Addresses in 'Securities against Misrule', pp. 74–8 above.

[3] In the margin of the copy, Bentham marked this statement and noted: 'Correct or omit.'

[4] i.e. Ali and Mustapha.

the United States frigate Philadelphia.[1] I mention this that in the event of his being at any time in your neighbourhood you may make reference to him for any thing that he happens to remember concerning me: I should rather have said, concerning my father: for at that time I was no more than thirteen years old.

There dined with him one day (I remember) at my father's| |other Gentlemen from your fleet, Dr. | |, Dr. | | and Mr. | |. I mention them for the purpose of multiplying the chances of your meeting with persons capable of conveying to you some conception of the sort of treatment your countrymen, though coming as enemies, experienced at my father's hands.[2]

§2. *Plan of operation, independently of any support from the Executive of the United States*

Having thus, in so far as time, space and faculties admitt, endeavoured to convey to you some conception of the nature of my resources for the execution of the intended Plan of operation, I will now lay before you a general sketch of the Plan itself.

The length of time that has elapsed since I left the country in question, and the uncertainty respecting the changes to which that interval may have given birth, impose on me, as you can not but see, the necessity of planning and thence of speaking by alternatives; looking forward to a chain of eventual measures one behind another: the second to be had recourse to should the first, upon my arrival, be found or deemed impracticable: and so in regard to the third and fourth.

1. First resource: personal application by me to the Sovereign himself: stating, in general terms, the idea of admitting the people at large to a share of power: backing it with such inducements as shall afford the fairest prospect of obtaining his concurrence. Say—*Application to the Sovereign*.

2. Second resource: application to his two sons abovementioned: directly or through the medium of my Brothers and Sisters, each of

---

[1] The United States had declared war against Tripoli in 1801 on account of her molestation of American shipping. On 31 October 1803, the *Philadelphia*, under the command of Captain William Bainbridge (1774–1833), attempting to maintain a blockade of the port of Tripoli, ran aground. It was subsequently captured by the Tripolitans and its crew taken hostage. They were released on the conclusion of peace in June 1805.

[2] Mohammed D'Ghies, described by the Americans either as Prime Minister or Minister of Foreign Affairs to the Pasha, was prominent in the negotiations which led to the conclusion of the peace between Tripoli and the United States and the release of Bainbridge and his crew: see *Naval Documents related to the United States Wars with the Barbary Powers*, 6 vols., Washington, 1939–44.

them to be tried in the first instance separately. Object of the application—engaging them to add their influence to mine: and, on failure of success, to concurr with me in the proposed ulterior measures for the security of both families. Say—*Application through the united families*.

3. Third resource. Application to the most influential persons, functionaries and others, for their co-operation as above: and eventually in ulterior measures. Say—*Application to influential persons*.

4. Application to a tribe of *Mountaineers*,[1] who, in a tract of mountainous country commencing at about 60 miles from the capital, preserve to this day a sort of comparative independence. Say—*Application to the Mountaineers*.

Now as to *inducements*.

As to the Sovereign, those which I have to present to his consideration consist principally of: 1. the universally acknowledged atrocity and unfitness of his eldest Son: 2. the destruction which would befall his whole family as well as the whole country, if, by support from Egypt or by any delusive means, that monster of cruelty should succeed in forming a party capable of seating him on the throne: 3. the utter impossibility of establishing any sure order of succession without recourse to a fundamental law in the establishment of which the whole body of the people shall have had a share: 4. the equal impossibility of giving encrease or even security to his revenue, unless by an encreased employment of capital;—a mode of expenditure to give to which no man has ever ventured, or will ever venture, to give encrease, under a form of government under which every *visible* encrease to capital is sure, sooner or later, to bring destruction upon the capital itself, if not upon the possessor.

As to the two sons, who are regarded as capable of filling the throne—hitherto, for any thing I have ever heard, they have been living in a state of mutual amity. But, on the decease of the present occupier of the throne, who could take upon himself to answer for two brothers, in such a *country*, in their *situation*, and with such *example* before their eyes. It is by what you would call the *murder* of his brother, as above mentioned, that the present Sovereign seated himself. See Tully's Letters from Tripoli.[2]

Now, suppose the concurrence of the Sovereign obtained, the following is the course that according to our customs will naturally be pursued.

In our country the Sovereign takes more frequently a visible part in public business than in the countries of Europe. Occasionally he exercises in public the functions of Judicature.

---

[1] i.e. the tribesmen of Gharian.
[2] See §1, pp. 155–6n above.

In case of concurrence, as above, he will accordingly repair to the principal Mosque, and there in his own person read a paper to the effect in question in the presence of the congregation, as in England and France in the case of a speech from the throne.

By the assistance of Mr. Bentham, a paper for this purpose has been prepared: a copy of it you will find in the Appendix under Letter A. It contains in general terms an engagement to call together a representative body of the people, for the purpose of their framing, in concert with him, a Constitutional Code. Of this paper I shall make a translation, and have it in readiness.[1]

---

[1] Presumably the first Address in 'Securities against Misrule', pp. 74–6 above. There is however a further address in Arabic with the following (grammatically imperfect) French translation in D'Ghies' hand at UC xxiv. 518 (n.d.), and it may be this which is referred to here: 'Portons jusqu'aux pieds du trône de l'éternel le tribut de nos louanges, rendons-lui des actions de grâce, car c'est lui qui nous a donné dans les cheveux blancs l'avis du déclin de not[r]e existence, c'est lui qui nous a donné l'esp[r]it, —flambeau resplendissant, c'est lui qui nous a donné les moyens de revenir de nos erreurs à la vérité—devoir incontestable, de suivre le bon système de nos prédécesseurs, de ne point nous écarter des principes prescrits par notre livre céleste; et de nous trouver alors entouré d'un rempart inat[t]aquable.

'C'est en réfléchissant bien à ces vrais principes, et à ces paroles divines, ô Souverains! que vous n'êtes que des bergers, que les peuples sont vos troupeaux et que chacun de vous doit rendre compte des brebis qui lui sont confiées: car celui qui ne fait pas son devoir est grandement responsable envers le Ciel, tandis que celui qui s'en acquitte trouv[e]ra une récompense inef[f]able. Mais dieu, clément et bienveillant, eu égard à notre faiblesse et au pouvoir séducteur de la tentation, a dit aussi: "ne faites rien de votre propre autorité, mais seulement d'après l'avis salutaire des gens de bien". Ces paroles ont été dites à Mahommed, dont l'esprit profond est distingué e[s]t généralement reconnu par les hommes célèbres de l'univers, combien à plus forte raison nous qui sommes si inférieurs à lui et qui prétendons suivre sa religion et les dogmes qu'elle prescrit, [ne] devons nous écarter du sens de ces paroles ni à perdre de vue ces avis salutaires, mais à nous y conformer au contraire avec la plus scrupuleuse attention.

'Puisque telle soit notre volonté et manière d'être, nous croyons qu'il est de notre devoir de l[a] faire connaître à nos peuples qui nous tiendron[t] lieu d'enfans; de leur marquer et tracer leurs droits et leurs devoirs pour pratiquer le bien et éviter le mal, de leur confirmer la liberté qui leur a été accordée par le Ciel et d'établir des bornes que les administrations ne puissent enfreindre. C'est à ces causes que nous avons voulu et arrêté que nous et nos successeurs pratiquassent ce qui suit, dans cet acte publique qui sera exposé dans toute l'étendue de notre royaume. 1e. de pratiquer ce précepte: le plus distingué et le plus noble d'entre vous sera celui qui fait le bien et évite le mal et il n'y aura pas d'autre distinction que celle-là: tous les enfans d'Adam quelque soit leur religion sont les mêmes, en se rappelant surtout la sent[e]nce suivante du prophète: "Celui qui fera tort à l'homme qui professe une autre religion, je me déclarerai son adversaire au jour du jugement dernier."

'2. Chaque compatriote a l[e] d[r]oit de parler et d'écrire ce qu'il jugera convenable [au] bien de sa patrie, sans pouvoir insulter aucune personne en la nommant, ni rien afficher sans l'approbation de l'autorité locale.

'3. Le devoir de chaque concitoyen est de respecter les vieillards, d'encourager la jeunesse, de protéger les orphelins, de se conformer strictement aux usages et aux loix du Pays en s'écartant des choses opposées et blâmables; que personne ne puisse faire tort à autre sans s'exposer à être réprimé et puni par nos loix, non plus que de pouvoir se venger soi-même de celui qui lui a fait tort sans être exposé à passer p[ou]r le coupable; son devoir étant de porter ses plaintes aux autorités locales pour quelqu'affaire que ce puisse être, selon les cas prévus et indiqués dans les tableaux dérivés de notre Constitution. Il est aussi d[u] devoir de chaque paroisse et quartier de les bien connaître et de veiller constamment au maintien de notre charte et traité avec nos peuples et qui établissent la vraie liberté et les d[r]oits de l'humanité en

What is but too evident, is that the obtainment of so great a concession can not but be precarious. As a succedaneum, how inadequate so ever, the next and only security obtainable at the hands of the Sovereign will be a Charter: a Charter having for its object the affording whatsoever feeble security against misrule can be afforded in a State the whole power of which—Legislative, Executive and Judicial, is acknowledged to be in the hands of a single individual. At the worst, it will however, in proportion to the degree of divulgation given to it, have the effect of pointing the attention of the people to all known acts of depredation at the expence of particular individuals or of oppression in any other shape. While the Sovereign remains possessed of his present unlimited power, promises, such as those which it is in the nature of a charter to give expression to, are all that can be given in the first instance: as to performance, it must take its chance. A paper for this purpose is drawing up with the assistance of Mr. Bentham. A sort of preamble, proposed for it, in the shape of another speech from the throne, as above, you will find in the Appendix under Letter B.[1]

Lastly as to the *Mountaineers*. I think of applying to that tribe, in preference to any other set of men, because it is among them, as being more or less habituated to resistance, that I expect to find the strongest disposition to unite, and the greatest facility for uniting, for such a purpose, in such sort as to form at once a body too strong to be mastered by any such force as could be sent against them on the sudden: and before they had time to receive such augmentation, as, while they remained free from attack, might gradually come in: which body would thus form a *nucleus* or support for all such accessions. For the purpose of engaging them, I have penned in French the substance of an Address which I have put into the hands of Mr. Bentham, in the view of his doing that by it which he has done already by the two Addresses above mentioned.[2] If, from individuals separately

prescrivant à chacun ce qui lui est permis ainsi que ce qui lui est défendu, de sorte qu'ayant cette parfaite connaissance s'il ne s'y conforme pas entièrement il mérit[e]ra d'être puni.

'N'ajoutons plus d'autres recommandations ni de preuves d'affections paternelles que nous sentons, que de prier dieu constamment et avec ardeur pour nous et vous, de nous diriger vers le bon chemin et de nous inspirer l'amour du bien.'

[1] Presumably the 'paper' is a reference to the provisions of 'Constitutional Securities', and the preamble a reference to the second Address, in 'Securities against Misrule', pp. 79–102 and pp. 76–8 above respectively.

[2] The text of this speech, in D'Ghies' hand, but with marginal summary paragraphs in Bentham's hand, is at UC xxiv. 536–7 (n.d.): 'Louanges à Dieu, Celui qui nous a accordé les moyens de découvrir la vérité, qui nous a réveillé[s] du sommeil léthargique où nous étions pour [nous faire] observer des choses essentielles qui ne pourraient échapper aux gens qui ont une profonde pénétration, qui a purifié notre âme et a levé le rideau dont elle était couverte, c'est-à-dire d'une obéissance aveugle et d'une humilité servile pour des personnes qui ne le méritent pas, et qui y a répandu les flammes du feu brillant de l'amour de la liberté pour célébrer cette noble religion M[ahométane] et détruire les palais des tyrans fondés sur les bases de l'oppres-

conversed with, I find sufficient encouragement, I shall *lithographize* and circulate this Address. If from communications made in consequence I receive sufficient ulterior encouragement, I shall then call a meeting, make a speech to them, and if the result be favorable, set up, or find some other person to set up, a standard, with the words 'The greatest happiness of the greatest number' in Arabic, headed by

sion. Chers frères, excellens compatriotes, et vous jeunesse sur qui repose l'espoir de la patrie, ouvrez les yeux sur la conduite de ces despotes souverains à qui Dieu a confié la liberté de notre sang et de nos biens; usurpateurs de leur puissance, ils en ont abusé, et semblables à Pharaon qui, dans sa longue existence, se croyait un Dieu, ils ont pu oublier qu'ils étaient des mortels et se sont crus des êtres célestes. On a vu briller dans leurs mains le Glaive qui verse le sang humain, ils n'ont envisagé d'autres vertus que dans les seuls moyens de nuire jour et nuit, de s'emparer des biens de l'orphelin, de renoncer à tout sentiment d'humanité et de les violer, ces droits si sacrés, de faire triompher l'agresseur, jouissant sur les débris de ses malheureux victimes, de s'abandonner au torrent de la méchanceté et de faire détruir[e] leurs peuples au moyen de guerre[s] intestines et ceux mêmes qui leur sont attachés et qui les exhortent de pendre et de tuer pour le moindre mouvement de colère et malgré l'évidence de la fausseté des accusations; mais quels sont donc les droits qu'ils prétendent avoir? Les voici, dans le passage suivant de l'alKoran: "Aimez Dieu, votre prophète et votre souverain et obéissez-leur", mais ils ignorent la vraie signification de ce passage, ils n'ont suivi ni les condition[s] ni les principes en vertu desquels ils peuvent jouir de ce privilège: ils ignorent encore les autre[s] passages que Dieu leur avait prescrits, c'est-à-dire le soin de leurs peuples ou frères, en ayant pour eux les attentions et les affections les plus tendres, qui ne peuvent être bien exprimées que par celles d'un bon père à l'égard de ses enfans: mais hommes les plus hypocrits qui existent, dissimulés, éloignés de la vérité seul[e] en vertu d[e la]quel[le] ils puissent jouir d'un privilège qui ne peut leur appartenir qu'en remplissant leurs devoirs et qu'ils ont méconnus en devenant à la fois juges et partis.

'Personne de nous n'est maître de soi-même ni de ses biens, n'a la libre volonté de faire ce qui lui plaît ni de réaliser l'espoir de la moindre chose, mais [chacun] doit être aveuglément soumis à *la Sainte volonté* de ses *tyrans*; ne vous éveillerez-vous pas, ô mes chers frères, du sommeil léthargique où vous êtes plongés, pour abolir cet esclavage et rétablir *votre liberté*; pour déchirer cette tissue d'horreurs, qui a couvert la terre jusqu'à ce qu'enfin tous les êtres qui existent en aient jeté des cris effroyables—les montagnes mêmes et leurs sommets n'y ont point été insensibles. Faites-vous gouverner suivant les préceptes du divin alKoran, en suivant les dogmes de notre noble prophète, sans accorder le pouvoir absolu à un seul, mais bien à des représentans choisis parmi les plus savants d'entre vous dans les droits des peuples, et présidés par le plus âgé et le plus éclairé; de cette manière vous améliorerez vos situations, vous assurerez vos fortunes, et vous jouirez d'une victoire céleste quand il existera parmi vous une seule et même opinion et une volonté bien décidée de vaincre ou de périr pour le bien de l'humanité et le bonheur de la patrie. Faites comme ont fait vos frères et voisins, les Anglais, les Français, les Espagnols, et les Portugais, sans faire cas de la conduite des lâches Napolitains, c'est-à-dire, que l'opinion n'étant pas chez eux généralement partagée, ni la valeur de cette noble liberté bien appréciée, ils se sont embar[r]assés au point de perdre une cause si précieuse. Mettez tou[t] votre espoir en Dieu, ayez l'énergie Mohammétane, armez-vous pour l'amour de Dieu, aidez-vous mutuellement pour fair[e] le bien général, n'aidez plus ces tyrans que Dieu vous a envoyé[s] pour vous punir de ce que vous tardiez si longtemps à secouer leur joug et à allumer le flambeau de ces grandes vérités (passage de l'alKoran); éveillez-vous, éveillez-vous mes chers compatriotes, ne perdez-vous pas un seul instant qui pourrait être employé à faire le bien? Vous attendez de Dieu la victoire—je pourrais dire qu'elle est déjà entre vos mains, il ne faut que le seul cri jeté par un ami de l'humanité qui a consacré sa vie à l'amour de Dieu; abolissez vos esclavages, rétablissez vos libertés selon la volonté qui nous en a été donné par le Ciel dans les divines paroles, "Au moment où vous jetterez le voile dont vous êtes couverts, vous verrez combien vous êtes nombreux et combien de personnes viendront à votre secours, l'épée en main et aussi soumises à vos ordres que redoutables à vos ennemis!"'

For the passage quoted from the Koran cf. sura iv, verse 59. In the margin, Bentham

165

a motto from the Coran, the most appropriate that can be found. Under this standard, should we find ourselves in sufficient force, we may march to the Metropolis, or whatever other spot may appear more proper to begin with.

This however supposes a provisional Constitution ready drawn up in such sort as to be capable of being proposed for acceptance: for to destroy a bad government, supposing it possible, without having a better in immediate readiness to substitute to it, would be to encrease the evil instead of remedying it. In case of success, whether it be with or without bloodshed, it will be my special care, as I am confident it would be that of both my Brothers, to preserve the Sovereign, property as well as person, as effectually as possible, from every harm that, consistently with the prosecution of the great public purpose, is not absolutely inevitable.

§3. *Weakness of Government—Facility afforded by it*

That you may see how clear the intended enterprize is of all such imputation as that of being a visionary one—a pursuit of ends without probable means—I find myself under the sad necessity of laying open before you the extreme weakness of the hand of government.

Throughout the whole dominion there may be perhaps about 6,000 or 7,000 men ordinarily employed with arms in their hands. But it is only in the collection of the taxes, under the orders of the several Agents of the Financier General, that they are employed. Such as they are, they are not with any tolerable degree of regularity enlisted, armed, paid or embodied, much less exercised and disciplined. They are individually employed as occasion calls: in each district, there may be any number of them today, and none at all tomorrow.

On the other hand, the rest of the people, as many as choose, are armed likewise: the Excisemen, as they may be called, armed each in his own way, and the rest of the people armed in that same way.

In no better assured condition is even the small number of men that serve the Sovereign himself for a body-guard, and constitute the only such guard he has. There may be from fifty to a hundred of them,

---

commented: 'Voici le texte à monarchie absolue: mais où et quel est le texte dont on pourroit se prévaloir en exhortant les peuples d'y appliquer le *frein* dont il s'agit?' The source of 'les divines paroles' has not been traced.

An uprising in Naples in 1820 had overturned the Bourbon monarchy and led to the establishment of a constitution based on the Spanish model of 1812, but the old regime had been restored by Austria in March 1821.

The marginal summary sheet is at UC xxiv. 60 (n.d. December 1822).

stationed in the palace, living upon the footing of menial servants: some free, some slaves. Numbers ever changing: some paid, some unpaid: of those who are paid, some pampered, some starving: the same individual sometimes gorged, sometimes for a length of time kept half-starved.

When for collection of tribute, for quelling an insurrection in the country itself, or for defence or offence against any foreign State or tribe, a body of troops is collected, and employed, by the Sovereign, a standard is set up. Thereupon, whatever be the inducement—personal attachment, hope of plunder, or fear—those who choose to take part in the expedition join it: and in this way to join in an expedition against the government would be just as easy as to join in an expedition in support of the government.

As to the disposition of the leading men, only as to what it was about 9 years ago can I speak from actual observation: but in that particular, I see no reason for anticipating a change, unless to the purpose in question it be a favorable one.

In such a state of things, how comes it, you may possibly feel disposed to ask—how comes it that down to this time no such enterprize has ever been set on foot? The answer is altogether simple. Of the virulence of the disease, as well as of its existence, every body has an acute perception. But of any thing in the shape of a remedy, it is altogether out of the question. To the application of a remedy, and that an apt one, a number of things would be necessary, no one of which is to be found amongst us any where: knowledge for instance of what *is* an apt remedy, skill to prepare it, union of the probity, skill and fortitude necessary to the apt application of it. As yet no such requisites have ever been to be found amongst us: nor is it likely there ever should without assistance, in the way of intellectual means at least, from more cultivated minds in Christendom.

To return to the *Mountain*. Whatever may be my present anticipations, of course no attempt of this sort should I make, in that quarter or any other, until by a visit made to it, I had by all manner of means satisfied myself that the disposition of men's minds was sufficiently favorable, and no effectual opposition likely to be made from other quarters.

§4. *Extension of the plan to the other States—its use and facility*

As to commencement, Tripoli is the only place for it: for, unhappily, no one can say how long it may be before any other of those countries has produced so much as a single individual, by whom, with or without aptitude for producing effect, any such enterprize will have been undertaken or so much as contemplated.

In Tripoli therefore it must commence if any where: but it follows not, by any means, that it must stop there.

If the change is good for any one State, so is it for every other: and in every State, the assurance of its preservation in that State will receive encrease from every instance in which it shall have been established in any other.

An Easterly course is not the course for it to take: at any rate in the first instance. In Egypt the arm of government is too strong: suffering from the depredations and oppressions of the despot, somewhat less intolerable: civil war, somewhat less frequent: the sense of universal insecurity, somewhat less acute.

1. Next to Tripoli on the West lies Tunis: to the North, the sea opposes its barrier: to the South, untraversable sands. In Tunis, the state of the government is not much less favorable. True it is, that in Tunis a vacancy in the throne is not quite so abundantly replete with evil as in Tripoli. In Tripoli, the calamity spreads over the whole country: in Tunis it is mostly confined to a handful of men, and those men foreigners. The lucrative situations are shared among a few hundred Turks: so therefore for the most part is the war. In Tripoli there are no Turks. It had been infested by them as Tunis is still: but about ten years ago, it was cleared of them by one stroke.[1]

Let us then suppose a Constitution established in Tripoli: with or without an hereditary head, a Representative body, with an Executive under it, as in your United States. The example of Tripoli would be no secret in the next neighbouring State. Supposing the impression made by it favorable, as soon as it appeared strong enough, and volunteers in sufficient number had been collected, then would be the time for a Tripolitan commander to advance to the frontiers of the dominion of Tunis, set up an appropriate standard on some convenient spot within the boundary line, and in all manner of ways circulate invitations for all who should feel inclined to adopt the Constitution of Tripoli, with or without modification, to cross the line and organize themselves. As to the Tripolitan army, only in case of necessity should it cross over to Tunis. Of what shall be regarded as constituting a sufficient warrant on the ground of necessity, no detailed description can, of course, here be given. Should the Constitution be established in Tunis, any such interference would be useless and mischievous. But, in case of contention, volunteers in support of such a Constitution as the one

---

[1] Turkish control had in effect been brought to an end by Ahmed Karamanli in 1711: see §1, p. 155n above, and 'Account of Tripoli', §2, pp. 4–5n above.

proposed might be permitted and even encouraged to go over. In case of failure, the dominion of Tripoli would of course be open to refugees, and lands should be allotted to them for their subsistence. On the occasion of the first elections, freedom of suffrage should in case of necessity be protected. But in that case, the difficulty would be to prevent its being violated on pretence of protecting it.

A manifesto should explain the views of the liberating government and serve as a security for its good behaviour. It should disclaim all accession of territory—in a word profit in any shape—at their expence to whom the aid was thus proffered. It should leave to their gratitude the reimbursement of any expence produced by the exertions made for their sake.

On that same occasion, should a federative Constitution, as in Your Union, be deemed mutually beneficial, as I suppose it would, it would say to them—'behold there an example of the felicity that results from it, and a model from which to work': the invitation to the people to join in this federative Union should accompany the invitation as above to form a Constitution for themselves. In that case, there seems not any great danger of their declining to adopt it. But in the event of their refusal, no endeavours should be used to force it upon them, nor need their acceptance of it be made a peremptory condition to the giving them such assistance as above. Apprized, as by that time they would be, of the unexampled felicity produced in Your Union by the admirable whole, there seems little danger of their being desirous to risk that felicity, by the defalcation of so manifestly useful a part. I say manifestly: for, so long as the Union exists, not to mention the encrease of defensive strength against every other power, and the lessening of the probability of offensive war against any other power, all possibility of mutual war would stand excluded.

2. Algiers. What has been said in regard to Tunis will apply with little variation to Algiers.

In Algiers, if on the part of the existing tyranny there would be a greater capacity for resistance, on the other hand, Tripoli and Tunis being united, there would be greater means for overcoming it. In Algiers there is, it is true, more territory and more population than in Tripoli and Tunis put together. Moreover, the quantity of the subject-matter of depredation extractible from the people in the shape of profits of government, and the actual number of the depredators, are, in a correspondent degree, greater: number of Turks with whom the plunderage is shared by the despot not much less than ten thousand: that being about the number habitually kept up by volunteer recruiting from Turkey, in the mode in use till of late in Tripoli, and still in Tunis. As to population, in the capital alone it is said to be not less than 100,000. As to disposable money, in Tripoli the Sovereign has no accumulated treasure. In Tunis as little. In Algiers, under every change, the constituted authorities have been in possession of a treasure to an unknown amount, the fruit of an accumulation begun as long ago as in the time of the Saracens and not supposed to have been ever interrupted by a total dissipation.

Spite of all this power of resistance, suppose the as yet unprecedented blessings of good government and general security already felt in Tunis as well as in Tripoli, and in Algiers the same course taken for offering to the people a participation in them, any effectual resistance on the part of the existing tyranny does not present itself as a result much to be apprehended. In the interval an institution which would have taken place of course in the Union between Tripoli and Tunis is an army, formed and kept up on Constitutional principles, but with all the advantage of European discipline. Think what could ten thousand Turkish banditti do, if, scattered in handfuls over the whole of that spatious territory, there were really any such large number—what could they do against so much as a tenth part of the number, disciplined in the European stile? But, instead of being less in number than the supposed undisciplined, the disciplined troops of the Union would of course be greater. For in neither dominion would the training have been confined to the capital: in both it would have had place in every district.

3. Morocco. On this country, it occurrs not that, on the present occasion, any separate consideration need be expended. What has been observed in relation to the three former States, may with little variation serve for this.

§5. *Assistance from U.S. Why and what desired*

Your disposition to afford the requested assistance will of course be influenced in no small degree by the correctness, as it appears to you, of our conceptions in relation to the value of such help, and the shapes in which we may reap the benefit of it.

Proof of probity of intentions on our part—saving in lives and property—certainty—promptitude—stability—instruction and guidance, the most apt that could be had from any quarter, as to the most probable means of securing those same beneficial results—as likewise in regard to constitutional legislation in case of success—all these advantages have presented themselves to my view as being among the natural fruits of the desired support and alliance.

First as to proof of probity of intentions. Nothing could be more inconsistent with your established character and so well-known policy, than either the making expensive conquests in a part of the globe so distant from yours, or the substituting one bad government to another—in a word the helping to set up any sort of government other than one as near as possible to your own, of the excellence of which you are so justly sensible. A manifesto on our part will make declaration of our views and intentions: a manifesto on your part, translated by us in Arabic and circulated along with our own, will make known yours.

Of the sincerity of your declarations in that behalf your Constitution and your history will afford to all parties the most conclusive evidence. It will be evidence to the natives: it will be evidence to foreign powers. The natives are the class of persons in whose instance the removal of suspicions is most material, because it is on their affections that the enterprize will depend at its very commencement. The antipathies produced by the differences in religion, government and manners might without explanation suffice to reduce very much, if not outweigh, the value of the assistance. But to give the requisite explanation on our part, in addition to that which you will give, will be our concern, and I have no fear as to the success of it.

Proof of goodness of intention on your part would be proof of the same quality on our part. Had we had any such view as that of setting up a despotism of our own in the room of that which we were hazarding our lives in the endeavour to remove, application to you for cooperation would be application for an obstacle, instead of a support. Yes, Sir, in *you* we should have so many witnesses in our favour: in *you* we should have so many sureties to the world for our good behaviour.

Saving in blood and property—certainty—promptitude—stability—all these advantages hang together, and will be effects of the same cause.

With a party holding out to you an inviting hand, a party in the estimation of Your own Agents sufficiently strong, or they would not accept the invitation—with such a party on your side and no power capable of opposing any effectual resistance any where, judge, Sir, with how small a force assistance, such as should with reference to all those several purposes be effectual, might be afforded by you. The smallest force could not be without its use: the greatest that could be allotted by Your Executive would render a service in exact proportion to its magnitude. If, as above, so far as depended upon force, the end could be compassed even without any such assistance, much more assuredly could it be compassed with the addition of such assistance, whatever it might be.

171

Lastly as to good guidance in legislation. Unspeakable would be the usefulness of a set of well-informed men, or even of a single well-informed man, from your country in this view. In him, besides an original *guide*, we should have an *oracle* to whom to apply in all cases of difficulty: an umpire, in all cases of difference of opinion.

In mentioning this, I mention a topic which will present a particular demand for consideration on your part. I mean to the end that in the selection made of naval and military men, fitness in relation to this civil purpose may be kept specially in view. Unhappily, under the most favorable circumstances, interchange of ideas on this subject, and with a degree of precision adequate to the purpose, can not but have no small difficulties to contend with. Your whole country contains not, I should suppose, at present so much as a single person who has any acquaintance with the Arabic: unless by accident, this or that person returned from a Consulate in North Africa. Acquaintance with the French language would afford an additional medium of communication, namely by means of such speakers of French in Tripoli who may at the same time be speakers of Arabic: an acquaintance with Italian and Spanish would in the same way be still more useful. As to English, our Sovereign has for a body Physician an Englishman, Dr. Dixon.[1] With the assistance of that gentleman, my brother Mohammed has for some time been studying English. I am inclined to hope he has made good progress: judging as I do from a letter I have before me written to him in that language: him I accordingly look to as an eventual translator and interpreter. Should any means of obtaining a little insight into the Arabic be procurable in your country—dictionary—grammar—vocabulary etc.—they should on this occasion be made the most of. Secrecy with regard to the particular purpose [will] be at the same time necessary: but of this presently.

With regard to the means of engaging extraordinary service, in this shape or any other, the difficulty you are placed under by your Constitution is not unknown to me. Your Executive has no money for secret services: not so much as promises can it make of money in the shape of gift or pension. But what it might I should suppose have to hold out, is hope—hope of eventual situations or commissions, such as in case of success would grow naturally out of the service.

---

[1] At UC xxiv. 37, Bentham noted: 'Dr Dixon has been Physician for about 7 years: appointed 2 months before Hassuna's departure. Age about 50: has a wife and children: teaches English to Hassuna's Brother Mahomet.' John Dickson, a Royal Navy Surgeon, had been in Tripoli since about 1814 (see Hanmer Warrington to Earl Bathurst, 29–30 July 1822, PRO FO 76/16, fo. 183): he was married to Elizabeth, née Dalzel (1793?–1862), who some years earlier, when living at Algiers, had written to the English press on the condition of British captives in the Barbary states.

§6. *Secrecy necessary—why—means of securing it*

The slightest hint will (I should suppose) suffice to remind you of the necessity of secrecy. Should any intimation of the design reach Tripoli before I am there, or before I am in readiness to give commencement to it, the colour in which it would present itself to the Sovereign could not but be in the highest degree unfavorable: it would have no one to explain it and present it in its true light; the destruction of the plan would be a certain consequence; that of the author little less so. The same would be the result should intimation of it be received by him, after my arrival, while I am occupied in any of those eventually succedaneous plans, which you have seen mentioned.

A consequence is—that such measures alone can be employed as can be taken and pursued without conveying to Tripoli any intimation of their object. I say to Tripoli: and, through the medium of the Consuls there, any hint in an American or European Newspaper might suffice to convey it to persons in Tripoli who would convey it to the Sovereign, each one thence with such colouring as suited his own views.

A further consequence, if I do not misconceive Your Constitution and its bearings upon this point, is—that the only measures which can be employed are such as it lies within the powers of Your Executive to employ without recourse to the Legislative.

True it is—that, subject to exceptions not worth mentioning to this purpose, the whole military force of your Country, by land and water, is at the command of your President: this I see in your Constitution.[1] But then in regard to supplies, of those which are already at his disposal, such part only as he would feel himself justified in applying to so extraordinary a service would be applicable to this purpose: nor without recourse to Congress could he make any addition to them. If then, in the opinion of Your Executive, it would not be advisable to take any step in the business, without the preliminary assurance of a greater force than could be employed in this service without application to Congress, here would be an insuperable bar to all hope of concurrence on your part. This however I can not but flatter myself will not be the case.

In the first place, such force, if any, as, without encrease of expence, you could eventually employ in the service—employ in

---

[1] See Art. II, §2 of the Constitution of the United States of America: 'The President shall be Commander in Chief of the Army and Navy of the United States, and of the Militia of the several States, when called into the actual Service of the United States. . . .'

action—or, though it were but in *shew*—might as before observed, how small so ever it were, be better than nothing.

In the next place, if so it be that you have a force already in the Mediterranean, or destined for the Mediterranean, this is already the thing needful: nothing is wanting but orders for the eventual application of it to this purpose.

In the third place, if, having at command a force over and above what would otherwise be employed in the Mediterranean service in general, you could employ it on condition of finding an ostensible reason capable of covering the true one, it will rest for your consideration whether the idea of pursuing the design of making acquisition of a port, whether from Spain by purchase or from the Greeks in return for support, or preserving your Mediterranean trade from annoyance by Greeks, Turks, and now French, Spaniards, Portugueze, etc., since the declaration of this new war,[1] might not be made to answer the purpose.

§7. *United States—their expected inducements for concurrence*

As to the considerations by which, on this occasion, determination may be given to the course to be taken on the part of Your Executive, in respect of acceptance or rejection, to have any thing like full knowledge of them, as well as to give them any thing like their due weight, belongs it is true to yourselves alone: yet neither does it seem to me altogether impossible but that in this or that particular instance it may happen to me to place this or that consideration in a point of view in which it might not otherwise have presented itself. At any rate, any thing in this way may assist in preserving this proposal from the imputation of being an altogether inconsiderate one, destitute upon the face of it of all claim to attention, and of all chance of obtaining its object.

1. In the first place comes *Security against North African Piracy*. From no other source could any thing like an entire, or in perpetuity so much as a partial, security for you against this plague be derived to you. To day the States in question leave you all of them unmolested, but tomorrow the molestation may by any or all of them be renewed. To day, you have treaties with them: but tomorrow those treaties may, any or all of them, be formally broken off or violated. Under governments such as ours, in a state of society and manners such as ours, the whole wisdom of years may at any time be set at nought, by

---

[1] Presumably that between Spain and Algiers referred to in §7, pp. 175–6 below.

the caprice or ungrounded passion of the moment: passion, Sir, grounded on false information—or even destitute of all ground. Upon this topic I see no need of enlarging. Though on your minds in your situation, the idea of this irritability with its consequences can not be so strongly impressed by observation from a distance as on ours it is by sad and continual experience, it is not without some assurance that I expect to find it sufficiently so for the purpose.

True it is that on your part no such security can be compleat unless and untill the plan has been accomplished in regard to all the States in question: more particularly in regard to *Algiers*, that being beyond comparison the most formidable. But the plan, you see, embraces them all, and every thing must have its beginning. Neither, were it to stop at Tripoli, would a perpetual security from the hostility of that State be at all times a matter of indifference to you. At any rate it was not so in the year 1804.[1]

It was but t'other day, and while some part of this letter was writing, that an article speaking of a rupture of Algiers with Spain appeared in the English papers. Whether that which is the lot of Spain one day may not be yours another day, it is for you to judge. The article is in the following words—

Morning Chronicle 28 Jany. 1823:[2]

'The Governor of Minorca notified to the Town Council of Port Mahon, on the 30th November, that the Dutch Consul at Algiers had been apprised, by the Dey's Minister of Marine, that a rupture had taken place between his Highness and Spain, and that, if the DEY'S corsairs should go to sea, they would capture whatever Spanish vessels they might chance to fall in with. On the 22d ult., the date of the latest advices from Algiers, there were fitting for sea at that port one vessel of 58 guns, one of 50, one of 36; an 18 gun brig, and two schooners.'

Thus far the Morning Chronicle. What the cause of this rupture may have been I can not take upon me to say. My surprize would not indeed be great were I to learn that the bringing of it about has been one of the modes in which the Holy Alliance has been making proof of its regard for the interest and happiness of the Spanish Nation:[3] and in that case the cause would have no immediate application to your case. But, so long as the cause is unknown, may not your State, as well as

---

[1] An allusion to the war of 1801–5 between the United States and Tripoli.

[2] The report appeared in the *Morning Chronicle* of 27 January 1823. The text here is reproduced from the original, rather than from the copy made for Bentham.

[3] The dispute concerned a long-standing debt which Algiers claimed from Spain. In June 1822 a combined Spanish and Dutch squadron had brought a message from the Spanish government to the Dey of Algiers demanding an equitable settlement, but upon receiving an unsatisfactory reply the Spanish had withdrawn their Consul.

every other, be included in the virtual menace to which it gives utterance?

2. In the next place comes the having a port in the Mediterranean for refuge: refuge against bad weather and naval accidents. This convenience has long been among the universally known objects of your desires and as yet fruitless endeavours. Very lately you have been trying to obtain it from Spain: so at least I have heard from more than one authentic source. Even from Tripoli, so long ago as the year 1804 or thereabouts, you took measures, and those strong ones, for obtaining it. What you then got was found not to answer the purpose, and you abandoned it.[1] Neither indeed, I have heard it said, would the port of Tripoli itself. But if not, might not some spot that would answer your purpose be found on some other part of the Coast? Is the negative sufficiently ascertained by any such surveys as you have made? If so, might not the coast of Tunis, or that of Algiers? In these cases it is true, after the regeneration of Tripoli, you would have to wait for that of those two States respectively.

As to Spain, supposing you to succeed in any negotiation with that State, there would be in the first place the expence of purchase, in the next place not unprobably the whole expence of construction: I mean as applied to fortifications and docks: and this, over and above the expence of such a fleet as you might think fit to send to take possession. In our case, the mere expence of such a fleet as that might not improbably suffice. If so, then the expence of purchase would be the whole of it saved: and in the article of construction, expence, to a greater or less amount, might not improbably be saved by such contribution as for the common benefit it might be in our power as well as inclination to afford.

Since this letter was begun, turning to a book published here within these few months, under the title of 'Narrative of an Expedition from Tripoli in Barbary, to the Western frontier of Egypt, in 1817, by the Bey of Tripoli; in Letters to Dr. Viviani of Genoa, by Paolo Della Cella M.D. . . . translated from the Italian, by Anthony Aufrere Esq.', (it is the one from which you will have seen a passage quoted in § 1 of this)[2] on page 177 I find these words—'The United States of America were at one period desirous of forming an establishment at Derna, which they offered to purchase of the Pacha of Tripoli; but their offer being

---

[1] An American expedition led by William Eaton (1764–1811), and supported by the deposed Ahmed, brother of Yusef Pasha, had marched from Egypt and seized the town of Derna on 27 April 1805. Since the main purpose was not to acquire a port but to secure the release of the crew of the *Philadelphia* (see § 1, p. 161n above), Derna was abandoned on the conclusion of peace in June 1805.

[2] See pp. 156–7n above. Except where otherwise noted, the text here is reproduced from the original, rather than from the copy made for Bentham.

rejected, and some misunderstanding having taken place upon other grounds, they forcibly seized it. Not long afterwards, however, from what motives I could not learn, they suddenly desisted from their enterprize and quitted the place, leaving behind them a battery with six pieces of cannon, and a water-mill which is still in use, and gives rise to much stupid wonder in such of our barbarians as happen to approach it.

'The want of a good harbour' (continues he) 'is probably the reason why no foreign power, desirous of having a stable footing in that part of the Mediterranean, has established itself at Derna; for besides that this bay offers no convenient or secure asylum for shipping, the road itself is intersected by sharp and rocky calcareous strata which project far into it under the water, and from their cutting or tearing the cables that rub against them, are by mariners denominated saws. But *towards the point of Cape Bon-Andrea, the sea forms a capacious bay where even large vessels may ride in safety during blowing weather.*'[1] Thus far the scientific traveller, by whom the spot was visited.

As to what may be termed *sentimental* inducements, it belongs not to me to preach to you upon any such texts. I mean the service you would render to all other States—the obligations you would confer on them—the gratitude of the minor States—the envy of the domineering ones—the confidence they would all of them see fresh reason to repose in your declarations—supposing them in this instance fulfilled by practice—the disinterestedness, in the only rational sense of the word, the generosity and true wisdom displayed by you—the universal admiration of which this constellation of merits would render you the objects—the blaze of glory with which you would be covered—the testimony which you would thus give to all nations of the matchless excellence of the only government which has ever yet had for its object, in deed as well as in profession, the greatest happiness of the greatest number.

§8. *Preliminary steps proposed to be taken by the U.S. Executive in case of concurrence*

Under this head what I have to propose is as follows—

1. That in case of your not deeming it fit to make communication of this address to Your Cabinet, you would be pleased to signify as much to me by the earliest opportunity by letters addressed as hereinafter mentioned.

---

[1] The italics are Bentham's, and do not appear in the original.

2. That, in case of your laying it before Your Cabinet, should the determination be in the negative, you would be pleased to give me information in like manner.

3. That in the event of their determination to enter into any measures in consequence of this proposal, you would be pleased to inform me[1] what it is, and in what events, and on what conditions, that they regard themselves as able and feel disposed to do, in furtherance of the design proposed.

4. That thereupon, with as much dispatch as may be, you would be pleased to give instruction to Your Consul or some other person at Tripoli to enter into a confidential and secret intercourse on this subject with me, and in case of my absence with any such other person or persons as in that case I shall have appointed: of which appointment notice shall accordingly have been given on my part to Your Consul or other such Agent.

5. That, in consideration of the uncertainty which, for some time, may attach upon the place of my residence, that is to say whether at the point of time in question I shall be in London or in Tripoli, or on my passage by sea or land between these two places,—you would be pleased to give the like instructions to Your Minister or some other Agent of yours in London to enter into the like communication with me, or in my absence with Mr. Jeremy Bentham, or in case of his decease with any person or persons whom for this purpose he shall have appointed: which person or persons may be known by application made to his Executors. It is with Mr. Bentham, or such his nominee, that when at Tripoli, and when in my way between Tripoli and London, I shall correspond, giving them a detailed account of my proceedings.

6. That if, at the time of such concurrence on your part as above, there be already a maritime force belonging to the United States cruizing in the neighbourhood of Tripoli, orders be sent to all commanders thereof, then and thenceforward until further order, to execute any such instructions as shall have been given to them in relation to this object, by Consul of the United States or such Your Agent as above.

7. That, in case of the setting up of the standard of liberty by myself or any of the constituted authorities of the State in prosecution of the plan hereinmentioned, should support to the enterprize be, in any shape, given by your armed force or any part thereof, instruction be given to Your Consul and the Commanders of Your forces to make known in the most effectual manner by proper manifestos and otherwise, that they will not at any time take permanent possession of the

---

[1] This word does not appear in Bentham's draft, but has been supplied by the copyist: see the Editorial Introduction, p. xxxii above.

country or (with such exceptions, if any, and on such conditions as shall be mentioned) any part of it, nor interfere by force or menace, direct or indirect, in the election of any representatives which it may please the people to choose, and that if necessary they will maintain the perfect freedom of all such elections to the utmost of their power, and that, with the exception of what in case of need would be done by any man rather than perish, no violence will be offered to the person or property of any individual by these auxiliaries other than what may be indispensably necessary for the support of the cause for which their assistance is called in. To an assurance to this effect I, and any party operating under my direction, in prosecution of the plan hereinabove explained, will give concurrence, certifying to the people our persuasion that the promise will be punctually observed.

8. That in consideration of the interruption or even utter miscarriage that might be the consequence of death or incapacity on the part of any such your first appointed Agent, as above, before his place could be supplied from Washington, provision be made of a sufficient number of Agents at Tripoli to follow one another in eventual succession: in which case for further security against eventual incapacity (considering the destruction which as above would be the natural consequence of any violation of secrecy antecedently to the open commencement of the enterprize, and that no person would be appointed by you for whom there were any apprehension on the score of probity) you will be pleased to judge whether it might not be of use that the several instruments by which appointment were respectively made of the several successive Agents were lodged in my hands or those of any substitute of mine in Tripoli, as above.

9. That with a view to the augmenting the number of persons qualified to afford us assistance or advice in relation to the formation of a Constitution, and at the same time to communicate information in regard to those useful branches of art and science which are as yet unknown to us, you would be pleased to afford such encouragement as it may lie in your way to afford to competent individuals to visit the several Barbary States in the character of Travellers, for the information of your own country and the rest of the world, and eventually of *Lecturers* in the several branches of useful art and science belonging to the department of physic—and in particular Natural Philosophy, Natural History, and the several branches on which the Medical art is dependent—for the instruction of our part of the world. In Tripoli, namely at the Universities, one or both of them, I can take upon me to promise them Auditors, as likewise purchasers at a profit for any moderately-priced apparatuses of which they had shewn the use.

1. In Tripoli, persons of the above description may be assured of a

most cordial and useful reception from me, if I am there at the time, and if not from my whole family.

2. In Tunis, by means of Letters from myself to persons of my acquaintance there, if I am in Tripoli at the time, and at any rate from my father, on the supposition of their being known to him at Tripoli.

3. In Algiers, from Khoja abovementioned, who, by means of his Son, will understand any thing you write to him in English. Mr. Bentham will I believe give you some particulars relative to this subject:[1] he and I have had frequent conferences on it: every thing he says to you on it you may consider as coming from me. A recommendation to Khoja at Algiers may perhaps be eventually of use, because it may happen that means of passage to Algiers may present themselves when there are none to Tripoli. Khoja (I have perhaps already mentioned) has the same affections and desires as myself: but of the particular design in question communication has not been made to him. Though there is nothing of magnificence in his establishment, his name and abode are known to every body in the town of Algiers. A letter directed to him in Arabic, or if in English inclosed in one to your Consul, would therefore find its way to him without difficulty.

---

[1] See 'Bentham to Adams', pp. 150–2 above.

GREECE: PRINCIPLES OF LEGISLATION AS TO CONSTITUTIONAL LAW[1]

---

[1] Further material on a similar theme, carrying the marginal sub-heading 'Fundamental Principles', is at UC xxi. 230–3 (12 February 1823).

§ 1. *Self-regard—its predominance universal and necessary*

To find the provisional Grecian Constitution in so high a degree conformable to the principle of the greatest happiness of the greatest
number has been matter of considerable and no less agreable surprize
to me.

In the examination of it a truth which should never for a single
moment be lost sight of is the universal prevalence and predominance
of the propensity to self-preference in human nature.

So far from this universality being matter of doubt, it will on consideration be found that the existence of it is indispensably essential to
the existence of the species: and that supposing it taken away the
species would within a few months, not to say weeks, vanish from the
face of the earth.

If this be correct, so far then from being a subject of well-grounded
denial, it is not so much as the subject of well-grounded regret, unless
the existence of the species were itself a subject of well-grounded
regret.

It is by its excess therefore and not by its existence that by this self-
preference harm is done.

Included in this self-preference is a propensity, and this a constant
one, on the part of each individual to sacrifice to his own self-
regarding interests all other interests put together.

In the case of a public functionary this sacrifice may without
impropriety receive for shortness the denomination of the *sinister
sacrifice*.

In the breast of every man considered with reference to any and
every other there are three sorts of affections: 1. self-regard: 2. social
sympathy: 3. antisocial antipathy. Self-regard, desire of his own
happiness, is in constant exercise: sympathetic regard, regard for the
happiness [of others], in frequent but less constant exercise: antipathetic regard—regard for the unhappiness of others—in still less
frequent exercise.

In the ordinary course of life, the influence of self-regard is stronger
and more efficient than that of those two extra-regarding affections
put together.

In self-regard is included the desire of possessing, in a quantity
altogether unlimited, the several external instruments of human
felicity, which thence may be also stiled the *objects of general desire*—
and by certain religionists have been designated by the appellation of
the good things of this world.

183

These are: 1. the matter of wealth in its several shapes: 2. power in its several shapes: and to these under most governments have been added 3. factitious dignity in its several shapes.

With the exception of such portions of wealth as have been the immediate fruits [of] his own labour, or of the labour of others made over to him freely, in exchange for the like fruits in other shapes, or gratuitously, no human being can obtain any portion of the matter of wealth but at the expence of all others, and more particularly at the expence of the last proprietors.

Considered in this point of view, every human being has in every other a possible enemy.

On the other hand, the quantity which by any single exertions of his own a man is able to obtain of these same instruments is small indeed compared with what it is in his power to obtain by the help of the exertions of others behaving towards him in a state of union.

Considered in this view, every human being has in every other a possible friend and helpmate.

In mankind in general, desire of acquiring fresh and fresh addition to the stock a man has of the external instruments of felicity grows stronger and stronger as the quantity of those that appear to him within his reach is greater and greater.

Of the aggregate stock of the external instruments of felicity in the possession of the political community in question, the quantity which its ruling functionaries taken in the aggregate have within their reach is in a manner unlimited: the ardency of their desire to make the utmost possible addition to that portion of the stock which they respectively possess as their own property to their own use is in like manner unlimited.

At the time and on the occasion of its formation every Constitution taken in the sense here in question has two great difficulties to contend with, extrinsic and intrinsic: self-regarding affection on the part of other political communities, and the like affection on the part of its own functionaries.

To the existence and force of the danger impending from without the members of the new Community never fail to be in an adequate degree sensible: they are accordingly [. . . ?] and constantly upon their guard against it.

But of the danger impending from within never in any instance have they yet [been], nor till at the end of a long course of sad experience are ever like to be, in any thing approaching to an adequate degree sensible.

§ 2. *Counter-assurance—its universality*

In every political community, old as well as new, this danger is not merely a danger impending, but an evil constantly operating and constantly extending, or at least striving to extend, itself.

From the ruling few the subject many are continually receiving the assurance that by each the felicity of all the others is an object pursued to the exclusion of, or at the least in preference to, his own.

In this assurance if in any instance there has been a particle of truth, the instances are so rare that for the purpose of any practical conclusion, and practical arrangement to be taken in consequence, they may be laid out of the account altogether, and without any evil consequence.

In the breasts of ruling functionaries in general the proportion between the strength [of] self-regarding affection and that [of] social affection which has for its object the aggregate body of the community in question is naturally subjected to variation by divers circumstances.

No new State has ever yet been formed but at a time of general danger and proportionate excitation. The time during which this danger is at the highest is the time at which the felicity of each individual member, whether in the situation of ruling functionary or only in that of subject citizen, is in the highest degree dependent on that of the whole: his property, his power, his personal liberty, his very life, he feels to be [in] a state of constant and immediate dependence upon the existence and power of the whole.

§ 3. *Self-sacrifice—how far exemplified*

In this state of things it is, if in any, that he feels really disposed to make sacrifices to any amount over and above those which he can not help making at the expence of his own particular interest to the universal interest: and in this state of things there are no bounds to the sacrifices of this kind which, in a certain state of excitation, this or that man may not feel really disposed to make. In the sacrifice of life, the sacrifice of the instruments of felicity all of them together is included: and of the disposition to make this all-comprehensive sacrifice instances are not altogether wanting, as the instances scattered as they are over the pages of history in no inconsiderable abundance sufficiently shew.

Having at this or that critical moment had within his own breast

185

experience of the actual propensity to this heroic sacrifice, the wonder would not be great, if, little as men are in the habit of any thing like an impartial scrutiny into the state and contents of their own minds, a man should here and there have been in existence by whom the assertion of a constant habit of preferring on every occasion, in case of competition, and to the extent of such competition, the universal interest to his own particular and self-regarding interest has been believed to be true.

Be this as it may, an assertion [of][1] this sort either explicit or implied is on all occasions to be found in the discourse, oral and written, of ruling functionaries of all classes under governments of all kinds: and in no instance is it to be found more decided and more vehement than in those in which, as demonstrated by actual conduct, it has been furthest from being true, and on the part of those by whom it has been thus allowed accompanied with the most perfect consciousness of its being compleatly false.

On the other hand such is the blindness and power of self-partiality that while occupied in the establishment of arrangements the most decidedly adverse to the universal interest and the most decidedly favorable to his own particular interest, nothing is more common than for a man to have succeeded, and with very little difficulty, in impregnating himself with the persuasion that the arrangement by which, by the supposition, a sacrifice has been made of the universal interest to such his particular interest has in fact been beneficial to the universal interest: for in this case the effect of the self-partiality will be to keep the mind steadily turned toward all arguments which tend to establish in it that convenient persuasion, and as steadily turned away from those of which the tendency is to shake it.

§4. *Sinister sacrifice—its modes*

The principal shapes in which sacrifice is made of the universal interest to the particular interest of ruling functionaries taken in the aggregate are as follows:

1. Attaching respectively to the most influential situations masses of power over and above what the universal interest necessitates. Say, viz. in the first place, creation of coercive power, in integrality, or in fractional parts, in excess. Note that all power is established at the expence of all individuals subject to it.

2. Attaching to these same situations masses of pecuniary emolu-

---

[1] MS 'to'.

186

ment in excess. Note that all pecuniary emolument bestowed on functionaries is bestowed at the expence of all who are made contributors to it.

3. Attaching to these same situations masses of factitious dignity. It will be seen presently that all factitious dignity is so much in excess.[1] Factitious dignity is bestowed at the expence of all who are not invested with it. And every fresh mass of factitious dignity is bestowed at the expence of all those who are already invested with it as well as of all those who are not invested with it.

For the bestowal of factitious dignity where any such condescension is manifested as the assigning of an apparent reason or pretence for it, the pretence consists in its being given in reward for meritorious service.

But, in so far as with relation to service in the shape in question dignity is a reward apt in shape, natural dignity, without any factitious assistance or embellishment other than that which consists in publicity, is a sufficient, rightly-seated and in comparison of all others accurately well-proportioned reward: whereas no factitious dignity, it being in each rank the same thing for all who are invested with it, no factitious dignity can ever, unless by mere accident, bear any thing like a correct proportion to service: and in practice may to any amount be seen to be conferred in such sort as to be altogether mis-seated: bestowed upon those by whom no service to the universal interest has ever been or so much as pretended to have been rendered, rendered in any shape: in such sort as to be, in respect of justice, on a footing exactly corresponding to punishment when inflicted on him by whom no offence has in any shape been committed.

4. Attaching to these same situations power of patronage in excess. Power of patronage is power of placing men in situations to which power of the coercive kind, or pecuniary emolument, or factitious dignity, or other power of patronage, severally or conjunctly, are attached. In this way, by one and the same situation, desire on the part of two different functionaries is excited and gratified: the functionary located and the functionary locating: the *protégé* and the *patron*.

Correspondent to every mass of effective power as above is a mass of obstructive, which if and when the obstruction proves effectual is preventive, power.

A mass of preventive power has of late years been stiled in one

---

[1] For a discussion of factitious dignity see 'Economy as applied to Office', Ch. 7, and 'Constitutional Code Rationale', Ch. 6, in *First Principles preparatory to Constitutional Code* (*CW*), pp. 48–52 and pp. 299–324 respectively.

word a *Veto*.[a] A power of suspension has the effect of a veto while it lasts: it may be stiled a *suspensive veto*.

A power of obstruction—a power to obstruct—has, in so far as it has any distinctly perceptible effect, the effect of a suspensive Veto: and by every instance of the exercise of a suspensive Veto the chance[?] of its proving an effective Veto is produced. For the production of this effect, the accident of intervening death is in the instance of every individual of itself sufficient.

5. Establishing in excessive number official situations in cases where the utility of the functions, thence of the offices, is unquestionable. Establishing needless Offices.

Examples. Keeping up a Stipendiary Land Military force in magnitude, that is to say in respect of number of men, greater than what is needful. So a ditto Naval force.

6. Employing a number of functionaries in the exercise of a function which would be exercised with equal or superior aptitude by a single individual. An arrangement of this sort may be termed *fractionalizing* an office. This arrangement has place wherever a function that might as well be exercised by an individual is committed to what in English is called a Board: in French, *un Bureau* or *un Conseil*. To the power of any single individual by whom a function of the same nature is exercised without the adjunction of any other, the power exercised by a member of such a board is as the fraction having for its denominator the number of the individuals of which the board is composed is to an integer. Nine Taylors, according to a vulgar English proverb more remarkable for addition than for truth, make a man: or thus, a Taylor is the ninth part of a man. With much more reason might this be predicated of the Members of those Boards by which some of the functions belonging to the Executive department are exercised: of this number are the Treasury Board, the Admiralty Board, the India Board, the Board of Trade. The vulgar proverb had its origin in vulgar error: it supposed men of that occupation inferior in courage to men of other occupations. In the case of the political boards the notion of deficiency in manhood has no small portion of truth in it: namely in so far as the elements [of] appropriate aptitude, moral and intellectual and active, are considered as so many elements of manhood. When the Presiding Member is laid out of the question, in the case of the Member of the Treasury Board not much injustice is done to him if he is set down as the $\frac{1}{5}$th. part of a man, of the Admiralty Board as $\frac{1}{6}$th., of

---

[a] From the Roman Verb in the active mood, present tense, first person singular, *Veto*, I forbid.

the India Board as $\frac{1}{7}$th., of the Board of Trade as $\frac{1}{10}$th., of the Ordnance Board as $\frac{1}{5}$.[1]

A power of obstruction—a mass of obstructive power—may be created with or without disguise: with or without a mask.

A power of obstruction is created in every instance in which to the exercise of any mass of effective power the concurrence of a certain individual or of an individual in this or that situation is rendered necessary.

It may be created with a disguise on it or without a disguise on it: with a mask on it, or without a mask. It is created without a mask where it is conferred on express terms. There are divers forms in which it may be created with a mask. An example is where to the validity of a public document the signature of a certain individual, or of an individual in a certain situation, is upon examination of the terms of the arrangement found to be necessary.

Whether in this mode any effective power of obstruction be conferred, and, if conferred, the degree and effective force of this power, will depend on the possession or non-possession of power in another shape by the individual whose signature is thus rendered necessary. For example on the part of the Monarch in a Monarchy it has the effect of an integral Veto: on the part of a person officiating only in the character of an arbitrarily displaceable Clerk or Scribe to this or that high functionary or body of functionaries it conferrs no effective power on the displaceable Clerk: the person or persons on whom it conferrs an effective power are he or they to whom it belongs to displace the Clerk if they so please.

Of an obstructive power in disguise in the Constitution in question, various instances will be pointed out. They are presented by the several articles 24, [25],[2] 30, 31, 36, 46, 54, 56, 57.[3]

In the whole list of external instruments of felicity there is not one that is not employable and employed as an instrument for the acquisi-

---

[1] Apart from the Ordnance Board, Bentham's figures are mistaken. At the time Bentham was writing, there were seven Commissioners of the Treasury (though their number was soon to be reduced to six) and five Commissioners of the Admiralty; the Board of Commissioners for the Affairs of India, known as the Board of Control, consisted of an indefinite number of Privy Councillors and two other persons appointed at the discretion of the Crown—it had about a dozen members, though its business had effectively been placed under the supervision of the President long before the meetings of the Commissioners had been formally abolished in 1816; the Committee of the Privy Council for Trade and Plantations, known as the Board of Trade, had a substantial number of *ex officio* and specially nominated members, but from the early nineteenth century the Board was usually only attended by the President and Vice-President; the Ordnance Board was presided over by the Master General and had five other members.

[2] MS '27'.

[3] For a discussion of obstructive power in the Greek Constitution see 'Observations', pp. 236–9 below.

tion of all the others. With money in hand a man acquires power: with power, money: where the community is saddled with the burthen of factitious dignity, with money or power in hand, factitious dignity: and with factitious dignity, either of these others.

No mass of obstructive power so inconsiderable but by means of it he may acquire money or power in any other shape. Give me this place or so much money and I sign my name, otherwise not. Thus a controul is formed: and by conditions annexed to the exercise or non-exercise of the function of applying this signature, effective power in any shape may be obtained.

In the school of Corruption—of misrule operating by corruption—men become expert in the *practice* of all these operations. But to practice them is one thing, to find names for them and bring to view their several natures and their effects in relation to each other is a very different thing. This is called theory: and is feared, an object of disgust and hatred—disgust on account of the labour requisite for the comprehending it: terror on account of the light it throws on the corrupt and sinister practice: practice which is the more and more likely to miss its ends if the more clearly the true nature and effect of it is understood.

JEREMY BENTHAM TO GREEK LEGISLATORS[1]

---

[1] A further sequence of material which Bentham composed under this heading, but which he seems to have excluded when finally organizing the text, is at UC xxi. 309, 304–8, 196–7 (22–3 February 1823). Related fragments are at UC xxi. 198 (22 February 1823) and xxi. 199 (25 February 1823).

Regenerative Legislators of Greece,

You enter upon your career under the most auspicious circumstances. Nothing to match them is to be found in history. Nothing to match them is to be found in present times. Obstacles which in other nations set up a bar to good government, and that bar an insuperable one, have no place in your case. You are not cursed with Kings. You are not cursed with Nobles. Your minds are not under the tyranny [of] Priests. Your minds are not under the tyranny of Lawyers.

Legislators! It is now more than five and fifty years since he [who] now addresses you first devoted himself to the service of mankind. He has served faithfully: he has toiled hard: he has had his sufferings: and he has not gone unrewarded! The grave is never out of his sight: nor is his cheerfulness ever diminished by it: he is contented with his lot: he has no complaint to make.

The sort of attention which, in his endeavour to serve you, he must call for at your hands, others in places correspondent to yours have given to him before.

Never is the day labourer, never is the helpless pauper, an object of contempt to me: I can not say the same thing of the purse-proud aristocrat: I can not say the same thing of the ancestry-proud aristocrat: I can not say the same thing of the official bloodsucker: I can not say the same thing of the man covered with the tokens of factitious honor: least of all can I say the same of a King. When a Monarch has thought to corrupt me and delude me, to degrade me to a level with the Castlereaghs, the Metternichs, the Hardenbergs and the Gentzs,[1] you may see at any time what he has got by it.

For the giving you honest advice, my situation is at the same time as favorable as it is possible to imagine, so favorable that a more favorable one can not be so much as imagined.

With no one of you all have I ever, either by word of mouth or by letter, directly or through the medium of any common friend or acquaintance, had any sort of intercourse: to me not one of you is or ever has been a source either of fear or hope.

Whatsoever the source of this advice be thought or supposed to be, I claim not, on the score of the whole or any part of it, any the least particle of praise. No self-sacrifice in any shape has the giving of it

[1] Robert Stewart (1769–1822), second Marquis of Londonderry, styled Viscount Castlereagh 1796–1821, British Foreign Secretary 1812–22, Clemens Wenzel Lothar Metternich-Winneburg (1773–1859), Austrian Minister of Foreign Affairs 1809–48, Karl August von Hardenberg (1750–1822), Prussian Chancellor 1810–22, and Friedrich von Gentz (1764–1832), publicist and confidante of Metternich, were major figures in European diplomacy in the years following the conclusion of the Napoleonic wars.

required at my hands. On many among you the object of it and effect of it, if it has any, may be to call for self-sacrifice, for sacrifice of personal interest to public, to an amount which lies not within the field of any calculation I can make: nothing can be more easy than to make a call upon others for such sacrifices: for Kings, nothing more difficult than to obey it.

After such observations as it here lies in my way to make—on human nature taken in the aggregate—and on human nature placed in political situations in particular, my expectation of producing by this part of my advice any effect whatsoever—my expectation of seeing a single needless or useless office struck off, or so much as a single atom of superfluous pay from any office, useful or useless, struck off—can not be very sanguine. But to me it belongs to offer the advice, to others, if it be good advice, to follow it.

Of the advice which I shall take the liberty of submitting to you, [two][1] distinguishable sets of observations will be seen to be the sources.

1. Observations made on human nature in general, on human beings in every situation in life, in all situations taken indis-criminately.

2. Observations made on the conduct of men, and particularly men in ruling and other influential situations, under such Constitutions as have had for their object or end in view the greatest happiness of the greatest number.

Grounding myself on these observations, the first piece of advice which I shall take the liberty of submitting to you is—not to suffer yourselves to be turned aside from any thing that follows by the observation that not the least atom of flattery in any shape is offered to you or any of you:

that the inducements by which on each occasion I expect to find your practice determined are no other than those self-regarding ones by which, with few or no exceptions, it has seemed to me that human conduct has in all places and at all times been determined:

that as I do not in the instance of any public man in any public situation look for willing self-sacrifice in any shape, so neither can I look for any such thing in your situation in the instance of you or any of you:

that accordingly I look not on any occasion for any such stile of con-duct as can with any propriety be termed disinterested, produced by any other cause than a man's own conception of what at the moment of action is in the highest degree conducive to his own interest:

that when in this or that situation a sacrifice has been thought or

---

[1] MS 'three'.

said to have been made by a man in this shape—a sacrifice of his own interest—the sacrifice has been nothing more than a sacrifice of his interest in one shape to his interest in another, the sacrifice of what at the moment has been in his eyes a lesser to what has been in his eyes at that same moment his greater interest: the sacrifice for example of pecuniary interest to reputation: of a certain sum of money to such a quantity of general good opinion and good will and good offices at the hands of other men as according to his calculation would be worth more.

You stand clear from the temptation afforded by distant dependencies: you stand exempt from the danger of splitting upon that rock. You stand out of the danger of being driven into enmity by the correspondent appetite.

In this respect you have the advantage over Spain, Portugal, England, France, and the Netherlands: in particular over Spain and Portugal.

Were but one individual to manifest in the management of his own concerns any such degree of unsoundness of mind, any such symptoms of mental derangement, as are seen manifested by the rulers of both those nations in the management of those affairs of others as have been committed to their charge, what tolerably honest and intelligent Judge is there that would pause for a single moment before he took the so flagrantly abused power out of such palpably unapt hands: injustice the most palpable, inconsistency the most flagrant, impossibility of success in the mad and mischievous enterprize most compleat!

In the three other cases the impossibility of good government, the injuriousness of the practice to the inhabitants of both countries— that which is the seat of nothing but subjection—and that which is the seat of government, that is of those by which the yoke is kept upon the necks of their distant and unknown brethren—is little less flagrant: but the mischief from the practice is not as near so vast: nothing that can be spoken of as ruinous is included in it. Both countries are plundered and oppressed that a few in the domineering country may be enriched: but in neither country are the inhabitants exposed to the danger of a foreign yoke—or of a domestic tyranny— so galling as is to be seen in so many other countries.

Should it happen to any one among you to stand up, to make profession and protestation of love to the country, probity and disinter[este]dness, in a word virtue in any shape, and on the ground of any such strings of word[s] uttered by him lay claim to public confidence in any shape more than would be bestowed upon the meanest citizen, or even the most notorious criminal, let the manner in which such waste of words is received by you be such as shall suffice to deter him and others from repeating any such experiment upon your credulity.

Protestations to any such effect are made with just as much facility by those in whose instance they are furthest from, as by those in whose instance they are nearest to, the truth.

You have not for your affliction any such unpunishable Depredator General, Oppressor General, Corrupter General, Deluder General, God upon earth, as that to which we cringe under by the name of Monarch—as in Germany, Italy, Russia, France, Denmark, the Netherlands, Sweden, Spain, Portugal and England. Standing on this pinnacle, you may look down with pity.

You have no Aristocratical cast of men to deal by you as the Helots were dealt with by the Spartans: men who, for the tyranny they experience at the hands of the despot, find a compensation in that which they concurr with him in exercising over their fellow slaves.

You are not inflicted with the plague of priests. For though a class of men who under that name pretend to that knowledge of the Almighty which it is not given to man to possess, yet you know them too well to suffer them to tyrannize over you: and ere long you will learn from the example of the Anglo-American United States that an established priesthood, paid at public expence by forced contributions, are no more necessary to the maintenance of piety than useful to the maintenance of morality: and as for the body, so for the soul, to those who think they have need of a physician you will leave the care of choosing one for themselves. Relieving your fellow citizens from all burthens imposed on them on this pretence, you will not forget the protection due to actual possession, nor suppose that possession derived by priests from priests is less entitled to protection than if it were derived by sons from fathers.

From this other eminence likewise, you may look down upon all those other nations whom I have brought under your review.

You are not as yet afflicted with the plague of lawyers. Ah, may you never be so unfortunate!

Judges you must have. But oh! place not in that necessary and worthily venerated station any man whose hand has been polluted by the gold of the wrongdoer. Advocates you must have—Yes, and hireling ones you must tolerate: for the weak in mind and body can not on every occasion command for this any more than any other purpose the assistance of gratuitous friendship. But let the avowed professor of insincerity—the indiscriminate defender of the injured and the injurer—be the last man you think of seating on the bench of justice.

Lay down the universal rule of action in the form of written law, the meanest understanding among you will find it an easier matter to learn from it all his rights and all his duties than the most learned and most acute of all lawyers that ever existed does in his endeavours to learn and, when paid, to teach that pretended unwritten law which, having in reality no existence, is essentially incapable of being learnt by any man.

You are not afflicted by the plague of spurious representatives: hundreds nominate[d] by their own creatures and dependents to plunder and oppress the millions. You have none of these bloodsuckers, these unpunishable malefactors, stigmatized and abhorred under the name of Borough-monger by all who are not their accomplices.

Stationed on this eminence, with the citizens of the Anglo-American United States on your side, you will look down upon all these other nations, but with the best-deserved scorn and contempt upon England and upon France.

In your struggle to free yourselves from the yoke of your Mahometan oppressors, you have no Monarchs, no Nobles, no Priests, no retainers of Monarchs, Nobles or Priests, to join with the arch-tyrants and do their utmost to keep, if that can not be to reseat[?], it on your necks. Your newly appointed Agents have therefore neither reason nor pretext for screening their malpractices in any shape from censure, by restraints on the liberty of public discussion and of the press. From imputations false in fact, as in the station of a private citizen, so in the situation of a public functionary in any department and any grade, protection will be given to reputation by the hand of law: for damage in any assignable and specific shape compensation will be awarded if produced by rashness, to which, if by wilful falshood, appropriate punishment will be added. But as in the Anglo-American United States, so with you, every man by whom any such imputation has been cast will be admitted to prove the truth of it: and considering that mischief capable of being done by functionaries is great in proportion to the power of which they are possessors or partakers, while defence against unjust imputation is in a correspondent degree easier, more indulgence will be shewn by you to ungrounded imputations upon public men than [to][1] the like upon private Citizens. Legislators! the stronger the protection a man has from any other source whatever, the less, not the greater, is the need he has of that which is afforded by the hand of law.

Legislators! though servants to all, think not that by that universality you are placed in any other condition than that of servants. Legislators? I denounce to his fellow citizens as an usurper that man

---

[1] MS 'by'.

who in any address made to them collectively or individually shall presume to use any such language as that of a master. Think not by any assumption of superiority of wisdom, either justification or excuse can be made for assumption of independent and irresistible power.

Look round you and wherever you see a crown you will see under it some empty-headed sensualist whose title to respect is composed of a mass of wealth, sufficient for the subsistence of some myriads of industrious and productive hands, poured into his lap as a reward for idleness, or for exertions many times worse than idleness.

Look round and satisfy yourselves that as no such selfishness, no such cruelty, no such hatred and contempt of benefactors, so no such ignorance of all useful things, no such prejudice, no such folly, no such absurdity, no such meanness, no such utter incorrigibility, is any where to be found comparable to that which is always to be found upon every throne, and in every knot of those hereditary vermin who are never tired of crawling under the throne so long as they have any hope of feeding upon what drops from it.

Legislators! All men in your situation have five trials to undergo; five temptations to contend against, five insatiable and corruptive appetites to hold in subjection if they are able: appetite for money, appetite for power, appetite for factitious honour and dignity, appetite for revenge, appetite for ease.

To no [one] of these appetites can any gratification be afforded to rulers, but at the expence of subjects. Hence the uncontestable maxim that the less the amount of the gratification afforded to them the better. Here then we have minimization of expence—one of the two specific ends into which the general end of government divides itself.

To all these temptation-applying appetites belong their respective instruments of gratification afforded to them by the structure of government.

Offices, invested with various masses of money and power, separate or in combination, are the instruments from the possession and use of which these two appetites receive their gratification. These two instruments of human felicity—these two objects of general not to say universal desire, must in some proportion or other, must of necessity, whatsoever be the expence and cost to subjects, be placed in the hands of rulers. Of these the utmost that can be said is that, it being at the expence of subjects that they are created, and the sum of the enjoyment of those by whom they are received and enjoyed being never so great as the sum of the suffering on the part of those at whose expence they are created, the less the quantity that can be made to suffice for the accomplishment of the universal and only proper end of government, the better.

Cupidity holds out to your grasp needless offices, useless offices, overpay of needful and useful ones and to ones called Sinecures: revenge, the ruin of all who by appeals to the people, your constituents, shall presume to call in question your faultless excellence—that faultless and matchless excellence which men in your situation have no where failed to arrogate to themselves. If, under these temptations, you sink, you will fall with others; if you stand firm, you will stand alone. To prove their fitness for command, men have been seen in various countries subjecting themselves to the bodily torture: none who could revenge themselves have as yet endured patiently that torture which by obloquy, always the severer the more merited, is inflicted on the mind.

Legislators! the occupier of every place which is not absolutely needful as well as useful is a public robber: so is the receiver of whatever pay is over and above that which is needful in every needful and useful place. Every occupant of a sinecure Office is moreover a swindler: receiver of money extorted from the people on a pretence altogether false.

When I say to you, endure with patience whatever obloquy is cast upon you—treat with nothing but silent contempt any appellatives of vague reproach—defend yourselves against specific imputations—defend yourselves with no other arms than counter-argument and disproof, I call not upon you for any thing more than what for these | | years[1] [has][2] been done by others in your place—I speak of all constituted authorities in the Anglo-American United States.

What is there in you that should render public virtue in you inferior to what it is in them? That which in them has for so many years been uninterrupted practice, to you is there any thing in it that is impossible? is not their nature yours likewise? is not possibility sufficiently proved by fact?

Those who cry out, restrain the licentiousness of the press, say in other words, give to me, and all those who are in league with me, success and impunity for all our crimes.

The next instrument of human felicity, created by rulers at the expence of subjects for their own use, is factitious honor or factitious dignity—call it which you please.

For this sort of article there is not in any the smallest quantity the least particle of use: much less is the employment of it, as in the case of those two others, matter of necessity. It is created at the expence

---

[1] Presumably since the expiration of the Sedition Act in 1801.
[2] MS 'does'.

of two different classes of the community: the members at large, and those persons [by][1] whom preeminent and extraordinary service, preeminent and extraordinary in quantity [and][2] quality, has been rendered to the public. In the instance of all those, appropriate honor and dignity—honor and dignity suited in quantity and quality to the nature of the service, are attached to it by the hand of nature. Thus all such factitious honor and dignity [is] productive of evil in a variety of shapes. 1. Oppression to the members of the community at large. 2. Injustice to the whole class of those by whom extraordinary service in any shape has been rendered. 3. Discouragement applied to the exertions of those by whom, were it not for the observation of such injustice, extraordinary service as above would have been rendered.

Of the manufacture of poison in this shape, I have the satisfaction of not being able to find any trace in your organic law.

Note that when the pretence of being contributory and necessary to the production of extraordinary public service is taken away, every pretence that could ever be imagined for the fabrication of this instrument of mischief is taken away: the characters of fraud and oppression are left upon the face of it in all their nakedness.[a]

With only one exception, no government but one having ever existed which had for its end in view the greatest happiness of any persons other than those among whom the powers of it were shared and destined to be shared,[3] no government having ever been in existence by which the interest and greatest happiness of those over whom, was not deliberately and on every occasion of competition constantly made a sacrifice to the interest real or supposed of those by whom the powers of it were exercised, hence it is that no government has ever existed by the very constitution of which, as well as by every act done in maintenance of it, provocation, constant, universal and perpetually repeated provocation, has not been given to all on whom and at whose expence the powers of it have been exercised. I say— the very constitution of it. For, take the instance of a Monarchy—a quantity of productive labour sufficient for the maintenance of fifty or a hundred thousand productive labourers, think of such a quantity extorted for the pampering of one individual, to the cramming with

---

[a] It is scarce needful to observe that in so far as by him by whom any such extraordinary service has been rendered, expence has been necessarily incurred, reimbursement of such expence is due, so as it be not to an amount greater than that of the value of the service rendered.

---

[1] MS 'to'.
[2] MS 'of'.
[3] Presumably the government of the United States of America.

enjoyment a single individual, in whose sensory [not] so much as double the quantity of real enjoyment which any one of those same useful individuals would have possessed had he been left unmolested can after all be forced.

Here then by the very act by which this quantity of labour is extorted and the fruit of it thus miserably wasted, depredation, oppression and waste are exercised upon this vast scale, while by the pretences made in the endeavour to exculpate it, an insult is offered to every mind to which they are addressed, and corruption and depravation produced in every mind by which acceptance is given to them. On no better nor other ground than that of the immense amount of the depredation and extortion practiced for his benefit, virtue and merit in every imaginable shape, and in every shape matchless in degree, are attributed and ascribed to him. With their own hands these creatures of the idol manufacture it, and when thus manufactured they are the first to fall down and worship it. Out of the materials of Vice in all its forms they make it, and it is to this compound that they give the name of consummate Virtue!

Thus much by simple existence. But every arrangement in detail, and every act exercised in the business of giving execution and effect to such arrangements, having for its object and effect that same sinister sacrifice, thus it is that, with scarce an exception worth mentioning, in the exercise of the powers of government scarce an act is done by which injury is not done, and provocation thereby given, to the great body of the people.

All this while provocation can not be offered, injury can not be done, but resentment, in the event of any favorable opportunity, resentment at the hands of the injured, can not but with more or less anxiety be looked for and apprehended. Among those whom on every day of the year they have been treating as enemies, all the causes of blindness that apply to such exalted stations can not altogether prevent [them] from beholding so many individuals prepared upon each favorable occasion to act in their own defence, and in so doing to act as enemies.

The robber beholds of course an enemy in every one whom he has robbed: the oppressor in every one whom he has oppressed: and robbery and oppression upon an all-comprehensive scale being at all times the constant practice of every such government—all sharers in the exercise of the powers of it being as such public robbers, differing only from those who are commonly denominated and punished as such no otherwise than by superior magnitude of the mischief done, and the impunity with which it [is] clothed, hence it is that in every individual who is not or does not look to be a sharer with them in the fruit of the sinister sacrifice they behold an irreconcileable enemy, one who as such is an object of hatred and contempt to them: hatred in respect of the resentment which they can not but regard as having its abode in his breast; contempt for the patience and pusillanimity with which he submitts to such treatment at their hands.

Meantime notwithstanding all the immense mass which they have in their hands of the means of force and intimidation, added to the immense mass of the matter of good in all its shapes—of the external instruments of felicity in all their shapes—of the objects of general desire in all their shapes, ever and anon in the career of their universally injurious practice, resistance is here and there experienced by their ever-craving and ever-intolerant will: and thus it is that a state of morbid excitation—in a word a state of constant inflammation—is the state of every such high-seated and domineering mind. A mind which is thus the seat of perpetual hatred—of ill-will towards men—is in a state of perpetual torment: a sort of torment to which no prospect of mitigation is open but that which it looks to derive from the idea of human suffering on the part of those in whom the dissocial passion beholds its objects.

On the other hand, where there is suffering there will naturally be complaint: where a system of depredation and oppression is in view, indignation will be awakened in every generous and sympathizing breast, even of those who do not regard themselves as having been struck by it with any special injury. By both these causes, complaint as opportunity offers is naturally elicited: indication is made of the several particular sufferings, indication is made of this or that arrangement as affording a prospect of eventual remedy. Desire of relief from suffering, desire of seeing an end to it, desire of compensation, desire of security for the future—desire of revenge at the expence of the authors—all those desires concurr in giving expression to such complaints. But by every such expression, fresh provocation is given to the confederacy of depredators and oppressors. An emotion to which the word *hatred* can not with truth be said to be inapplicable, considering that by this word not any the slightest degree is excluded, is excited in every injured breast to which the cause of its sufferings is an object of attention and regard: hatred in respect of the course of injury perpetually inflicted and sustained: contempt incidentally in respect of the character of those who on this or that particular occasion are seen [to be] instrumental to the infliction of it, and the symptoms of folly and absurdity by which this or that particular injurious act is so frequently seen to be accompanied.

As by the words *hatred* and *contempt* no determinate degree of the respective emotions, affections and passions indicated by them respectively is marked out, nor consequently any degree how slight and gentle so ever excluded, hence it is that to take for the subject of discussion any one existing arrangement of government in the country in question, or any one act performed by any of the individuals among whom the powers of government are shared, and at the same time to hold it up to view in the character of one by the contemplation of which a sentiment of disapprobation has been produced, to do this without doing that by which a tendency to produce hatred at least towards those by whom the supposed pernicious arrangement is supported, or the supposed pernicious act been exercised, is plainly impossible.

Meantime of any observation made whether in oral discourse or in writing on the established arrangements or incidental acts and measures of those by whom the powers of government are exercised, the only possible use is the indication of this or that arrangement or this or that practice in the character of a proper object of disapprobation, on this or that account on each occasion mentioned: and thus doing that in relation to which its tendency to bring the government or the governors, one or both, into hatred and contempt can not consistently with truth be denied.

This being considered, to interdict under penalties all public discussion of the measures of government and to interdict by the like penalties every thing that has a tendency to bring the government and governors into hatred and contempt are thenceforth but two different names for exactly the same thing.

By every arrangement, by every measure, by which endeavours are used to stifle the liberty of public discussion, especially through the medium of the press, rulers, in proportion to the success with which such endeavours are attended, provide for the gratification not merely of the appetite for revenge, but for the more effectual and consummate and perpetual gratification of all those maleficent and dissocial passions to the influence of which I have been representing them as standing exposed, and at the same time to the utmost of their power yielding themselves: appetite for money, appetite for power, appetite for factitious honor and dignity: not to speak of the appetite for ease with which the list of universally [. . . ?] temptations will have to close. For by these same means of penal restrictions, while in case of violation, and in proportion to violation, gratifying the appetite for vengeance, in proportion to observance, they will have secured against opposition every avowed opinion, really or only pretendedly entertained,[1] and not only against punishment but against restraint

---

[1] i.e. every avowed opinion of rulers will have been secured against opposition.

every act of depredation by which money has injuriously been obtained, every act of oppression by which power has been injuriously exercised, every act of imposture by which, to the prejudice of true honor, true dignity—the reward of really extraordinary and meritorious public service—factitious honor and dignity has in any of its infinitely diversified and essentially mischievous and justly comtemptible forms been conferred and received.

From all this it will moreover appear—

1. That if in any country there be to be found among its laws or judicial practices one by which penalties are denounced on him whose endeavours shall be by any discourse uttered in letter or speech to bring into hatred or contempt the government or any of the persons among whom the powers of government are shared, proof is hereby given of the most manifest and irrefragable kind that all persons by whom any such liberty shall be exercised as that of expressing disapprobation of the system or practice of government or governors or any part of it are to all persons by whom a part has been taken in the establishment of such law or practice, or in the making application of it, objects of hatred and contempt: insomuch as that this is an open declaration of war against all such members of the community as refuse to submitt themselves to every extremity of depredation and oppression in the character of slaves.

2. That if there can be any just ground for hatred on the part of any one man towards any other, it is not possible for any set of men by their conduct to furnish a more just and proper ground for that dissocial yet unhappily never altogether avoidable sentiment than is afforded by the giving existence, support or execution to such a law.

In a word, that by a law to any such effect even so much as the pretence of good government, the very pretension to act otherwise than by the compleat sacrifice of the happiness of the whole community besides to the sinister interest of the ruling few, is abandoned and denied, and that not to entertain wishes and upon every favorable occasion use endeavours for the utter subversion and destruction of such a government is to join with it in making interminable war upon human happiness.

When in speaking of all these several corruptive appetites I have brought to view the observation that all men in your position—all legislators—have had to maintain a contest—have had incumbent on them the task of endeavouring to keep them in subjection—what I have meant to say is that in the instance of each such government the greatest happiness of the greatest number of the members of the community in the character of subjects has been in proportion to the success of any such endeavours as may be conceived to have been directed by rulers to the keeping them within subjection, within due bounds: and that accordingly endeavours the most strenuous possible to that effect ought in every instance to have been used.

What I do not mean to say is—that in the instance of any government, unless there be one exception, have any such endeavours ever been used.

On the contrary, of every government as yet known—the main end of all endeavours has been the greatest happiness of those by whom the powers of government have been exercised: in no instance the greatest happiness of those over whom and at the expence of whom [the] powers of government have been exercised.

Now then, by what criterions can you put yourselves in a way to know in what instances and thence to what extent robbery in all these several shapes has been committed? Legislators! I will tell you. I will put you in possession of two such criterions.

The first is—Proof deduced from the universal and incontestable constitution of human nature that from the possession of the instruments of felicity in question on the part of rulers over and above a certain describable quantity nothing but evil can ensue to subjects. Say for shortness, proof from theory or proof from universal experience.

The other is—Indication of instances in which in the case of this or that other government the business of government is carried on as well or better with a less quantity of the expensive article in question than in this or that other government with a larger quantity.

Now as to the use capable of being made of particular experience. The following rule may serve for the expression of it:

Rule of economy as applied to the number of Offices.

If, for the performance of a certain portion of the business of government in the state in question Offices in a certain number having been created, indication has been given of any other political state in the government of which, for the performance of that same portion of business, not so many Offices have place, the difference between the whole number of Offices having place in the government in question and the whole number having place in the political state so referred to, say for shortness the pattern state, is superfluous, and belongs to the head of needless and useless Offices, and the expenditure made in respect of them is so much expenditure in waste.

OBSERVATIONS BY AN ENGLISHMAN ON A PASSAGE IN RAFFANEL'S *HISTOIRE DES ÉVÉNEMENS DE LA GRÈCE*, PARIS, 1822: CHEZ DONDEY-DUPRÉ IMP. LIB., EDITEURS, P. 429 ETC.[1]

---

[1] The relevant passage, C.D. Raffenel, *Histoire des événemens de la Grèce*, Paris, 1822, pp. 429–40, which is a French translation of the Greek Constitution of 1822, is reproduced below.

Chapitre Iᵉʳ. — *De La Religion.*

Art. 1ᵉʳ. La religion de l'état est la religion orthodoxe de l'église d'Orient (grecque).

Cependant toutes les religions sont tolérées, et leurs cérémonies sont librement exercées.

Chapitre II. — *Droit public des Grecs.*

2. Tous les indigènes de la Grèce, professant la religion chrétienne, sont Grecs, et jouissent de tous les droits politiques.

3. Les Grecs sont égaux devant la loi, sans distinction de rang ni de dignité.

4. Tout étranger établi ou habitant momentanément la Grèce, y jouit des mêmes droits civils que les Grecs.

5. Une loi sur la naturalisation sera prochainement publiée par le gouvernement.

6. Tous les Grecs peuvent être appelés à tous emplois. Le mérite seul détermine la préférence.

7. La propriété, l'honneur et la sûreté de chaque citoyen sont placés sous la sauvegarde de la loi.

8. Les contributions aux charges de l'état sont réparties dans la proportion de la fortune de chacun. Aucun impôt ne peut être exigé qu'en vertu d'une loi.

Chapitre III. — *Forme du gouvernement.*

9. Le gouvernement est composé de deux corps: le sénat législatif et le conseil exécutif.

10. Les deux corps concourent à la formation des lois. Le conseil peut refuser sa sanction aux lois adoptées par le sénat, de même que celui-ci peut rejeter les projets de loi proposés par le conseil.

11. Le sénat législatif est composé des députés élus par les diverses provinces.

12. Le nombre des députés au sénat sera déterminé par la loi des élections.

13. La loi des élections, qui sera publiée par le gouvernement, contiendra les deux dispositions suivantes:

1º. Les représentans doivent être Grecs;

2º. Ils doivent avoir trente ans accomplis.

14. Les députés de toutes les provinces et îles libres de la Grèce sont admis, dès que leurs pouvoirs sont reconnus valables par le sénat.

15. Chaque année, le sénat nomme son président et son vice-président à la majorité des voix.

16. Il nomme, de la même manière et pour le même temps, un premier et un second secrétaires, et des sous-secrétaires.

17. Le sénat est renouvelé chaque année.

18. Le conseil exécutif est composé de cinq membres, choisis hors du sein du sénat législatif, et d'après les règles établies par la loi spéciale concernant la formation de ce conseil.

19. Chaque année, le conseil nomme son président et son vice-président à la majorité des voix.

20. Il nomme huit ministres, savoir: l'archi-chancelier de l'état, chargé des relations extérieures; les ministres de l'intérieur, des finances, de la justice, de la guerre, de la marine, des cultes et de la police.

21. Il nomme aussi à tous les emplois du gouvernement.

22. Les fonctions du conseil ne durent qu'un an.

CHAPITRE IV. — *Du sénat législatif.*

SECTION Ier. — *Pouvoir législatif du sénat.*

23. Attendu l'urgence et l'importance des besoins de l'état, le sénat législatif doit continuer cette année ses travaux sans interruption.

24. Le président fixe l'ouverture des séances et en détermine la durée.

25. Il peut convoquer, en cas de besoin, le sénat à des séances extraordinaires.

26. En cas d'absence du président, le vice-président en remplit les fonctions.

27. Les deux tiers des memb[r]es suffisent pour constituer le sénat.

28. Les résolutions du sénat sont prises à la majorité des voix.

29. En cas de partage, la voix du président détermine la majorité.

30. Tous les actes du sénat sont signés par le président et contre-signés par le premier secrétaire.

31. Le président transmet les résolutions du sénat au conseil, et les soumet à son approbation.

32. Si le conseil refuse sa sanction ou propose des amendemens, le projet est renvoyé au sénat, avec les motifs de son refus, ou les amendemens proposés, pour y être de nouveau discuté. Après ce nouvel examen, le projet est encore porté au conseil, qui l'adopte ou le rejette définitivement.

33. Le sénat reçoit et examine toutes les pétitions qui lui sont adressées, quel qu'en soit l'objet.

34. Tous les trois mois, le sénat forme dans son sein autant de comités qu'il y a de ministères.

35. Sur la désignation du président, chacun de ces comités est attaché à une branche du service public, et prépare les projets de loi qui sont relatifs à cette branche.

36. Tout membre du sénat peut proposer un projet de loi écrit, que le président renvoie à l'examen du comité compétent.

37. Le sénat reçoit les projets de loi que le conseil exécutif lui envoie, et les approuve, les modifie ou les rejette.

38. Toute déclaration de guerre et tout traité de paix seront soumis à l'approbation du sénat; et en général, tous traités que le conseil exécutif ferait avec une puissance étrangère, sur quelque matière que ce soit, ne seront obligatoires qu'autant qu'ils seront approuvés par le sénat.

Les trèves et les armistices de peu de jours ne sont pas compris dans cette disposition.

39. Au commencement de chaque année, le conseil soumet à l'approbation du sénat l'état approximatif des dépenses de l'année et des moyens de les couvrir; à la fin de chaque année, il présente aussi à l'approbation du sénat le compte exact des recettes et des dépenses.

Cependant, les circonstances rendant impossible la présentation d'un état approximatif pour cette première année, le sénat fournira aux besoins de la guerre et des autres dépenses publiques, sauf l'approbation du compte exact qui lui sera soumis à la fin de l'année, conformément à la seconde disposition de cet article.

40. Le sénat approuve ou rejette les propositions d'avancement dans les grades militaires faites par le conseil.

41. Il approuve ou rejette aussi les propositions faites par le conseil, pour récompenser les grands services, civils ou militaires.

42. Le sénat réglera le nouveau système monétaire, et le conseil fera battre les monnaies au nom de la nation.

43. Il est expressément défendu au sénat d'approuver aucun traité qui pourrait porter atteinte à l'indépendance politique de la nation; et s'il venait à sa connaissance que le conseil se fût engagé dans quelque négociation criminelle de cette nature, il devra mettre le président en accusation, et, en cas de culpabilité reconnue, le déchoir de ses fonctions.

44. Les journalistes ont le droit d'entrée dans toutes les séances du sénat, excepté les comités secrets qui pourront avoir lieu toutes les fois que cinq membres les demanderont.

SECTION II. — *Des secrétaires du sénat.*

45. Le premier secrétaire du sénat est chargé de la rédaction de tous les actes de ce corps, et en tient un recueil exact.

46. Il reçoit du président les résolutions du sénat, et les transmet au conseil.

47. En cas d'absence du premier secrétaire, le second secrétaire le remplace.

Section III. — *Pouvoir judiciaire du sénat.*

48. Si un ou plusieurs des membres du sénat étaient accusés d'un délit politique, une commission de sept membres, nommée à cet effet par le sénat, prendra connaissance de cette accusation, et en fera un rapport par écrit. Si la commission juge l'accusation admissible, le sénat s'emparera de l'affaire. Si l'accusé est condamné à la majorité des deux tiers des voix, il sera déclaré déchu de sa dignité, et renvoyé devant le tribunal suprême de la Grèce pour y être jugé comme simple citoyen.

49. Aucun sénateur ne peut être arrêté qu'après avoir été condamné pour un délit ou pour un crime.

50. Lorsqu'un membre du conseil exécutif sera accusé d'un délit ou d'un crime politique, le sénat nommera dans son sein une commission composée de neuf membres, qui fera un rapport conformément à l'article 48. Si la commission est d'avis d'admettre l'accusation, et si le sénat, qui, dans ce cas, reste saisi de l'affaire, condamne l'accusé à la majorité des quatre cinquièmes des voix, le président déclarera le condamné déchu de sa dignité, et le renverra devant le tribunal suprême de la Grèce, qui le jugera comme il est dit à l'article 48.

51. Lorsqu'un ou plusieurs ministres seront accusés d'un crime ou d'un délit politique, ils seront jugés dans les formes et de la manière prescrite par l'article 48.

Chapitre v. — *Du conseil exécutif.*

Section Iᵉʳ. — *Pouvoir exécutif du conseil.*

52. Le conseil exécutif, pris en corps, est inviolable.

53. Si le corps entier du conseil exécutif venait à se rendre coupable d'un crime ou d'un délit politique, le président serait jugé et puni, conformément à l'article 43; et, après la nomination d'un nouveau président, les autres membres seraient séparément poursuivis, jugés et punis, conformément à ce qui est établi dans l'article 50.

54. Le conseil fait exécuter les lois par les ministres.

55. Il sanctionne ou rejette les projets de loi adoptés par le sénat législatif.

56. Il propose des projets de loi au sénat qui les discute. Les ministres ont le droit d'assister à cette discussion; et le ministre aux attributions duquel est relatif le projet discuté, doit toujours y être présent.

57. Tous les actes et décrets du conseil sont signés par le président, contre-signés par le premier secrétaire, et scellés du sceau de l'état.

58. Le conseil dispose des forces de terre et de mer.

59. Il pourra publier les instructions qu'il juge convenables, et faire appliquer les lois qui concernent l'ordre public.

60. Il pourra aussi prendre les mesures nécessaires à la tranquillité

publique dans toutes les matières de police, pourvu qu'il en instruise le sénat.

61. Il pourra, avec le consentement du sénat, faire des emprunts tant dans l'intérieur que hors de l'état, et donner en garantie des fonds du domaine public.

62. Il pourra également, avec le consentement du sénat, aliéner une partie desdits fonds du domaine public.

63. Il nomme les ministres et en fixe les attributions.

64. Les ministres sont responsables de tous les actes de leur département; par conséquent, ils ne doivent exécuter aucun acte ni décret contraire aux droits et aux devoirs proclamés par le présent acte.

65. Le conseil nomme tous les employés du gouvernement auprès des puissances étrangères.

66. Il doit instruire le sénat de ses relations avec les états étrangers, et de l'état intérieur de la Grèce.

67. Il a le droit de changer les ministres, et tout employé dont il a la nomination.

68. En cas d'urgence, il convoque le sénat en session extraordinaire.

69. Lorsqu'il aura été commis un crime de haute-trahison, le conseil pourra prendre les mesures extraordinaires qu'il jugera nécessaires, quel que soit le rang des personnes accusées.

70. Le conseil pourra encore, dans ce même cas, faire, si les circonstances l'exigent, des promotions et des nominations provisoires dans les grades militaires, lesquelles seront soumises à l'approbation du sénat, lorsque la tranquillité sera rétablie.

71. Dans ce cas, le conseil présentera au sénat, dans le délai de deux jours, un rapport exact et par écrit des motifs qui l'ont mis dans la nécessité de prendre des mesures extraordinaires.

72. Comme il dispose des forces de terre et de mer, le conseil peut, en tems de guerre, prendre encore des mesures extraordinaires pour se procurer des logemens, des vivres, des habillemens, des munitions, et tout ce qui est nécessaire aux armemens de terre et de mer.

73. Il présentera au sénat un projet de loi sur les décorations à donner, en récompense des services rendus à la patrie.

74. Le conseil exécutif est chargé d'entretenir les relations avec les puissances étrangères, et peut entreprendre et suivre toute espèce de négociation. Mais les déclarations de guerre et les traités de paix ou autres doivent être soumis à l'approbation du sénat.

75. Cependant il peut faire toutes conventions de trèves de courte durée, conformément à l'article 38, sauf la communication qu'il en doit au sénat.

76. Au commencement de chaque année, il présentera au sénat un état approximatif; et à la fin de chaque année, un compte exact et détaillé des revenus et des dépenses de l'année courante. Ces deux comptes sont dressés par le ministre des finances, et accompagnés de toutes les pièces justificatives.

Néanmoins, pour cette année, les comptes seront faits comme il est dit à l'article 39.

77. Les résolutions du conseil sont prises à la majorité des voix.

78. Dans aucun cas, et sous aucun prétexte, le conseil ne pourra entrer dans aucune négociation, ni conclure aucun traité capable de porter atteinte à l'indépendance politique de la nation. Au cas d'un pareil crime, le président du conseil est poursuivi, déchu et puni, comme il est dit à l'article 53.

79. Le conseil proposera un projet de loi sur l'uniforme des troupes de terre et de mer.

80. Il présentera encore un projet de loi pour régler la solde des troupes de terre et de mer, et pour fixer les appointemens de tous les employés du gouvernement.

SECTION II. — *Mode de poursuite contre les membres du conseil.*

81. Dès que l'accusation d'un délit politique, portée contre un membre du conseil, a été admise par le sénat, l'accusé est déchu de ses fonctions; l'instruction et le jugement sont poursuivis d'après les dispositions de l'art. 50.

82. Aucun des membres du conseil ne peut être arrèté qu'en vertu d'une condamnation; en cas de destitution ou d'absence d'un conseiller, si les voix sont partagées dans une délibération, la voix du président détermine la majorité.

83. L'accusation contre un ou plusieurs ministres, admise par le sénat, entraîne leur destitution, et l'instruction de leur procès sera poursuivie, conformément à l'art. 51.

84. En cas de crimes de haute-trahison, le conseil pourra former, dans le lieu où siégera le gouvernement, une commission centrale et extraordinaire, chargée de connaître de ces crimes, jusqu'à la formation du tribunal suprême de la Grèce.

CHAPITRE VI. — *Du Pouvoir judiciaire.*

85. Le pouvoir judiciaire est indépendant des pouvoirs législatif et exécutif.

86. Il est composé de onze membres élus par le gouvernement, et qui choisissent leur président.

87. Une loi sur l'organisation des tribunaux sera prochainement publiée.

88. Cette loi fixera l'étendue de leur ressort, et les formes générales de procédure qu'ils doivent suivre dans l'instruction des procès.

89. Cette loi sera basée sur les cinq dispositions suivantes:

1°. Un tribunal suprême sera formé et établi dans la ville où siégera le gouvernement. Ce tribunal connaîtra, sans appel, des crimes de haute-trahison et des attentats contre la sûreté de l'état.

2°. Des tribunaux généraux seront établis dans tous les chefs-lieux des gouvernemens locaux. On pourra appeler des jugemens de ces tribunaux au tribunal suprême.

3°. Il sera établi un tribunal inférieur dans chaque arrondissement. On pourra appeler de leurs jugemens au tribunal général du chef-lieu. Les tribunaux inférieurs ne peuvent point connaître des délits politiques.

4°. Il sera établi, dans chaque commune ou village, un juge de paix qui connaîtra de toute affaire n'excédant pas la somme de cent piastres, et de tous les différends de famille.

5°. Les juges de paix peuvent être accusés devant les tribunaux d'arrondissement; ceux d'arrondissement devant le tribunal du chef-lieu, et ceux du chef-lieu devant le tribunal suprême.

90. Le conseil exécutif est chargé de former une commission qui sera composée d'hommes recommandables tant par leurs lumières que par leurs vertus. Cette commission sera chargée de la rédaction des lois qui formeront les Codes civil, criminel, commercial, etc. Ces lois seront soumises aux discussions et à l'approbation du sénat et du conseil.

91. En attendant la publication de ces lois, les jugemens seront rendus d'après les lois de nos ancêtres, promulguées par les empereurs grecs de Byzance, et d'après les lois publiées par le gouvernement actuel.

Quant aux affaires commerciales, le Code de commerce français aura force de loi en Grèce.

92. La torture est abolie.

La confiscation est également abolie pour tous les citoyens.

93. Après l'organisation entière du corps judiciaire, aucun citoyen ne peut être arrêté sans l'ordre spécial du tribunal compétent, excepté en cas de flagrant délit.

CHAPITRE VII. — *Articles supplémentaires.*

94. Les go[u]vernemens locaux, établis avant la convocation du congrès national, sont soumis à l'autorité du gouvernement suprême.

95. Corinthe est déclaré le siége du gouvernement provisoire. En cas d'un changement exigé par des circonstances particulières, ce changement est arrêté par le sénat et le conseil.

96. Le sceau de l'état porte pour signe distinctif Minerve, ornée des symboles de la sagesse.

97. Les couleurs nationales, tant pour les drapeaux de terre que pour les pavillons de mer, sont le blanc et le bleu.

98. L'arrangement des couleurs dans la formation des drapeaux et des pavillons sera déterminé par le conseil.

99. Le gouvernement doit prendre toutes les mesures pour donner des soins paternels aux veuves et aux orphelins des hommes morts pour la patrie.

100. Il doit aussi des honneurs et des récompenses à toutes les actions éclatantes et à tous les services marquans rendus à la patrie.

101. A la fin de la guerre, il devra encore accorder des récompenses à ceux

qui auront contribué à la régénération de la Grèce par des sacrifices pécuniaires, et accorder des gratifications à ceux que des efforts généreux pour ce noble objet auront plongés dans l'infortune.

102. La présente loi organique sera imprimée et distribuée dans toute l'étendue de la Grèce. L'original sera déposé aux archives du sénat législatif.

Donné à Epidaure, le 1ᵉʳ. (13) janvier, l'an 1822, et le 1ᵉʳ. de l'indépendance.

The Spanish Constitution is in possession of the honor of being taken for a model on all those occasions on which, with a view to the bettering the condition of the whole people in the aggregate, a new system of Constitutional law has been endeavoured to be introduced and established, to the exclusion of the several forms of government under which discontent has in such sort had place as to engage a portion of the people to join in encountering the hazards of the enterprize.[1]

For this honor this same body of law has been indebted, partly to its goodness, relation being had to the greatest happiness of the greatest number; partly to the urgency of the occasion, which rendered it matter of indispensable necessity to set up in the room of the form of government which it was thought necessary to pull down, some other form to which expression had already been given by a determinate assemblage of words. It was necessary men should have settled from the first what they were to fight for, as well as under direction of what individuals they were to continue to fight, or the commencement given to the fighting carried on against those whom the war found in the possession and exercise of the powers of government could not have any beneficial result.

This Spanish Constitution had its good points. According to the *projet* in question, the framers of the Grecian Constitution have already put themselves in possession of some of those good points, or for aught appears, may without difficulty do so in regard to all the others. The Greek Constitution (so I will call it for shortness) has in it other good points which the Spanish Constitution perhaps could not have had, certainly can not be seen to have.

The Spanish Constitution has several very bad points from which the Greek Constitution has the happiness of being free.

---

[1] The Spanish Constitution of 1812, overturned in 1814 by Ferdinand VII (1784–1833), King of Spain from 1808, but restored by the revolution of 1820, had formed the basis for new constitutions in Naples in 1820 and Portugal in 1821, and had been briefly proclaimed in Piedmont in March 1821.

Upon the whole, reference had to the greatest happiness of the greatest number, the Greek Constitution seems greatly preferable to the Spanish. It is even greatly preferable to the Portugueze, though by the Portugueze considerable improvements have been made upon the Spanish.

On the other hand, relation always had to the abovementioned exclusively and uncontrovertibly right and proper end of government, considerable imperfections, or say points of inaptitude, (such they have appeared) have been found in it. Of some of the most important of these, in so far as time admitts, for the pressure is extreme, indication will on the present occasion be made. By some other occasion the design may perhaps be compleated. To those by whom alone any amendment can be applied to any such imperfections, no indication made of them can, in the nature of the case, be other than unpleasant: they can no more escape being so than bitter physic can escape being so to a child. But it is only on such terms that any attempt to afford relief to any disorder of the body politic can ever be made.

By aptitude and inaptitude, what is here, on each occasion, meant—is aptitude or inaptitude with reference to the purpose of producing such greatest happiness, or say *maximum* of felicity, as above.

When against this or that arrangement a charge of inaptitude is made, the source of the proof by which the charge is considered as supported is referable either to the head of *general* experience; or to that of *particular* experience: general experience, viz. of those points in human conduct and disposition which have been perceptible in all places at all times; particular experience, namely the experience afforded, either by well-organized States in which the Constitution is eminently conducive to the above all-comprehensive and exclusively justifiable end, and the people, in so far as depends on the state of the government, prosperous, happy, contented, and in the most enthusiastic degree attached to that universally understood source of all their happiness; or in this or that ill-organized State by the sufferings therein produced by this or that bad arrangement, by which a sacrifice has been made of the interest and happiness of the greatest number to the interest, real or supposed, and happiness, enjoyed or expected, of the ruling and otherwise influential few. If time permitts, I may perhaps suggest this or that additional article having for its object the making addition to such features of aptitude as the body of law in question appears to be already in possession of.

217

I. Apt arrangements inserted in the Spanish Constitution, as likewise in the Grecian[1]

1. Virtual declaration of the exclusively right and proper end of government—the greatest happiness of all the members of the community: namely, without exception in so far as possible, and in so far as by a conflict of interests it is rendered impossible, the greatest happiness of the greatest number.

In the Spanish, the recognition is made by Articles 4 and 13.[2] In the Grecian it is made not quite so expressly as could have been wished. It seems however contained in it by implication: namely in Article 2, and Article 3, and Article 6, and Article 8. In agreement with this last is Art. 8 in the Spanish.[3]

2. By Articles 35, 18, 21, 25, etc., the Spanish Constitution gives the right of suffrage on the occasion of the Election of the Representatives of the people sitting in the Assembly of the Cortes, as also certain other Representative bodies of subordinate authority, to all *Citizens*.[4] The definitional matter, having for its object the ascertaining what individuals shall to this purpose be regarded as *Citizens*, is not quite so clear and satisfactory as could be wished.

That given by the Grecian Constitution, namely in Article 2, seems rather more so. 'Of all natives of Greece' (*indigènes*) 'professing the Christian religion, it is declared that they are Greeks, and that they are in the enjoyment of all *pol[it]ical rights*.' Among these political

---

[1] A fragment with the marginal sub-heading 'Introduction: Good points in Greek Constitution' is at UC xxi. 191–2 (12 February 1823).

[2] The clauses of the Spanish Constitution to which Bentham refers are reproduced from a translation which was soon to appear appended to 'Preliminary Discourse, read in The Cortes at the presentation of The Projêt of the Constitution, by the Committee of the Constitution', *The Pamphleteer*, xxii (1823), 1–87 (see the Editorial Introduction, p. xxxix above).

'Art. 4. The Nation is obliged to preserve and protect, by wise and just laws, the civil liberty and the property, besides all other legitimate rights, of all individuals belonging to it.

'Art. 13. The object of the Government is the happiness of the nation; since the end of all political society is nothing but the welfare of all individuals of which it is composed.'

[3] 'Art. 8. All Spaniards are . . . bound, without any distinction whatever, to contribute, in proportion to their means, to the expenses of the state.'

[4] 'Art. 35. The parish elective meetings shall be composed of all citizens settled and resident in the district of each respective parish, including the secular ecclesiastics.

'Art. 18. Those are Spanish Citizens who descend from parents both of the Spanish dominions of either hemisphere, and are settled in any town or district of the same.

'Art. 21. Those also are citizens who are the legitimate offspring of foreigners settled in Spain, who, born in the Spanish dominions, have never quitted them without the leave of government, and who having completed their twenty-first year, have settled in any town of the same dominions, exercising therein any profession, office, or useful branch of industry.

'Art. 25. The exercise of the same rights [i.e. of citizens] is suspended, in the first place, in virtue of any judicial prohibition from physical or moral incapacity. 2. In cases of bankruptcy, or of debtor to the public. 3. In the state of domestic servitude. 4. From not holding any employment, office, or known means of living. 5. From having undergone a criminal prosecution. 6. From the year one thousand eight hundred and thirty, all those who claim the rights of citizenship must know how to read and write.'

rights, I can not but conclude it was intended to comprize the right of contributing by their respective suffrages to the election of representatives to sit in the body stiled the legislative Senate. To the *Election?* but by what individuals in the character of Electors? According to the inference I have drawn as above, all natives of Greece. But after looking for some direct expression as to this point, I have the mortification of not finding any. Nothing do I find that bears on it in any more particular manner than does Article 11th. in which it is said, 'The legislative Senate is composed of the deputies elected by the different provinces.'[1]

[II.][2] *In the Grecian Constitution, Articles in which features of supposed inaptitude have been observed*[3]

First come Articles 9 and 10, concerning the so-declared two component parts of the government: namely the body termed the *Legislative Senate*,[4] and the body termed the *Executive Council*.[5] In the

---

[1] This sequence, as originally written, was continued by UC xxi. 209 (26 February 1823), but Bentham noted that this sheet was 'Not employed', that is not included in the material sent to Greece.

[2] MS '*III*'. Bentham had originally intended 'Unapt arrangements inserted in the Spanish Constitution, and not in the Grecian' (see pp. 252–4 below) to form the second part of the essay, but reversed the order in the version sent to Greece.

[3] An earlier draft discussing some of the themes in this section is at UC xxi. 280–2, 273–6, 234–6, 277, 283–7, 289, 288 (16–18 February 1823). Related fragments are at UC xxi. 278 and 279 (17 February 1823).

[4] The following passage discussing part of Article 13, providing that the deputies elected to the legislative senate 'doivent avoir trente ans accomplis', is at UC xxi. 181–2 (9 February 1823): 'Art. 13. Exclusion of all under 30 years of age from the Legislative Senate.

'1. For the exclusion no reason has been found. Every political exclusion is generally bad, or no otherwise rendered good than by some special cause and that an adequate one.

'2. Fit or unfit, a man under that age is not so likely to be elected as a man above that age because not likely to be so much and so advantageously known. That to the number of a majority such relative non-adults should be chosen is compleatly improbable.

'On no occasion, by a minority can any considerable mischief be done.

'3. At an age even junior to that at which a person is admitted to the compleat management of his own affairs he might without danger be admitted to such a part in the management of the affairs of the Nation. In doing mischief [to] his own affairs he has nobody to oppose him: in doing mischief to the affairs of the Nation, he has every other to impede him: and a majority stops him definitively.

'4. Much wisdom is not shewn by the man who shall say—"By those to whom every thing that exclusively regards the individual in question is perfectly known, his aptitude for the situation in question will not in question be so well known as by men to whom nothing that regards him is individually known."

'5. From the commencement of all history, no example to justify an exclusion of this sort has ever been or can ever be produced.

'6. The less advanced the age, the greater the probability of an adequately strong propensity to an occasional sacrifice of a man's personal interest to the universal interest: the stronger in a word the force of sympathetic affection operating on the national and other enlarged scales: the more advanced, the more constant the preponderance of personal, domestic and other comparatively narrow interests over the universal interest.

'7. Whatever reason there might be for excluding a person from eligibility to a function in the

 [*See p. 220 for n. 4 cont. and n. 5.*]

appellations respectively given to these two bodies, there seems to be an inconsistency: and, on considering them in themselves, one of them, namely the one stiled the Executive Council, seems to be useless: and forasmuch as in regard to political power, there can not be any portion which if useless is not also mischievous, hence it will be seen to follow, that, in the instance of the body here in question, if it be useless it is worse, indeed much worse, than useless.

First as to the inconsistency of the denominations. To the body intended, as it should seem, to be chosen immediately by the people is attached the appellation of *Legislative Senate*. But no sooner are the functions of the body termed *Executive Council* brought to view, than it appears that to the Senate stiled Legislative no more than one out of two equal shares in the power of legislation in the highest grade is given, the other share being given to the body stiled the *Executive Council*. The consequence is—that to the whole of that power which, by the appellation of *Executive* given to it, one should be disposed to regard as designed subordinate (the business of the Executive power being to give execution and effect to the *will* entertained and declared by the legislative) is added a share in that same superior power. So that here is a body of functionaries which is at the same time placed in subordination to and in coordination with another body to which, by its appellation, it is indicated as being purely subordinate. Moreover thus it is that so far from being in effect subordinate, this declared subordinate is in effect greatly superior in power to its so-declared superordinate, which effective superiority will appear to have place most incontestably when the powers given to the so-stiled Executive Council are brought to view in detail, as they will be presently.

Now then as to the inaptitude of the body itself, and of the arrangements by which existence is given to it.

Of all the arrangements that have application to it, the only one that in my eyes wears the character of aptitude is Article 22 in which the

exercise of which he stands single, there is none for the like exclusion in the case of one in the instance of which he is but one out of a multitude.

'8. The case in which at an age at which a human being is not so fit for government as a quadruped would be is yet admitted to a function on which all others depend, and in the exercise of which he is single, is that to which no exclusion has, under any of the governments now distinguishing themselves by the appellation of legitimate, place in any instance. This single consideration would of itself suffice for the demonstration of the utter inaptitude and absurdity of every such form of government.

'Say that though the nominal power commences the instant of birth, the real does not till a number of years afterwards, the absurdity is somewhat lessened but is far indeed from being removed. In every instance the functionary in that situation is admitted to do as he pleases with the affairs of every body else at an age at which no individual is permitted to take his own affairs into his management.'

[5] An earlier draft in which Bentham considered the Executive Council is at UC xxi. 184–9 (12 February 1823).

functions of this body are declared not to endure beyond the term of a year. Here then, should it be found unapt, is a door left open for the exclusion of it.

First as to the person or persons by whom members of this body have been, or are to be, chosen: this is more than I can find any mean of determining.

In Article 18, after saying that the number of its members is *five*, it is said that they are chosen *hors du sein du sénat législatif*. Here is a fault somewhere: namely either in my acquaintance with the French language, or else in the translation made into that language from the Greek original. Is it that the members of this Council *must be* or that they *must not be* members of the Legislative Senate at the time when the choice is made? This is a doubt to which I must confess myself unable to find the solution. But in either case the objections I see applying to it apply with not much less than equal force.

From the remainder of this same Article, I see that the manner in which the Council is to be formed is a matter which remained to be settled according to a set of rules to be established by a special law as yet not made.

Be these rules what they may, I proceed to shew why in the first place this body is in my view of the matter useless.

It is itself composed of five Members. By these *five* (per Article 20) are to be appointed *eight* other functionaries, under the name of Ministers. Number of functionaries thus belonging to the Executive Department, adding the two grades together, 13. To these same five belongs moreover (per Article 21) the power of placing functionaries in all the other employments of government. Note that by whom they shall respectively be liable to be displaced is not mentioned.[1]

Now of these thirteen, eight at least are I say altogether useless. For proof I appeal as above to *particular experience*: the experience afforded by the only Constitution that ever really had for its object or end in view the greatest happiness of the greatest number: I mean the Constitution of the Anglo-American United States. Here at the head of the Executive Department you have a single person, *the President of the United States*. To him alone belongs the direction of the whole business of that Department. To him belongs the direction to be given to, the command over, the whole Military force of the Country by Sea and Land.[2] To him belongs the placing and at his pleasure the

---

[1] The copyist has crossed out this sentence, and added the following phrase to the end of the preceding sentence: 'to which by Article 67 is added the power of displacing them'.

[2] In the margin, Bentham noted at this point: 'Constitution Art. | |.' The President was appointed Commander in Chief of the Army and Navy of the United States by Art. II, §2 of the Constitution.

displacing of the four *Ministers* stiled *Secretaries* by whom, in subordination to the President and the Legislative Assembly stiled *the Congress*, the whole civil power of the confederacy is exercised: namely 1. Secretary of State, 2. Secretary of War, 3. Secretary of Navy, 4. Secretary of Finance.[1] If the business of the Greek Nation is but carried on with a degree of aptitude and success not very much below that with which it is carried on in that confederated Commonwealth, the Grecian will be a happy people. Nothing approaching to it has yet been seen any where else; no: nor ever will be on any other condition than that of imitating it. Now then, supposing my advice on the subject asked for, it would be this. Take some one individual—for example the President of that same Executive Council—give him the power possessed in the Anglo-American Commonwealth by the functionary whose title is *President of the United States*. This done, take four other individuals, say for example the four other Members of the so-stiled Executive Council, and give to them respectively the functions and powers possessed respectively by the abovementioned Secretaries. Call them Secretaries or Ministers as you please: but on account of the collateral ideas associated with the two denominations respectively, my recommendation would be to call them *Secretaries* and not Ministers. Under the appellation of *Secretaries* they present to my imagination the images of so many responsible instruments of good government, under a free and happy people: under the name of Ministers, the ever mischievous and profligate tools of a Monarch, leagued or not leagued with a set of sub-despots in the condition of Aristocrats, having for their sole business the exercise of depredation and oppression in all their forms over, and at the expence of, all the other members of the community who are not sharers with them in the spoil.

Be this as it may, having these five functionaries thus equipped with power, no need have you either of the Executive Council with its five Members or of your eight Ministers of State.

Note that seeing that four[2] Secretaries are sufficient for conducting, under the President, the whole of the business of the Executive Department in the Anglo-American United States, not merely four, but even fewer than four, should be sufficient in Greece.[3] For whether it be population or territory that is considered, but more especially if it

---

[1] See the Constitution of the United States, Art. II, §2. The three Departments of State, Treasury, and War and Navy had been created by Congress in 1789; the Departments of War and Navy had been separated in 1798 to bring the total to four.

[2] Bentham had originally written 'five', but the copyist has altered the total to 'four'.

[3] In the margin, the copyist has made the following addition at this point: 'were it not for a Secretary or a Minister of Justice which I should see reason to add, tho' no such functionary was found requisite in those United States'.

be territory, think how small the scale is upon which every thing that has place, has place in Greece, when compared with the vast scale upon which population, but more particularly territory, has place in that only as yet known seat of Good Government!

In holding up to view the state of government in that federative democracy as a model for imitation, I mean not that the imitation should be undiscriminating. In that hitherto matchless seat of practical wisdom and experienced felicity, the machinery of government has not however as yet all that simplicity of which it appears to me susceptible. The President is placed in his situation—not by those to whose declared will it is designed that on every occasion he should as far as in his power give execution and effect, but by the suffrages of a set of appropriate Electors nominated by the legislatures of the several confederated Commonwealths: and the time of his continuance in Office is four years. For my part, I see not any evil that would be likely to arise, if, in your case at the beginning of each year, this Chief of the Executive Department were elected by the Members of the legislative body, meaning your so-stiled Legislative Senate, the negative on their proceedings being supposed taken away by the abolition of the so-stiled Executive Council as above. True it is that, with the exception of the time and labour bestowed as it seems to me without equivalent profit, I know of no evil as having actually been produced by the interposition of these two bodies of Electors. But so admirably well-adapted to its object in its essential points is the machinery of that Constitution, and in particular such is the tutelary force of that grand corrective of all political evil, the power of public opinion, supported by the all-comprehensive body of appropriate and ungarbled information, continually poured in upon it by the vast multitude of the public journals, that in the excellency of the whole taken together any little imperfections that may have place in this or that particular part find in practice an effectual corrective. But when a newly formed, or rather about to be formed, state is the subject of consideration, principles should be looked out for: and to all such arrangements as are seen employed in any other political State, the manifest prosperity of which holds it out as an object of imitation, a careful scrutiny should be applied, lest, in regard to such good effects as are produced by the whole machinery taken together, this or that part, of which when considered by itself it will be plain that nothing but obstruction can be afforded, be numbered among those efficient causes by which every good effect discernible in the aggregate result has in reality been produced.

Looking out for a ruling principle, on this occasion then, what I ask is—What is the design and use, in so far as it has any, of the

Executive department? Answer, I know of but one: and that is—to give execution and effect to the will declared by a superior department, namely that to which is generally given the name of the *Legislative*.

As to the Greek government, under the Constitution in question it is out of all question a Representative Democracy. Now in every such Commonwealth I behold three authorities one under another, meaning in the case of each that which is supreme in its own grade. So many of these authorities as there are thus standing in a line one to another, so many situations may be spoken of as existing, or so many *Departments*. In the first and highest situation stand the members of that department which I stile the *Constitutive*: next below them, the members of that which I stile the *Operative*. Constitutive is a term of relation: the department to which it bears relation and reference is that same Operative. To the members of the Constitutive department it belongs then to choose and place in their situation, and at certain intervals, if such be their pleasure, to displace, the several members of the Operative department. Under the business which I consider as belonging to this same Operative department I consider as included the whole of the business of government: one part alone excepted, namely that which consists in determining who the individuals are by whom all the rest of the business shall be done: this being understood, that in the business of the Operative department are included that of the legislative and that of the Executive.

Here a sort of paradox—a sort of apparent inconsistency—presents itself: in the scale of power, those, *over* whom all power is exercised, superior to those, *by* whom all power is exercised. The inconsistency is however only in the expression: for in fact the like has place in every political state to which the name of a Representative democracy is applied or applicable. On all days in the year but one, and on that one day to all effects but one, the members of the *Constitutive* department are subject to those of the *Operative*: but to that one effect on that one day the subordination is reversed, and the members of the Operative department are subject to those of the Constitutive. It were hard indeed, if possibility were not sufficiently proved by fact.

Now then as to the Operative department, it is by the necessity of the case that it stands divided, as above, into the two departments stiled the legislative and the Executive. Not that of these two departments the Executive is to be understood as being coordinate with the legislative any more than the legislative alone or the legislative and the Executive taken together are to be regarded as coordinate with the Constitutive. No, it is matter of absolute necessity that, with reference to one of them, namely the legislative, the other, namely the Executive, should be subordinate. For the legislative department being established, why is it that any part of the[1] business of the Operative department is committed to any functionary or set of functionaries other than those by which that of the legislative department is to be done? Is it that the functionaries employed in the legislative department may find in another department a man or set of men by whom controul or obstruction in any shape may in any event be opposed to their power? a man or set of men by whom the giving execution and effect to any will, which they have concurred in the formation of, may be subjected to frustration or even to delay? No such thing. The reason why that which is taken out of their hands, is accordingly taken out of their hands is—or at any rate the only reason on which its being so can be justified, is—simply this: namely that when the business turned over, and as it were turned down, to the Executive department has, the whole of it, been taken out of their hands, as much is left in their hands as it is physically speaking, supposing due attention paid to it, possible for them to go through: indeed, as in the American United States experience has amply shewn, more than they do or can go through without continually subjecting large portions of it to a delay by which serious inconvenience, in particular and assignable shapes, is continually produced, as also the ultimate frustration of many a useful design, for want of the faculty of applying to it that portion of time [before that period] at the expiration of which its original feasibility deserted it. In the Executive department of that same Government, look to the four Secretaries of State acting immediately under the President. See them staggering, each of them, under the load of the business which is continually pouring in upon their shoulders. This done, conceive the aggregate mass of their respective businesses added to the mass of business at present executed by the legislative assembly stiled the Congress. Say then whether the mere division of the load of business, without any such design as that of dividing power between two sets of conflicting functionaries with opposite interests and consequently opposite wills, has not been the true and only beneficial effect which has been experienced from these arrangements, at least by which the business of the Executive department has been placed in hands different from those which stand charged with the business of the legislative.

The will of the greatest number being supposed to be under the guidance of the true interest of the greatest number, constantly, and by sufficiently apt means, aiming at the production of the greatest

---

[1] The words 'of the' have been added by the copyist.

225

happiness of the greatest number (and on no other supposition can the existence of a representative democracy be justified), behold then, in respect of subordination and dependence as between authority and authority, department and department, the only state of things the production of which, in so far as possible, can be justified. It is that by which the conduct of every subordinate functionary is placed in a state of as strict and absolute dependence as is possible on the aggregate will of those among whom the supreme power of the state is shared: and these are the members of the Constitutive body—the individuals contributing by their respective suffrages to the constituting and placing in their respective places the several functionaries among whom the power of the principal, called the legislative, branch of the Operative department is shared. Now, of the conduct of the several members of the Supreme legislative body, the dependence on the aggregate will of their immediate and only superiors—the possessors of shares in the supreme Constitutive power, can not, it will readily be admitted, be too strict. Why? e'en because it is to no other end than that of giving execution and effect to that which, on each occasion, it is supposed, could the details of the case have been before them, with sufficient time for consideration and discussion, would have been *their* will with relation to the subject in question—it is no other end than this, that this department with its subordinate power is created, the functionaries belonging to the superior and supreme department, namely the Constitutive, being by other and still more indispensable occupations—namely that of providing for all classes taken together the means of continuing their existence, prevented from taking direct and particular cognizance of that which requires to be done.

Thus necessary is the strictest and most absolute dependence of the conduct of subordinates on the will of superiors as between the members of the legislative department on the one part and those of the Constitutive on the other part. But for this same reason not less so is it as between the conduct of the members of the Executive department and the declared will of the members of the Legislative department. Why? because exactly proportioned to the strictness of the dependence of the conduct of this department which stands third in rank on the declared will of the members of its immediate superordinate—the department second in rank—will be the strictness of its dependence on the necessarily presumed will of the members of the superior department of all—of that department so constituted that the interest of all its members is the same thing with the universal interest. In the Executive Department let the number of grades one [under] another be ever so great, the demand for the strictest dependence possible, and the reason for it, will remain unchanged. Suppose for example, a single Functionary at the head of it, and under an appropriate name, say in the language of the Anglo-American Union the President, occupying to himself the highest grade. Immediately under him, in the next grade, [four][1] functionaries by the name of Secretaries or Ministers, placed at the head of so many sub-departments: Landed branch of the Military force, Naval branch of the Military force, Foreign affairs, and Finance:[2] each with others under him in so many different grades, forming a chain of indefinite length composed of so many links as there are grades.

As to the mischief resulting from any deficiency in the strictness of dependence, the civil, the *Non-military*, department stands in principle on the same footing as the Military. The only difference is that which regards time. To what purpose is the Lieutenant General added to the General, the Major General to the Lieutenant General, the Brigadier General to the Major General, and so on down to the lowest grade? Is it that, by the occupant of each inferior grade, obstruction and delay may be opposed to the will manifested by his immediate superior, and so on up to the will of those who have no superior? No: but that with greater certainty, and if possible even with greater promptitude, the superior will, and at length the supreme will of all, may in each instance receive execution and effect.

To return to the Operative department taken in the aggregate. If by the possessors of the power of the Constitutive department, the power detached from their own and given by them to the members of the Operative department, and in the first instance to the legislative branch of it, were not thus detached and parted with, no power at all would they be able to exercise. As to the remnant which after the detachment thus made remains to them, there is nothing of splendor in it; but such as it is, it is found to answer to perfection the great and universal purpose—the purpose of all who share in it: they are therefore not losers but gainers, even in the article of power, by the sacrifice, if such it can be called, which they thus make.

The case of agency on this largest scale, compare it, in this respect, with the case of agency on an individual scale. By whom would any such supposition be entertained, as that the interest of an individual would be the better served, if, after appointment made by him of an agent for the management of a certain portion of his affairs, such agent should have it in his power to appoint, and should appoint accordingly, sub-agents who should have the power of opposing

[1] MS 'five'. Bentham himself listed only four functionaries: the copyist added a fifth.

[2] In the text at this point, the copyist has made the following addition: 'to which, in the case of Greece, I would add Justice'.

obstruction, delay, and eventual frustration, to any operation which he might deem it for his interest to have performed? and this without its being ever in his power to remove any such obstruction so created? By whom would any such supposition be for a moment entertained, as that a proposition for the interposition of any such irremovable instrument of irremovable obstruction could ever have had a regard for the interest of the individual in question for its efficient cause? Assuredly by no one whatsoever.

Thus then, for a principle of incontestable utility, in the most extensively public as in the most private management, we have the principle of *absolute and all-pervading dependence*: dependence, namely of all *agents* upon their common *principal*.

If this explanation has been rather of the longest, and perhaps rather longer than was necessary, and even than it would have been had there been time for shortening it, the practical importance of it will be found proportionable. It will operate as a source of simplicity carried to its maximum: it will operate as a sponge upon immense masses of the most mischievous complication in an endless diversity of forms. It will rid the Greek Constitution of its Executive Council, of one half of the number of its *Ministers of State*. It will rid it of its eleven Members of the Judiciary power, established by Articles 85 and 86.

It will suffice of itself to prove the impossibility, that in the English form of government the power exercised by the King, or the power exercised by the House of Lords, should ever have[1] had for the end of its creation the greatest happiness of the greatest number, or so much as the happiness of any individual other than the several sorts of person by whom those powers have been and are exercised and their several connections. It will rid the country of both these sources of misrule and misery, so soon as the eyes of the greatest number are sufficiently open to the only sound principles of the art and science of government; that is to say if the supreme Constitutive power be lodged in the hands of all who are capable of bearing a part in the exercise of it, instead of being engrossed by a minute fraction of that number almost all of them listed in the service of misrule by a community of corrupt and sinister interest.

It will render similar service to France, in the eyes of all Frenchmen who can endure to look at it.

It will rid the Spanish constitution of its King: and of that vast reservoir and fountain of the matter of corruption, the Council of State with its forty members, all of them creatures of the Monarch.

It will render similar service to Portugal.

---

[1] The word 'have' has been added by the copyist.

It will render service even to the Constitution of the Anglo-American United States, matchless as it is as yet, and little short of the summit of absolute perfection as it is. It will clear it of its Senate: a mass of useless, and thence worse than useless, complication: introduced by a natural and not illaudable timidity, at a time when principles were as yet unsettled, and no sufficient stock of experience as yet obtained: established in imitation of that parent government, which, not without reason, was universally regarded as the best, or to speak more properly the least bad, government that, till the Anglo-American Government had had time to manifest itself, had ever been exemplified.

In this same Senate, set down by the side of the Assembly composed of the immediate Delegates of the people, I see a source of factitious delay, of waste of time on the part of the Members and their Electors, of waste of money given in the name of pay. In various shapes I see more evil done by it than I can here find time to bring to view. Applied to the power of the President, I see his responsibility diminished by it. I see him choosing subordinates under a secret necessity of letting the Members of this body into a share of the patronage. I thereby see in it a natural source of corruption applied to the power of the Assembly of Representatives. I see it opposing, to an indefinite amount, obstruction to the will of the Members of the Constitutive body as manifested by their Delegates. In its Members, continuing in that situation as they do for six whole years, I see a source and seat of aristocratical feeling and prejudice. A set of men, not placed immediately by the people, but by another set of men who have been placed by the people—this set of men, paid at the expence of the people, may, every one of them, in spite of the people, continue for six years together in the practice of delaying or defeating arrangements proposed by the people's immediately deputed delegates, whose faculty of running counter to the will of the people lasts not, in the instance of any one of them, more than two years. Nor would these two years have been more than one, had it not been for the vast quantity of time necessary to be consumed in travelling between the seat of election and the seat of government. Accordingly in Spain, that authority lasts but for one year. And so in Portugal.[1] From an authority thus constituted, the best that can be hoped for is inefficiency: the more efficient, the more maleficent. I see not a single good effect produced with it that would not be better produced without it. The Spanish Constitution has no such *Second Chamber*, as the phrase is, to throw obstruction in the way of all the proceedings of the first: and

---

[1] Under both the Spanish Constitution (Art. 108) and the Portuguese Constitution (Art. 41), elections to the Cortes were in fact to be held every two years.

from the omission none but good effects have ever been found. To the Portugueze Constitution the same observation applies with at least equal force. I see nothing but its existence that seems capable of being alledged in support of its existence. But of any utility that may be supposed to belong to it, a most simple and convincing test is that which the Citizens of that only seat of good government have at all times in their hands: a test which even any one such Citizen has it in his power at any time to make application of. Let him look over the history of the proceedings of Congress since the first introduction of this part into the machinery of its Constitution. Let him note in the first place what in his eyes are the apt arrangements to which it has applied its obstruction, and which notwithstanding such obstruction have been established. Let him note down in the second place the apt arrangements which have as yet remained excluded by it. Let him note in the third place the unapt arrangements which have as yet been kept excluded by it, and which would have been established if it had not been in existence. My expectation would be to find in each of the two first lists some articles, and in the last either none or next to none.

True it is that only to a representative democracy having for its end in view the greatest happiness of the greatest number, and to that end to the giving advancement to the interest, and execution and effect to the will declared as far as it can be declared, of the greatest number, can application be made of this principle of absolute and universal dependence with any advantage. Applied to any such form of government as the English, it would be the consummation of despotism and misrule: it would give to the laws, were they ever so much worse than they are, a strength altogether irresistible. But whatsoever remains useful in the English government has its source not in the strength but in the weakness of the laws. So inexorably hostile to the interests of the greatest number are those laws and judicial practices which belong to the constitutional branch of the field of law, that rather than that those parts should not be weak, it is desirable that the whole should be weak together, and so intensely mischievous are they, that the weakness of the whole can not be too great. Accordingly in the general texture of the laws such a degree of weakness and comparative inefficiency has place as is scarcely to be found in any of the purely despotic Monarchies. This salutary weakness has for its cause partly the anxiety of the Aristocracy to give to themselves security against arbitrary power in the hands of the Monarch, partly the arrangements made by the Members of the Judiciary for the purpose of keeping screwed up to its utmost pitch that uncertainty on which their sinister emolument and no less sinister power depend.

To keep on foot the delusion by which the whole system, taken in the aggregate, is represented as being not only comparatively but positively good—good, not only when compared with despotism under its various modifications, but with the best form of government imaginable—to keep on foot this delusion, a substitute to the only true principle above-mentioned has been invented and held up to view. It is that which holds out the *division of power* among rulers as the most efficient if not the only security for good government: meaning in this case by power the supreme power in its highest grade: the division of it, namely among divers authorities, two or more: any such power as an universally applying Constitutive power in the hands of the greatest number, as above, not being recognized as that which either has or ought to have place any where in the machinery of government.

This principle has this much of good in it, that, though incompatible with the only good form of government, it has at times operated as a palliative, how feeble soever, to the mischief produced by a bad one.

True it is, that where, between one functionary or set of functionaries and another, a power which is independent of that of the people is shared out, a case there is in which such division, in so far as it has place, has a tendency to be productive of effects beneficial to the interest of the people. This is—where the power so divided is the Supreme power in the State, say the power of legislation in the highest grade, and the mode of division such that no valid act can be performed by the one of these authorities without the concurrence of the other. In this case the power is fractionized: the whole power is the integer, and each of them has a fractional part of it. Thus in the English Government the whole of this power is divided into three fractions: to the King belongs one, to the House of Lords another, to the House of Commons another. In the case of each of those two Houses, the fraction is moreover further fractionized: to each Member belongs a fraction of that of the House he sits in: which fraction is thus a subfraction of the whole. In a case of this sort, this same good tendency what does it depend upon? It depends upon those disagreements and those contests which in such a case are so natural, and have been so universally exemplified. Every such contest having for its subject-matter the obedience of the people, each party has found itself under a necessity more or less urgent of courting the good will of the people. The consequence has been that when between the parties so contending a cessation of hostility and a compromise in some shape or other has had place, they have both of them found themselves under the necessity of concurring in the establishment of some arrangement from which the interest and condition of the people has received some more or less beneficial service.

Under the sense of this necessity it was that on the occasion of their contest with King John the Members of the great Aristocratical body of the time, the Barons, in the termination they put to that contest by the Charter which they succeeded in exacting from him, admitted the great body of the freemen into the benefit of some portion of the security, such as it was, which it professed to establish. But, what seems probable, is—that the portion of the population to which this security was on that occasion extended, formed in those days by far the smallest portion of the whole.[1]

Thus again on the occasion of that conflict which in the year 1688 substituted one race of Monarchs to another, when the Aristocracy of the country obtained for itself not only security against arbitrary power in the hands of the Monarch, but a share coordinate with his own in the power belonging to the legislative and judicial departments, they could not altogether avoid admitting the great body of the people to the benefit of some share of the security obtained for themselves in respect of person and property. For their own share they gave themselves that security which was afforded by the undisturbed possession of their till then disputed and precarious share in the Supreme power as above: to the people, they knew better than to give to them any such security: in place of it what they gave them was— that tissue of vague, unobligatory and ineffective generalities called the *Bill of Rights*.[2] From men so situated how could any thing better have reasonably been expected? By a genuine representation of the people, the power of the people would have been encreased, whereby that of these their rulers would immediately have been diminished, and peradventure ultimately abolished. The system of sham representation, as if it had been the people's only safeguard, was therefore most carefully, and in all its plentitude, preserved.

With the conflict between the King on the one part and the two branches of the Aristocracy on the other ceased all chance of ulterior benefit to the interest and condition of the people. Whatsoever real benefit had ever resulted to the people from that same division of power became purely nominal as soon as the contention between the parties sharing in it ceased. No sooner did that contention cease by the establishment of a new succession of Monarchs, than a partnership between the formerly contending parties took its place: a partnership, the stock of which was at all times composed of such part of the property of the people as could be extracted from the owners on pretence of making provision for the expences of government. True it

[1] Chapter 39 of Magna Carta, first issued by John, King of England, in 1215, provided that no freeman should be proceeded against except by due process of law.
[2] For the Bill of Rights see 'Securities against Misrule', p. 23n above.

is that notwithstanding this bond of strength a sort of comparative weakness remained, in which the people have found a source of comparative advantage. To the single-headed despot by whom, as in the Continent, all the powers of government would have been exercised succeeded in these islands a many-headed despot: and in the constitution of this beast of prey there is a sort of weakness which prevents him from driving on in the career of depredation and oppression at a pace quite so rapid as that which has every where been kept up by a single-headed one. In this retardation consists the only real benefit derived from the supposed sole and sufficient security for good government: for, sooner or later, the arrival of the vehicle at the bottom of the abyss is not less certain in the one case than in the other, unless in the mean time a government in the hands of the people should by some means or other be made to take [the] place of a government in the hands of their natural and for ever implacable enemies.

Any division which it might be proposed to make of the supreme power in the State, has it or has it not a tendency to lodge any part of that same power in the hands of the great body of the people? If not, in what way is it possible that by that same great body any benefit should be reaped from it? If yes, suppose such tendency ripened into act: the consequence is—a portion of the power, but no more than a portion, becomes lodged in the hands of the people. But from this portion, be it ever so considerable, how is it possible [that][1] any benefit can be reaped by them greater than or even so great as that which would be reaped by them from the whole? In a word how can a chance of a part be equal in value to the possession of the whole? Yet on this chance of a part, and it has been seen how feeble an one, depends the utmost benefit which can ever have been supposed derivable by them from any division made of the supreme power in question, they by the supposition not having any share in it.

Take now the converse of the above case. Suppose the whole of the supreme power already in the hands of the people: and then let it be seen whether any benefit could be produced to them by any scheme of division by which this or that portion of it were lodged in other hands. Take for example the Anglo-American United States. In that seat of good government and consequent felicity, the whole of the Supreme power is in the hands of the people: the supreme Constitutive in the hands of the greatest number: the supreme Operative, supreme Legislative and Executive included, in the hands of agents of theirs, placed by them, some in an immediate, others in an unimmediate

---

[1] MS 'than'.

way, sooner or later all displaceable, and those who have most power regularly displaced by them. Add now a King, with a veto upon every act of the legislative body, and the power of placing and displacing all subordinate functionaries belonging to the Executive department. Here then would be division of power: a division, so far as it went, agreeing with that which has place in England. To the people in question what would be the benefit of it? By the most anxious scrutiny could any the smallest possible particle of benefit be found derivable from it?

At the very commencement of his reign the least you could do for him (it is the least that has any where been done for him[1]) is—to take from the producers, and pour into his lap, a mass of property equal to that which suffices for the subsistence of several thousands of them in the same time. But if instead of thousands they were, as in England and France, myriads, never would the allowance thus made to him be, for never has it any where been found, sufficient. No sooner were he installed than he would begin to do as George the third did all his life, and as George the fourth is doing now: George the third who, in the course of his reign, forced the people at nine different times to pay his debts: George the fourth who in the same career is outstripping his father.[2] The offices placed at his disposal would not be numerous enough, nor rich enough. To fill up the deficiency, he would talk of honour and dignity, and plunge the country into war: he would talk of trade and commerce, and build nests of lucrative offices in distant dependencies: he would conquer colonies for the sake of wars: and wage wars for the sake of colonies.

If, for the conferring the supposed benefit of the people, by taking power out of their hands and lodging it in the hands of men with interests unchangeably opposite to theirs, what is as yet supposed to be done is not yet sufficient, to the defalcation thus already made from their power, add another. For the necessary support of so necessary an ingredient in good government as a Monarchy, establish an hereditary aristocracy, establish a House of Lords. But, not being exclusively dedicated to the service of God by vows of celibacy, the men thus made into great men will to the customary extent be blessed with sons and daughters. The fathers will all of them have dignity to

---

[1] MS alt. in the hand of the copyist: 'this supposed Idol of your creation, whom Blackstone invests, in so many words, with the attributes of the Almighty'. An allusion to William Blackstone, *Commentaries on the Laws of England*, 4 vols., Oxford, 1765–9: see especially i. 230–70.

[2] The debts of George III (1738–1820), King of Great Britain and Ireland from 1760, were paid by Parliament in 1769, 1777, 1784, 1786, 1802, 1804, 1805, 1814 and 1816. George IV was notorious for his extravagance: Parliament had paid his debts in 1783 and 1787, and in 1795 had appointed commissioners to establish a sinking fund in order to liquidate further debts which he had contracted.

support: their Honourable and Right Honorable children will all of them remain honoured with the corresponding burthen. Here then is a demand for more lucrative offices, and as the indispensable sources of new offices, more wars and more distant dependencies.

Nor is this all. For these and so many other honourable men, factitious honor and dignity in all its innumerable shapes must be provided, or merit in all its shapes must go unrewarded. By the sole and infallible judge of merit in all its shapes, titles of honor must be scattered around, and with or without garters, stars and ribbons.

In company with the correspondent merit, this honor and dignity you have in whatsoever quantity you deem requisite. For its support, unfortunately, each title and each ornament requires money: but you know already where and how to get it.

Still though you have your House of Lords, you have not as yet any such quality in it as *holiness*. No holiness without Bishops. Over a competent number of them, place a competent number of Archbishops; you may thus condense any additional quantity of holiness into one and the same receptacle. In every desirable degree of plenitude every one of these receptacles may be and will have been made full of the Holy Ghost: but to accomplish this plenitude a proportionable quantity of the[1] manna of unrighteousness must have been forced into their unwilling pockets: and to be forced into those sacred pockets it must have been forced out of the profane pockets of the people.

The most important arrangement in this system of the division of power remains yet behind. It consists in the depriving the vast majority of the people of those *votes* which constituted their share in that supreme Constitutive power, which on the supposition we set out with was divided among them all in equal portions. By the minute remnant, the greater part of it in the hands of the Members of the so-called House of Lords, will thereupon be chosen another House of Lords who for distinction sake you may call a House of Commons. This fundamental defalcation accomplished, accomplishment is given to that form of Government which in England, where no such document as a Constitutional Code is in existence, is known by the name of the *matchless Constitution*: and sure enough its match is not any where to be found. In regard to money matters, would you see by the light of experience the effects of the change? Look to England and behold annual expence of government, exclusive of interest of national debt, £St.18,577,636: annual interest of national debt, £St.30,921,494: the debt in the shape of a perpetual annuity to that

---

[1] The word 'the' has been added by the copyist.

amount: an annuity, the whole of it indeed redeemable, but redeemable at a time that never can come.[1]

By any warning given against *open negatives* upon the power of the people, the service rendered would be very incomplete without the addition of a like warning against latent ones. With or without design, a negative of this latent sort may be seen given in and by several of the Articles of the Greek Constitution: namely Articles 24, 25, 30, 31, 36, 46, 54, 57. In regard to any such negative, such *veto* as it has been called, mark in the first place one general effect of it. This is— the investing the possessor with the faculty of obtaining in the way of compromise a share in every power to which it is applicable: which share he applies of course to his own purposes, whatever they may happen to be.[2]

In this latent form, be the proposed arrangement or measure what it may, a negative upon it is given to every functionary by whom, on pain of its being of no effect, this or that act must have been done in relation to it. Now then if so it be that the functionary on whom this power of controul has been conferred is in a state of perfect official dependence—a mere copying Clerk or Scribe, suppose, whose continuance in his situation is altogether and at all times dependent upon the will of some higher functionary, the possible negative thus given may perhaps be in little or no danger of becoming an efficient one. But, if so it be that the functionary thus gifted is a person in a situation of declared or virtual independence, in this case it is not rendered the less efficient but rather the more efficient a negative by its not being an openly declared one.

Now then for the instances.

First as to all operations together, taken in the lump.

1. By Article 24: 'To the President, namely of the so-stiled Legislative Senate, it belongs to determine the day on which each Session

---

[1] In a memorandum at UC xxi. 212 (4 March 1823), Bentham remarked: 'What was said in the paper against the division of power system on the subject of the amount of the interest of the English National Debt and the annual expence of Government may perhaps require correction: viz. by notice to be taken of the expence of management, and of the interest of the unfunded debt.' Pinned to this sheet is the following note in the hand of Francis Place (1771–1854):

Expenditure 1822 · · ·	49,499,130	total ⎫	49,400,000
Interest on debt · · ·	30,921,494	⎬ not including Sinking fund.	4 · · · · · · · ·
Government · · · · · ·	18,577,636	⎭	53 · · · · · · · ·

Expense of Management nearly 4,000,000: of this the management of the inland part is nearly 1,000,000£.

Net Receipt 1822 · · ·	54,414,650	
	4 · · · · · · · ·	Management
	58 · · · · · · ·	

[2] A fragment on the topic of 'Antecedent or Precedential veto' is at UC xxi. 190 (11 February 1823).

of that Assembly shall commence; as also the day on which it shall terminate.' If then he determines no such day, no such Session can have place: moreover if, such having been his pleasure, so it be that a Session having commenced and for a certain time continued, his pleasure in this behalf has changed, he declares such his pleasure accordingly, and from that time a negative is put by him in the lump upon all such proceedings of the Assembly as would otherwise have succeeded. True it is that by Article [15][1] to that same Senate itself it belongs to choose this same high-seated functionary. But, when the choice has been made, such, as above, is the state of dependence in which that body has been placed under this its own offspring: dependence for its very existence. Now then, an act of this sort of parricide suppose it to have been committed: the consequence is—that what is left of the powers of government falls of itself into the lap of the so-stiled Executive Council with its five Members, acting as they are to do in a perpetually secret conclave.

Supposing him to have (under Article 24) put an end to the existence of these his creators, by Article 25 he is empowered to bestow upon them at any time a new existence. 'In case of need' (says this 25th. Article) 'he may convoke the Senate to enter upon an extraordinary Session.' Thus it rests at all times at his choice whether to sell existence to them at his own price, or to leave them in a state of annihilation. If and so long as they are sufficiently obsequious, he suffers them to act accordingly: if refractory, he lays them asleep: and so *toties quoties*. Thus far as to the latent negative or *veto* in the hands of the President on the operations of the so-stiled Legislative Senate taken in the aggregate.

Now as to the several operations taken in detail.

1. By Article 30th., 'Every Act of the Senate is signed by the President and countersigned by the principal Secretary.' Suppose then an Act the tenor of which does not suit his views: what is the consequence? He withholds his signature, and no such Act can come into existence.

Moreover in this same power he has a sharer, it has been seen, in the principal Secretary.

2. A second means of applying the President's particular Veto is put into his hands by the next Article, Article 31. 'The President' (it says) 'transmitts the Resolutions of the Senate to the Council' (meaning the Executive Council) 'and submits them to its approbation.' Good. But in the mean time though inexplicitly they have not the less effectually been thus submitted in the first place to the approbation of this same

---

[1] MS '17'.

all-powerful functionary. Do they suit his views, he transmitts them accordingly: do they thwart his views, he keeps them where they are. President of so-stiled Legislative Senate to President or other most influential member of the so-stiled Executive Council—'You see this Resolution: what will you give me if I transmitt it to you?—what will you give me if I keep it back?' The language will naturally be the very quintessence of decorum: and so it may be, while this and nothing else is at the bottom of it.

3. Article 36, after saying that 'Every Member of the Senate may propose a project of law in writing', goes on and says, 'which the President refers to the examination of a Committee'. Suppose then introduced in this manner a project of law which has the misfortune not to suit the views of this great functionary, what becomes of it? He receives it, omitts to forward it to any Committee, and there is an end of it. It is thus stifled in embryo.

4. So much for the President of the so-stiled Legislative Senate. Now again for the Principal Secretary of that same body. In and by Art. 46 he is once more let in for an equal share with the President as above in the negative which we have seen the President put in possession of by Article 31 with regard to all Resolutions of that same Senate. 'He', (the principal Secretary) says the Article, 'receives from the President the Resolutions of the Senate and transmitts them to the Council'—namely the so-stiled Executive Council. Thus then, if it be the pleasure of the President not to deliver them to the Principal Secretary, or of the Principal Secretary not to transmitt them to that same Council, there is an end of these same Resolutions.

Mark now the secret perils which every offspring of the wisdom of the so-stiled Legislative Senate has to encounter and surmount before it can come into existence. Instead of birth comes abortion, if either to the so-stiled *Executive Council*, that is to say to three out of its five Members, or to the President of the so-stiled Legislative Senate, or to the Principal Secretary of that same Legislative Senate, it has the misfortune to be an object of displeasure, or even of indifference.

But the list of its perils is not yet at an end. When it has passed through these, and (under Article 32) received existence from the hands of the so-stiled Executive Council, if as affairs turn out so it happens that to three of the five Members of which the so-stiled Executive Council is composed it afterwards ceases to be agreable, it is consigned to a sleep, to which there is no assignable termination. For, says Article 54, 'The Council causes the laws to be executed by the Ministers.' Suppose then a law which, to the Minister by whom execution and effect should be given it, happens to be disagreable or an object of indifference: if so it be likewise to three out of the five

Members of the so-stiled Executive Council, they have but to let the law pass unnoticed, and so long as this is the case with it, it sleeps. Suppose it even to be agreable to the Minister, still if it fails or ceases to be so to any three of these five great functionaries, I would not give much for any benefit that rested upon it.

One concluding peril is yet behind. Be the arrangement what it may, in vain might it suit the views of a majority of the so-stiled Legislative Senate; in vain might it moreover suit the views of four-fifths of the five Members of the so-stiled Executive Council. If the President of this same Council is not one of them, he has but to with[h]old from the Act his signature and there is an end of it. For, by Article 57, 'Every Act and decree of the Council is signed by the President, countersigned by the Principal Secretary and sealed by Seal of the State.'

Here we see moreover given another latent *veto* with this additional hand for the reception of it. This same Secretary of this same Council of five, is he or is he not of the number of its Members? To that question no answer have I found.

But now a word as to this same *Seal of the State*. This seal is either in the hands of some one person, or in the joint hands of divers persons. Who is that one person? or who are these divers persons? For in him or them resides another latent negative. In the English Government different seals are in the custody each of them of some one individual functionary. Of these several functionaries, each one, so long as the seal is in his keeping, has not only an effective but an acknowledged Veto upon all acts which for their validity require upon the face of them an impression of the appropriate seal.[1] True it is, that to the King it belongs to take each seal out of any one pair of hands and place it in any other. But, so long as it remains in the hands of any person other than the King, that person has an effective *veto* upon all such acts as require an impression of that same seal to make them valid: and so long as it remains in the hands of the King alone, no binding force will be attributed to any act bearing an impression made with it: to render the act valid, in addition to such impression, the counter-signature of a subordinate functionary in whose custody the seal is will be deemed requisite.

On the occasion of the warnings herein above given, the governments chosen for examples have been the only good one, and among the bad ones the least bad that could be found. Against those which have place in Russia, Austria and Prussia all warning would on the

---

[1] In the text at this point, the copyist has added: 'Take for instance great Seal and privy seal.' The Lord Chancellor had custody of the Great Seal and the Lord Keeper of the Privy Seal had custody of the Privy Seal.

present occasion have been needless and therefore useless. The only forms of government against which any such warning presented a chance of being useful are those bad forms that have some good in them, and that one good form which has some bad in it. Among the bad forms which have some good in them have been mentioned the Spanish, the Portugueze and the English: the one good form that has a small sprinkling of bad in it is that of the Anglo-American United States.

So far as concerns the English Government (for Constitutional Code and therefore Constitution it has none) the books against which it may be of use that the Greeks should have warning are Montesquieu, Blackstone, and De l'Olme:[1] of that pretended Constitution, the sort of colouring given to it considered, the several descriptions given in these several works may be termed *the romance*. Tacitly or expressly, one supposition pervades them all, namely that in the formation of the government in question the greatest happiness of the greatest number was the end really in view: the greatest happiness of those *over* whom and not the greatest happiness of those *by* whom the power is exercised: a sort of fact by the assumption of which they assumed that which neither ever has been, nor, consistently with the existence of the species, ever could have been, true. One only state of things is there in which it ever has been or ever can be true: and that is the state of things in which without material difference the persons by whom and the persons over whom the power is exercised are the same.[2]

To return to this same so-styled Executive Council and the positive mischiefs with which I see it pregnant. In it I see lodged, as per article 21, the power of location with relation to all the offices in the State: all the offices of course included to which either power or emolument in any shape jointly or separately are attached, as also the power of dislocation with relation to those same offices. To this same so-styled Executive Council is moreover given an uncontrol[l]ed negative upon every Legislative act proposed by the so-styled Legislative Senate. On the several Members of the Legislative Senate, a measure of confidence more or less considerable may not without just ground attach itself. For the several Members will have each of them his constituents, his patrons and superiors to whom as such, with a degree of effect proportioned to the value he sets upon their good opinion, good

---

[1] Charles Louis de Secondat, Baron de la Brède et de Montesquieu, *De l'esprit des loix*, Geneva, [1748], especially Book XI, Ch. vi (first published in an English translation in 1750); Blackstone, *Commentaries on the Laws of England*; Jean Louis Delolme, *Constitution d'Angleterre*, Amsterdam, 1771 (first published in an English translation in 1775).

[2] The remainder of this part of the essay is in the hand of the copyist, but bears some corrections in Bentham's hand.

will, and good offices in all shapes, with or without such prospect as he may have or not have of continuance in such a situation as the case may be, he will feel himself responsible: for, the contrary not being said, what I take for granted, is—that to every thing that passes in this same Legislative Senate, with the exception of such temporary and partial concealment as it may be deemed necessary to give now and then to such parts of the business as shall on that account be assigned to Sittings denominated accordingly secret, whatever degree of publicity can be given, will be. On the other hand, in the situation of the so-styled Executive Council, with its number of Members no greater than 5, I see no such responsibility, consequently no such ground for confidence: on the contrary, but too strong a ground for complete distrust—a complete withholding of confidence. In them I see the Members of an everlastingly secret Conclave: a set of men engrossing in their own hands the whole of that power which is conferred by the uncontrol[l]ed disposal of the matter of good in all its shapes applicable in the character of matter of reward to the remuneration, which is as much as to say to the purchase, of service in all imaginable shapes to the aggregate of their several particular and sinister interests, at the expence and by the sacrifice of the universal interest. With the whole of this power in their hands, with the addition of a share in Legislative power equal to that of the body to which the appellation of Legislative Senate is exclusively attributed, I see them at work upon the appropriate moral aptitude—the political probity, of the several Members of the so-styled Legislative Senate: and, in the first place, upon the comparatively few to whom their preeminence in the faculty of public speaking will secure the leading share in the conduct of every part of the public business. For some time perhaps in the case of the majority, the value of his share in the universal interest may in the breast of each man outweigh the value of any particular and sinister interest by which he may be solicited to seek to gratify it[1] at the expence of the universal interest. I mention this state of things that it may be seen not to have been overlooked: but it is not in the nature of man, especially of man in any such situation, that it should have place to any considerable extent for any long continuance. These halcyon days being at an end, what then is the state of things that follows them? It is one that gives birth to a league between the 5 Members of the so-styled Executive Council on the one part and the leading Members of the so-styled Legislative Senate on the other: a league for the conjunct advancement of their joint and several particular and sinister interests. Now then as to offices with emolument

---

[1] i.e. his own interest.

attached, what are the dictates of this same conjunct sinister interest? That which the sinister interest of the Members of the so-styled Executive Council dictates is, with respect to the offices with emolument attached, that the number of them and the quantity of emolument attached to each be as great, and on the other hand the quantity of time and labour necessary to be bestowed on each be as small, as possible. This, were it only that in this way they might each of them have in his hands in the most ample quantity the means of providing for his own favorites and dependents, especially for those for whom, had it not been for this means, he would have had to provide at his own expence. Exposed exactly to the same temptation is the probity of the Members, especially of the leading Members, of the so-styled Legislative Senate. But by no means can any one of them thus give advancement to his own share in the conjunct sinister interest otherwise than by giving to his suffrage and discourse the direction which will contribute, as above, to the advancement of the conjunct sinister interest of the Members of the so-styled Executive Council, and thus it is that by the conjunct influence of these confederated sinister interests, the Members of the community at large, and in particular those by whose labour the whole mass of the good things thus disposed of is produced, will be loaded with burden after burden, so long as their physical faculty of producing and giving up, or at least, so long as their faculty of enduring depredation and oppression with patience, remains unexhausted.

Such being the present evil, now then as to the applicable remedy. It is a very simple one. Take any single man—for example him whom you would otherwise have made President of this same so-styled Executive Council, give to him the whole of the patronage, with the exception of such parts of it as may, without preponderate inconvenience, be detached from his office on special grounds; place under him 4 other persons, for example the 4 other Members of that same Executive Council: giving to each his separate Department as above,[a] with more or less of the patronage belonging to it; you thus break down the phalanx: to every purpose legal as well as moral each one of them is now fully responsible for his own acts: the eye of the public bears fully and separately on the conduct of each.

Now then as to the 11 functionaries to whom, by article 86, I see given the whole of that power which, by article 85, is styled the Judicial power.[1] If the power thus given to them, whatever it be, is

---

[a] See above, p. [228].

---

[1] An earlier draft in which Bentham discussed Articles 85 and 86 is at UC xxi. 193–5 (16 February 1823).

exercised by them no otherwise than in conjunction, what has been said, as above, on the subject of the 5 Members composing the so-styled Executive Council will, so far as regards responsibility, be found applicable to them. By what means they are to come into such their situation—I mean in whose will or wills they are to behold the efficient cause of their possession of it, is more than I can see. By article 86, they are to be elected by the *Government*. But this word *Government*, what individual, what Body or what Bodies, were meant to be indicated by it? Not the Legislative Senate: to this Body no such appellation do I see any where attributed: not the so-styled Executive Council: for neither to this Body do I see that same appellation any where attributed. True it is that in article 21, of this Body it is said that it nominates to all the offices (*emplois*) of the Government. If therefore to the question, by whom are these 11 fractions of a Judge or of a Minister of Justice to be placed in such their situation? it were made necessary to find an answer, mine would be, by the Members of this same so-styled Executive Council.

But now comes to mind one of the 8 functionaries styled in Article 20th. *Ministers*, namely the Minister of Justice. As towards the functions committed to the joint exercise of these 11, what is the relation which the function this so-called Minister of Justice is intended to exercise bears?

As to the Minister of Justice, him I have work for, him I should be glad to keep, but as for these 11, unless it be for one of them somewhere in the character of Judge in a single-seated Judicatory, no one of these have I any work for: much rather would I give to each of them for doing nothing the whole of the emoluments intended for him, than for bearing his part in the business, whatever it may be, that was intended for the whole. As to the arrangement made in Article [85][1] in which the Judiciary power is designed and declared to be in a state of independence as well with relation to the Legislative power as with relation to the Executive power, such independence is in direct contrariety with my principle of absolute and universal dependence on the supreme power of the whole, as above.

But hereupon it becomes necessary I should proceed to state what the sort of arrangement is which I should propose to make with relation to the business of this department.

Now as to the plan I would propose for a Judiciary.

The whole territory of the state, say on the present occasion Greece, I would divide into Judicial Districts: the number, of course, not at present determinable: each such Judicial District into Judicial

---

[1] MS '83'.

sub-districts, for the demarcation of which extent of territory and of population should conjunctly be taken into account.

For the sake of simplicity and uniformity, and for a further reason that will soon be visible, the limits of these several Judicial Districts should be the same as those of the several Election Districts, by each of which a Member is sent to the Legislative Senate. The limits of the several Judicial sub-districts may perhaps be the same with those of the several Election sub-districts into which it may be convenient that the Election districts be divided, for the purpose of collecting, at so many voting offices, the several parcels of votes, which are from thence to be transferred altogether to the Election district voting office, at which the aggregate number of the votes given in that district are collected, sorted, and counted. Whether, of any of these Judicial sub-districts, there shall be any ulterior division into sub-sub-districts must remain to be determined by particular local considerations. For these Judicial districts, the only source of division I should employ is—the territorial; no such source as that which has so generally been employed, and which may be termed the logical or metaphysical: a source taken from the nature of the Judicial business done: no such division, for example, as that between civil and penal suits or causes, or that between civil and ecclesiastical suits or causes, between commercial and non-commercial suits or causes: no such division as that under English Law, and thence under the English-bred Law of some of the Anglo-American United States, between Law cases and Equity cases. Reason. From any such principle of division spring two great evils: one is, needless and useless addition to the number of Judicatories: the other is, in the case of this or that suit or cause, doubt and contestation [as] to the cognizance of which of two or more Judicatories it appertains. To this general rule, a few exceptions, but to no very considerable extent in the aggregate, will be of necessity suggested by the peculiar circumstances in which some classes of public functionaries find themselves placed. For example, in the land branch of the Military service, there will be certain classes of offences to which the power of the ordinary local Judicatories will not be found applicable; and so in the case of the Maritime branch of that same service. But it follows not that because, in these particular cases, it is necessary that offences belonging to these particular classes be withdrawn from the cognizance of the ordinary Judicatories, they should be so in any cases to which the necessity does not extend.

The boundaries, and thence the contents, of the several fields of Jurisdiction being thus settled, now as to the efficient causes of placement and displacement—of location and dislocation—as well as the number of the functionaries by whom the Judicial situations in those several fields of Jurisdiction shall be occupied.

As to number. In each Judicatory, one Judge and no more. Reason 1st. Responsibility thus alone entire: not fractionalized and thus dissipated, appropriate moral aptitude thus maximized. Reason 2d. Expence minimized. In England, there are single-seated Judicatories, there are four-seated Judicatories, and there are many-seated Judicatories. Those in which, all circumstances taken together, the business is regarded as being of the highest importance are of the single-seated class. Where there have been and are two Judicatories of concurrent jurisdiction, one a single-seated Judicatory, the Chancery—the other a four-seated Judicatory, the Court of Exchequer—the single-seated Judicatory, notwithstanding the two or three stages of appeal crowded into it, has at all times received much more business than the four-seated one, the Court of Exchequer. The Judicatory in which, at all times, the greatest liberties have been taken with the most obvious and indisputable rules of Justice, is that of the twelve great Judges, composed of the population of the three great Westminster Hall Courts.[1] Not one of these functionaries would, in any single-seated Judicatory, have dared to deliver any such decisions as are so many of those in which all have joined, screened from the public eye by concealment, silence, and the delusive trappings with which he and his associates are bedecked. In Scotland, when there were fifteen of them sitting together in the highest Judicatory, it was still worse.[2] In a word, the probability of good Judicature is everywhere not directly, but inversely, as the number of the Judges. Few moral rules have ever received so full a proof from experience.

In each Judicatory, efficient cause of location, the choice made, and will declared, by the Minister of Justice. Efficient cause of dislocation, votes to that effect by the majority of the Electors appertaining to the Judicial district or sub-district as above, as the case may be. This, without cause necessarily assigned. The Electors being, on each day after giving their votes on the occasion of the election of a representative in the Legislative Assembly, called upon to give their votes for or against the existing Judge, but not in favour of any other person in the character of a Candidate for that same situation. In case of a majority for displacement, obligation on the Minister of Justice to place another individual in that same Judicatory, but with power to place in any other Judicatory the so-displaced Judge. On the part of

---

[1] i.e. the Court of Exchequer Chamber, consisting of the Judges of the Courts of King's Bench and Common Pleas and the Barons of the Exchequer.

[2] Before the Administration of Justice in Scotland Act of 1808 (48 Geo. III, c.151), the Court of Session was in theory a unitary court whose fifteen judges sat and deliberated together.

the Electors, no specific assigned cause for such displacement need be made necessary, but in the nature of the case no proposition to that effect could ever be made with any prospect of success without assigned causes in abundance. Power to the Minister of Justice to propose to any Judge at any time, and accept, his resignation, and upon refusal or silence to displace him, assigning or not assigning a specific cause or causes. Power to the so-displaced Judge to stand forth in public for the vindication of his character, and to contest the existence or the sufficiency, or both, of any causes so assigned. On this head some provisions of detail would be found requisite.

Reasons why the power of location should, in regard to all these Judicatories, be in the hand of a single person, the Minister of Justice:[1] 1. the object of the judicial system taken in the aggregate being to give and secure execution and effect to the whole body of the Law all over the territory of the state taken in the aggregate, one main business of the Minister of Justice will be, according to the measure of his ability, to secure consistency and symmetry in the plan and mode according to which such execution and effect is given or professed to be given in every such field of Jurisdiction throughout the state.

The power of displacement with reference to each such Judicatory being, as above, given to the majority of the Electors, why not, in preference to the Minister of Justice, give to that same body the power of placing likewise? Answer—1. after experience, in case of inaptitude, a body of that description may without difficulty be duly qualified for a decision declaring, in general terms, the existence of such inaptitude. Antecedently to such experience, no sufficient grounds for pronouncing a decision in affirmance of such aptitude can they have had. 2. In the case of an unapt choice, no sufficient responsibility would attach upon any individual in the character of a promoter of it. 3. For the sake of a chance of placing in so desirable a situation a confederate of his own, a leader having influence over the people might be apt to raise ungrounded clamour against a sufficiently apt Judge.

Question. Why when a Judge has thus been displaced by his justiciables—the electors—give the Minister of Justice the power of placing him in another district?

Answer. Because what may naturally enough happen is, that the conduct by which such displacement by a majority of the electors in the district in question has been produced has, though contrary to the particular interest or supposed interest of those same persons, been necessary to the support of the universal interest: for example the

---

[1] Bentham proceeds to give only one reason.

giving execution and effect to laws calling for sacrifices, by contributions in the shape of money, money's worth, or personal services, for the maintenance of the Government against its adversaries of all classes.

As the only effectual preventive of delay, power to every Judge to appoint Deputies in any number to sit at the same time with himself for the dispatch of business in different causes, but let no emolument be receivable by any such Deputy at the expence either of the public or of individuals. No doubt can be entertained of willingness on the part of a sufficient number of sufficiently apt individuals to undertake so honorable an office. The having served in such office might and should be made a necessary qualification for the being placed in the office of Judge. The choice thus proposed to be made of a Deputy should be declared to the parties and objections received. The principal Judge should not be sitting at home unoccupied while any such Deputy of his was sitting, for if such inaction were allowed two evils might follow: 1. to save his own reputation, a partial Judge might assign the function in this or that particular case to some connexion of one of the parties who for the sake of the profit, from partiality, would be content to submit to the disrepute: 2. the office of principal Judge might moreover be converted into a sinecure. In case of sickness such power of deputation is matter of absolute necessity.

To exclude partiality and all suspicion of it, it should be a declared object of endeavour to keep the Judge clear of all local connection in the way of interest or sympathy, hence it should be a general rule that no Judge should continue such in any one district for any long time, say for more [than] 3 years, nor be appointed Judge in any district in which he already has connexions of a certain description, to be specified; and his being known or suspected to have subsequently formed any such connexions may be stated as warrantable grounds for a proposition for his displacement as above, but no such connexion should be stated as a necessary efficient cause for his displacement, and provision might be made by means of which, in pursuance of a desire not much short of universal expressed by his justiciables, his continuance in that district might be prolonged.

As to the composition of the Jury, the exclusion of two evils, viz. partiality to the prejudice of the party in the right, vexation by attendance to the injury of the Jurors themselves, will be the leading ends in view. To secure a majority, the number should in every case be odd: less therefore than three it can not be. The greater the number more than three, the more extended the vexation. For securing impartiality, and thus far appropriate moral aptitude, not indeed to a certainty, that being impossible, but the best possible chance in favour of it, appointment by lot (provided the numbers of those included in the Lottery be sufficiently ample and indiscriminately taken) will suffice: for augmenting the chance of appropriate intellectual aptitude, viz. knowledge and judgment, the following course may be taken. The whole number of individuals in the district liable to serve as Jurors, divide into two classes—viz. the more erudite and the less erudite: for a Jury of three, take one from the more erudite class: to the influence of understanding on understanding, where moral inaptitude is not suspected, trust for his opinions being taken as a guide by his less erudite colleagues.

The class of persons in which it is desirable that Judges be chosen is *that* of Judge-deputes, as above—viz. such by which, in the discharge of that function, the highest degree of appropriate aptitude, in its several branches, has been manifested: the class of persons in which it is desirable that Judges should *not* be chosen is *that* of hireling advocates. In the breast of the hireling advocate, the chance of inaptitude, in that shape in which it is opposed to appropriate moral aptitude, is at its maximum: it amounts to a moral certainty. He lets himself out to hire indiscriminately to the party injured, or the injurer, to the guiltless man unjustly accused, or the malefactor, according as he happens to be retained: but it is uniformly on the side of the party in the wrong that his predilection ranges itself. In the party who, being in the wrong, is conscious of his being so, he looks for his best Customer; and, in case of success, the more flagrantly his client is in the wrong, the more illustrious the triumph of his advocate: the more conspicuous the proof afforded of the union of appropriate active with appropriate intellectual aptitude, with reference to the function of defeating the ends of Justice. Whatsoever falshood or insincerity in any other shape the advocate has occasion to defile himself with, the deluded public suffers him to scrape off from his own shoulders, and lay upon those of his client: his whole life is thereby a life of falshood and insincerity. Exclusions applied to the faculty of giving testimony, on the ground of moral inaptitude, are, if ever sincerely intended, a very foolishly devised instrument for avoidance of mendacity and thence of deception and injustice.

But if there were a sort of man on whom a note of eminent untrustworthiness should be put for the instruction and guidance of a Jury, it should be the hireling advocate. When the man, impregnated to the very marrow with the practice of mendacity and the love of injustice, is raised to the Judicial Bench, an appropriate masquerade dress is put upon him, and the silly and deluded multitude behold in him justice personified. Oftener has the black mare been rendered white by dipping, than the hireling advocate converted, by a seat on the Judicial

Bench, into a lover of Justice. Every now and then in England passes the following scene. Advocate or Judge to witness—'Do you believe in the existence of a God?' Witness to Judge—'Yes'—Judge, thereupon, to Advocate—'Proceed with him, he is a good witness'—Advocate or Judge to Witness—'Do you believe in the existence of a God?'— Witness—'No': Judge—'Out with him: his testimony is not receivable'. Thus, then, if the Atheist will, to so indefensible a question, give a false answer, he is admitted: but if his regard for truth be such that he will not give a false answer, he is held out as an object of reproach—a man to whose testimony no regard can safely be given, and, as such, rejected. But to the man of habitual mendacity, any such man of conspicuously and painfully manifested veracity is an object of the deepest hatred and vengeance; and, to gratify this malignant passion, he scruples not to make sacrifice of the injured party whose misfortune it has been to have need of the testimony of this too veracious witness.

In a country in which a sort of imaginary law, called unwritten, and which has so much more writing belonging to it than that which is called written, has place, the choice made of Judges from the order of Advocates has an unhappily existing reason, adequate or inadequate, as well as a pretence. There being no rule of action really in existence, the hireling advocate is the only sort of man who can be regarded as an adept in the art of speaking of the case, whatever it be, in a manner that supposes the existence of a rule of action, and in the use of that jargon which has been employed in palming upon the public that fiction in the character of a truth. To him alone is sufficiently familiar that branch of the thieve's cant. The care of keeping on foot this disastrous reason, this unhappy necessity, is one cause of the care taken by the fraternity of Lawyers to keep the rule of action from ever receiving real existence. By the impossibility of defending himself, by his own powers, against those injuries which the fraternity are in league to inflict on him, a man is thus under the deplorable necessity of purchasing, at the ruinous price set upon it, their essentially treacherous assistance. Bonaparte, being a Despot, was, by the vigor of his mind, enabled to add to his vulgar triumphs two transcendental ones: triumphs over the two bitterest and most mischievous enemies of the human race—established priests and lawyers. Over the lawyer tribe, the main cause and token of his triumph was the establishment of a really-existing body of law, having for it's object not indeed the greatest happiness of the greatest number, but of the one, Napoleon Bonaparte: it sacrificed, wheresoever competition appeared to show itself, the interest of all to the interest of that one. But, had it been several times worse than it is, France would still have beheld and felt in it a matchless benefit.[1] The Citizens of the Anglo-American United States have thrown off the yoke of a Monarchy, have thrown off the yoke of an Aristocracy, have many of them thrown off the yoke of an established priesthood. But the yoke of the hireling advocate still presses upon their necks: their courage has been sufficient to free them from the yoke of the English Monarch: but their wisdom has not yet been sufficient to liberate them from the yoke imposed upon them by the most corrupt and profligate of his tools.

Oh weakness! Oh inconsistency! You have given yourselves a rule of action accommodated to your own interests on the Constitutional branch of the field of Law; you leave it to your natural and irreconcileable enemies to plunder you under the cloak of an imaginary rule of action, imported from a foreign and enslaved country, a system of fiction accommodated to their own particular and sinister interests to the sacrifice of your's.

In every Judicial District, there will, in the most prosperous state of human nature, be but too many who, being by the inaptitude opposite to appropriate intellectual and appropriate active aptitude laid under an incapacity of giving adequate support to their own cause, even on the supposition of the justice of it, will be at the same time lying under the inability of finding, if ever, in sufficient time an adequate gratuitous advocate. For persons thus situated, there seems an indispensable necessity of providing a pair of official advocates, one for each side of the cause. Call the one, the pursuer's advocate general: call the other, the defender's advocate general. On the part of the Judge, no degree of appropriate aptitude in all its branches that in his place can be realized, or so much as imagined, can supersede altogether the demand for assistance in those other shapes. In causes of the simplest nature, yes: but in causes of a certain degree of complexity, no: in this or that instance, a necessity will arise for such communication and such arrangement of Documents as the time of the Judge could not suffice for. Moreover, the inexorable and predetermined impartiality of the Judge would scarcely be compatible with the reception of that unrestrained confidence of which the case of a party, how compleatly soever in the right, may occasionally have need. By the single-seatedness of every Judicatory as contrasted with the many-seatedness so generally established—by this single-seatedness, combined with the gratuitousness of the service rendered by deputies, room will be left for reconciling the allotment

---

[1] Napoleon Bonaparte (1769–1821), First Consul of France 1799–1804, Emperor of the French 1804–14, had been responsible for the codification of French law: the so-called *Code Napoléon* consisted of *Code Civil* (1804), *Code de Procédure Civile* (1806), *Code de Commerce* (1807), *Code d'Instruction Criminelle* (1809) and *Code Pénal* (1810).

of sufficient salaries to these two subsidiary functionaries, with a reduction in the expence of the whole of the establishment, as compared with that with which it would be charged by hitherto-established usage. To these two functionaries should also be given the power of appointing unpaid deputies: neither in these situations, any more than in that of Judge, is man exempt from sickness. To the faculty of enlarging and contracting itself as need requires may be given the appellation of elasticity: needful as is this quality, never till Bentham wrote did any such conception as that of planting it in the Judicial Establishment enter into the head of any as yet known publicist.

Proper[1] and only proper model of Judicial procedure, the domestic. For, in domestic procedure, there are no hireling advocates interested in the obstruction and defeat of the ends of justice. For the collection of evidence, powers which are not to be found in the domestic Judicatory will in many instances be necessary to the public Judicatory. These powers must of course be supplied. But in this supply lies almost the only difference requisite. In domestic procedure, the only natural procedure has its model. In every father, his children and his other servants, if he has any, behold their Judge. Contradistinguished in it's name, because opposite as to the ends to which the course of it has been directed, must be the course of procedure by far the most extensively as yet in use: call it the technical—such is the name by which, even by it's inventors, it has been characterized. For technical, say on any occasion unjust—you need not fear misnaming it.

Sittings uninterrupted. No day in the year exempt. On what day is Justice less necessary than another? On what day is injury inactive? What relaxation has the medical man? But to the Judge moderate relaxation might be given by allowing the substitution of a Deputy for a limited number of days. As to Deputy, see [above].[2] Doors of the Judicatory constantly open to all visitants. Structure of it, specially adapted to the giving to the greatest number possible the best accommodation possible. Let such visitants be considered as a Committee of the public opinion tribunal appointed for the purpose of securing more or less responsibility on the part of the Judge: they may at the same time be considered as a Committee of the universal body of electors in whom resides the supreme power of the State—the constitutive. Let this be the spot in which the suitors waiting their turn to be heard in the several causes have their appointed station: power to all who

---

[1] In the text above this paragraph, Bentham has added the heading: 'Judicial Procedure'.
[2] MS 'below'.

choose to take notes and give publicity to them through the public Journals, subject to compensation in case of injurious falsehood through negligence or rashness, and moreover in case of mendacity to punishment. Whether in any and what cases a temporary concealment should be allowed is a consideration of subordinate importance and would require appropriate details.

In addition to all such casual and unofficial Inspectors, an official Committee of that same universally inspecting Tribunal—a constantly existing body of assessors to the Judge—should, under the name of a Jury, useful ideas having become associated with that name, be provided. Of this Jury the decision might either be obligatory, as according to present practice, on the Judge, or not. One great service will be rendered by it in either case: namely the imposing on the Judge a sort of moral necessity to lay open to the public ear the grounds of every thing that he does. For this reason the Jury should be in attendance whensoever the Judge himself is in attendance, for if the intentions of a Judge are evil, a single moment in which he acts by his own uncontrol[l]ed authority may suffice to deprive the party who is in the right of the benefit looked for at the hands of a Jury.

In Judicature, where there is no publicity, there is no justice: no tolerably adequate security for the giving due execution and effect to the laws, whatsoever they may be. That justice should have been the object where the doors of a Judicatory have been kept regularly closed is not possible. The object of the arrangement has been the sacrifice of the universal interest of all men in the character of justiciables, to the particular and sinister interest—either of the Judge, or of the despot, whose creature and instrument he is, or both together. Judicature has for it's only right and proper ends, these: main and positive end, giving execution and effect to the Laws, whatsoever they may be: collateral and negative ends, avoidance of all needless delay, expence, and vexation in other shapes: all needless delay is injustice while it lasts.

[III.][1] *Unapt arrangements inserted in the Spanish Constitution, and not in the Grecian*

In the first place stand all those articles by which power is lodged in the hands of a single individual in the situation of *Monarch*. To enumerate them would here be useless. The least mass of power that was ever given to a functionary, to whom that appellation was at the same time given, has always sufficed to place him in a state of incontestable and implacable hostility with the interest and greatest

---

[1] MS '*II*'. See p. 219n above.

happiness of the greatest number of the members of which the community is composed. Money, power, factitious honor and dignity, faculty of gratifying the appetite for vengeance, faculty of enjoying the perfection of *ease*—whatsoever of the external instruments of felicity in any of these shapes happen to be conferred on that one individual at the expence of the greatest number, that which in actual felicity he gains bears no sort of proportion to what they lose. So much for the article of expence in the case of that form of government: now as to relative and appropriate aptitude, say appropriate moral aptitude, appropriate intellectual aptitude (knowledge and judgment included) and appropriate active aptitude. While the exercise of all the other functions of government is made dependent on the will of that one individual, there exists not so much as a single function for the exercise of which every individual in that so mischievously elevated situation is not, by that very situation and by that vast mass of the external instruments of felicity so heaped upon it, rendered, in an eminent degree, more flagrantly and unquestionably unapt than any other individual in the whole community would be found to be: supposing him not below par in respect of original intellectual power, nor destitute of those intellectual acquirements which in Scotland are obtained by men in the situation of day labourers. Thus it is, that in every Monarchy all the rest of the people are made *victims* to, and the sport of, the will of the very worst man among them—of a man who in every intelligible sense of the word *worst* is rendered so by the mere circumstance of being situated where he is.

As, in his eyes at least, his interest is sure to be, at all times, in a state of immutable opposition to the universal interest, so having [it] on every occasion of competition in his power to make sacrifice of the universal interest to his particular interest, and these occasions spreading over the whole field of government, so it is that he has for his constant and uninterrupted occupation what may be termed the making of the *sinister sacrifice*. By this same appellation let it accordingly be characterized. And note that the more enormous the quantity he possesses of the aggregate of those same instruments, the more craving and insatiable is his appetite for more and more. The more extensive the sinister sacrifice is which he has made, the more extensive is the ulterior sacrifice of the same kind which it is his wish and constant endeavour to make, so long as there is any thing as yet left unsacrificed. Think on this occasion of Napoleon Bonaparte. Think of the allied despots who have succeeded to all his bad qualities without any of his good. Think of those allied despots, not forgetting the one who was the avowed partaker of their wishes and endeavours though alas! the forms of his government did not admitt of his being in form a party to their holy league.[1]

Mahometan and Jewish Natives. First as to Mahometans.[2] In relation to this part of the population, what is the most eligible course that can be taken: the government being supposed established in the hands of the Christian part?

To put them all to death surely can not be in contemplation: as little to export them all by force. In some number or other, absolute and relative, relative in relation to that of the Christians, they will continue in the territory of the State.

Here the first object or end in view is that which is dictated by *Self-regarding prudence*. Against hostility on their part, when reduced to the condition of subjects, every necessary precaution must of course be taken.

The next object or end in view is that which is dictated by *Effective benevolence*. Treat them with as much kindness as the indispensable regard for your own safety will permitt.

The more closely the matter is looked into, the greater will be seen to be the extent to which the dictates of effective benevolence will, in this instance, be found to coincide with those of self-regarding prudence.

Provided no Mahometan be admitted to a seat in the Legislative Assembly, or even if the multitude of seats capable of being filled by Mahometans were limited to a certain small number, so small as to be considerably short of being equal to the number filled by Christians, votes in the Election of Members of the Legislative Assembly need not be refused to them. Such of these Mahometan votes as could not be given in favour of Mahometans in the situation of candidates for seats in the Representative Assembly would, of course, be given to such Christian candidates as were regarded as being in the highest degree friendly to the Mahometan part of the population of the whole.

In this or that Election District, say even in any number of Election

---

[1] An allusion to the Holy Alliance established by the sovereigns of Austria, Prussia and Russia in 1815, but which George, Prince Regent of Great Britain (later George IV, King of Great Britain and Ireland) stated he could not accede to on account of 'the forms of the British Constitution'.

On the following sheet (UC cvi. 380), Bentham noted: 'Memm. To the transcribed copy of the matter in the preceding sheet was added in J.B.'s hand a short article descriptive of the bad points in the Council of State contained in the Spanish Constitution: with notice of the like instrument of mischief in the Portugueze.

'Also a very short article simply noticing as mischievous the divers stages of Election in the Spanish Constitution which it is taken for granted will not have been or be adopted in the Grecian.'

No draft of this material appears to have survived.

[2] Bentham did not go on to discuss separately the position of the Jews.

Districts, suppose the Mahometan votes to out-number the Christian, still no real inconvenience can ensue so long as in the Representative Assembly the non-Christians did not at any time out-number the Christians. If, however, any apprehensions on this score should notwithstanding be entertained, a very simple and inoffensive remedy might be provided; namely by making the age at which a Mahometan is permitted to vote, by any number of years that might be thought fit, more advanced than that at which a Christian is admitted to vote.

Strange it were, if by such treatment, the Mahometans were not rendered good Citizens. By the faculty of voting, even supposing no Mahometans were allowed to sit as Representatives, they would be raised to a situation high in dignity, as well as security, in comparison of the highest which any of them can occupy[1] at present. To no Christian could in that case any Mahometan be, as such, an object of contempt.

In the mean time and until that happy change shall have been acknowledged to have taken place, one precaution is suggested by the indispensable care of self-defence. Of the Christian portion of the population the male part will, I take for granted, be trained, without any exception, in the military stile to the use of arms: trained, in the European form of military exercise, in the use of the musquet and the bayonet in companies and batallions. The operations performed in the course of this exercise being in their nature public, men of both portions of the circumcised race might, without the hardship of domestic inquisition, be interdicted from the right of taking part in any such exercise. They might even be interdicted from having fire-arms of the length of musquets in their possession. But, as to swords and pistols, these they might, it should seem, without danger have the liberty of keeping in their houses and wearing about their persons, in the character of instruments for self-defence. Arms capable of being carried in secret, and by that means used as instruments of aggression, such as daggers and pistols, might, such of them as were small enough to be kept concealed, be comprized in the interdiction.

In regard to marriage, there seems to be no reason why a man of this persuasion should in future be allowed to keep under the bonds of that contract any more women than one. In a limitation of this kind there will be no invasion of religious liberty. In the Koran the having more than one is not made matter of obligation: in a word the sort of pluralism in question is an injustice in which, even where Mahometanism reigns, a very small number of men are partakers in comparison of the whole. The first wife should accordingly while living

---

[1] In the text at this point, the copyist has added: 'even in a Mahometan country'.

be the only wife. Over any other woman whom a man might engage to live and cohabit with him, no power should be allowed to him.

So in regard to succession. For simplicity sake the plan of distribution applied to property upon the death of the possessor should be the same in the case of a Mahometan as in the case of a Christian. Neither in this would there be any invasion of religious liberty, so long as the power were left to a man of this persuasion to give to his property by his last will and testament that course, whatever it be, which is given to it by the Mahometan law.

CONSTITUTIONAL CODE: MATTER OCCASIONED BY GREECE[1]

[1] An earlier draft of this material is at UC xxi. 264–70 (18 February 1823). Related fragments are at UC xxi. 260–2 (21 February 1823).

§1. *Proper end of government, what*

For designating the aggregate number of all the Members of which the political community in question is composed, say for shortness, the people.

According to the principle of utility, or say rather the greatest happiness principle—the only right and proper end of government, the only object fit to be aimed at in the formation of a body of Constitutional law, or any other branch of the law, is the greatest happiness of the whole people.

It is but to a small and undefinable extent that by any measure of law or government the happiness of all can be promoted without any defalcation from the happiness of some one or more.

This being the case, the only object that in general can be aimed at with success is the greatest happiness of the greatest number:—of the greatest number of the whole people.

§2. *Competent judges of what is most conducive to that end, who: viz. all or greatest number*

The greatest happiness of the greatest number requires that the arrangements of government by which the conduct of the whole people [is][1] regulated should be conformable as far as may be to the *will* of all such as are not on this occasion under an incapacity of forming a well-grounded judgment as to the question what arrangements are most likely to be productive of the greatest quantity of happiness on the part of the greatest number.

§3. *From contributing to the formation of that judgment and consequent will, shall any and who be excluded?*

If on the ground of inaptitude in relation to this matter any class of persons be proposed to be excluded from the faculty of making manifestation and giving efficiency to this will, it lies upon the person proposing the exclusion on the one hand to prove the fact of incapacity, to make good the charge of incapacity, in the instance of this class, and on the other hand to shew that no equal incapacity has place in the instance of any class which he proposes shall be admitted.

[1] MS 'are'.

In the instance here in question there are [four][1] classes of persons to whose will there seems not any chance that any efficiency should be allowed by those in whom the physical strength of the community has its seat. These are:

1. Persons of the female sex.
2. Non-adults of the male sex.
3. [Non-readers.
4.] Persons of the Mahometan persuasion of whatsoever age.

§4. 1. Females

As to persons of the female sex, if the only proper mode of receiving the declaration of a person's will, namely that of *secret suffrage openly delivered*, be employed, no reason consistent with the principle of general utility as above can be assigned why they or any of them, being of relatively mature age, should stand [excluded]. But no pre-possession, howsoever adverse to the principle of general utility, can on the sudden be eradicated: and it would be idle to propose to all that to which acceptance it is certain would not be given by any one.

§5. 2. Non-Adults

As to persons of an age short of relative maturity, to draw between the class of persons that shall stand excluded on this ground and the class to whom admission shall be accorded any line that shall not be in a considerable degree arbitrary is manifestly impossible. That on the part of a child of an age at which the faculty of loco-motion has not yet developed itself such incapacity is entire is manifest beyond dispute. But to say at what age such incapacity is at an end and the corres-pondent capacity has its beginning is not possible even in the instance of any one individual—much less in the instance of an indefinitely large multitude of individuals all of them liable to differ from one another in this respect even when they are all of them at exactly the same age.

For cutting this Gordian knot, analogy and uniformity unite in suggesting an expedient. For giving efficiency to a person's will in relation to the concerns and happiness of all, take that period, be it what it may, which another branch of the rule of action makes choice

---

[1] MS 'three'. Bentham discussed non-readers in addition to the three other classes he listed below.

of for giving commencement to the efficiency of his will as applied to the regulation of his own private concerns, of his conduct in his private and personal capacity: the period at which his own person, and any property destined by the law for his support, begins to be at his own disposal.

By the Imperial Roman law and, as I should expect to find, by the Imperial Greek law which was derived from it, the age at which maturity to this private purpose is understood to commence is an age as far advanced as that of 25 years. Under the principle of utility a function by which so large a portion of the community at a time of life at which sensibility is at the highest pitch stands excluded from the faculty of self-government, each individual being subjected to the arbitrary individual [will] of another, seems altogether indefensible. It had its origin in the selfish tyranny by which the domestic justice of the Roman law was characterized: that same law by which the life of the offspring was down to the latest period committed to the mercy of the father.

By the law of England the person and property [of] each individual are placed at his or her disposal at the age of one and twenty years. From the defalcation thus made of a period of four years from the domestic slavery established all over the continent of Europe by the Roman Law, no inconvenience has ever yet been felt or so much as been pretended to be felt.

This same law, which refuses to the youthful person the disposal of his or her person till a period of [one] and twenty years has been accomplished, concedes to him or her the disposal of his or her property by will at an age as early as that of 14 Years. But the exclusion being but temporary and if life continues sure to cease, it seems needless to disturb the simplicity of the arrangement in search of a degree of precision the attainment of which by any such arrangement is not possible. Say then at once age of maturity to the purpose here in question one and twenty years: or if any alteration be made let the age fixed upon be rather earlier than later.

In vain would it be said—the affairs of the whole community being so much more important than the affairs of any one individual member of it, a greater degree of maturity should be required for the age at which efficiency is given to the will of the individual with relation to the affairs of the whole than that at which efficiency is given to it with relation to no other than his own individual affairs. In vain: for, 1. were any such proportion to be regarded the effect would be to continue the exclusion to no one can say how advanced a period, nor could any indication in favour of one in preference to any other be found. 2. A more conclusive and satisfactory answer is this. In the case in which efficiency is given to the will of the individual in relation to his own personal affairs and with a view to his own personal happiness, the result of this efficiency is the entire power over the subject-matter in question: whereas in the other case it is no more than a minute fraction of that same power: a fraction which is saved from being productive of any such sensibly bad effect as is producible by want of sufficient maturity in the other case: preserved namely by the multitude of indisputably maturer wills by which it is so sure to be outnumbered. Suppose the formation of it possible, an universal league of all alledged immature wills, suppose the wills from 18 to 21 years of age, would not when set against the whole number of mature wills, all of them interested on the other side, be productive of any effect.

Inaptitude alone, howsoever compleat and incontestable, will not, on this occasion, present of itself any adequate ground for exclusion. The ground will be wanting if, by reason of the smallness of the number in whose instance the cause of incapacity has place, added to the want of assurance that the incapacity would have for its effect the placing of the suffrage of the person on the side adverse to the public interest, all sensible effect from the incapacity would as it were be drowned. For where in case of dispute the question of the inaptitude requires to be solved by appropriate evidence, here by every such enquiry a course of litigation must be commenced: litigation from which, in addition to what is natural, factitious delay, vexation and expence are inseparable: and thus a real and sensible evil is introduced under the notion of excluding that which, if it be to be stiled an evil, is but nominally so, not being sensible.

§6. *3. Non-readers*

If by exclusion put upon comparative incapacity, comparative capacity can and will be given to any class of persons, the greatest happiness principle requires that such exclusion be established. Thus for instance between a class of persons comparatively incapable and a class of persons comparatively capable, the art of reading furnishes a clear line of demarcation. Suppose but that by every individual desirous of it adequate means and time for the acquisition of it have been possessed, no scruple need be made of putting an exclusion to the purpose here in question on all such as shall not have given manifestation in some appropriate and appointed mode of their being in possession of it. For here whatsoever exclusion has place being the effect of the work of the individual himself on whom the exclusion is put, no injury is thereby done to him personally, and by his voluntarily submitting to be excluded from the exercise of this right his inaptitude is sufficiently proved.

But by that same fruitful art by which a man is thus in so conspicuous a degree rendered fit for taking a part in the management of the public affairs of the whole people, and thus making provision for the universal happiness, he is at the same time rendered incomparably more fit than he could otherwise be for the taking charge of his own personal and other private affairs—for making provision for his own happiness and that of those whoever they may be whose will is rendered more or less dependent on his by the hand of nature.

§7. 4. Mahometans

By the term Mahometans are designated a class of persons forced on this occasion into notice by circumstances peculiar to Greece in contradistinction to the other Christianity-professing nations and political states of Europe.

By self-preservation—an altogether unopposable law—by that and nothing else, for neither can any thing else be requisite, are men of this class excluded from the faculty of giving any degree of efficiency to their will to the purpose here in question. The character in which they stand subjected to the exclusion is that of enemies: natural and, for a time, unhappily irreconcileable enemies. In their case so long as the danger from admission continues, so long must the exclusion be continued. So long it must be, but not a moment longer ought to be. No sooner has the danger ceased than self-regarding prudence joins with effective benevolence in dictating the removal of the antisocial bar.

So much for the general principle. As for the particular arrangements which it presents itself as indicating, a little further on they will find themselves in their place.[1]

With reference to them the grand problem is—consistently with universal safety and thus with universal happiness, by what arrangement from necessary enemies to convert them into actual friends?

Note that on this occasion it is only to the efficiency of man's *will* that for the purpose in question exclusion can in any instance be regarded as necessary to be put. To whatsoever contribution can be offered in the shape of the fruits of human understanding as offered to understanding not so much as any plausible reason can be assigned

---

[1] See 'Observations', pp. 254–6 above.

why any exclusion should be opposed. Thus it is that neither to females, to infants, nor to Mahometans does the greatest happiness of the greatest number either require or admitt that the faculty of manifesting opinion by the way of written discourse should be interdicted.

§ 8. *Necessary to maximization of greatest number's happiness is maximization of the efficiency of ditto's will*

What is here meant to be designated by the word the people being thus explained, the enquiry proceeds as follows.

The greatest happiness of the people requires that in the formation of the arrangements by which the conduct of the people is to be regulated, the greatest degree of efficiency be at all times given to the will of the people that the nature of the case admitts of.

For in no body of men other than the greatest number of the people will either any will be found assignable [in][1] which a stronger desire to produce the greatest happiness of the people is to be found, or any understanding possessing a more intimate knowledge of that which is in the highest degree conducive and contributory to the production of such greate[st happiness]. Take any other class of persons, whether smaller or larger, exterior or interior, with reference to such greatest number, the desire of such other class would be the production of its own greatest happiness whatever became of the happiness of the people in question: such would be the desire, and such the constant endeavour in consequence.

Suppose, though there be no reason for the supposition, suppose on the part of the other class a truer and more extensive and accurate knowledge of that which is in the highest degree conducive to the happiness of the people in question than has place on the part of the people themselves, still this knowledge would not be productive of that same desirable effect: whatsoever appropriate knowledge, judgment and active talent was possessed by this other class would be employed in the augmentation of the felicity of such other class, and to the diminution of the felicity of the class in question, in so far as such diminution on the one part, such augmentation on the other, promised to be effected.[2]

[1] MS 'by'.

[2] Bentham noted at this point, '☛ Insert here inaptitude of the *one* and the *many*', but no corresponding material is indicated on the plan or appears to have been written. For such a discussion see for instance 'Supreme Operative', in *First Principles preparatory to Constitutional Code* (*CW*), pp. 149–226.

§9. *Means of maximizing efficiency of greatest number's will, Operation by Delegates: their inducement to operate towards the proper end*

What remains to be seen is—in what degree and by what means the maximum of efficiency can in the nature of the case be given to the will of the people.

That which it is not physically speaking in their power to do in any political community large enough to maintain its independence—and in particular in any such political community as that of Greece—is to take any part in the individual arrangements by which their own greatest happiness is to be produced, which have for their objects the production of such their greatest happiness.

The obstacles to their taking any such part are manifest and altogether insuperable. [1.] Unless the necessary means of subsistence be produced, all arrangements taken for the security of it against invasion would be fruitless and absurd. But with the continuity of the labours necessary to the production of the means of subsistence, any thing like an equal continuity in the labour of giving existence to the political arrangements necessary to the security of this when produced, is on the part of the greatest number, in point of physical possibility, absolutely incompatible.

2. If all could find time, no place would hold all or more than a minute part of all while conjunctly occupied in the formation of the general will.

It being therefore physical[ly] impossible that the body of the people should in their own persons respectively endeavour to give efficiency to their respective wills in the production of the arrangements which have for their object the production of their greatest happiness, the utmost that remains within the field of physical possibility as capable of being done for this purpose, is that this endeavour of theirs be made by them by proxy: that is to say that, in the greatest number possible, they should concurr in the choice of substitutes, or say delegates, for that purpose, being for this purpose distributed into groupes, each groupe concurring in the choice of one such delegate.

The way in which, by expression and effect given to the several individual wills, contribution is made to the universal happiness is this. If the result depended upon himself each individual would give expression and effect to such will as in his judgment would in the highest degree be conducive to his own greatest happiness, whatsoever became of the happiness of others, and consequently on most if not all occasions at the expence of the happiness of all others.

Witness the practice of the Monarch in all Monarchies. But, in so far as the effect of it is by others seen or thought to be detrimental to their own happiness, the will of each individual finds an opponent and bar in the will of every other, and in the will of all together a bar absolutely insuperable. On the other hand, in so far as the effect of each one's will is by every other individual seen or thought to be conducive to his own greatest happiness, the will of each one finds a support and coadjutor in the will of every other: in a word each separate and sinister interest finds a bar, and that an insuperable one, in every other separate and sinister interest: but each man's share in the universal interest finds an ally and coadjutor in every other man's share in the universal interest.

Thus in the choice of delegates. Every elector, if it were in his power to find [a] Candidate who, in the event of his becoming a delegate, in the part taken by him in the body of delegates would give support to the separate and sinister interest of him the elector to the exclusion and thence at the expence of all other interests, [would][1] be sure to give his vote to that same Candidate and to no other. To some Electors it may accordingly happen to find each of them some such Candidate, and all of them one and the same Candidate: and thus it may by possibility happen that among the Delegates there may be here and there one who by community of sinister interest stands engaged to support the separate and sinister interest of this or that Elector at the expence of every other: and in a purposely corrupt system of representation, such as that of England is become and that which has been forced upon the people of France, the Monarch or the Aristocracy having under their command the wills of so many Electoral bodies, this state of things is to a ruinous degree exemplified.

But under a system of representation having for its end in view the greatest happiness of the greatest number—a system arranged for example as in general are those that have place in the Anglo-American United States, no such purposed sacrifice of universal interest to the separate interest of a few does or ever can have place. Let a man pitch upon a Candidate who is generally regarded as the most apt of all those who are willing to be constituted Delegates for the seat in question, he finds in a sufficient number of others an effectual concurrence: let a man fix upon a Candidate on whom he could depend for the pursuing upon all occasions his the Elector's separate and sinister interest at the expence of every other, he would not find Electors in sufficient numbers to place him in the seat.

---

[1] MS 'will'.

As it is in the case of the people, in their quality of Electors, on the occasion of the choice of a Delegate to be their representative in the operative Assembly, so is it in the case of those same Delegates on the occasions on which they are occupied in the choice of arrangements proposed to receive the force of law. And thus it is that the universal good is the result of the continual conflict amongst the jarring elements of separate and sinister interests, desires and endeavours. To any imaginable amount self-sacrifice may in fact have place: but to the production of the greatest happiness of the greatest number not so much as a single instance of it is necessary in the general course of business.

§ 10. *Hence two bodies each possessed of supreme power in its own line: viz. Supreme Constitutive and Supreme Operative. But the Supreme Operative must be subordinate to and dependent for its power on the Supreme Constitutive*

On this occasion, the proper object of all arrangements taken for the enabling the people thus to act by delegation is the production of such arrangements as it may be presumed would be taken by the people themselves had they respectively sufficient time for the making them, in addition to sufficient time for qualifying themselves for the making of them by means of appropriate information in all its various shapes.

Of the mode of election best adjusted to this end mention will be made a little further on in its place.[1]

At present suppose for argument sake this best mode found and carried into practice.

Here then we have already two distinguishable bodies of men in the government. 1. The people at large by whom, for the taking of these arrangements of detail by which their greatest happiness is to be provided for, a set of functionaries have been provided: [2.] functionaries placed by the choice or election made of them for that purpose: substitutes, delegates, functionaries, who in point of physical possibility might be chosen out of any assemblage of men but who most naturally and, as to the greater portion at any rate, most beneficially will have [been] chosen by them from among themselves. In these immediate delegates of the people is conceived as yet to reside the whole of the power just-mentioned: call it the *Operative power*: to

---

[1] Bentham did not go on to consider this topic here: for his most detailed discussion of election procedure see *Bentham's Radical Reform Bill, with Extracts from the Reasons*, London, 1819 (Bowring, iii. 558–97), which he intended to incorporate into *Constitutional Code* (see *Constitutional Code*, vol. I (*CW*), p. 48n).

the people at large remains and resides the power of determining at all times in what individuals that same Operative power shall have place: in a word to constitute them what with relation to that function they are: call it the *Constitutive power*.

§ 11. *Of the Supreme Operative the strictness of dependence on the will of the Supreme Constitutive should be maximized*

Of the delegation thus made by the people of operative power the sole use and object being by the supposition the giving effect by means of those substitutes to that which would be their will had they time for forming it, it follows that for this purpose the dependence of the conduct of those substitutes to the will of those same [principals],[1] in so far as they have time and means of forming it, can not be too absolute and entire.

§ 12. *From the Supreme Operative must be detached the Supreme Executive: remains above it, the Supreme Legislative*

So much for the set of substitutes chosen in the first place. But by the same cause, namely want of time and appropriate information in detail, the physical possibility of going through in its entirety the whole of the business so allotted to the abovementioned possessors of the operative power stands in like manner excluded: details of the arrangements which require to be made for defence of the people against external adversaries by land and water—details of the arrangements for defence against internal adversaries in the character of criminals—details of the arrangements necessary to be made for the exaction and distribution of the pecuniary supplies necessary for the purchase of the things and persons applied to the purposes of such national defence—by these indications thus briefly given, proofs sufficient of the impossibility in question are already brought to view. In addition to the necessity of clearing the hands of the people at large of the whole of the operative part of the business of government, thus comes the necessity of clearing of large portions of it the hands in which at the first step the whole of the operative part was lodged or regarded as if lodged.

At the first step we had one operative power acting in subordination, and in the strictest possible subordination, for such it was neces-

---

[1] MS 'principles'.

sary it should be or the end in view could not be accomplished—in the strictest possible subordination to the constitutive power. At the second step as above we have now a detached hand or set of hands to which by the operative power a portion of its functions is committed: in the conduct of which delegate or delegates of the second order the strictest subordination as towards the will of its immediate principal, and thereby towards the will of the original principal, is for the like reason indispensable. The portion of power thus detached from the operative power call it the Executive. But while by the operative power a certain portion of its functions is thus detached and committed to a delegate or set of delegates of its own appointment, at the same time whatsoever is not thus detached from it is of course by it reserved to be exercised by itself. The portion of operative thus detached being termed the Executive power, call the portion thus reserved the Legislative power. Here then we have the division of the whole mass of operative power in the community into two portions: the supreme Operative power, ordinarily in use to be designated by the appellation of legislative power or supreme legislative power; and the Executive power.

Thus we have already a chain of political subordination consisting of three links. [1.] Link the first or basis of the whole, the all-embracing constitutive power: subordinate to none; 2. link the second, the legislative or supreme legislative power: subordinate to the constitutive power and to that alone; 3. link the third, the supreme Executive power: subordinate to the legislative or supreme legislative power, and thence to the supreme [constitutive][1] power, but not to any other: subordinate to the legislative to the end that it thus may be so to the all-embracing constitutive power, and not for any other purpose, for the sake of any other end.

Of this chain, up to what precise number the total succession of links may require to be extended can not for any state, much less for every political state, [or] for the political state here in question, be determined for all times by any general rule. But whatsoever be the length of it, relation being constantly had to the greatest happiness of the greatest number, rules for the direction of the structure of the several links will be found not incapable of being grounded on a sufficiently satisfactory foundation.[2]

[1] MS 'Operative'.
[2] The following passage marked 'Inserendum' is at UC xxi. 259, 257–8 (21 February 1823). Bentham did not indicate where he intended to insert it, but it seems most appropriately placed here: 'Objection. Under this system, by which it is assumed that for securing the greatest happiness of the greatest number the surest course is to order matters that the conduct of all be rendered as nearly as may be conformable to the will of the greatest number, no such effect can ever be produced in any country in which, by the united influence of force, intimidation,

§ 13. *Subordinate proper ends: 1. Expence minimized*

To form a ground and foundation for these rules one indisputable matter of fact must in the first place be brought to view. This is that, be the political state in question what it may, a quantity of things to be applied to the purpose of national defence in its several branches as above will of necessity require to be provided, and the stock of them kept up: also things of other sorts for the subsistence of any functionaries whose whole time is allotted to the purpose, at any rate if there be not in sufficient number any set of persons who, having in their

corruption and delusion, [the greatest number] have been reduced to and at this moment in question continue in a state of the most pernicious error as to the means by which alone the end can be attained and accomplished, the desirable effect can be produced. By the conjunct imposture of Priests and Lawyers, the greatest number have been taught and persuaded to think that a form of government, in which depredation and oppression in all other shapes to the profit of their rulers have by those same rulers been screwed up to the highest pitch possible, is not only a good government, but the very best government—the only one in justification of which any thing reasonable can be said. This being the case, a government which has really for its object the greatest good of the greatest number neither is nor ever can be regarded by them in any other light than that of a bad and unendurable government: so bad that all attempts to cause it to have place ought to be resisted by every individual, though the sacrifice of his whole fortune, with the addition of that of his life, were the certain consequence.

'An objection of this sort, it must be confessed, admits but of one answer. The will to which, if the greatest happiness of the greatest number is the result of it, effect will have been given by the arrangements taken in pursuit of that end will be—not that which at the commencement of the change, while minds are as yet in their state of debasement, would be their will—but that which it may be presumed will be their will by the time that a rational regard for the only proper end of government, together with a right conception of the means most contributory to that end, have been attained by them. Happily as to what will be their wills, when once there has been time for the impressing on their minds this salutary conception and the impression has been made accordingly, there can not be any reasonable particle of doubt. Official aptitude maximized, public expence minimized—when once proposed, who can refuse to recognize in these two short phrases the designation of the two minor ends immediately subordinate to and included in that same universal end? Among the most ignorant and prejudiced of men, who is there that does not on every occasion obtain whatever it is that he wants for the smallest price at which he finds it in his power to obtain it? What man therefore so ignorant or so prejudice[d] as not to recognize the advantage of obtaining at the like low prices all such services as he stands in need of at the hands of his rulers?

'Every mercantile man sells as dear as he can: every mercantile man buys as cheap as he can what he buys. If he could get for nothing, and this without suffering more than equivalent either by law or in reputation, for nothing he would get it. Every man who lives by the wages of his labour—by the sale of his services, gets as much for them as he can get for them. The official functionary, whose services real or pretended are rendered not to any individual to the exclusion of the rest but to all individuals taken together, does in his place what the day labourer does in his—sells them at the highest price which he finds it possible to get for them. Favoured by his peculiar situation, favoured by the long-protracted influence of force, intimidation, corruption and delusion, the Monarch sells at a price to which no others bear any proportion his worse than useless services. In this what cause is there for wonder? The wonder would be if it were otherwise. But by being so far from wonderful [it] is not the less disastrous: it calls not the less for all exertions that can be made with safety for the substituting equality and security to a state of injustice and universal sufferance.'

own property the means of subsistence, can all of them together be induced to allot to that same purpose a sufficient quantity of time. Of things at large and means of subsistence in particular, in so far as thus employed, is composed the necessary *expence* of government.

In no political state has it ever been found—in no political state does it seem likely that it should ever be found—that the things and services of persons requisite for the abovementioned purposes could by possibility be obtained at all times in sufficient abundance at the hands of persons parting from them without experiencing any sensation of reluctance. But in so far as the operation of affording the matter of expence in this or any other shape has reluctance for its accompaniment, all expence is evil: in all political states as yet in existence this evil has been very considerable: and in most political states hitherto in existence it has been and continues to be so considerable as to be every [thing] but intolerable.[1]

§ 14. *2. Aptitude maximized*

Correspondent to the three branches or species of power above brought to view are so many departments: say the constitutive, the legislative, the executive departments.

In each department the degree in which accomplishment is given to the abovementioned all-embracing and sole justifiable end of government, the greatest happiness of the greatest number, will be as the relative or appropriate aptitude of the several functionaries employed in it.

Now there may be brought to view two immediately subordinate and consequently minor ends of government included in the abovementioned all-embracing end: Aptitude maximized; expence minimized. Into the compass [of] these four words for memory sake may be condensed the designation of these two immediately subordinate and practically consecutive ends or fit objects of pursuit on the occasion of all political arrangements.

Aptitude—appropriate aptitude—is a term of reference: of the object to which on this occasion it is intended to bear reference abundant mention has already been made—the greatest happiness of the greatest number.

Of appropriate aptitude as thus defined, three immediate branches all distinguishable from one another will be found observable:

---

[1] There is no text corresponding to the following marginal summary, which belongs here: 'Hence one end of minor extent immediately subordinate to greatest happiness etc.: namely expence minimized.'

appropriate moral aptitude, appropriate intellectual aptitude, and appropriate active aptitude.

By appropriate moral aptitude, in so far as perfect, understand on the part of the functionary in question the disposition and thus the desire and endeavour to contribute on every occasion, in the exercise of his function, to the utmost of his power to the attainment of the so often mentioned all-embracing and only proper end.

As to the motives, or say the inducements, by which this desire and endeavour have been produced, or say secured, the degree of desire and endeavour being given, they are in themselves as immaterial with reference to the end as in most instances they are difficult to discover, ascertain and demonstrate.

On the part of the majority of the delegates in a representative government constituted upon the abovementioned principles, appropriate moral aptitude will generally speaking be in a sufficient degree possessed: between the personal interest of the functionary and his share in the universal interest, such is the connection as to render the existence of this quality in a sufficient degree probable.

On the part of the ruling functionaries in a pure Monarchy, in a pure Aristocracy—or in any government in which there is a mixture either of Monarchy or of Aristocracy, it is impossible. It is [. . . ?] with that constantly [. . .?] self-preference, on which the whole species depends for its existence.

Of appropriate intellectual aptitude there are again two distinguishable branches: 1. appropriate knowledge, or say information, and appropriate judgment: say in other words scientific aptitude, and judicial aptitude.

Of appropriate moral aptitude the degree will depend upon the conjunct effective force of [two][1] distinguishable causes: namely original or innate disposition, and superventitious inducements.

The sources by which these inducements will principally be furnished are: 1. the force of the popular or moral sanction, as applied by the Public Opinion Tribunal: 2. the force of the political including the legal sanction, as applied by the power of the judicial tribunals and by the other powers exercised by the several functionaries of government. In addition to the force of these sanctions may be added or set the force of the sympathetic sanction acting on a scale commensurate to that of the whole community and having for its object the happiness of the whole, and the force of the religious sanction. But as applied to the conduct of public functionaries the force of these two sanctions does not always exist in any perceptible quantity, and where it has

---

[1] MS blank.

place is not exposed to any such principle of measurement as has place in the case of the two sanctions abovementioned.

Of appropriate scientific aptitude the degree will be in the conjunct ratio of the effective force of [three][1] causes: 1. innate disposition as above: 2. absence or presence of apt means and sources of information: 3. effective force of such inducements the tendency of which is to engage the individual in the endeavour to become possessed of appropriate aptitude in the shape here in question by the application of such means to their respective ends.

Of appropriate active aptitude the degree possessed by the functionary in question will in like manner be in the conjunct ratio of innate aptitude, and the effective force of the inducements by which, in the situation it has happened to him to occupy, he has been led to give added vigour to his innate appropriate aptitude, and at the same time to make application of it to operations bearing more or less analogy to the functions of the Office with relation to which his appropriate aptitude is considered.

Exposure to the effective force of the several sanctions here just mentioned as capable of furnishing inducements promotive of appropriate aptitude, whether with relation to the exercise of a public function such as the above, or to a person's general conduct in life whether invested or not with any such public function, is commonly termed responsibility—his responsibility.[2]

Responsibility is, according to the nature of the sanction by which the inducements are regarded as afforded, distinguishable into political including legal responsibility, and moral responsibility, the degree of it being the degree of his exposure to the action of the popular or moral sanction, as applied by the Public Opinion Tribunal.

Note that to each such sanction belong two distinguishable branches—the punitory or say penal, and the remuneratory: the penal, in the case where the inducement is constituted by the eventual expectation or fear of pain; the remunerative, in the case where it consists in the eventual expectation or hope of pleasure, that is to say of the possession of any such things as are commonly regarded as instruments of pleasure or of good in its other shape, exemption from pain.

Note however that by any eventual expectation of the matter of good, whether in its positive or its negative shape as above, the sort of condition commonly designated by the word responsibility is [not] regarded as being brought to view.[3]

---

[1] MS blank.

[2] A fragment on the topic of responsibility is at UC xxi. 263 (11 February 1823).

[3] There is no text corresponding to the following marginal summary, which belongs here: 'in

§ 15.[1] *Rules or Maxims of Constitutional Law as to what regards Official subordination*

In a representative democracy, as between grade and grade from the highest down to the lowest, the dependence of each on that to which it is immediately subordinate, and thence on that to which all others are subordinate, can not be too comprehensive.[2]

This admitted, it follows that it is not [for] the purpose of diminishing, but only for the purpose of encreasing, the strength of the supreme or any such intermediate authority that any portion of power is given to any authority under the supreme.[3]

Another consequence is—that to any exercise given to its power by that authority which stands highest in the Operative department, viz. that of the Legislative Assembly, no act of usurpation, no unconstitutional exercise of power, can consistently be ascribed. Such exercise of its power may like every other exercise be expedient or in any degree inexpedient. But on the mere ground of its being in ordinary cases exercised by the Executive department, and in this or that extraordinary case by the Legislative department, anti-constitutional it can not be. On the contrary, whatsoever be the case or cases in which it has happened to the Executive authority in any grade to have omitted to give execution and effect to the declared will of the Legislative, in every such case, if so it be that without its special interference such execution and effect can not be given, it appertains to the functions and duty of the Legislative to interfere accordingly and by its own immediate order cause that to be done which without such order ought to have been done.

Another consequence is—that, so far as it produces any effect at all, in no part of the chain of subordination can an effect mischievous upon the whole fail of being produced by any scheme of division by which, ere an arrangement of government can be made, an agreement has [to be][4] effected between two authorities between which the

point of force, expectation or hope of pleasure can not in this way stand on a par with fear of pain or of loss of pleasure'.

[1] For the material used in this section see the Editorial Introduction, p. xlii above.

[2] The marginal summary differs slightly from the text at this point: 'The supreme power, viz. the Constitutive, being in competent hands, viz. all the members of the community, the dependence of all other authorities on *that* can not be too absolute.'

[3] There is no text corresponding to the following marginal summary, which belongs here: 'Immediately under the Supreme Constitutive is the Supreme Operative. As from the Supreme Constitutive is detached the Supreme Operative, so from the Supreme Operative the Supreme Executive, leaving over it the Supreme Legislative. Only for want of time, not for diminution of power, is Supreme Operative detached from Supreme Constitutive, so therefore Supreme Executive from Supreme Operative.' [4] MS 'been'.

power of giving effect to any such arrangement has for this purpose been perfectly divided. In a word, it is by subordination as opposed to coordination that whatever good has place is produced: it is by coordination as opposed to subordination that whatever evil has place is produced.

In regard to an absolute Monarchy what no one is backward to acknowledge is—that what strength it has depends altogether on the strictness of subjection [and] dependence which the conduct of every subordinate functionary has on the will of his immediate superior, and thence on that will to which it is the duty of all other wills to conform themselves. But if such strictness is thus necessary to strength in a Monarchy, much more so must it be in a democracy of which it is the essential character (besides that the power which in an absolute Monarchy is condensed into one hand is divided in the first place betwixt two bodies, the highest of them composed of all the Members of the community) that in the highest grade of the Operative department no arrangement can be made till a will of the whole body has been formed, after a collision, to the length [of] which there is no determinate limit, amongst the wills of the several Members. Such in this respect being the natural and necessary and unavoidable disadvantage against which every representative democracy as such has to contend, every thing ought of course to be done by which it can be lessened, nothing by which it can be encreased.

If what is above be admitted, it will follow that in any state in which there exists a body constituting a real and efficient representation of the people, no effects but such as are of a mischievous nature can be produced, either by the addition of a Monarch not chosen by the people and endowed with coordinate power in legislation with or without power belonging to the Executive department, or of a body of men not chosen by the people, and thus forming a second House independent of the people, or even of a body of men chosen by the people and forming a second House also dependent on the people.

What will also be seen is—that in neither of the two former of these three cases can the form given to the Constitution have had the greatest happiness of the greatest number either for its object or for its effect. The bodies and individuals respectively whose greatest happiness it can not but have had for its object, to the neglect and sacrifice of the greatest happiness of the greatest number, can not but have been in the one case the individual to whom, in the other the body to which, have been committed such vast powers altogether independent of the will of the people.

Another thing which it is believed will also be seen is—that of the third of the three forms, howsoever the greatest happiness of the greatest number may have been the object, it can not have been to so great an extent the effect as if this surplusage ingredient in the composition of the Constitution had been omitted.[1]

---

[1] The argument in the marginal summary diverges from that in the text at this point: 'The end pursued by every individual being his own greatest happiness, the end pursued by all will be the greatest happiness of all: the end exclusively pursued by the few, the ditto of those few: the end exclusively pursued by the one, the ditto of that one. But the happiness of the *few* can not be maximized but the ditto of the rest must be diminished: still less that of the *one*.'

CONSTITUTIONAL CODE

CHAPTER VIII. OF THE PRIME MINISTER

§5. *Term of Service*[1]

Art. 1. The Prime Minister's term of service is one year, reckoning from the commencement of the first solar year that commences after the authorization of the Constitution, delineated in this Code.

Art. 2. The Prime Minister of the first year is not relocable till an interval of two years has had place, since the termination of that his year of service.

Art. 3. The Prime Minister of the second year is not relocable, till an interval of one year has had place since the termination of that his year of service.

Art. 4. On no succeeding year, is any person who has served in the situation of Prime Minister relocable, until an interval of one year has elapsed since the termination ⟨of his⟩ then last year of service.

Art. 5. For the case in which, by reelection otherwise than according to these four articles, or by omitting to perform a fresh Election, or otherwise, the endeavour shall be used to keep the same individual in this Office, see §2.[2]

Rationale to Ch. VIII, §5
Art. 1. {reckoning from the commencement, etc.}

Question 1. Why, to the first solar year of service, that commences after the commencement of the Constitution, attach a fraction of the preceding year, thus making the term of service longer in this instance, than in any succeeding one?

Reasons.

1. For the sake of symmetry. That, in the instance of this office as well as in that of every other, the term of service having the same commencement, the conception formed of the whole system may be so much the clearer, the maximum of simplicity in this particular being substituted to such useless complication as might otherwise have place to an ⟨indefinite ex⟩tent.

2. That, for the purpose of making appropriate provision for all

---

[1] Bentham inserted the following note at this point: 'Col. S. is requested to substitute what follows to the Section sent on a former occasion.' For Leicester Stanhope and his dealings with Bentham see the Editorial Introduction, pp. xlii–xliii above.

[2] According to a contemporary plan of *Constitutional Code* at UC xxxviii. 9, this section was entitled 'By whom and how located'. Cf. *Constitutional Code*, vol. I (*CW*), Ch. VIII, §5, Art. 4, p. 156.

exigencies, the times of the periodical changes may, to the greatest possible extent, be in a clear form present to the minds of all persons in any way interested.

3. That, at the commencement of the system, when as yet no experience of it's manner of working has been obtained, there may be more or less time for the making of any such preparatory arrangements, as, when once settled, will naturally supersede the demand for time for that purpose in all succeeding years.[a]

Art. 2. {interval of two years.}

Question 1. Why, during this interval, render the Prime Minister incapable of being relocated: thus taking from the Legislature, during this time, the faculty of relocating an individual who, in their estimation, may be endued with a degree of appropriate aptitude, in all it's shapes, perfectly adequate, and superior to what they expect to find in any other individual.

Reasons.

1. In order to give to the Electors the faculty of taking experience for the ground of their judgment:—of having at least two tried men to choose out of: experience, apposite and appropriate; men who have already served in the very situation, with relation to which the judgment as to their respective degrees of appropriate aptitude, absolute and comparative, is to be formed. But for this temporary non-relocability clause this faculty would, it will be seen, be, in all probability, altogether wanting.

2. For this purpose, the least intervals that can suffice are those here proposed: namely, in the case of the Prime Minister of the first year, an interval of two years; in the case of the Prime Minister of the second year, an interval of one year. This will appear from the following statement.

Anno 1 of the Constitution, as above, location commences: relocation, none.

Anno 2 of the Constitution, Prime Minister of year 1 not relocable: some other person is located, who thereby becomes Prime Minister of year 2.

---

[a] ☞ Note, other official situations there are to which the additions thus proposed to the first term of service that has place after the commencement of the Constitution applies with equal propriety: to these, it will accordingly be applied by the writer of this: and as to that which has come upon the carpet in the part already sent, perhaps Col. S.[1] will have the goodness to make the correspondent amendment. These ⟨are:⟩ 1. that of a Member of the Legislature: 2. Mem⟨ber of⟩ the Sub-Legislatures.

---

[1] Leicester Stanhope.

CHAPTER VIII. OF THE PRIME MINISTER

Anno 3 of the Constitution, Prime Minister of year 1 continues non-relocable. Prime Minister of year 2 is also non-relocable.

Thereupon, comes in Prime Minister of year 3, who makes a third man capable of being eventually relocated, and thence acting as rival to, and in the character of a *tried* man, as Competitor to and with the two others.

Anno 4. Prime Minister of year 1 now becomes relocable. Prime Minister of year 2 becomes also relocable: his interval having for the pur⟨pose of⟩ the competition been thus short⟨ened. Prime⟩ Minister of year 3 is not ⟨relocable.⟩ Here then Prime Minister of year 1 and Prime Minister of year 2 have each other for Competitors. For Competitors they have moreover at the same time men in general, with scarce an exception: but these two are the only men who, with relation to the individual situation in question, and it's duties, can with propriety be stiled *tried* men: men, of whose conduct in that same situation, experience has been had. On this plan, even if as soon as he has become relocable, every man is accordingly relocated, still there will always be two at least of these tried men to choose out of: and in proportion as such relocation fails of taking place, every year will add one to the number of competitors. If to an interval of two years, it should be judged best to substitute an interval of three years in the case of the first Prime Minister, and thereafter an interval of two years in the case of the next, the number of tried Competitors will thus receive proportionate encrease.

3. Of the competition thus established, and ⟨. . .⟩ alternate possession, which, as between ⟨Competitor⟩ and Competitor, ⟨. . .⟩ (ordinary approach to equality in respect of appropriate aptitude being understood to have place between them) emulation will be among the natural results. Thus with relation to Official duty, so far as the emulation has place, those whom it finds to a certain degree apt, it will render continually more and more so.

4. In the one or say in every one out of Office, the Competitor who is in Office will have a naturally watchful censor, constantly upon the alert, in the endeavour to spy out any feature of imperfection in his conduct, and lay it before the public eye.

5. Upon any plan upon which an individual once located in this Office continues in it without interruption for a succession of years, the longer he continues the greater will be the facility, thence the stronger the temptation, to join in organizing, in concert with the leading Members of the Legislature, or even by habit, without concert, to fall into, a course of corrupt co-operation, having for it's effect the encreas⟨ing the⟩ amount of the mass of the mat⟨ter⟩ of depred⟨ation⟩ gathered at the public expence, in the way brought to

281

view in the Rationale to Ch. V on the Constitutive authority.[1] On this supposition, the Prime Minister locates in the lucrative situations at his disposal the connections of the Members of the Legislature, as they successively come into authority; while the Members in the necessary number concurr in adding to the lucrativeness and number of those same situations, that the mass of emolument, in which they are sharers, may thus receive continual encrease.

True it is, that on the thus proposed alternation plan, as in the case of the English East India Company, not to speak of other less known Companies, between those who for the time are *in*, and those who for the time are *out*, of office, a like system of confederacy and concert will be liable to have place. Still, under such an alternation as that here in question, the sinister result is not near so ⟨likely⟩ to take place as if the po⟨ssession⟩ were, for a succession of years, lodged without variation in one and the same hand, or in the same set of hands, permanently associated and organized by authority of law.

In respect of the probability of efficient competition and emulation, the plan here proposed has not, it is believed, any where, in respect of principle, any exact precedent. In this case, it is between individual and individual. In the case of the East India Company, no such competition as between one tried individual and another ever has place. Of a body of 24, one fourth go out every year, and an equal number take their places. But those who come in are always as many as are alive and choose to do so of those who went out before: for it is by the influence of the majority who stay in, that the minority who come in afresh are constantly located by their common constituents, the body of proprietors. Thus, then, ⟨tho⟩ugh there is an interval of non-ser⟨vice,⟩ there is no interval of *non-influence*: and hence as to the plan of Government, whatsoever be it's degree of aptitude, it has no means of bettering itself: no person is there by whom the *melioration-suggestive function* can be exercised with any tolerable prospect of success.[2]

Various, and little less than all-embracing, will be the shapes in which appropriate intellectual aptitude, knowledge and judgment included, not to speak of appropriate active aptitude—will be neces-

[1] For a discussion of this topic see 'Economy as applied to Office', Ch. 2, §§ 3–9, in *First Principles preparatory to Constitutional Code* (*CW*), pp. 17–26.

[2] Bentham inserted the following note at this point: '☛ If what is here said of the East India Company is in any particular incorrect, Col. S[tanhope] is requested to make the requisite correction, or if incorrigible to cancel it: the post will not allow time for ascertaining the matter here.' Bentham's statement was perfectly accurate. The executive body of the East India Company, the Court of Directors, was elected by the Court of Proprietors: of its twenty-four members, six retired each year and were not eligible for re-election until the following year. It had become customary for the Directors in office to unite to promote the return of the six Directors who had retired the previous year.

sary to the apt exercise of the functions of this almost all-embracing Office; including as it does in it's field of operation every thing but the Judiciary. From a glance at the ensuing or preceding list of Sub-Ministers, with the indications given of the functions belonging to their respective Offices,[1] some general conception of the nature and extent of the business of it may for this purpose be obtained. Of this business, one part and no more than one part, will be the locating persons in the several immediately subordinate Offices, and to that purpose forming an estimate of the appropriate aptitude, absolute and comparative, of all the several individuals whose situations and occupations afford, antecedently to actual appropriate experience, any presumptive evidence of aptitude on ⟨. . .⟩ to their several official ⟨. . .⟩. True it is, that be the person placed in the highest situation who he may, great is the reliance which, in relation to all aspirants, he can not avoid placing upon reports received from other quarters: but still the better his own acquaintance is with the several branches of the business, the better grounded will be the judgment which, after all, it will be necessary for him to form for himself as between report and report, great as the multitude of mutually conflicting ones can not but be.

While the need of appropriate aptitude is so great, scanty, on the other hand, is the supply of which a first choice can obtain any reasonable probability. Of this first choice, naturally, not to say necessarily, the object will be some one of the individuals towards whom, by services in that shape in which the effects of public service are alike conspicuous to all eyes, the admiration and ⟨grati⟩tude of the people at large have been ⟨. . .⟩ shape can be ⟨. . .⟩ than that of military service. But not to speak of the various circumstances by which appropriate aptitude, even in that very line, is rendered a consequence so far from being a necessary one of the most brilliant success—(such as superior aptitude of all those under his command, inaptitude general or accidental, on the part of the opposing enemy, together with accident in an infinite variety of shapes)—transcendent is the aptitude which a man may really possess in relation to those points on which success in that line of service depends, and at the same time be as much below par in respect of the aggregate of those points of aptitude of which appropriate aptitude in relation to the functions belonging to those several civil departments in question is composed.

Whatsoever were the degree of inaptitude manifested (such flagrant

---

[1] According to the plan at UC xxxviii. 9, in Ch. X 'Of the Sub-Ministers severally' Bentham discussed the functions of eleven Sub-Ministers: Election, Legislation, Army, Navy, Interior Communication, Preventive Service, Indigence Relief, Education, Domain, Foreign Relation and Finance.

manifestations ⟨of⟩ moral inaptitude excepted as in a situat⟨ion . . .⟩ as this can not be regarded ⟨. . .⟩ non-relocation, if relocation were admitted, can scarcely be regarded as probable.

On grounds ever so decidedly adequate, great would be the reluctance to subject to the mortification of a dismissal any such person as the general favourite here supposed. Great even in the Legislature itself: in that situation in which the inaptitude in question would be more clearly discernible than in any other: still greater in that of the people without doors: a situation into which any tolerably clear and at the same time correct conception in relation to the subject could scarcely have made it's way; and a step of this sort which, if it depended on themselves alone, the Legislature might be not disinclined to take, they might be restrained from taking by the in general salutary fear of the displeasure of their Constituents. In name, non-location, in effect the operation would be dislocation: to a great military character, such as that supposed, ⟨it⟩ would be *cashiering*: few are they ⟨. . .⟩ themselves to give support to any such proposition if put to the vote: still fewer they who, unless under the stimulus of personal enmity, would so far hazard their popularity as to bring it forward. To every one it would be manifest, that, to a tried man such as that in question, a proposition for setting up as a competitor any untried man, would in effect and design be a motion for dislocation.

Signal indeed is the inaptitude with which, great the length of time during which, for want of a temporary non-relocability clause, under the annual Election System, various branches of the public service have been known to have been oppressed: to the observation of the writer of this, examples of this sort, more than one, have in the course of his life presented themselves. This too in cases in which, in favour of the relatively unapt functionary, there has been no such plea of antecedent service as in the case here in question there could scarce fail to be.

From the proposed change of hands in ⟨. . .⟩ no fear either of stagnat⟨ion or⟩ of fluctuation need be entertained: of stagnation in the business, or of fluctuation as between principle and principle in respect of the ends, with a view to which, or the mode in which, it is conducted. The *will* to which the functionary is intended and enabled to give execution and effect is not his own will, but the will of the Legislature. As to the general plan for the conduct of the business of the Government, if it be not in the Legislature itself, or in the Office of the Legislation Minister, that it originates, it will be in that of the Finance Minister: in that Office, into which the money for every thing is to come, and from whence it is to issue, it being as it were the heart in which the circulation of the vital fluid has it's source. In the way of expenditure, of whatever is done in the several Sub-departments under the Prime Minister, the source will naturally be in those same Sub-departments respectively. Against any flagrant course of misconduct, the superintending power of the Legislature, and in dernier res⟨ort⟩ that of the Constitutive authority, can scarce fail to afford an adequate security. But ⟨against a⟩ more or less unapt choice ⟨of⟩ such subordinates as are to be located by a superordinate, small indeed is the security which, by any such controuling force, can be afforded. For that which really is, or at any rate may be made to wear the appearance of being, a mere error in judgment, neither can punishment nor disgrace in any shape be applied. Setting aside corrupt concert, as above, between Prime Minister and the Legislature, the difference between an apt man and an unapt one, and then between apt and unapt conduct in general, will in this situation commonly turn—not so much upon moral, as upon intellectual inaptitude.

INDEX OF SUBJECTS

Note. The following is a unified index which refers to the texts of all the essays included in the volume, without identifying the particular work in question.

References to Bentham's notes and to editorial notes are given by means of the page number(s) followed by the letter 'n'.

The symbol 'v.' is used to indicate 'as distinct from' or 'as opposed to'. Other abbreviations for frequently occurring words and phrases are as follows:

app. apt.	appropriate aptitude
fac. dig.	factitious dignity
f(s).	functionary(ies)
govt(s).	government(s)
gtst. h.	greatest happiness
gtst. no.	greatest number
p.o. trib.	public opinion tribunal
rep. dem.	representative democracy

ABSOLUTE MONARCHY: strength of, 275. *See* MONARCH(S), MONARCHY(IES)

ACCIDENTS: to be inserted in newspaper at Tripoli, 50

ACCUSATIONS: received by judicatory, 54–5, 60; belong to logical field of power of judicatory, 55; received by newspaper, 61; grounded on wrongs, 66; embraced by field of jurisdiction of judicatories v. that of p.o. trib., 66–7; in mixed monarchy, against party in power preferred by party in expectancy, 70–1; maxim no man bound to accuse himself, 81–2n

ACKNOWLEDGEMENT OF RIGHTS: ambiguity of, 76–7n; means of publicity for, 77n; means of achieving, 77n

ACTION(S): produced by real not avowed opinion and affection, 45; gtst. h. only measure of goodness and badness of, of rulers, 78

ACTIVE APTITUDE: element of app. apt., 188; in advocate, union of, with intellectual apt. to defeat ends of justice, 248; active inapt. and provision of official advocates, 250; in monarchy, 253; branch of app. apt., 271–2; degree of, 273; necessary to exercise of functions of prime minister, 282–3

ACTIVE TALENT: possessed by class other than gtst. no., 264

ADMINISTRATION: cause of disagreement in monarchy: disagreement amongst members of, 69

ADVICE: facility of yielding to, psychological cause by which concession may be produced, 107, 108

ADVISERS: of sovereign and concurrence in concession, 107–8; of sovereign and representation of danger with which improvement pregnant, 138

ADVOCATE(S): arguments of, heard by judicatory, 55, 61; arguments of, received by newspaper, 62; judges should not be chosen from class of hireling, 248–50; in each judicial district, provision of official, 250–1; in domestic procedure, no hireling, 251. *See* LAWYERS

AFFECTION(S): social, active force for surmounting indolence, 43; check applied to misrule by real, not avowed, 45; morality and felicity dependent upon sympathetic, 50; in breast of every man three sorts of, 183; proportion between strength of self-regarding and social, in ruling fs., 185; less advanced the age, stronger the sympathetic, 219n

AFRICA: in Northern, printing press never been in use, 32; state of countries of North, 159–60; security from North African piracy, 174–6. *See* BARBARY

AGE: in Tripoli, validity of certificate of, 21; under Greek Constitution, exclusion of all under thirty years of, from Legislative Senate, 219–20n; in Greece, at which Mahometan v. Christian permitted to vote, 255; non-adults excluded from giving efficiency to will, 260–2; infants not interdicted from faculty of manifesting opinion, 263–4

AGENCY: on largest v. individual scale, 227–8; in United States, operative power in hands of agents of people, 233–4

ALGIERS: foundary in, 19; Tripoli in state of amity with, 21; circumstances of, 149, 150–2; value of security against misrule not unknown to people, 149; extension of plan to, 169–70; most formidable of North African states, 175; rupture with Spain, 175–6; United States' acquisition of port from, 176; reception of travellers and lecturers, 180. *See* AFRICA, BARBARY

ANGLO-AMERICAN UNITED STATES: *See* UNITED STATES OF AMERICA

ANTIPATHETIC REGARD: affection in breast of every man, 183

APPETITE(S): for matter of corruption, 70; legislators have corruptive, to hold in subjection, 198–205; of monarch for external instruments of felicity, 253

APTITUDE AND INAPTITUDE: app. apt. probably not deficient in one of children of Pasha, 6; certificate of apt. of notary, 15; apt. of phrase securities against misrule, 24n; apt. of codes of European law deficient, 34–5; apt. on part of public speaker, 40; apt. of newspaper being given, usefulness will be as extent of diffusion, 46; endeavour of govt. to obstruct communication is avowal of inapt., 72; security in proportion to app. apt., 126; elements of app. apt. and members of political boards, 188–9; defined with reference to gtst. h., 217; apt arrangements in Spanish and Greek Constitutions, 218–19; inapt. in Greek Constitution, 219–52; unapt arrangements in Spanish, not in Greek Constitution, 252–4; on ground of inapt., classes of persons excluded from giving efficiency to will, 259–64; apt. maximized, end of govt., 270n, 271–3; app. apt. of prime minister and temporary non-relocability, 280–5. *See* ACTIVE APTITUDE, INTELLECTUAL APTITUDE, MORAL APTITUDE

ARABIC: translations of works into, 111; standard with words gtst. h. of gtst. no. in, 165; United States' manifesto translated in, 171; in United States, acquaintance with, 172

ARGUMENT(S): heard by judicatory, 55, 61; received by newspaper, 62

ARISTOCRACY: Greeks have no aristocratical cast, 196; in United States, Senate source of aristocratical prejudice, 229; in England, anxiety of, to give themselves security against arbitrary power of monarch, 230; in England, conflict of, with monarch, 232–3; establishment of hereditary, for support of monarchy, 234–5; in United States, yoke of, thrown off, 250; electoral bodies under command of, 266; moral apt. of ruling fs. in, 272. *See* NOBILITY

ARMS: capable of giving increase to physical force, 64; liberty to keep, 83–4; right to use of, 87; faculty of applying, as means of relief against oppression, 116–17; in England, by law people deprived of means of resistance by possession of, 117n; suppression of practice of carrying, 120n; in Barbary, on part of people possession of, 145; armed force in Tripoli, 145–6, 166–7; intimidation of Pasha with armed force, 148; in Greece, Christian population trained to use of, 255. *See* DISARMAMENT

ARMY: *See* MILITARY

ATTENDANCE: exclusion of evil in composition of jury: vexation by, 247; jury in, whenever judge in, 252

AUSTRIA: warning against form of govt. of, 239–40

BANISHMENT: example of misrule, 26; as vexation v. oppression, 26–7; security against injurious, 84, 90–2; mysterious disappearance and suspicion of, 94; secret, as mode of oppression, 119; as cause of disappearance, 133–4; no immediate hope of remedy for slaves on subject of, 135

BARBARY: powers plague to United States, 145; longing for emancipation from despotism, 145; Constitution of United States established in, 154; encouragement of competent individuals to visit, 179–80. *See* AFRICA, ALGIERS, MOROCCO, TRIPOLI, TUNIS

BASHAW: *See* SOVEREIGN

BENEVOLENCE: in Greece, kindness towards Mahometan natives dictated by effective, 254, 263

BILL OF RIGHTS: and security of governed, 23n; English indebted to, for security against misrule, 140; given to people by aristocracy, 232

BIRTH(S): fs. of govt. placed by, 28; to be inserted in newspaper at Tripoli, 51; nominal power of monarch commences at, 220n

BODY: force operating on, 55; security against suffering in, 84; vulnerable point of man, 99–100; oppression operates on goods and, 120–1. *See* PERSON

BOUNTY: in case of newspapers, less mischievous than prohibition, 52

BRITISH EMPIRE: p.o. trib. of, composed of all persons belonging to, 57. *See* ENGLAND, SCOTLAND

CADI: *See* KADI

CALUMNIES: not in a way to be inflicted by sovereign, 79n

CAPITAL: subsistence of labourers v. profit of capitalist, 37–8; matter of good applied as reward, 56; in Tripoli, application of, 109; examples of undertakings requiring permanent employment of, 109–10; in Europe, accumulation of, 110; in Tripoli, quantity of, can never receive increase but from increase in security, 110; circumstances of change in Tripoli constitute pump for, 111; in Tripoli, increased employment of, 162

CENSORSHIP: right of, 85–6

CHARTER(S): and oppression, 25–6; as subject of notification, 126–8; v. contract, 126–7n; in England and France, of promise, 140–1; as security obtainable at hands of Pasha, 164

CHEAPNESS: circumstance on which circulation of newspaper depends, 46

CHRISTIANITY: comparisons of Mahometan and Christian states to be inserted in newspaper at Tripoli, 51; Christian and money in Mahometan countries, 146; existence of security against misrule in Christendom, 149; in Greece, govt. established in hands of Christian part of population, 254–6

CIRCULATION: operation applicable to notification of suffrages of p.o. trib., 44; circumstance on which, of newspaper depends, 46–50; diffusion given to judgements of judicatory, 61; diffusion of evidence by newspaper, 61; diffusion to judgement and will given by newspaper editor, 63

CIRCUMCISION: register of acts of, to be kept by imams and notaries, 51

CITATIONS: not essential to ends of justice, 55

CIVIL LAW: claims and oppositions in, 54–5; no division between civil and penal or civil and ecclesiastical suits, 244

CLAIMS: received by judicatory, 54–5, 60; belong to logical field of power of judicatory, 55; grounded on rights, 66; embraced by field of jurisdiction of judicatories v. that of p.o. trib., 66–7

CLASS: interest of consuming, in opposition to that of producing, 67

CODIFICATION: in European govts., small extent of, 32; apt. of European codes of law deficient, 34–5; assent of monarch to new constitutional code notified through speech from throne, 40; collateral use of proposed arrangements: matter for penal code, 134; in Tripoli, representative body in concert with Pasha to frame constitutional code, 163; in England, no constitutional code, 235, 240

COERCION: and security, 44

COLONIES: *See* DISTANT DEPENDENCIES

COMMERCE: in Tripoli, judicatory of, 11; proposed system of communication contributory to increase of, 130–1

COMMERCIAL LAW: no distinction between commercial and non-commercial suits, 244

COMMINATION: unlawful, and banishment, 90

COMMON LAW: standard of reference of judicial decisions composed of anterior decisions, 32–3

COMMUNICATION: incapacity of p.o. trib. of acting in concert counteracted by facility given to means of, 71–2; except in dem., object of supreme operative body to obstruct, for political purposes, 72–3; liberty of communicating information, 85–6; obstruction of, of information prohibited, 86; in Tripoli, employment of capital and means of, 109; faculty of communicating as means of relief against oppression, 116–17; in England, by law people deprived of means of, 117n; obstruction of intellectual, as mode of ultra-oppression, 119; in Tripoli, establish system of, between office of Kadi, judicatories and mosques, 130; object of proposed system of, 130–1

COMPENSATION: desire of, of oppressed party, 43; to take place of barren punishment, 53; person contributory to injurious imprisonment compelled to furnish, 89; person contributory to injurious banishment compelled to furnish, 91; person presenting record of disappearance without justification responsible to purpose of, 95; person concerned in misuse of private writings responsible to purpose of, 96; awarded for damage to reputation from false imputations, 197; in case of injurious falsehood in publicity of judicial proceedings, 251–2

CONCEALMENT: security against evil at hands of those to whom publicity disagreeable, 41–2

CONCESSION: chance in favour of, 103–4, 135–8; probability of, on part of monarch, 105–9; persuasives for Pasha's concurrence in, 109–11; in England, of Magna Carta, 128–9n; chance of, answering purpose, 138–41

CONDITION(S) IN LIFE: in Tripoli, 21–2; by no religion shall justifying cause be made for suffering in respect of, 79; injurious inspection of private writings liable to cause evil to, 96n; vulnerable point in man, 99–100

CONFINEMENT: example of misrule, 26; as vexation v. oppression, 26–7; security against secret, 84, 88–90; injurious, prohibited, 86; person contributory to injurious banishment punished by imprisonment, 91; passports, registration and exposure to arbitrary, 91; mysterious disappearance and suspicion of, 94; secret, as mode of oppression, 119; as cause of disappearance, 133–4; no immediate hope of remedy for slaves on subject of, 135

CONSTANCY: circumstance on which circulation of newspaper depends, 46–7

CONSTITUTIONAL LAW: in England, depravity of penal branch of, 83n; in Tripoli, security can never receive increase but from change in constitution, 110; inter-community of penal law, judicial procedure and, 132–4; in Tripoli, establishment of popular constitution, 146; Constitution of United States established in Barbary, 154; extension of constitution of Tripoli, 168–70; difficulties on formation of constitution: self-regarding affection on part of other political communities and on part of fs., 184; Spanish Constitution taken for model where new system of, introduced, 216; in England, inexorably hostile to interests of gtst. no., 230; in England, no constitutional code, 235, 240; in United States, accommodated to interests of citizens, 250; in formation of, only fit object is gtst. h. of people, 259; no exercise of legislative power unconstitutional, 274; gtst. h. and form of constitution, 275–6

CONSTITUTIVE DEPARTMENT: *See* CONSTITUTIVE POWER

CONSTITUTIVE POWER: females excluded from share in, by tyranny and prejudice, 58; to members of, belongs to choose members of operative department, 224; conduct of subordinate fs. placed in state of dependence on will of constitutive body, 225–7; power detached from constitutive and given to operative department, 227; in United States, Senate opposing obstruction to will of constitutive body, 229; in hands of gtst. no. not recognized by division of power principle, 231; in United States, in hands of gtst. no., 233–4; vast majority of people deprived of share in, 235; visitants to judicatory considered as committee of, 251; resides in people, 267–8; strictness of dependence of operative power on will of, maximized, 268–9; first link in chain of political subordination, 269; degree in which end of govt. accomplished in constitutive department as app. apt. of fs., 271; operative detached from, 274n; as security against misconduct, 285

CONTRACT: v. charter, 126–7n

CORAN: *See* KORAN

CORONER'S INQUEST: use of, 133

CORRUPTION: inclination to, on part of judge, 34; appetite for matter of, 70; strife between those in possession of, and those in expectancy of, 70–1; presumption of exercise of, by f., 98; theory v. practice of, 190; monarch as Corrupter General, 196; in monarchy, produced by pretences, 201; in United States, Senate source of, 229; influence of, on will of gtst. no., 269–70n; corrupt co-operation between prime minister and legislature, 281–2

DEATH(S): to be inserted in newspaper at Tripoli, 51; as cause of disappearance, 133–4. *See* HOMICIDE

DEBILITATION: example of misrule, 26; example of oppression, 27; security against national, 87. *See* DEFENCELESSNESS, DISARMAMENT, ENFEEBLEMENT

DEBTS: of George III and George IV, 234. *See* NATIONAL DEBT

DECEIT: instrument by which depredation committed, 97; exclusions to faculty of giving testimony, foolishly devised instrument for avoidance of deception, 248–9

DECLARATION OF THE RIGHTS OF MAN: and security of governed, 23n

DEFAMATION: absurdity of exclusion put upon testimony of party defamed in action for, 81n

DEFENCELESSNESS: security against national, 83–4. *See* DEBILITATION, DISARMAMENT, ENFEEBLEMENT

DEFENCES: received by judicatory, 55, 60

DELAY: applications for, not essential to ends of justice, 55; and appointment of agents, 227–8; in United States, Senate source of factitious, 229; judge to appoint deputies to prevent, 247. *See* DELAY EXPENSE AND VEXATION

DELAY EXPENSE AND VEXATION: right and proper end of judicature, avoidance of, 252; inseparable from litigation, 262

DELEGATES: people should choose, 265–7; operative power resides in, of people, 267–8; moral apt. of, in rep. govt., 272

DELINQUENCY: and absurdity of exclusion put upon testimony, 81–3n

DELUSION: inspired by splendour that environs sovereign, 136; monarch as Deluder

General, 196; division of power principle keeps on foot, by which English system represented as good, 231; influence of, on will of gtst. no., 269–70n

DEMOCRACY: *See* REPRESENTATIVE DEMOCRACY

DENMARK: afflicted by monarch, 196

DEPENDENCE: principle of absolute, 228–31, 243; under Greek Constitution, of Legislative Senate on President, 237; strictness of, of operative power on will of constitutive maximized, 268. *See* SUBORDINATION AND SUPERORDINATION

DEPRAVATION: in monarchy, produced by pretences, 201

DEPREDATION(S): where suffering of oppressed attended with profit to oppressor, oppression has effect of, 27; evil produced by, v. that produced by barren vexation, 27–8n; characteristic occupation of ultra-indigent and ultra-opulent, 67–8; in monarchy, monarch is arch-depredator, 68; and law, 71; and application of securities, 79n; system of laws and securing of governed from, 82n; security against official, 97–9; where oppression bears on property, vexation designated by more particular name of, 100n; extortion of service considered as, 100–1n; as oppression when benefit to oppressor is among results, 115–16; except in United States, for benefit of ruling few chief object of govt., 116; in England, by law people deprived of knowledge of instances of, 117n; vexation by official, as mode of oppression, 119; as accompaniment of war, 132; desire of sovereign to commit act of, 137–8; charter will point attention of people to acts of, 164; in Egypt, of despot, 168; in Algiers, quantity of, 169; monarch as Depredator General, 196; in monarchy, exercised upon vast scale, 201; indignation awakened by system of, 202; rulers' acts of, secured against punishment and restraint, 203–4; sole business of ministers, exercise of, 222; in England, retardation of, 233; gtst. no. taught that form of govt. in which, screwed up is best, 270n; co-operation between prime minister and legislature for increasing matter of, 281–2. *See* SPOLIATION

DESIRE(S): wishes of judge guided by interest, 33; of compensation and vengeance of oppressed party, 43; declaration of, included in judgement, 63; satisfaction of, for matter of corruption impossible, 70; of sovereign to commit act of depredation or vexation, 137–8; external instruments of felicity as objects of general, 183–4; of ruling fs. to make addition to external instruments of felicity they possess, 184; in no body other than gtst. no. stronger, to produce gtst. h., 264; universal good is result of conflict among sinister, 267; moral apt. as, to contribute to gtst. h., 272

DESPOTISM: in Barbary, longing for emancipation from, 145; in Tripoli, continues because nothing better proposed, 146; in Tripoli, insecurity and indigence perpetuated by, 156; applied to English form of govt., principle of dependence would be consummation of, 230; in judicature where no publicity, object has been sacrifice of universal interest to sinister interest of despot, 252

DIFFUSION: *See* CIRCULATION

DIGNITY: app., attached to extraordinary service by hand of nature, 200; reward of extraordinary and meritorious service, 204; in Greece, by faculty of voting, Mahometans raised to situation high in, 255. *See* FACTITIOUS DIGNITY, NATURAL DIGNITY

DISAPPEARANCE: security against mysterious, 94–6; mysterious, as mode of oppression, 119; course of procedure for ascertaining cause of, 133

DISARMAMENT: security against national, 87; suppression of forcible means of relief against oppression, 117. *See* DEBILITATION, DEFENCELESSNESS, ENFEEBLEMENT

DISCONTENT: effect of depredation, 116; rulers' apprehension of, on part of people, 131–2

DISCUSSION: in Greece, no reason for restraints on liberty of public, 197; interdiction of public, 202–4

DISPOSITION: innate, as cause of apt., 272–3

DISTANT DEPENDENCIES: Greeks stand clear from temptation afforded by, 195; symptoms of mental derangement manifested by rulers of Spain and Portugal in management of, 195; impossibility of good govt. in case of, 195; colonies and war, 234

DISTRIBUTION: operation necessary to publication of ordinances, 38–9

DISTRICT(S): Tripoli to be divided into, 75; state divided into judicial, 243–4; electors in judicial, and dislocation of judge, 245–7; continuance of judge in, 247; in every judicial, provision of official advocates, 250–1; in Greece, Mahometan v. Christian votes in election, 254–5

DOCUMENTS: See WRITINGS

DOMINION: prospect of extending, psychological cause by which concession may be produced, 108

DRAFTSMAN: See LEGISLATOR(S)

DURATION: of notification depends upon permanence of signs employed, 126

EASE: appetite for, of legislator, 198, 203; faculty of enjoying, conferred on monarch at expense of gtst. no., 253

EAST INDIA COMPANY: location of officials, 282

ECCLESIASTICAL LAW: no division between civil and ecclesiastical suits, 244

ECONOMY: rule of, as applied to no. of offices, 205

EGYPT: Tripoli bounded by, 3; Tripoli in a state of amity with, 21; subjugation of Tripoli by, 147; state of govt. in, 168

ELASTICITY: in judicial establishment, 251

ELECTION: females and, of possessors of supreme operative power, 58; armed force of United States not to interfere in, of representatives, 178–9; apt arrangement in Spanish and Greek Constitutions: right of suffrage in, of representatives of people, 218–19; limits of judicial district same as, districts, 244; and dislocation of judge, 245–7; visitants to judicatory considered as committee of electors, 251; in Greece, Mahometans to have votes in, of members of representative assembly, 254–5; interests of electors and delegates, 266–7; of fs. for taking arrangements of detail by which gtst. h. to be provided for, 267; of prime minister, 279–85. See SUFFRAGE(S)

EMOLUMENT: See PAY

ENFEEBLEMENT: national, as mode of ultra-oppression, 120. See DEBILITATION, DEFENCELESSNESS, DISARMAMENT

ENGLAND: choice of jury, 14–15; board and lodging in universities, 17; security of governed and force, 23n; memorials which stand in place of law, 33; confusion in law reports and treatises, 34; evil produced by neglect of effect of abridgement of labour, 37; newspapers most instructive, 52; press example of p.o. trib., 57; in newspapers fruit of labours of sub-committees of p.o. trib., 60; functions of official judicatory compared with those of newspaper, 60–4; taxation of newspapers, 73; exclusion put upon testimony, 81–3n; sovereign's inducement to dismiss fs., 104; circumstances of change in Tripoli published in newspapers, 111; travellers from, drawn to Tripoli, 111; means of relief against oppression, 117n; sentence of execution passed on King by p.o. trib. declared irregular, 122–3; original contract of Whig Monarchists a fiction, 127n; concession of Magna Carta, 128–9n; use of habeas corpus and coroner's inquest, 133; English indebted to Magna Carta and Bill of Rights for security against misrule, 140; Six Acts do not extend to Barbary, 145; insertion of articles in newspapers, 150, 159; war with Algiers, 151; speech from throne, 163; English as medium of communication in Tripoli, 172; boards by which some of functions of executive exercised, 188–9; in respect of distant dependencies, Greece has advantage over, 195; afflicted by monarch, 196; Greeks will look down with scorn and contempt upon, 197; riddance of King and House of Lords, 228; application of principle of dependence would be consummation of despotism and misrule, 230; division of power principle, 231–6; seals in custody of fs., 239; warning against form of govt. of, 240; distinction between law cases and equity cases, 244; judicatories in, 245; existence of God and receipt of testimony, 249; choice of judges from advocates, 249–50; age of maturity by law of, 261; system of representation purposely corrupt, 266; location of officials in East India Company, 282. *See* BRITISH EMPIRE

EQUALITY: of external instruments of felicity, 53; and h., 78

EQUITY: and prevention of deperition of evidence, 13–14; no distinction between law cases and equity cases, 244

EUROPE: Franks of most European nations in capital of Tripoli, 3; in European govts. under common law, standard of reference of judicial decisions composed of anterior decisions, 32–3; confusion in law reports and treatises, 34; apt. of codes of European law deficient, 34–5; evil produced by neglect of effect of abridgement of labour, 37; speech from throne in constitutional monarchies, 40; United States' newspaper less known than English, 57; govts. and extinction of classes of members of p.o. trib., 58–9; security of property, 108–9; accumulation of capital, 110; sovereign of Tripoli illustrious among sovereigns of, 110–11; means of relief against oppression, 117n; condition of English distinguished from inhabitants of, 140; in Barbary, perception of security under European govts., 145; in Greece, Christian population trained in European form of military exercise, 255; domestic slavery established over, by Roman Law, 261

EVIDENCE: prevention of deperition of, 13–14; received, compelled, collected and stored by judicatory, 55, 61; received, impressed and diffused by newspaper, 61; compelled, collected and stored by newspaper, 62; afforded by deeds v. that afforded by words, 72; seizure of writings and obtainment of, 96–7; injunction of secrecy, of depredation, 97–8; where object of seizure of papers is furnishing, vexation not oppression, 120n; instructions respecting, in case of homicide, 126; in Tripoli, no adequate means for collection of, 133–4; collection of, and domestic v. public judicatory, 251. *See* TESTIMONY

EVIL: *See* GOOD AND EVIL

EXAMINATION: conducted under auspices of English equity, 14; of witnesses in case of unlawful homicide, 92–4

EXECUTIVE DEPARTMENT: *See* EXECUTIVE POWER

EXECUTIVE POWER: in Tripoli, in hands of single individual, 164; business of, to give execution and effect to will of legislative power, 220, 223–4; business of executive department included in that of operative, 224; should be subordinate to legislative, 224–5, 226–7; in United States, in hands of agents of people, 233–4; under Greek Constitution, independence of judiciary with relation to, 243; detached from operative, 268–9, 274n; degree in which end of govt. accomplished in executive department as app. apt. of fs., 271; interference of legislative with, 274; mischievous effects produced by monarch with or without, 275

EXPECTATION: fear is, of eventual evil, 41; inducement constituted by, of pain and pleasure, 273

EXPENDITURE: by proposed arrangements remedy not applied to misrule in shape of lavish, 115; made in respect of needless and useless offices is waste, 205

EXPENSE: in Tripoli, of sovereign v. that of govt., 20; in Tripoli, provision for, of judicatory and universities, 20; and distribution of ordinances, 38–9; public recitation not necessarily attended with, 39; of operations preparatory to publication, 43–4; of record of disappearance defrayed by judicatory, 95–6; depredation at, of individual v. that at, of govt., 97; in Tripoli, of letter-post, 130, 131; obtainment of wealth at, of others, 184; of power, pecuniary emolument, fac. dig., 186–7; minimized, end of govt., 198, 270–1, 270n; instruments of felicity created by rulers at, of subjects, 198–205; in England, of govt., 235–6; in each judicatory one judge, thus, minimized, 245; no emolument at, of public receivable by deputies of judge, 247; single-seatedness and, of judicial establishment, 250–1; external instruments of felicity conferred on monarch at, of gtst. no., 253; co-operation between prime minister and legislature for increasing depredation gathered at public, 281–2. *See* DELAY EXPENSE AND VEXATION

EXTERNAL INSTRUMENTS OF FELICITY: *See* INSTRUMENTS OF FELICITY

EXTRACTION: operation applicable to notification of suffrages of p.o. trib., 44

FACTITIOUS DIGNITY: as external instrument of felicity, 183–4; mode of sinister sacrifice: attached to influential situations, 187; employable as instrument for acquisition of money and power, 190; appetite for, of legislator, 198, 199–200, 203; provided for hereditary aristocracy, 235; conferred on monarch at expense of gtst. no., 253. *See* DIGNITY, NATURAL DIGNITY

FACTITIOUS HONOUR: *See* FACTITIOUS DIGNITY

FAVOURITES: vexation at hands of, most to be apprehended, 104; and divulgation of instances of oppression, 104

FEAR: obstacle to publicity of transgressions, 41–2; cause of influence of p.o. trib.: of ultimate obstruction, 122–3; cause of influence of p.o. trib.: of inferior sufferings, 124; penal inducement constituted by, of pain, 273

FEDERALISM: invitation to people of Tunis to join in federative union with Tripoli, 169

FELICITY: *See* HAPPINESS, INSTRUMENTS OF FELICITY

FEMALES: not excluded from p.o. trib., 58; excluded from giving efficiency to will, 260; no interdiction of faculty of manifesting opinion, 263–4

FEZZAN: in subjection to Tripoli, 3, 7; population of, 3–4

FICTION: and p.o. trib., 28, 121, 125; and members of p.o. trib., 56–7; in England, original contract of Whig Monarchists a, 127n; in England and United States, of rule of action, 249

FICTITIOUS ENTITY: p.o. trib. apt to present itself as, 54

FIELDS OF POWER: of judicatory: geographical v. logical, 55

FINANCE MINISTER: of Tripoli, 6, 20; of Fezzan, 7; and origin of general plan for conduct of govt., 284–5

FINANCIAL ESTABLISHMENT: of Tripoli, 20–1

FORCE(S): legislative arrangements established for security of governed generally trusted to, 23n; operating on body v. that operating on mind, 55–6; as element of power, 64; of judicatories v. that of p.o. trib., 65–6; instrument by which depredation committed, 97; case of people oppressed by military, not considered, 120n; of public opinion only, not included in, of govt., 121; degree of notoriety measure of, of p.o. trib., 121–2; in Tripoli, armed, 145–6, 166–7; intimidation of Pasha with armed, 148; assistance afforded by United States with, 171, 173–4, 178–9; means of, in hands of sharers in exercise of powers of govt., 202; in United States, military, at command of President, 221; influence of, on will of gtst. no., 269–70n; app. apt. and exposure to, of sanctions, 272–3

FRACTIONALITY: *See* INTEGRALITY AND FRACTIONALITY

FRANCE: choice of jury, 15; security of governed and force, 23n; newspapers worth little, 52; *Lit de Justice*, 107; circumstances of change in Tripoli published in newspapers, 111; Constitutional Charter as security for misrule, 140–1; speech from throne, 163; French as medium of communication in Tripoli, 172; preservation of United States' trade from annoyance by, 174; in respect of distant dependencies, Greece has advantage over, 195; afflicted by monarch, 196; Greeks will look down with scorn and contempt upon, 197; riddance of monarch, 228; triumph of Bonaparte over priests and lawyers, 249–50; system of representation purposely corrupt, 266

FREQUENCY: circumstance on which circulation of newspaper depends, 46, 47; degree of, of newspaper dependent on variety, 47

FUNCTIONARY(IES): in Tripoli, all, subject to judicatories, 10; of govt. as agents of community, 28; minds of, operated on by p.o. trib., 28; power of p.o. trib. as supposed by, 30; as receivers of information of transgressions, 41–2; in rep. govt., importance of function of newspaper editor v. that of official, 45–6; every disagreement among, is addition to power of p.o. trib., 69; appeal to p.o. trib. is to act as accuser either of, or of form of govt., 70–1; in every govt. but dem., see in p.o. trib. an adverse power, 72; security for appeal to public opinion and power of law on conduct of fs. and non-fs., 80–1; power without limitation given to, whose signatures necessary to validity of passport, 91; depredation and, 97; presumption of exercise of intimidation or corruption by, 98; and acknowledgement of receipt of money, 98–9; and acknowledgement of exaction of service, 100–2; vexation at hands of, most to be apprehended, 104; vexations and oppressions presented as liable to be practised by, 105–7; remedy to depredation if exercised by subordinate, 119n; app. apt. of, as instruments applicable to purpose of notification, 125–6; sinister sacrifice on part of public, 183; desire of ruling, to make addition to external instruments of felicity they possess, 184; difficulty on formation of constitution: self-regarding affection on part of, 184; proportion between strength of self-regarding and social affection in ruling, 185; disposition of ruling, to sacrifice particular to universal interest, 185–6; sacrifice of universal interest to particular interest of ruling, 186–90; protection given by law to reputation of, from false imputations, 197; conduct of subordinate, placed in state of dependence on will of constitutive body, 225–7; negatives on power of people given to, 236–9; election of, for taking arrangements of detail by which gtst. h. to be provided for, 267; subsistence of, and expense of govt., 270–1; app. apt. of, and gtst. h., 271–3

GAGGING: example of misrule, 26; example of oppression, 27; security against national, 80–3, 85–7. *See* SILENCING

GENOA: Genoese in capital of Tripoli, 3

GERMANY: afflicted by monarch, 196

GOD: power of sovereign given by, 78; monarch as, upon earth, 196; not given to man to possess knowledge of Almighty, 196; existence of, and receipt of testimony, 249

GOOD AND EVIL: fear of evil and sovereign, 24n; private v. public v. mixed evil, 26–7; evil produced by depredation v. that produced by barren vexation, 27–8n; evil produced by neglect of effect of abridgement of labour, 37–8; fear is expectation of eventual evil, 41; evil consequences of violation of moderation, 49–50; prospect of, forces operating on mind, 55–6; subjection to evil as element of power, 64–5; magnitude of, at disposal of judicatories v. that of p.o. trib., 65–6; and field of jurisdiction of judicatories v. that of p.o. trib., 66–7; matter of good in shape of matter of corruption, 70; gtst. h. only measure of goodness and badness of actions of rulers, 78; evils producible by action of individuals v. those producible by sovereign, 79n; prevention of evil to person and property, 83; shape of evil in case of injurious inspection of private writings, 96n; and production of intimidation, 97–8; United States only good govt., 148; good govt. as means of relief from insecurity, 159; destruction of bad govt. without better in readiness is to increase evil, 166; in Greece, obstacles to good govt. have no place, 193; impossibility of good govt. in case of distant dependencies, 195; fac. dig. productive of evil in variety of shapes, 200; matter of good in hands of sharers of powers of govt., 202; division of power amongst rulers as security for good govt., 231–6; good and bad in forms of govt., 239–40; evils from division of cases between judicatories, 244; probability of good judicature inversely as no. of judges, 245; exclusion of evils in composition of jury, 247–8; universal good is result of conflict among sinister interests, 267; good form of govt. regarded by gtst. no. as bad, 270n; all expense is evil, 271; remunerative inducement constituted by hope of good, 273

GOODS: oppression operates on body and, 120–1

GOVERNMENT(S): in Tripoli, expense of sovereign v. that of, 20; security against bad, 23n; fs. of, as agents of community, 28; in European, under common law, standard of reference of judicial decisions composed of anterior decisions, 32–3; European, and extinction of classes of members of p.o. trib., 58–9; rep. dem. only form of, which has gtst. h. for object, 68; appeal made to p.o. trib. by members of, 69; appeal to p.o. trib. is to act as accuser either of fs. or of form of, 70–1; in every, but dem., interest of ruling few in opposition to general interest, 72; endeavour of, to obstruct communication is avowal of inapt., 72; English govt.'s taxation of newspapers, 72–3; except in United States, those by whom opposition made to those by whom powers of, exercised numbered among delinquents, 82n; liberty to converse on form of, 83; depredation at expense of, 97; no service exacted on account of, without acknowledgement, 100–2; in Tripoli, insecurity under form of, 108; loans obtained by, of Tripoli for establishment of public works, 110; except in United States, depredation for benefit of ruling few chief object of, 116; check to power of, applied by publicity, 118; force of public opinion only force not included in force of, 121; punishment in power of p.o. trib.: opposition to laws and practice of, 124; regularity in acts of, 124–5; form of charter v. contract given to commencement of rational, 126–7n; power of public opinion only check to power of, 129; expense of letter-post to, lessened by pay received for letters sent by individuals, 130; in Barbary, perception of security under European, 145; United States only good, 148; insecurity accompaniment of, such as Tripoli's, 154; United States only, in which gtst. h. object really pursued, 159; good, as means of relief from insecurity, 159; destruction of bad, without better in readiness is to increase evil, 166; in Tripoli, weakness of, 166–7; extension of plan to, of Egypt, Tunis, Algiers, Morocco, 167–70; in Greece, obstacles to good, have no place, 193; impossibility of good, in case of distant dependencies, 195; specific end of, minimization of expense, 198–9; interest of those over whom powers of, exercised made sacrifice to interest of those by whom powers exercised, 200–1; resistance to will of sharers of powers of, 201–2; production of hatred and contempt towards, 202–4; in instance of each, gtst. h. in proportion to success of endeavours by rulers to keep corruptive appetites in subjection, 204–5; right and proper end of, 217, 259; apt arrangement in Spanish and Greek Constitutions: declaration of right and proper end of, 218; business of, and operative v. constitutive departments, 224; in English form of, impossibility that power exercised by King or House of Lords had gtst. h. for end, 228; applied to English form of, principle of dependence would be consummation of despotism and misrule, 230; division of power amongst rulers as security for good, 231–6; warning against forms of, 239–40; particular interest and maintenance of, 246–7; arrangements of, by which conduct of people regulated conformable to will of gtst. no., 259, 264; subordinate proper ends of, 270–3; gtst. no. taught that form of, in which depredation and oppression screwed up is best, 270n; minor ends of, 270n. *See* ABSOLUTE MONARCHY, MIXED MONARCHY, MONARCHY(IES), REPRESENTATIVE DEMOCRACY, REPRESENTATIVE GOVERNMENT

GOVERNORS AND GOVERNED: legislative arrangements established for security of governed v. governors generally trusted to force, 23n; condition of, and phrase securities against misrule, 24n; object of system of laws as gtst. h. of governors, 82n; production of hatred and contempt towards governors, 202–4. *See* RULER(S), SUBJECTS

GRAMMAR: taught in Tripolitan universities, 16; subject of study in Mahometan universities, 158

GREATEST HAPPINESS: *See* HAPPINESS

GREECE: in Mahometan universities study of mathematics, logic, rhetoric, derived from translations of Greek, 158; United States' acquisition of port from, 174; preservation of United States' trade from annoyance by, 174; provisional Constitution conformable to gtst. h. principle, 183; obstructive power in Constitution, 189; obstacles to good govt. have no place, 193, 196–7; Greeks stand clear from temptation afforded by distant dependencies, 195; no reason for restraints on liberty of public discussion and press, 197; five trials of legislators, 198–205; Constitution preferable to Spanish, 216–17; apt arrangements in Constitution, 218–19; inapt. in Constitution, 219–52; Legislative Senate, 219–20, 221, 223, 236–9, 240–2, 243, 244; Executive Council, 219–23, 228, 237, 238–9, 240–2; Ministers, 221–3, 228, 238–9; President of Executive Council, 222, 223, 239, 242; Judiciary, 228, 242–52; President of Legislative Senate, 236–8; Secretary of Legislative Senate, 237, 238; Secretary of Executive Council, 239; Minister of Justice, 243, 245–7; unapt arrangements in Spanish Constitution not in Greek, 252–4; Mahometan and Jewish natives, 254–6, 263–4; age of maturity under Greek law, 261

HABEAS CORPUS: use of, 133

HAPPINESS: gtst. h. not taken for object of pursuit by commentaries on Koran, 34; gtst. h. proper end of legislation, 34–5; gtst. h. of monarch object of pursuit of authors of codes of law, 35; of ruling one or few more or less connected with, of many, 35n; apt. of newspaper as measured by gtst. h. being given, usefulness will be as extent of diffusion, 46; felicity dependent upon sympathetic affection, 50; gtst. h. standard of reference in comparisons of Mahometan and Christian states, 51; gtst. h. right and proper end of social action, 53; application of gtst. h. principle, 53; rep. dem. only form of govt. which has gtst. h. for object, 68; by every disagreement among members of govt. service rendered to gtst. h., 69; in mixed monarchy, sinister interest of component parts acts in constant opposition to gtst. h., 69–70; and equality, 78; gtst. h. only right and proper end of ruler, 78; liberty to express whatsoever contributory to gtst. h., 80; gtst. h. and object of system of law, 82n; right of giving publicity to facts where conception contributory to gtst. h., 85–6; sensibility to h. of subjects, psychological cause by which concession may be produced, 107n, 108; regularity v., 124; gtst. h. and power of p.o. trib., 125; United States only govt. in which gtst. h. object really pursued, 159, 177, 221; in United States, felicity produced by Constitution, 169; provisional Greek Constitution conformable to gtst. h. principle, 183; regard and desire of, 183; assurance from ruling few that felicity of all others is object pursued, 185; at formation of state, felicity of each in highest degree dependent on that of whole, 185; gtst. h. in proportion to success of endeavours by rulers to keep corruptive appetites in subjection, 204–5; apt. and inapt. defined with reference to gtst. h., 217; gtst. h. right and proper end of govt., 218; will of gtst. no. aimed at production of gtst. h., 225–6; in English form of govt., impossibility that power exercised by King or House of Lords had gtst. h. for end, 228; gtst. h. and exercise of power, 240; in France, object of law gtst. h. of Bonaparte, 249–50; monarch in state of hostility with gtst. h. of gtst. no., 252–4; right and proper end of govt. is gtst. h. of people, 259; gtst. h. requires that arrangements of govt. by which conduct of people regulated be conformable to will of gtst. no., 259, 264; gtst. h. principle and exclusion upon incapacity, 262–3; people and arrangements by which gtst. h. produced, 265; way contribution made to universal, by expression given to individual wills, 265–7; election of fs. for taking arrangements of detail by which gtst. h. to be provided for, 267; error of gtst. no. as to means by which gtst. h. attained, 269–70n; app. apt. of fs. and gtst. h., 271–3; gtst. h. and form of constitution, 275–6. *See* INSTRUMENTS OF FELICITY

HOLY ALLIANCE: and rupture of Spain with Algiers, 175–6; despots of, succeeded to bad qualities of Bonaparte, 253–4

HOMICIDE: example of misrule, 26; as vexation v. oppression, 26–7; security against secret and unlawful, 84, 92–4; mysterious disappearance and suspicion of, 94; secret, as mode of oppression, 119; instructions respecting evidence in case of, 126; hope of remedy for slaves on subject of, 135. *See* DEATH(S)

HONOUR: *See* DIGNITY, FACTITIOUS DIGNITY, NATURAL DIGNITY

HOUSE OF COMMONS: p.o. trib. and committees of, 28; fraction of legislative power belongs to, 231; another House of Lords, 235

HOUSE OF LORDS: riddance of, 228; fraction of legislative power belongs to, 231; establishment of, for support of monarchy, 234–5; House of Commons another, 235

IDEAS: association of, formed from physical association, 47

IMAGINATION: p.o. trib apt to present itself as offspring of, 54

IMAM(S): in Tripoli, attached to each mosque, 12; and validity of certificate of age, 21; and representation to sovereign, 42–3n; register of acts of circumcision to be kept by notaries and, 51; notice of confinement attested by, 89; on death of every person notice given to, 92; in case of unlawful homicide, examination made by, 92–4; and publication of record of disappearance, 95

IMPARTIALITY: circumstance on which circulation of newspaper depends, 46, 48–9

IMPRESSION: given to judgements of judicatory, 61; of evidence by newspaper, 61; to judgement and will given by newspaper editor, 63

IMPRISONMENT: *See* CONFINEMENT

INDIGENCE: ultra-indigent as enemies of body politic, 67–8; in Tripoli, perpetuated by despotism, 156

INDOLENCE: obstacle to publicity of transgressions, 41, 43

INDUCEMENT(S): necessary to obtain consent of sovereign to concession, 104; restraining v. impelling, in case of advisers, 108; to depredation has place at all times, 116; furnished for compliance with legislative arrangements, 132–3; to concurrence of sovereign of Tripoli, 162; United States', for concurrence, 174–7; practice determined by self-regarding, 194; by which desire to contribute to gtst. h. secured, 272; superventitious, as cause of apt., 272–3

INFLUENCE: depredation and official, 97; prospect of extending, psychological cause by which concession may be produced, 108; cause of, of p.o. trib.: fear of ultimate obstruction, fear of inferior sufferings, 122–4

INFORMATION: furnishing of, of transgressions, 41–4; liberty of communicating, 85–6; obstruction of communication of, prohibited, 86; of confinement, 88–90; presence of means of, as cause of scientific apt., 273

INJURY(IES): personal, or, to marital or paternal rights not in a way to be inflicted by sovereign, 79n; of reputation by false imputations, 80; exercise of rights and corporal, 86–7; done to people in exercise of powers of govt., 201

INSTRUMENTS OF FELICITY: equality of external, 53; labour means by which external, brought into existence, 58; self-regard includes desire of possessing external, 183–4; sacrifice of, 185; each external, employable as instrument for acquisition of others, 189–90; created by rulers at expense of subjects, 198–205; external, conferred on monarch at expense of gtst. no., 253

INTEGRALITY AND FRACTIONALITY: mode of sinister sacrifice: fractionalizing office, 188–9; case in which division of power beneficial to interest of people: fractionization of legislative power, 231; responsibility of judge not fractionalized, 245

INTELLECTUAL APTITUDE: odium attendant on obstruction of communication in ratio of, 72; element of app. apt., 188; augmentation of, of jury, 247–8; in advocate, union of active apt. with, to defeat ends of justice, 248; intellectual inapt. and provision of official advocates, 250; in monarchy, 253; branch of app. apt., 271–2; branches of, 272; degree of, 273; necessary to exercise of functions of prime minister, 282–3; moral inapt. v. intellectual inapt., 285

INTELLECTUAL WEAKNESS: implied in case of being misled by bad advice, 106

INTENSITY: of notification depends upon impressiveness of means, 126–8

INTEREST(S): wishes of judge guided by, 33; effect of abridgement of labour on, of operative hands, 37–8; articles sent in to newspaper by those whose, served, 52; will of members of judicatory acted upon by ruling, 54; ruling, of judicatory v. that of p.o. trib., 56; real net, is actual ruling, 56; and field of jurisdiction of judicatories v. that of p.o. trib., 66–7; division of, in p.o. trib., 67; of p.o. trib. in accordance with that of gtst. no., 69; by every disagreement among members of govt. service rendered to public, 69; in mixed monarchy, sinister interest of component parts acts in constant opposition to, of gtst. no., 69–70; in every govt. but dem., of ruling few in opposition to general, 72; of all to put down govt. which endeavours to obstruct communication, 72; of lawyers to maximize delinquencies, 82n; of gtst. no. and strength of laws, 82–3n; propensity on part of each individual to sacrifice all other, to own self-regarding, 183; sacrifice of particular to universal, 185–6; sacrifice of universal, to particular, of ruling fs., 186–90; call for sacrifice of personal, to public, 194; sacrifice of, 194–5; of those over whom powers of govt. exercised made sacrifice to, of those by whom powers exercised, 200–1; of people v. that of ruling few, 217; conflict of, 218; less advanced the age, greater probability of sacrifice of personal, to universal, 219n; of constitutive body same thing with universal, 226; of individual and appointment of agents, 227–8; in England, constitutional law inexorably hostile to, of gtst. no., 230; case in which division of power beneficial to, of people, 231–6; under Greek Constitution, sacrifice of universal to particular, 241–2; particular, of electors of district and dislocation of judge, 246–7; local connection of judge in way of, 247; in France, object of law: of Bonaparte, 249–50; in United States, constitutional law accommodated to, of citizens, 250; monarch in state of hostility with, of gtst. no., 252–4; of electors and delegates, 266–7; in rep. govt., connection between, of f. and universal, 272. *See* SINISTER INTEREST(S), SINISTER SACRIFICE, UNIVERSAL INTEREST

INTIMIDATION: instrument by which depredation committed, 97; presumption of

exercise of, by f., 98; of Pasha with armed force, 148; means of, in hands of sharers of powers of govt., 202; influence of, on will of gtst. no., 269–70n
IRRIGATION: in Tripoli, employment of capital for, 109–10
ITALY: Italians in capital of Tripoli, 3; Italian as medium of communication in Tripoli, 172; afflicted by monarch, 196

JEW(S): in capital of Tripoli, 3; and money in Mahometan countries, 146; Jewish natives in Greece, 254, 255
JUDGEMENT(S): formed, expressed and executed by judicatory, 55, 61; formed and expressed by newspaper editor, 62–3; given impression and diffusion by newspaper editor, 63; execution and effect given to, by members of p.o. trib., 63–4; execution and effect given to, in case of judicatories v. that in case of p.o. trib., 65; supposition that monarch misled by false statements rather than unwise, 106; punishment in power of p.o. trib.: obstructions to execution of, 124; as to arrangements productive of h., 259–64. See INTELLECTUAL APTITUDE
JUDGE(S): under common law, makes choice of such writings as appear best adapted to his purpose, 32–3; difficulty of, and corruption of, in applying commentaries on Koran, 34; necessity of collection of ordinances as guide to, 35; Tripoli to be divided into districts and in each, placed, 75; fact of detention at extraordinary prison made known to, 89; person under confinement may be produced before, 90; notice of sentence of banishment pronounced by subordinate judicatory sent to office of head, 91; and notification of record of disappearance, 94–5; application of penal law in case of oppressor of sufficient power to be formidable to, 105; lawyers not to be made, 196–7; under Greek Constitution, 243; in each judicatory, one, 245; location and dislocation of, 245–7; power to, to appoint deputies, 247, 251; local connection of, 247; class of persons in which, chosen, 248–9; app. apt. of, cannot supersede demand for assistance of advocates, 250; and committee of p.o. trib. as jury, 252; in judicature where no publicity, object has been sacrifice of universal interest to sinister interest of, 252. See KADI
JUDICATORY(IES): judicial establishment of Tripoli, 8–11; in Tripoli, of commerce, 11; in Tripoli, districts of mosques form sub-districts of, 12; in Tripoli, financial districts coincide with judicial districts, 20; in Tripoli, provision for expense of, 20; and publicity of transgressions, 42; expense of transmitting depositions from, to, 44; proceedings of, to be inserted in newspaper at Tripoli, 51; morality and h. depend upon notoriety of rule of action referred to by, 53; parallel between p.o. trib. and, 54–73; functions of, 54–5; power of, 55–6; ruling interest of, 56; functions of p.o. trib. v. those of, 60–4; power of p.o. trib. v. that of, 64–73; copy of proclamation of rights to be sent to, 77n; register of confinement to be kept at office of, 88; any person may repair to, and require of judges that person under confinement be produced, 90; notice of sentence of banishment pronounced by subordinate, sent to office of head judge, 91; suspicion of confinement, homicide or banishment, entry made in register book of, 94; and notification of record of disappearance, 95–6; and seizure of writings, 96; general statement of service exacted of indeterminate individuals deposited at, 102; register of merit to be kept in, 102; punishment in power of p.o. trib.: obstructions to execution of judgements of, 124; places for notification, 127–8; report of reading of charter in, 128; in Tripoli, possible sources of notification, 129–30; establish letter-post between office of Kadi, mosques and, 130; in England, emolument and power of judiciary depend on uncertainty, 230; plan for judiciary, 243–52; evils from division of cases between, 244; one judge in each, 245; location and dislocation in, 245–7; single-seatedness, and expense of judicial establishment, 250–1; visitants to, considered

as committee of p.o. trib., 251–2; political including legal sanction, as applied by judicial tribunals, as cause of moral apt., 272–3; judiciary not included in field of operation of prime minister, 283

JUDICATURE: where no regularly sanctioned ordinances, other matter referred to for purpose of, 32–6; civil v. penal branch of, 54–5; sub-committees of, of p.o. trib., 60; in Tripoli, functions of, exercised by sovereign, 162; probability of good, inversely as no. of judges, 245; in, where no publicity no justice, 252

JUDICIAL ESTABLISHMENT: *See* JUDICATORY(IES)

JUDICIAL POWER: in Tripoli, in hands of single individual, 164; under Greek Constitution, independence of, 243

JUDICIAL PROCEDURE: intercommunity of constitutional law, penal law and, 132–4; domestic v. technical, 251

JUDICIARY: *See* JUDICATORY(IES)

JURISDICTION: fields of, of judicatory, 66–7, 244; consistency in every field of, 246

JURY(IES): in Tripoli, England and France, choice of, 14–15; composition of, 247–8; hireling advocate and instruction of, 248–9; committee of p.o. trib. as, 252

JUSTICE: hostility of those deprived of means of subsistence exercised under notion of retributive, 37; functions necessary to ends of, 54–5; sub-committees of, of p.o. trib., 60; fac. dig. productive of evil in shape of injustice to those by whom extraordinary service rendered, 200; in advocate, union of active with intellectual apt. to defeat ends of, 248; for technical procedure say unjust, 251; in judicature, where no publicity, no, 252

JUSTICE MINISTER: under Greek Constitution, 243; and location and dislocation of judges, 245–7

KADI: in Tripoli, minister of justice and religion, 7, 8–9; election of imam confirmed by, 12; and validity of certificate of age, 21; deposition stating act of oppression of sovereign made before, 42–3n; proceedings of judicatory of, to be inserted in newspaper at Tripoli, 51; and notification of record of disappearance, 94–5; report of reading of charter given to, 128; establish letter-post between judicatories and office of, 130. *See* JUDGE(S)

KING(S): *See* MONARCH(S)

KNOWLEDGE: *See* INTELLECTUAL APTITUDE

KORAN: and commentaries taught in Tripolitan universities, 17; standard of reference in judicial decisions, 33; quoted by sovereign of Tripoli, 74, 77; subject of study in Mahometan universities, 158; standard headed by motto from, 165–6; having more than one wife not made matter of obligation in, 255

LABOUR: effect of abridgement of, on interest of operative hands, 37–8; means by which external instruments of felicity brought into existence, 58; forced, is loss, 100–1n; increase in produce of soil and increase in quantity of, 110; and obtainment of wealth, 184; in monarchy, quantity of productive, extorted for pampering one individual, 200–1

LABOURER(S): profit of capitalist v. subsistence of, 37–8; in Scotland, intellectual acquirements obtained by day, 253; day, sells services at highest price, 270n

LAND: in Tripoli, price of, 21

LANGUAGE: fiction interwoven with texture of, 28; poverty and confusedness of, 29; moderation of, circumstance on which circulation of newspaper depends, 46, 49–50; p.o. trib. apt to present itself as offspring of, 54; Latin a favourite, to English lawyers, 81n; imperfection of, 121

LAW(S): taught in Tripolitan universities, 16; real right comes from really existing, 23n; security most needed where no violation of, needed for accomplishment of misrule, 23–4n; sanctionment wanting to, 32; assent of sovereign to any particular, notified through speech from throne, 40; and depredation and oppression, 71; security for appeal to power of, 80–3; interest of gtst. no. and strength of, 82n; in England, by law people deprived of means of relief against oppression, 117n; vexation and provision made by existing, 117, 119n; punishment in power of p.o. trib.: opposition to, 124; written v. unwritten, 196–7; and protection of reputation from false imputations, 197; in England, weakness of, 230; no distinction between law cases and equity cases, 244; object of judicial system as execution of, 246; written v. unwritten, and choice of judges, 249; where no publicity, no security for execution of, 252; in formation of, only fit object is gtst. h. of people, 259. *See* CIVIL LAW, COMMERCIAL LAW, COMMON LAW, CONSTITUTIONAL LAW, ECCLESIASTICAL LAW, LEGISLATION, PENAL LAW, ROMAN LAW

LAWYERS: in Tripoli, four sects among, 10; Latin a favourite language to English, 81n; contributed to establishment of exclusion put upon testimony, 82n; Greeks not under tyranny of, 193, 196–7; triumph of Bonaparte over, 249–50; imposture of, on gtst. no., 270n. *See* ADVOCATE(S)

LEGAL SANCTION: gives impunity to master who murders slave, 135

LEGISLATION: legislative arrangements established for security of governed generally trusted to force, 23n; gtst. h. proper end of, 34; inducements furnished for compliance with legislative arrangements, 132–3; assistance afforded by United States: good guidance in, 170, 172; under Greek Constitution, negative of Executive Council upon, 240; mischievous effects produced by monarch endowed with co-ordinate power in, 275. *See* ORDINANCE(S)

LEGISLATION MINISTER: and origin of general plan for conduct of govt., 284

LEGISLATIVE DEPARTMENT: *See* LEGISLATIVE POWER

LEGISLATIVE POWER: in Tripoli, in hands of single individual, 164; in Greek Constitution, shared by Legislative Senate and Executive Council, 220; executive department to give execution and effect to will of legislative department, 223–4; business of legislative department included in that of operative, 224; executive should be subordinate to, 224–5; members of legislative body dependent on will of constitutive, 225–6; power detached from constitutive and given to legislative department, 227; case in which division of power beneficial to interest of people: fractionization of, 231; in United States, in hands of agents of people, 233; under Greek Constitution, independence of judiciary with relation to, 243; remains over executive power, 269, 274n; degree in which end of govt. accomplished in legislative department as app. apt. of fs., 271; no exercise of, unconstitutional, 274; legislature and relocation of prime minister, 280–5; term of service of member of legislature, 280n

LEGISLATOR(S): extensive views of legislative draftsman v. those of sovereign, 137; call for self-sacrifice on part of Greek, 194–5; five trials of, 198–205; term of service of, 280n

LEGISLATURE: *See* LEGISLATIVE POWER

LETTER-POST: proposed institution for notification, 129–32

LIBERTY: in Tripoli, no permanent security for, 108; at formation of state, of each dependent upon power of whole, 185; in Greece, no reason for restraints on, of public discussion and press, 197; by every measure to stifle, of public discussion, rulers provide for gratification of appetites, 203–4; limitation of marriage and succession of property v. religious, 255–6

LIFE: in Tripoli, no permanent security for, 108; in Tripoli, insecurity of, 156; at formation of state, of each dependent upon power of whole, 185; sacrifice of, 185

LITERACY: non-readers excluded from giving efficiency to will, 260, 262–3

LOANS: obtained by govt. of Tripoli for establishment of public works, 110

LOCATION AND DISLOCATION: under Greek Constitution, power of, with relation to offices of state, 240–2; of judges, 244–7; relocability of prime minister, 279–85

LOGIC: taught in Tripolitan universities, 16; subject of study in Mahometan universities, 158; logical source of division and judicial districts, 244

LOSS: *See* PROFIT AND LOSS

LOTTERY: appointment of jurors by, 247–8

MADHHABS: in Tripoli, two possess authority, 10; four obtained pre-eminence, 33–4

MAGNA CARTA: concession of, 128–9n; English indebted to, for security against misrule, 140; extracted from King by Barons, 232

MAHOMETANISM: comparison of Mahometan and Christian states to be inserted in newspaper at Tripoli, 51; money in Mahometan countries, 146, 149; on vacancy, Mahometan throne object of scramble, 154; power of sovereign in Mahometan state, 155; in Mahometan nations, order of succession to throne not fixed, 156; subjects of study in Mahometan universities, 158; Mahometan natives in Greece, 254–6; Mahometans excluded from giving efficiency to will, 260, 263–4

MALES: births of, ascertained by register of acts of circumcision, 51

MANUFACTORIES: in Tripoli, employment of capital in, 109

MARRIAGE: in Tripoli, 21–2; in Greece, Mahometans to be allowed one wife, 255–6

MATHEMATICS: taught in Tripolitan universities, 16; subject of study in Mahometan universities, 158

MEDICINE: encouragement to lecturers in, to visit Barbary states, 179–80

MELIORATION-SUGGESTIVE FUNCTION: in East India Company, no person by whom, can be exercised, 282

MENTAL DERANGEMENT: cause of disagreement in monarchy: of monarch, 69; symptoms of, manifested by rulers of Spain and Portugal in management of distant dependencies, 195

MERIT: register of, 102; fac. dig. as reward for meritorious service, 187; ascribed to monarch, 201; dig. as reward of meritorious service, 204

MILITARY: land establishment of Tripoli, 19; naval establishment of Tripoli, 19–20; communication of transgressions to, 42; circumstance favourable to concession: demand for, service, 107; faculty of applying, discipline as means of relief against oppression, 116–17; in England, by law people deprived of means of resistance by practice of, exercises, 117n; case of people oppressed by, force not considered, 120n; Tripolitan army and extension of plan, 168–9; army formed from union of Tripoli and Tunis, 170; force of United States at command of President, 173, 221; land and naval forces as examples of needless offices, 188; execution and effect of superior will in, department, 227; in branches of, service, certain classes of offences to which power of ordinary judicatories not applicable, 244; in Greece, Christian population trained in European form of, exercise, 255; app. apt. and, service, 283–4. *See* FORCE(S)

MIND: forces operating on, 55–6; vulnerable point of man, 99–100; concession depends partly on monarch's state of, 107–8

MINES: in Tripoli, employment of capital in digging of, 110

MINISTER(S): of Tripoli, 6–7; in rep. govt., with exception of function of principal, importance of that of newspaper editor greater than any official, 45–6; under Greek Constitution, 221–3; functions belonging to, 283. *See* ADVISERS, FINANCE MINISTER, JUSTICE MINISTER, KADI, LEGISLATION MINISTER, PRIME MINISTER

MISRULE: *See* RULE AND MISRULE

MIXED MONARCHY: disagreement between component parts is essence, 69–71; change from, to rep. dem., 127n; in France, lot of people under, 141. *See* MONARCH(S), MONARCHY(IES)

MODERATION: circumstance on which circulation of newspaper depends, 46, 49–50

MONARCH(S): publicity as remedy to evils produced by, and agents, 25; charters as safeguards against, 25–6; gtst. h. of, object of pursuit of authors of codes of law, 35; speech from throne of, 40; as arch-depredator, 68; causes of disagreement in monarchy: disputed succession, minority of, mental derangement of, disagreement among members of family of, 69; and causes of disagreement in mixed monarchy, 70; and charter v. contract, 126–7n; in France, community declared dependent on will of, 140–1; on part of, obstructive power with mask has effect of veto, 189; Greeks not cursed with Kings, 193, 196; for Kings nothing more difficult than self-sacrifice, 194; title to respect of, composed of wealth, 198; virtue and merit ascribed to, 201; nominal v. real power of, 220n; ministers as tools of, 222; riddance of, 228; in England, anxiety of aristocracy to give themselves security against arbitrary power of, 230; in England, function of legislative power belongs to King, 231; in England, conflict of aristocracy with, 232–3; addition of King to govt. of United States, 234; in state of hostility with interest and gtst. h. of gtst. no., 252–4; practice of, 265–6; electoral bodies under command of, 266; sells services at price to which no others bear proportion, 270n; mischievous effects produced by addition of, in state where efficient representation of people, 275. *See* ABSOLUTE MONARCHY, MIXED MONARCHY, MONARCHY(IES), SOVEREIGN

MONARCHY(IES): phrase securities against misrule employable under, 24n; publicity only security against misrule under, 25–6; speech from throne in constitutional, 40; monarch is arch-depredator, 68; causes of disagreement in, 69; sufferings of people under, 123; on part of monarch in, obstructive power with mask has effect of veto, 189; quantity of productive labour extorted for pampering one individual, 200–1; inapt. and absurdity of, 220n; establishment of hereditary aristocracy for support of, 234; in United States, yoke of, thrown off, 250; app. apt. in, 253; moral apt. of ruling fs. in, 272. *See* ABSOLUTE MONARCHY, MIXED MONARCHY

MONEY: waste of public, example of misrule, 26; heart of man of opulence no less full of virtue than purse of, 38; depredation has place where f. obtains, 97; f. to acknowledge receipt of, 98–9; circumstance favourable to concession: on part of sovereign extraordinary demand for, 107; increase in produce of soil and increase in quantity of, laid out in shape of capital, 110; in Mahometan countries, 146, 149; disposable, in Tripoli, Tunis, Algiers, 170; United States' executive no, for secret services, 172; employable as instrument for acquisition of power and fac. dig., 190; appetite for, of legislator, 198–9, 203; in United States, Senate source of waste of, 229; conferred on monarch at expense of gtst. no., 253

MORAL APTITUDE: odium attendant on obstruction of communication in ratio of, 72; element of app. apt., 188; under Greek Constitution, of members of Legislative Senate, 241; of judge maximized, 245; securing of, in jurors, 247–8; in hireling advocate, chance of moral inapt. at maximum, 248; in monarchy, 253; branch of app. apt., 271–2; as desire to contribute to gtst. h., 272; degree of, 272–3; moral inapt. v. intellectual inapt., 285

MORALITY: dependent upon sympathetic affection, 50; depends upon notoriety of rule of action referred to by judicatories, 53; established priesthood not useful to maintenance of, 196

MOROCCO: Tripoli in state of amity with, 21; communication of good govt. to, 148; value of security against misrule not unknown to people, 149; extension of plan to, 170. *See* AFRICA, BARBARY

MOSQUE(S): in Tripoli, number, districts and officials of, 12–13; public recitation in, 40; register of acts of circumcision to be kept by imams and notaries of, 51; copy of proclamation of rights to be sent to, 77n; notice of confinement attested by imam of nearest, 89; and publication of record of disappearance, 95; general statement of service exacted of indeterminate individuals deposited at, 102; register of merit to be kept in, 102; places for notification, 127–8; report of reading of charter in, 128; in Tripoli, possible sources of notification, 129–30; establish letter-post between judicatories and, 130; in case of Pasha's concurrence, people convened to principal, 148; in case of concurrence, Pasha to read paper in principal, 163

MOTIVE(S): *See* INDUCEMENT(S)

MUFTIS: in Tripoli, attached to Kadi's judicatory, 8–10

MULTIPLICATION: operation necessary to publicity of ordinances, 36; in Tripoli, mode of, and existing scribes, 38; followed by distribution, 38; operation applicable to notification of suffrages of p.o. trib., 44; in Tripoli, of written instruments by printing presses, 129–30

NATIONAL DEBT: in Tripoli, absence of, 21; of England, 235–6

NATURAL DIGNITY: apt reward for meritorious service, 187. *See* DIGNITY, FACTITIOUS DIGNITY

NATURAL HISTORY: no cognizance of, taken in Mahometan universities, 158; encouragement of lecturers in, to visit Barbary states, 179–80

NATURAL PHILOSOPHY: no cognizance of, taken in Mahometan universities, 158; encouragement of lecturers in, to visit Barbary states, 179–80

NAVY: *See* MILITARY

NEGLIGENCE: rulers restrained from, by apprehension of discontent on part of people, 131–2

NETHERLANDS: in respect of distant dependencies, Greece has advantage over, 195; afflicted by monarch, 196

NEWSPAPER EDITOR(S): motion in which decision of p.o. trib. originates made by, 45; in rep. govt., importance of function of, 45–6; advantage to, of impartiality between parties, 48; for keeping up of impartiality, employment of two, 49; head of members of p.o. trib., 57; president of sub-committee of general superintendence of p.o. trib., 59–60, 73; allegation of misdoing made by, 61; forms and declares opinion, 62–3; gives impression and diffusion to judgements, 63; importance of, 64

NEWSPAPER(S): only effectual instrument of operations applicable to notification of suffrages of p.o. trib., 44–6; circumstances on which circulation of, depends, 46–50; plan for conducting, at Tripoli, 50–1; literary capital requisite antecedently to commencement of, 52–3; how to maximize usefulness of, 53; in English, fruit of labours of sub-committees of p.o. trib., 60; functions of official judicatory compared with those of English, 60–3; in England, taxation of, 73; circumstances of change in Tripoli published in, 111; in Tripoli, altogether wanting, 129; insertion of articles in English, 150, 159; in Algiers, setting up of, 151. *See* PRESS(ES)

NOBILITY: Greeks not cursed with nobles, 193. *See* ARISTOCRACY

NOTARY(IES): in Tripoli, attached to judicatories, 9; in Tripoli, functions of, 11, 13–16, 22; deposition stating act of oppression of sovereign made before, 42–3n; register of acts of circumcision to be kept by imams and, 51

NOTIFICATION: effect of publicity, 28–9; subjects for, 29–31; sounds of, 40; assent of monarch to new constitutional code or particular law notified through speech from throne, 40–1; transgressions as subject-matter of notificative operations, 41–4; suffrages of p.o. trib. as subject-matter of notificative operations, 44–6; of mysterious disappearance, 94–5; subjects of, 125; instruments of, 125–6; circumstances on which efficiency of, depends, 126–8; proposed institutions for, 129–32. *See* NOTORIETY, PUBLICITY

NOTORIETY: degree of, measure of force of p.o. trib., 121–2; security cannot be taken away without, 136; of violation of promises of sovereign, 138, 139–41. *See* NOTIFICATION, PUBLICITY

OBEDIENCE: power constituted in direct ratio of, 30; ultimate punishment in power of p.o. trib.: withdrawing, 122–3; and notoriety of ordinances, 139–40; in Tunis, people in state of passive, 149

OBLIGATIONS: rules imposing, in vain if from non-fulfilment no penal consequence, 79n

OBSTRUCTION(S): cause of influence of p.o. trib.: fear of ultimate, 122–3; punishment in power of p.o. trib.: to exaction of taxes and execution of judgements, 124; power of, 187–8, 189; and appointment of agents, 227–8; in United States, Senate opposing, to will of constitutive body, 229, 230

OFFENCES: to be inserted in newspaper at Tripoli, 50–1; punishment and exciting commission of, 80–1; penal inducements provided in vain unless description of, furnished, 132–3; in branches of military service, certain classes of, to which power of ordinary judicatories not applicable, 244. *See* TRANSGRESSIONS

OFFICES: mode of sinister sacrifice: establishing needless, fractionalizing, 188–9; appetites for money and power receive gratification from possession of, 198–9; rule of economy as applied to no. of, 205; and war, 234; under Greek Constitution, power of location with relation to, 240–2

OPERATIVE DEPARTMENT: *See* OPERATIVE POWER

OPERATIVE POWER: females and election of possessors of supreme, 58; except in dem., object of supreme operative body to obstruct communication for political purposes, 72–3; business of, 224; divided into legislative and executive departments, 224–5; power detached from constitutive and given to operative department, 227; in United States, in hands of agents of people, 233–4; resides in delegates of people, 267–8; strictness of dependence of, on will of constitutive maximized, 268; executive detached from, 268–9, 274n

OPINION(S): suffrages of p.o. trib. as, produced in minds of members, 30; check applied to misrule by real and not avowed, 45; formed by judicatory, 55, 61; formed and expressed by newspaper editor, 62–3; execution and effect given to, by members of p.o. trib., 63–4; execution and effect given to, in case of judicatories v. that in case of p.o. trib., 65; right of declaring, on conduct, 85; no interdiction of faculty of manifesting, 264. *See* PUBLIC OPINION TRIBUNAL

OPPOSITIONS: received by judicatory, 55, 60

OPPRESSION(S): and charters, 25–6; is vexation produced by hand armed with legal power, 26–7; two stages of, 27; where suffering of oppressed attended with profit to oppressor, has effect of depredation, 27; and notification, 30; subject of suffrages of p.o. trib., 30–1; transgressions as acts of, 41; publicity of transgressions and security against vengeance of oppressor, 42; publicity of act of, of sovereign of Tripoli, 42–3n; desire of compensation and vengeance of oppressed party, 43; plead of coercion against wrath of oppressor, 44; and law, 71; system of laws and securing of governed from, 82n; inhibition of carrying of arms to prevent, 83–4; securities against official, 99–100; divulgation of instances of, 104; supposition avoided of, practised by command or with knowledge of sovereign, 105–7; as vexation having men in power as its authors, 115–16; means of relief against, on part of people, 116–17; in England, means of relief against, 117n; simple v. ultra, 118–20; mode of operation on part of oppressive hand, 120–1; greater the suffering produced by act of, greater no. of individuals likely to take cognizance, 121–2; ultimate punishment in power of p.o. trib. to inflict on oppressors: withdrawing obedience, 122–3; shapes of, as subjects of notification, 125; security against, object of proposed system of communication, 130; rulers restrained from acts of, by apprehension of discontent on part of people, 131–2; violation of promise on part of sovereign not to give oppressive orders, 139; resistance lawful to act of, declared criminal and punishable, 139–40; charter will point attention of people to acts of, 164; in Egypt, of despot, 168; monarch as Oppressor General, 196; fac. dig. productive of evil in shape of, 200; in monarchy, exercised upon vast scale, 201; indignation awakened by system of, 202; rulers' acts of, secured against punishment and restraint, 203–4; sole business of ministers, exercise of, 222; in England, retardation of, 233; gtst. no. taught that form of govt. in which, screwed up is best, 270n

OPULENCE: *See* WEALTH

ORDINANCE(S): subject of publicity and for notification, 29; operations necessary for publicity and notification of, 31–2, 36, 38–41; where no regularly sanctioned, other matter referred to for purpose of judicature, 32–6; for promoting publication to be forcibly imperative, 44; notoriety of, 139–41

PAIN(S): *See* PLEASURE(S) AND PAIN(S)

PANOPTICON: in Tripoli, employment of capital for erection of, 110

PARTY(IES): advantage to newspaper editor of impartiality between, 48–9; arguments of, heard by judicatory, 55, 61; arguments of, received by newspaper, 62; in mixed monarchy, competition for power between, 70–1; absurdity of exclusion put upon testimony of, defamed in action for defamation, 81n; exclusion of evil in composition of jury: partiality to prejudice of, in right, 247–8; in wrong best customer of hireling advocate, 248

PASHA: *See* SOVEREIGN

PASSPORT: egress prohibited without, 91–2

PATRONAGE: mode of sinister sacrifice: power of, in excess attached to influential situations, 187–8

PAY: ruling interest of members of judicatory depends on, 54; spies require to be more highly paid than soldiers, 59; expense of letter-post to govt. lessened by, received for letters sent by individuals, 130; in Tripoli, of sovereign's armed domestics, 146; mode of sinister sacrifice: attaching pecuniary emolument in excess to influential situations, 186–7; in United States, Senate source of waste of money given in name of, 229; in England, emolument of judiciary depends upon uncertainty, 230; under Greek Constitution, power of location with relation to offices with emolument attached, 240–2; under Greek Constitution, emoluments of judges, 243; no emolument at expense of public receivable by deputies of judge, 247; members of legislature, in corrupt co-operation with prime minister, increase emolument of situations at his disposal, 281–2

PENAL LAW: accusations and defences in, 54–5; provisions of, interspersed with securities, 79n; in England, depravity of constitutional branch of, 83n; application of, in case of oppressor of sufficient power to be formidable to judge, 105; intercommunity of constitutional law, judicial procedure and, 132–4; collateral use of proposed arrangements, matter for penal code, 134; no division between civil and penal suits, 244

PEOPLE: newspaper editor as representative of, 46; addresses of sovereign of Tripoli to, 74–8; and exclusion put upon testimony, 82–3n; sufferings of, matter of indifference to sovereign, 104; in Tripoli, meeting of persons chosen by, security against civil war, 109; in Europe, change made for better in condition of, work of necessity, 111; means of relief against oppression on part of, 116–17; in England, by law, deprived of means of relief against oppression, 117n; vexation produced by men in power made known to, 118; case of, oppressed by military force not considered, 120n; sufferings of, under monarchy, 123; and charter v. contract, 126–7n; controlling power of, 131–2; in France, lot of, under mixed monarchy, 141; in Barbary, possession of arms on part of, 145; in Tunis, disputed succession not disastrous to, 147; in case of Pasha's concurrence, convened to principal mosque, 148; in Tunis, in state of passive obedience, 149; in Barbary, value of security against misrule not unknown to, 149; application to sovereign of Tripoli stating idea of admitting, to share of power, 161–2; charter will point attention of, to acts of depredation and oppression, 164; invitation to, of Tunis to join in federative union with Tripoli, 169; in Algiers, quantity of depredation extractible from, 169; armed force of United States not to interfere in election of representatives chosen by, 178–9; provocation given to, by exercise of powers of govt., 200–1; interest of, v. that of ruling few, 217; in United States, Senate not placed immediately by, 229; case in which division of power beneficial to interest of, 231–6; negatives on power of, 236–9; in monarchy, made victim to worst man among them, 253; right and proper end of govt. is gtst. h. of, 259; arrangements of govt. by which conduct of, regulated conformable to will of gtst. no., 259, 264; means of maximizing efficiency of will of, 265–7; constitutive power resides in, 267–8; use of delegation made by, of operative power, 268; mischievous effects produced by addition of monarch or second house in state where efficient representation of, 275

PERSON: by no religion shall justifying cause be made for suffering in respect of, 79; inhibition of meeting for prevention of evil to, 83; injurious inspection of private writings liable to cause evil to, 96n; where, depends upon changeable will, no one safe, 110; preservation of, of Pasha from harm, 166; disposal of, and age of maturity, 260–2. See BODY

PETITION OF RIGHT: and security of governed, 23n

PHRASEOLOGY: apt. of, of rule of action, 34–6

PIETY: established priesthood not necessary to maintenance of, 196

PIRACY: security from North African, 174–6

PLEASURE(S) AND PAIN(S): in mind of sovereign, pain attached to idea of opposition to his will, 103; and penal and remuneratory branches belonging to each sanction, 273

POLICE: in towns of Tripoli, 11

POLITICAL GAGGING: See GAGGING

POLITICAL INCLUDING LEGAL SANCTION: by prime minister impulse given to, 45–6; as cause of moral apt., 272–3; responsibility and exposure to force of, 273

POPULAR OR MORAL SANCTION: as cause of moral apt., 272–3; responsibility and exposure to force of, 273

PORTUGAL: preservation of United States' trade from annoyance by, 174; in respect of distant dependencies, Greece has advantage over, 195; afflicted by monarch, 196; Greek Constitution preferable to Portuguese, 217; riddance of monarch, 228; no second chamber, 229–30; warning against form of govt. of, 240

POSSESSION: protection due to actual, 196. *See* PROPERTY

POVERTY: obstacle to publicity of transgressions, 41, 43–4

POWER(S): of Pasha opposed by social and religious sanctions, 5; oppression is vexation produced by hand armed with legal, 26–7; constituted in direct ratio of obedience, in indirect ratio of resistance, 30; importance of newspaper editor in application of, of p.o. trib. as check upon misrule, 45; in general no aversion excited in minds of men in, by publication of misdeeds, 50–1; equality of, 53; of judicatory and ruling interest of members, 54; of judicatory, fields of exercise of, and means of efficiency, 55–6; of p.o. trib. measured in same elements as that of judicatory, 56; of p.o. trib. universally recognized, 56–7; of judicatories v. that of p.o. trib., 64–73; in mixed monarchy, competition for, 70–1; of sovereign given by God, 78; security for appeal to, of law, 80–3; except in United States, those by whom opposition made to those by whom, of govt. exercised numbered among delinquents, 82n; acts of, prohibited as violations of rights of giving expression and publicity, 86–7; exercises of, prohibited as violations of right to use arms, 87; without limitation given to fs. whose signatures necessary to validity of passport, 91; depredation and official, 97; oppression is vexation by means of, 99; vulnerable point of man, 99–100; application of penal law in case of oppressor of sufficient, to be formidable to judge, 105; love of, psychological cause by which concession may be produced, 107n, 108; oppression is vexation having men in, as its authors, 115–16; remedy applied to vexation insofar as men in, concerned in production, 117–18; commensurate to obedience, 122–3; inferior punishments in, of p.o. trib., 124; of p.o. trib. as check to, of govt., 125; of public opinion as only check to, of govt., 129; strength of sense of controlling, of people in breasts of rulers, 131–2; disposition on part of despot to barter, for security, 147; in Algiers, shared among ten thousand Turks, 149; of sovereign of Tripoli without distinct limit, 155; application to sovereign of Tripoli stating idea of admitting people to share of, 161–2; in Tripoli, whole, of state in hands of single individual, 164; as external instrument of felicity, 183–4; at formation of state, of each dependent upon, of all, 185; mode of sinister sacrifice: creation of, in excess, 186; of patronage, 187; obstructive v. preventive v. suspensive, 187–8; fraction of, exercised by member of board, 188–9; of obstruction, 189; mischief capable of being done by fs. in proportion to, 197; assumption of superiority of wisdom no justification for assumption of independent and irresistible, 198; appetite for, of legislator, 198–9, 203; interest of those over whom, of govt. exercised made sacrifice to interest of those by whom, exercised, 200–1, 205; resistance to will of sharers, of govt., 201–2; production of hatred and contempt towards those by whom, of govt. exercised, 202–4; if useless, political, is mischievous, 220; nominal v. real, of monarch, 220n; detached from constitutive and given to operative department, 227; in English form of govt., impossibility that, exercised by King or House of Lords had gtst. h. for end, 228; in England, anxiety of aristocracy to give themselves security against arbitrary, of monarch, 230; in England, of judiciary depends upon uncertainty, 230; division of, principle, 231–6; negatives on, of people, 236–9; gtst. h. and exercise of, 240; under Greek Constitution, of location with relation to offices of state, 240–2; in branches of military service, certain classes of offences to which, of ordinary judicatories not applicable, 244; to judge to appoint deputies, 247; supply of, for collection of evidence to public judicatory, 251; conferred on monarch at expense of gtst. no.,

253; mischievous effects of division of, 274–6. *See* CONSTITUTIVE POWER, EXECUTIVE POWER, FIELDS OF POWER, JUDICIAL POWER, LEGISLATIVE POWER, OPERATIVE POWER, SUPREME POWER

PREJUDICE: females excluded from share in constitutive power by, 58; in United States, Senate source of aristocratical, 229

PRESS(ES): in Tripoli, lithographic, preferable for multiplication of ordinances, 36; in Tripoli, employment of, and existing scribes, 38; practically free in England, legally and practically free in United States, 57; in Tripoli, established in universities and judicatories, 129; in Greece, no reason for restraints on liberty of, 197; restraint of, and impunity for crimes, 199; by every measure to stifle, rulers provide for gratification of appetites, 203–4. *See* NEWSPAPER(S)

PRICE(S): to be inserted in newspaper at Tripoli, 50; of services, 270n

PRIEST(S): Greeks not under tyranny of, 193, 196; triumph of Bonaparte over, 249–50; in United States, yoke of established priesthood thrown off, 250; imposture of, on gtst. no., 270n

PRIME MINISTER: impulse given to political sanction by, 45–6; term of service, 279–85. *See* MINISTER(S)

PRISONS: and information of confinement, 88–90. *See* PANOPTICON

PROBITY: *See* MORAL APTITUDE

PROCEDURE: *See* JUDICIAL PROCEDURE

PROCLAMATION OF RIGHTS: *See* ACKNOWLEDGEMENT OF RIGHTS

PROFIT AND LOSS: profit of capitalist v. subsistence of labourers, 37–8; incapacity of p.o. trib. of acting in concert counteracted by advantage afforded by means of profit, 71–2; forced labour and, 100–1n; in Tripoli, application of capital to source of profit, 109; in Tripoli, to sovereign by surrender of claim to ownership of mines, 110; in Europe, diminution in rate of annual profit in return for use of capital, 110

PROHIBITION: every tax operates as, 52

PROMISE(S): concession amounts to giving of, on part of sovereign, 138–9; secondary class of, giving notoriety to violation of primary class, 139–40; usefulness of monarchical, 140–1; while Pasha possessed of unlimited power, all that can be given, 164

PROPERTY: by no religion shall justifying cause be made for suffering in respect of, 79; inhibition of meeting for prevention of evil to, 83; security against infringement of, 84; exercise of rights and damage to, 87; injurious inspection of private writings liable to cause evil to, 96n; vulnerable point of man, 99–100; in Tripoli, insecurity of, 108, 156; where, depends upon changeable will, no one safe, 110; preservation of, of Pasha from harm, 166; at formation of state, of each dependent upon power of whole, 185; in Greece, succession of, 256; disposal of, and age of maturity, 260–2. *See* POSSESSION

PRUDENCE: in Greece, necessary precaution against hostility on part of Mahometan natives dictated by self-regarding, 254

PRUSSIA: warning against form of govt. of, 239–40

PUBLIC: object of regard of man of opulence, 38; no emolument receivable at expense of, by deputies of judge, 247

PUBLIC INSTRUCTION ESTABLISHMENT: of Tripoli, 16–19

PUBLICITY: remedy for misrule, 25–6, 27–9; subjects of, 29–31; operations necessary to, of ordinances, 31–2, 36, 38–41; difficulties as to giving, to transgressions, 41–4; means of, for acknowledgement of rights, 77n; liberty to publish on religion, 79–80; right of giving, to facts where conception contributory to gtst. h., 85–6; check to power of govt. applied by, 118; enables force of p.o. trib. to bring itself into action, 121; means of, in England v. Tripoli, 128–9n; and natural dignity as apt reward for meritorious service, 187; in Greece, given to

Legislative Senate, 241; of judicial proceedings, 251–2; in judicature, where no, no justice, 252. *See* NOTIFICATION, NOTORIETY

PUBLIC OPINION TRIBUNAL: constituted by all by whom cognizance taken of public affairs, 27–8; publicity is instrument of, 28; suffrages of, subject of publicity and for notification, 29, 30; power of, 30–1; suffrages of, as subject-matter of notificative operations, 44–6; parallel between judicatories and, 54–73; ruling interest of, 56; members of, 56–9, 121; standing committee and sub-committees of, 59–60; functions of official judicatories v. those of, 60–4; power of judicatories v. that of, 64–73; democratical v. aristocratical section, 67; addition to members of, 68–9; appeal made to, by members of govt., 69–71; incapacity of acting in concert, 71–3; security for appeal to public opinion, 80–3; public opinion sole remedy against misrule, 121; degree of notoriety measure of force of, 121–2; ultimate punishment in power of: withdrawing obedience, 122–3; inferior punishments in power of, 124; irregularity in acts of, 124–5; power of public opinion only check to power of govt., 129; in cases of violation of promises of sovereign, appeal made to, 139–41; in United States, power of public opinion, 223; visitants to judicatory considered as committee of, 251–2; committee of, as jury, 252; popular or moral sanction, as applied by, as cause of moral apt., 272; responsibility and exposure to force of popular or moral sanction as applied by, 273

PUNISHMENT: *See* REWARD AND PUNISHMENT

RANK: cause of disagreement in monarchy: disagreement of members of administration with other men of opulence and, 69

READING: *See* LITERACY

RECITATION: operation necessary to publicity of ordinances, 39–41

RECORDATION: record of disappearance, 94–6. *See* REGISTRATION

REGARD: *See* ANTIPATHETIC REGARD, SELF-REGARD, SYMPATHETIC REGARD

REGISTRATION: operation necessary to publicity of ordinances, 32; operation applicable to notification of suffrages of p.o. trib., 44; egress prohibited without, 91–2

RELIGION: religious establishment of Tripoli, 12–16; sub-committees of, of p.o. trib., 60; security against vexation on account of, 79–80; religious tyranny established by Elizabeth I, 81–2n; vexation on account of, as mode of oppression, 118–19; limitation of marriage and succession of property v. religious liberty, 255–6

RELIGIOUS SANCTION: opposes checks to power of Pasha, 5; as cause of moral apt., 272–3

REPRESENTATIVE DEMOCRACY: fs. of govt. placed by suffrages of rest of community, 28; importance of function of newspaper editor, 45–6; ultra-indigent and ultra-opulent can never be extirpated, 67–8; in every govt. but dem., interest of ruling few in opposition to general interest, 72; except in dem., object of supreme operative body to obstruct communication for political purposes, 72–3; change from mixed monarchy to, 127n; authorities in, 224–5; subordination between authority and authority, 225–7; application of principle of dependence, 230; subordination in, 274–6

REPRESENTATIVE GOVERNMENT: phrase *securities against misrule* employable by sovereign representative body, 24n; importance of function of newspaper editor, 45–6; granting of representative assembly by sovereign amounts to promise, 138; representative system to be proposed to Pasha, 147–8; if established in one Barbary state, would spread over others, 149; in Tripoli, representative body in concert with Pasha to frame constitutional code, 163;

armed force of United States not to interfere in election of representatives, 178–9; Greeks not afflicted by spurious representatives, 197; apt arrangement in Spanish and Greek Constitutions: right of suffrage in election of representatives of people, 218–19; in Greece, Mahometans to have votes in election of members of representative assembly, 254–5; system of representation and interests of electors and delegates, 266–7; moral apt. of delegates, 272; mischievous effects produced by addition of monarch or second house in state where efficient representation of people, 275–6

REPUTATION: by no religion shall justifying cause be made for causing suffering in respect of, 79; injury of, by false imputations, 80–1; injurious inspection of private writings liable to cause evil to, 96n; vulnerable point of man, 99–100; psychological causes by which concession may be produced: love of, prospect of extending, 107n, 108; law and protection of, from false imputations, 197; of judge and appointment of deputies, 247

RESERVOIRS: in Tripoli, employment of capital in, 110

RESISTANCE: force and, 23n; power constituted in indirect ratio of, 30; security of rulers against, of subjects as object of govt., 116; against oppression on part of people, 116–17; in England, by law people deprived of means of, 117n; rulers without fear of, 118; and notoriety of ordinances, 139–40; in Tripoli, Mountaineers habituated to, 164; experienced by sharers of powers of govt., 202

RESPECT: ultra-opulent objects of, 67; title to, of monarch composed of wealth, 198

RESPONSIBILITY: and furnishing of information of transgressions, 42; in United States, of President diminished by Senate, 229; under Greek Constitution, of members of Legislative Senate and Executive Council, 240–2; of judge, 245, 251; and location of judge, 246; as exposure to force of sanctions, 273

REVENGE: appetite for, of legislator, 198, 203. See VENGEANCE

REVENUE: derived from newspapers worst of all sources, 52; in Tripoli, Pasha's, consists in tax on produce of soil, 110; receipts of post establishment not to be made source of, 130; in Tripoli, increase and security to, 162

REWARD AND PUNISHMENT: punishment attached to acts pernicious to community or disagreeable to rulers, 35n; person furnishing information of transgressions subject to punishment in case of mendacity or temerity, 42; active forces for surmounting indolence, 43; compensation to take place of barren punishment, 53; punishment adapted to misdoing, 53; prospect of, operating as forces on mind, 55–6; ultra-indigent and ultra-opulent and exposure to punishment, 67; punishment and counter-securities, 80–1; punishment and accident of delinquency being known, 81n; rigour of punishment and reluctance to contribute to execution, 82n; punishment and violations of rights, 85–7; punishment of person contributory to injurious imprisonment, 89–90; punishment of person contributory to injurious banishment, 91; punishment of person presenting without justification record of disappearance, 95; punishment of person concerned in misuse of private writings, 96–7; rulers without fear of punishment, 118; ultimate punishment in power of p.o. trib.: withdrawing obedience, 122–3; inferior punishments in power of p.o. trib., 124; punishment and violation of promises of sovereign, 139; resistance lawful to act of oppression declared criminal and punishable, 139–40; fac. dig. as reward for meritorious service, 187; punishment for damage to reputation from false imputations, 197; rulers' acts of depredation, oppression, imposture, secured against punishment, 203–4; punishment in case of mendacity in publicity of judicial proceedings, 251–2; penal and remuneratory branches belong to each sanction, 273; punishment cannot be applied to error in judgement, 285

RHETORIC: taught in Tripolitan universities, 16; subject of study in Mahometan universities, 158

RIGHT AND WRONG: and deperition of evidence, 14n; gtst. h. right and proper end of social action, 53; gtst. h. only right and proper end of ruler, 78; apt arrangement in Spanish and Greek Constitutions: declaration of right and proper end of govt., 218; exclusion of evil in composition of jury: partiality to prejudice of party in right, 247–8; party in wrong best customer of hireling advocate, 248; right and proper ends of judicature, 252; right and proper end of govt., 259

RIGHT(S): securities v., 23n; and sovereign, 24n; claims grounded on, 66; embraced by field of jurisdiction of judicatories v. that of p.o. trib., 66–7; ambiguity of acknowledgement of, 76–7n; of people acknowledged by sovereign, 78; injuries to marital or paternal, not in a way to be inflicted by sovereign, 79n; of giving expression and publicity to facts whose conception contributory to gtst. h., 85–6; to use of arms, 87; apt arrangement in Spanish and Greek Constitutions: right of suffrage, 218–19. *See* WRONGS

ROMAN LAW: age of maturity under, 261

RULE AND MISRULE: security against misrule, 23n; security most needed where no violation of law needed for accomplishment of misrule, 23–4n; phrase securities against misrule employable in every state of society, 24n; publicity as remedy for misrule, 25–6; shapes of misrule, 26–7, 115–20; check applied to misrule by real not avowed opinion and affection, 45; importance of newspaper editor in application of power of p.o. trib. as check upon misrule, 45; legitimate rule and transformation of men into mutes, 58–9; misrule caused by form of govt., 71; securities against misrule acknowledged by sovereign, 78; by proposed arrangements remedy not applied to misrule in every shape, 115; public opinion sole remedy against misrule, 120–1; rulers restrained from acts of misrule by apprehension of discontent on part of people, 131–2; English indebted to Magna Carta and Bill of Rights for security against misrule, 140; in France, Constitutional Charter as security for misrule, 140–1; in Barbary, value of security against misrule not unknown to people, 149; charter as security against misrule obtainable at hands of Pasha, 164; theory v. practice of misrule operating by corruption, 190; in England, King and House of Lords sources of misrule, 228; applied to English form of govt., principle of dependence would be consummation of misrule, 230

RULER(S): security most needed where laws at command of, 23–4n; two stages in oppression by hand of, 27; h. of ruling one or few more or less connected with h. of many, 35n; and subjects of British Empire compose p.o. trib., 57; and extinction of classes of members of p.o. trib., 58–9; in every govt. but dem., interest of ruling few in opposition to general interest, 72; gtst. h. only right and proper end of, 78; liberty to converse on conduct of, 83; except in United States, depredation for benefit of ruling few chief object of govt., 116; not determinately unwilling to see provision made against secret vexation, 117–18; strength of sense of controlling power of people in breasts of, 131–2; security afforded against individuals and, 134; desire of ruling fs. to make addition to external instruments of felicity they possess, 184; assurance from ruling few that felicity of all others is object pursued, 185; proportion between strength of self-regarding and social affection in ruling fs., 185; disposition of ruling fs. to sacrifice particular to universal interest, 185–6; sacrifice of universal interest to particular interest of ruling fs., 186–90; symptoms of mental derangement manifested by, of Spain and Portugal in management of distant dependencies, 195; gratification afforded to corruptive appetites of, at expense of subjects, 198; instruments of felicity created by, at expense of subjects, 198–205; interest of people v. that of ruling few, 217;

division of power amongst, as security for good govt., 231–6; gtst. no. taught that form of govt. in which depredation and oppression screwed up by, is best, 270n. *See* GOVERNORS AND GOVERNED

RULING FEW: *See* RULER(S)

RULING ONE: *See* MONARCH(S), RULER(S), SOVEREIGN

RUSSIA: no chamber-pots in gentlemen's houses, 18; afflicted by monarch, 196; warning against form of govt. of, 239–40

SANCTIONMENT: operation necessary to publicity of ordinances, 32; wanting to law, 32

SANCTION(S): *See* POLITICAL INCLUDING LEGAL SANCTION, POPULAR OR MORAL SANCTION, RELIGIOUS SANCTION, SOCIAL SANCTION, SYMPATHETIC SANCTION

SCHOOL(S): of Tripoli, 18–19; Hill's, at Hazelwood, 150, 151–2

SCOTLAND: board and lodging in universities, 17; highest judicatory in, 245; intellectual acquirements obtained by day labourers, 253. *See* BRITISH EMPIRE

SCRIPTION: operation necessary to publicity of ordinances, 32

SECRECY: security against secret confinement, 88–90; amounts to confession that promotion of sinister interest object of what is done, 136; United States' executive no money for secret services, 172; of plan necessary, 173–4; under Greek Constitution, 241; no reason consistent with utility why females excluded from secret suffrage, 260

SECRETARY(IES): under United States' Constitution, 221–2; term preferred to minister, 222; in Greece, fewer than four sufficient, 222–3

SECURITY(IES): legislative arrangements established for, of governed generally trusted to force, 23n; against misrule, 23n; v. rights, 23n; most needed where no violation of law needed for accomplishment of misrule, 23–4n; phrase, against misrule employable in every state of society, 24n; publicity as, against misrule, 25–6; publicity as, against transgressions of fs., 30; and apt. of phraseology of rule of action, 34; efficiency of, 39; sovereign of Tripoli to recite, 40–1; concealment as, against evil at hands of those to whom publicity disagreeable, 41–2; publicity of transgressions and, against vengeance of oppressor, 42; and coercion, 44; equality consistent with, of external instruments of felicity, 53; acknowledged by sovereign, 78; in general v. in detail, 79n; application of, and evils producible by action of individuals and those producible by sovereign, 79n; in favour of nation, 79–84, 85–7; against vexation on account of religion, 79–80; against national gagging, 80–3, 85–7; against national defencelessness, 83–4, 87; in favour of individuals, 84–5, 88–102; against secret confinement, 88–90; against injurious banishment, 90–2; against secret and unlawful homicide, 92–4; against mysterious disappearance, 94–6; against misuse of private writings, 96–7; against official depredation, 97–9; against official oppression, 99–100; against extortion of personal service, 100–2; chance in favour of obtaining concession of, 103–4; in Tripoli, insecurity under form of govt., 108–9; meeting of persons chosen by people, against civil war, 109; in Tripoli, quantity of capital can never receive increase but from increase in, 110; of rulers against subjects and foreign powers as object of govt., 116; dependent on will of sovereign, 116n; modes of oppression against which, provided, 118–20; in proportion to app. apt., 126; fixed on firmer basis by contract than charter, 126–7n; against oppression and injury object of proposed system of communication, 130; applied to war, 132; afforded against rulers and individuals, 134; extension of, to slaves, 134–5; English indebted to Magna Carta and Bill of Rights for, 140; in France, Constitutional Charter as, for misrule, 140–1; in Barbary, perception of, under European govts.,

145; disposition on part of despot to barter power for, 147; in Barbary, value of, against misrule not unknown to people, 149; insecurity accompaniment of govt. such as Tripoli's, 154; in Tripoli, insecurity of property and life, 156; in Tripoli, insecurity perpetuated by despotism, 156; good govt. as means of relief from insecurity, 159; in Tripoli, to revenue, 162; charter as, obtainable at hands of Pasha, 164; in Egypt, sense of insecurity, 168; against North African piracy, 174–6; in England, anxiety of aristocracy to give themselves, against arbitrary power of monarch, 230; division of power amongst rulers as, for good govt., 231–6; where no publicity, no, for execution of laws, 252; in Greece, by faculty of voting, Mahometans raised to situation high in, 255; unless means of subsistence produced, arrangements for, of it absurd, 265; legislature and constitutive authority as, against misconduct, 285

SELF-PREFERENCE: *See* SELF-REGARD

SELF-REGARD: predominance universal and necessary, 183–4; proportion between strength of self-regarding and social affection in ruling fs., 185; practice determined by self-regarding inducements, 194; in Greece, necessary precautions against hostility on part of Mahometan natives dictated by self-regarding prudence, 254, 263

SERVICE(S): security against extortion of personal, 84, 100–2; depredation has place where f. obtains beneficial, 97; depredation and rendering of, 97–8; circumstance favourable to concession: on part of sovereign extraordinary demand for personal, 107; extortion of personal, as mode of oppression, 119; forced, as accompaniment of war, 132; United States' executive no money for secret, 172; fac. dig. as reward for meritorious, 187; fac. dig. created at expense of those by whom extraordinary, rendered, 199–200; reimbursement of expense of extraordinary, 200n; dig. as reward of extraordinary and meritorious, 204; price of, 270n; term of, of prime minister, 279–85

SILENCING: suppression of peaceful means of relief against oppression, 117. *See* GAGGING

SINGLE AND MANY-SEATEDNESS: in judicatories, 245, 250–1

SINISTER INTEREST(S): in mixed monarchy, component parts share in, 69–70; secrecy amounts to confession that promotion of, is object of what is done, 136; under Greek Constitution, 241–2; system of fiction accommodated to, of lawyers, 250; in judicature where no publicity, object has been sacrifice of universal interest to, of judge or despot, 252; each, finds a bar in every other, 266; of electors and delegates, 266–7. *See* INTEREST(S)

SINISTER SACRIFICE: in France, monarch promises to forbear making, 140–1; on part of public f., 183; modes of, 186–90; making of, constant occupation of monarch, 253–4

SLAUGHTER: inhibition of carrying arms to prevent, 84

SLAVES: descriptions of, inserted in newspapers, 50; extension of securities to, 134–5; in body-guard of Pasha, 166–7

SOCIAL SANCTION: opposes checks to power of Pasha, 5; by newspaper editor impulse given to, 45–6; and murder of slave by master, 135

SOLDIERS: spies require to be no less numerous and more highly paid than, 59; employed as letter carriers, 131

SOVEREIGN: of Tripoli, 4–6, 155–61; and rights, 24n; and fear of evil, 24n; and acts of oppression, 26–7; act of oppression exercised by, subject of suffrages of p.o. trib., 31; and public recitation, 40; of Tripoli to recite securities, 40–1; publicity of act of oppression exercised by, of Tripoli, 42–3n; in comparison few misdeeds committed by orders of, 50; addresses of, of Tripoli to people, 74–8;

evils producible by action of individuals v. those producible by, 79n; depredation and command of, 98; check to doing of will of, 103; security against vexation at hands of, object of arrangements, 103–4; object of sentiment of sympathy in, 104; and divulgation of instances of oppression, 104; supposition avoided of vexations and oppressions practised by command or with knowledge of, 105–7; degree of proneness of, to take offence in such sort as to refuse concurrence in arrangements, 107–9; persuasives for Pasha's concurrence in concession, 109–11; securities dependent on will of, 116n; remedy applied to vexation insofar as, concerned in production, 117; may deprive successors of oppression on account of religion, 118–19; no remedy to depredation if exercised by, 119n; charter as free and sole act of, 126–7n; funds of, never sufficient for personal expenses, 131; probability of consent of, 135–8; concession amounts to giving of promises on part of, 138–41; armed force of, of Tripoli, 145–6, 166–7; family of Pasha and disputed succession, 147; proposals to Pasha, 147–8; situation of family of, of Tripoli, 154; application to, of Tripoli stating idea of admitting people to share of power, 161–2; inducements to concurrence of, of Tripoli, 162; in case of concurrence, of Tripoli to read paper in principal mosque, 163; preservation of, of Tripoli from harm, 166; of Tripoli and secrecy of plan, 173. *See* MONARCH(S)

SPAIN: Spanish as medium of communication in Tripoli, 172; United States' acquisition of port from, 174, 176; preservation of United States' trade from annoyance by, 174; rupture with Algiers, 175–6; in respect of distant dependencies, Greece has advantage over, 195; afflicted by monarch, 196; Constitution taken for a model, 216; Greek Constitution preferable to Spanish, 216–17; apt arrangements in Constitution, 218; riddance of King and Council of State, 228; no second chamber, 229–30; warning against form of govt. of, 240; unapt arrangements in Constitution not in Greek, 252–4

SPIES: employment of, for preventing conversation taking dangerous direction, 59

SPOLIATION: inhibition of carrying arms to prevent, 84. *See* DEPREDATION

SUBJECT MANY: *See* SUBJECTS

SUBJECTS: and rights, 24n; and rulers of British Empire compose p.o. trib., 57; sensibility to h. of, psychological cause by which concession may be produced, 107n; in Europe, change made for better in condition of people in character of, work of necessity, 111; security of rulers against, as object of govt., 116; in Tripoli, in state of insecurity in respect of property and life, 156; assurance from ruling few to subject many that felicity of all others is object pursued, 185; gratification afforded to corruptive appetites of rulers at expense of, 198; instruments of felicity created by rulers at expense of, 198–205. *See* GOVERNORS AND GOVERNED

SUBJECTS CORPOREAL AND INCORPOREAL: of judicatory, 55

SUBORDINATION AND SUPERORDINATION: under Greek Constitution, subordination of Executive Council to Legislative Senate, 220; executive should be subordinate to legislative, 224–5; conduct of subordinate fs. placed in state of dependence on will of constitutive body, 225–7; supreme operative subordinate to supreme constitutive power, 267–8; links in chain of political subordination, 268–9; subordination in rep. dem., 274–6. *See* DEPENDENCE

SUB-RULING FEW: *See* RULER(S)

SUBSISTENCE: effect of abridgement of labour on means of, 37–8; unless means of, produced, arrangements for security of it absurd, 265; of fs. and expense of govt., 270–1

SUFFRAGE(S): in rep. dem., fs. of govt. placed by, of rest of community, 28; of p.o.

317

trib., subject of publicity and for notification, 29, 30; power of p.o. trib. as number of, 30; of p.o. trib. and influence of understanding and will, 30—1; internal v. external, 31n; of p.o. trib. as subject-matter of notificative operations, 44—6; representative system on basis of universality, secrecy, equality, annuality of, to be proposed to Pasha, 147—8; apt arrangement in Spanish and Greek Constitutions: right of, 218—19; no reason consistent with utility why females excluded from secret, 260. *See* ELECTION

SUPERORDINATION: *See* SUBORDINATION AND SUPERORDINATION

SUPREME CONSTITUTIVE: *See* CONSTITUTIVE POWER

SUPREME EXECUTIVE: *See* EXECUTIVE POWER

SUPREME OPERATIVE: *See* OPERATIVE POWER

SUPREME POWER: division of, 233—6; dependence on, 243

SWEDEN: afflicted by monarch, 196

SYMPATHETIC REGARD: morality and felicity depended upon sympathetic affection, 50; object of sentiment of sympathy in sovereign, 104; affection in breast of every man, 183; less advanced the age, stronger the sympathetic affection, 219n; local connection of judge in way of sympathy, 247

SYMPATHETIC SANCTION: as cause of moral apt., 272—3

TALENT: circumstance on which circulation of newspaper depends, 46n; variety of newspaper little dependent upon, 47. *See* ACTIVE TALENT

TAXATION: every tax operates as prohibition, 52; in England, of newspapers, 73; in Tripoli, tax upon produce of mines, 110; in Tripoli, Pasha's revenue consists in tax on produce of soil, 110; punishment in power of p.o. trib.: obstruction to exaction of taxes, 124; tax on social intercourse, 130

TESTIMONY: absurdity of exclusion put upon, 81—3n; of witnesses in case of unlawful homicide, 92—4; exclusions to faculty of giving, foolishly devised instrument for avoidance of mendacity, 248—9. *See* EVIDENCE

TIMIDITY: psychological cause by which concession may be produced, 107, 108

TRANSGRESSIONS: subject of publicity and for notification, 29; publicity as security against, of fs., 30; difficulties as to giving publicity to, 41—4. *See* OFFENCES

TRANSMISSION: *See* CIRCULATION

TRIPOLI: territory and population of, 3—4; chief of, 4—6; members of administration, 6—7; judicial establishment, 8—11; police, 11; religious establishment, 12—16; public instruction establishment, 16—19; military land establishment, 19; naval establishment, 19—20; financial establishment, 20—1; relation to other powers, 21; conditions in life, 21—2; phrase securities against misrule applicable, 24n; instead of regularly sanctioned ordinances, other matter referred to for purpose of judicature, 32—6; multiplication of ordinances, 36; existing scribes not to be thrown out of employment, 38; sovereign to recite securities, 40—1; publicity of act of oppression exercised by sovereign, 42—3n; plan for conducting newspaper, 50—1; literary capital requisite antecedently to commencement of newspaper, 52—3; addresses of sovereign to people, 74—8; sovereign's inducement to dismiss fs., 104; insecurity under form of govt., 108—9; persuasives for Pasha's concurrence in concession, 109—11; means of relief against oppression, 117n; notification of charter, 126—8; means of notification narrow, 129; funds of sovereign never sufficient for personal expenses, 131; no adequate means for collection of evidence, 134; probability of consent of sovereign, 135—8; revolution to commence in, 145, 167—70; family of sovereign and disputed succession, 147; proposals to Pasha, 147—8; value of security against misrule not unknown to people, 149; danger of civil war, 154; reigning family, 155—61; application to sovereign stating idea of admitting people to share of power, 161–2; application to Mountaineers, 162, 164; inducements to concurrence of sovereign, 162; in case of concurrence, Pasha to read paper in principal mosque, 163; weakness of govt., 166–7; communication in, 172; sovereign and secrecy of plan, 173; hostility to United States, 175; United States' acquisition of port from, 176–7; and preliminary steps to be taken by United States executive, 177–80. *See* AFRICA, BARBARY

TUNIS: Tripoli bounded by, 3; Tripoli in state of amity with, 21; disputed succession not disastrous to people, 147; circumstances of, 149; value of security against misrule not unknown to people, 149; plan extended to, 167–9; army formed from union with Tripoli, 170; United States' acquisition of port from, 176; reception of travellers and lecturers, 180. *See* AFRICA, BARBARY

TURKEY: subjection of Tripoli to, 4–5, 155, 168, 169; dependence of sovereign of Tripoli on Porte at an end, 146; Tunis under domination of few hundred Turks, 147, 149, 168, 169; in Algiers, power shared among ten thousand Turks, 149, 169; preservation of United States' trade from annoyance by, 174

TYRANNY: females excluded from share in constitutive power by, 58; religious, established by Elizabeth I, 81–2n

UNDERSTANDING: p.o. trib. and influence of, 30–1; jurors and influence of, 248; no exclusion opposed to fruits of, 263–4; in no body other than gtst. no. any, possessing more intimate knowledge of that conducive to gtst. h., 264

UNITED STATES OF AMERICA: security of governed and force, 23n; productions of printing press extensively diffused, 31–2; descriptions of slaves inserted in newspapers, 50; next to English, newspapers most instructive, 52; press legally and practically free, 57; except in, those by whom opposition made to those by whom powers of govt. exercised numbered among delinquents, 82n; circumstances of change in Tripoli published in newspapers, 111; except in, depredation for benefit of ruling few chief object of govt., 116; Barbary powers plague to, 145; only good govt., 148; Constitution established in Barbary states, 154; only govt. in which gtst. h. object really pursued, 159, 200, 221; in North Africa, govt. approaching that of, means of relief from insecurity, 159; felicity produced by Constitution, 169; assistance desired from, 170–2; and secrecy of plan in Tripoli, 173–4; inducements for concurrence, 174–7; preliminary steps to be taken by executive, 177–80; and established priesthood, 196; with citizens of, Greeks will look down upon other nations, 197; man by whom imputation cast admitted to prove truth of it, 197; defence of constituted authorities against imputations, 199; executive department, 221–3; division of business of executive, 225; Senate as mass of useless complication, 229–30; supreme power in hands of people, 233–4; warning against form of govt. of, 240; distinction between law cases and equity cases, 244; yoke of hireling advocate, 250; end in view of systems of representation, 266

UNIVERSAL INTEREST: in Tripoli, portion of revenue allotted to service of, a minimum, 20; and interest of p.o. trib. v. that of official tribunals, 56; secrecy amounts to confession that promotion of sinister interest, not, object of what is done, 136; sacrifice of particular interest to, 185–6; sacrifice of, to particular interest of ruling fs., 186–90; less advanced the age, greater probability of sacrifice of personal interest to, 219n; interest of constitutive body same thing with, 226; under Greek Constitution, sacrifice of, 241–2; and dislocation of judge, 246–7; in judicature where no publicity, object has been sacrifice of, 252; interest of monarch in opposition to, 253–4; each man's share in, finds ally in every other man's, 266; and system of representation, 266–7; in rep. govt., connection between interest of f. and, 272

UNIVERSITY(IES): subjects taught in Tripolitan, 16–17, 158; chief and teachers of Tripolitan, 17; board and lodging of students in Tripoli v. that in Britain, 17–18; vacations and lectures in Tripolitan, 18; in Tripoli, provision for expense of, 20; intelligence of lectures read in Tripolitan, 111; in Tripoli, possible sources of notification, 129–30; lecturers in art and science at Tripolitan, 179

UTILITY: in case of newspaper, depends upon impartiality, 48; more uncertain the effect of security, the less the, 92; test of, of United States' Senate, 230; for principle of, say gtst. h. principle, 259; no reason consistent with, why females excluded from secret suffrage, 260; and age of maturity, 261

VARIETY: circumstance on which circulation of newspaper depends, 46, 47–8

VENGEANCE: publicity of transgressions and security against, of oppressor, 42; desire of, of oppressed party, 43; not incapable of being satiated, 116; security of rulers against, of subjects as object of govt., 116; faculty of gratifying appetite for, conferred on monarch at expense of gtst. no., 253. *See* REVENGE

VETO: effective v. suspensive, 187–8; on part of monarch, obstructive power with mask has effect of, 189; on power of people, 236–9; under Greek Constitution, of Executive Council upon legislation, 240

VEXATION(S): political evil suffered by determinate individuals, 26–7; evil produced by depredation v. that produced by barren, 27–8n; security against, on account of religion, 79–80; where passport necessary, has no certain limit, 91; oppression is, by means of power, 99–100; security against, object of arrangements, 103–4; classes of persons at whose hands, most to be apprehended, 104; supposition avoided of, practised by command or with knowledge of sovereign, 105–7; as evil effects of misrule, 115–16; particular v. all-comprehensive, 117; remedy applied to, insofar as men in power concerned in production, 117–18; on account of religion, as mode of oppression, 118; by official depredation as mode of oppression, 119; provision against, in shapes of confinement, banishment, homicide, made by existing law, 119n; when, inflicted, oppression operates on body and goods, 120–1; where object of seizure of papers is furnishing evidence, not oppression, 120n; modes and acts of, as subjects of notification, 125, 127; security afforded against, by rulers and individuals, 134; desire of sovereign to commit act of, 137–8; exclusion of evil in composition of jury: by attendance, 247–8. *See* DELAY EXPENSE AND VEXATION

VIRTUE: heart of man of opulence full of, 38; profession of, 195–6; ascribed to monarch, 201

WAR: inevitability of civil, in Tripoli, 6; engaging in unnecessary, example of misrule, 26; and depredation v. destruction, 27–8n; on death of Pasha, danger to nation from civil, 109; by proposed arrangements remedy not applied to misrule in shape of unnecessary, 115; security applied to, 132; between England and Algiers, 151; in Tripoli, danger of civil, 154, 156; in Egypt, frequency of civil, 168; in United States, possibility of mutual, excluded by federal union, 169; law against public discussion is open declaration of, 204; and offices and colonies, 234

WASTE: of public money, example of misrule, 26; and application of securities, 79n; in monarchy, exercised upon vast scale, 201; expenditure made in respect of needless and useless offices is, 205; in United States, Senate source of, of time and money, 229

WEALTH: heart of man of opulence full of virtue, 38; equality of, 53; interest of extra-opulent few in opposition to that of many, 67; ultra-opulent as enemies of body politic, 67–8; cause of disagreement in monarchy: disagreement of members of administration with other men of opulence, 69; vexations and oppressions presented as liable to be practised by men of opulence, 105; and oppression, 116; composed of things or services, 119n; as external instrument of felicity, 183–4; labour and obtainment of, 184; title to respect of monarch composed of, 198

WILL(S): p.o. trib. and influence of, 30–1; of members of judicatory acted upon by ruling interest, 54; formed, expressed and executed by judicatory, 55, 61; declaration of, included in judgement, 63; given impression and diffusion by newspaper editor, 63; execution and effect given to, in case of judicatories v. that in case of p.o. trib., 65; of sovereign and existence of rights, 76–7n; motive for publicity of proclamation of rights, to bind, of sovereign, 77n; check to doing of, of sovereign, 103; where person and property depends on changeable, no one safe, 110; securities dependent on, of sovereign, 116n; in France, community declared dependent on, of monarch, 140–1; resistance to, of sharers of powers of govt., 202; business of executive power to give execution and effect to, of legislative power, 220, 223–4; conduct of subordinate fs. placed in state of dependence on, of constitutive body, 225–7; in United States, Senate opposing obstruction to will of constitutive body, 229; arrangements of govt. by which conduct of people regulated conformable to, of gtst. no., 259, 264; classes of persons excluded from giving efficiency to, 259–64; means of maximizing efficiency of, of people, 265–7; strictness of dependence of operative power on, of constitutive maximized, 268; influence of force, intimidation, corruption, delusion, on, of gtst. no., 269–70n; prime minister to give execution to, of legislature, 284

WISDOM: assumption of superiority of, no justification for assumption of independent and irresistible power, 198

WISH(ES): *See* DESIRE(S)

WITNESS(ES): in Tripoli, as assessors to notary, 14–15; expense of collecting depositions of, 43–4; collection of evidence from, by newspaper, 62; examination of, in case of unlawful homicide, 92–4; veracity of, 249

WORSHIP: liberty to perform, 79

WRITINGS: security against misuse of private, 84–5, 96–7; seizure of, prohibited, 86; violation of private documents as mode of ultra-oppression, 120; no interdiction of faculty of manifesting opinion by means of written discourse, 264

WRONG: *See* RIGHT AND WRONG

WRONGS: accusations grounded on, 66; embraced by field of jurisdiction of judicatories v. that of p.o. trib., 66–7. *See* RIGHT(S)

INDEX OF NAMES

Note. The following is an index of names of persons and places appearing in the introduction, text, and notes; the last (whether Bentham's or the editor's) are indicated
by 'n'. Under Bentham's name only references to his other works are indicated.

Abinger: *See* Scarlett
Abu Hanifa: 10 & n, 11n, 21–2, 33n
Abu Shiaib, Mohammed: 10
A'Court, William, 1st Baron Heytesbury:
  xvi
Adam: 163n
Adams, John Quincy: xxxi & n, xxxii,
  xxxiii, 145n
Africa, African: xvii, xviii–xix, xxx, xxxi
  & n, 21, 32, 149, 156n, 158, 159,
  172, 174
al-Ahmar, Mustapha: 7n
Ahmed ibn Hanbal: 10 & n, 33n
Ahmed, Pasha of Tripoli (1711–45): xx,
  3n, 4–5n, 155n, 168n
Ahmed, Pasha of Tripoli (1795): xx, 4n,
  5n, 6n, 156n, 176n
Ahmed, Sidi: 7n
Aleppo: 160n
Alexandria: 160 & n
Algiers, Algerian: xxxii–xxxiii, 6 & n,
  19, 21, 149–52, 155, 159, 169–
  70, 172n, 174n, 175–6, 180
Ali V Khoja, Dey of Algiers: 151 & n
Ali, Pasha of Tripoli (1754–95): xx, 4n,
  5n, 6n
Ali, Pasha of Tripoli (1832–5): xx, 5 &
  n, 146–7, 148 & n, 156 & n, 157
  & n, 160 & n, 161–2
Ancona: xliii
Anglo-American United States: *See*
  United States of America
Arabia, Arabic: xxvin, xxix, xxxiii,
  xxxiv, 3, 4, 5n, 10, 111, 150, 151,
  163n, 165, 171, 172, 180
Argenson, Marc René, Marquis de: xvii
Aristotle: 16
Arudj al-Din: 149n
Astros: xli
Athens: 146n
Austria, Austrian: 166n, 193n, 239–40,
  254n

Awlad Mohammed, Dynasty of: 3n

Bainbridge, William: 160–1
Barbarossa: *See* Arudj al-Din, Khayr al-
  Din
Barbary: xvi & n, xix, xxxii, xl, 145,
  149, 154, 172n, 179
Barca: 5–6n
Basra: 10
Bathurst, Henry, 3rd Earl: xvin
Beechey, Frederick William: xix
Bengazi: 5–6n, 7n, 8, 157n
Bentham, Jeremy
  Chrestomathia: 150n
  *Codification Proposal addressed to All
    Nations Professing Liberal Opinions*:
    xvii & n
  Constitutional Code: xv & n, xvii,
    xxvn, xxixn, xxxiv, xlii–xliii, 66n,
    267n, 279n
  'Constitutional Code Rationale': xxin,
    187n
  'Economy as applied to Office': 64n,
    187n, 282n
  Elements of the Art of Packing: 15n
  'First Lines of a Proposed Code of Law
    for every nation compleat and
    rationalized': xxixn
  *First Principles preparatory to Constitu-
    tional Code*: xvn, xxin, xxiin, 64n,
    187n, 264n, 282n
  *An Introduction to the Principles of
    Morals and Legislation*: xlivn
  Letters to Count Toreno: 64n
  Radical Reform Bill: 267n
  'Supreme Operative': xxii, 264n
  Traités de législation civile et pénale: xvi
    & n, xxvin, xxixn
  'Travellers for Tripoli': xviii, xix
Bentham, Samuel: xvii
Birmingham: 52n, 150
Blackstone, Sir William: 234n, 240 & n

Blaquiere, Edward: xxxvi & n, xxxvii, xxxviii & n, xl & n, xli

Bonaparte, Napoleon, Emperor of the French: 249–50, 253

Bornu: xix

Bowring, Sir John: xviiin, xix, xxv–xxvi, xxxin, xxxvi & n, xxxix & n

Britain, British: xv–xvi, xix, xxx & n, xxxin, xxxiv, xxxv, 19n, 23n, 57, 122, 146n, 160n, 172n, 193n, 254n

Brixton: 150

Brussels: 158

al-Bukhari: 77n

Burchell, William John: xix & n

Burghol, Ali: xx, 5n, 6n, 155n

Byron, George Gordon, 6th Baron: xliii

Cairo: 10 & n, 160n

Cambridge: 17

Canning, George: xxxn

Cape Bon-Andrea: 177

Caramania: 4n, 155

Castlereagh: *See* Stewart

Charles I, King of England, Scotland and Ireland: 23n, 123 & n

Clapperton, Hugh: xix

Colls, John Flowerdew: xvn, xxii, xxxiiin, xxxix, xl & n, xliii, li

Constantinople: 14

Cyrenaica: 6n

Cyrene: 5–6n

Dalzel: *See* Dickson

Damietta: 160n

Darnis-Zarine: 6n

Delolme, Jean Louis: 240 & n

Delphi: 20

Denham, Dixon: xix

Denmark: 196

Derna: 5–6n, 7n, 8, 157n, 176–7

D'Ghies, Fatima: 5n, 147 & n, 157, 158, 160, 161

D'Ghies, Hassuna: xv–xviii, xx–xxi, xxiii, xxvi–xxxvi, xl–xli, 5n, 11n, 17n, 19n, 22n, 52n, 76n, 111n, 146–80

D'Ghies, Khadija: 5 & n, 147 & n, 157 & n, 158, 160, 161

D'Ghies, Mohammed (brother of Hassuna): 158, 160, 161, 166, 172 & n

D'Ghies, Mohammed (father of Has-

suna): xvi & n, xxxiv–xxxv, 7 & n, 52n, 146–7, 149, 152, 157–8, 159, 160, 161 & n, 180

Diana: 20n

Dickson, John: 172 & n

Dickson, née Dalzel, Elizabeth: 172n

Diya-al-Din Pasha, Kur Yusuf: 160n

Doane, Richard: xxxiiin, xxxvn, xxxix & n, xl, xliii, li

Dragut: 5n

Dumont, Pierre Étienne Louis: xvin, xxix

Eaton, William: 176n

Edgbaston: 52n

Edinburgh: 17

Egypt: xxxv, 3, 6n, 21, 147, 156, 160 & n, 162, 168, 176n

Eldon: *See* Scott

Elizabeth I, Queen of England and Ireland: 81–2n

England, English: xvi, xviin, xxviii, xxix, xxxin, xxxiii & n, xxxiv, xxxv & n, xxxvi, xxxvii, xl, xli & n, 4, 12, 13, 14–15, 17, 18, 20, 23n, 28, 33, 34, 37, 52 & n, 57 & n, 60, 73 & n, 81–3n, 104, 111, 117n, 122–3, 127n, 128–9n, 133, 140, 145 & n, 146, 150, 151 & n, 155, 159–60, 163, 165n, 172 & n, 175, 180, 188–9, 195, 196, 197, 228, 230–3, 234, 235–6, 239 & n, 240 & n, 244, 245 & n, 249, 250, 261, 266, 282

Epidauros: xxxvi

Europe, European: xxx, xxxiiin, xxxv, xxxvi, xl, 3, 19, 32, 34, 37, 40, 57, 58, 108, 110–11, 117n, 140, 145, 146, 147, 149, 155, 158, 162, 170, 173, 193n, 255, 261, 263

Exmouth: *See* Pellew

Ferdinand VII, King of Spain: 216n

Fessatou: 9

Fezzan: 3 & n, 4, 5n, 7 & n, 12, 16, 74–102

France, French: xvi & n, xviin, xxiii, xxvii, xxviii, xxxiii, xxxv, xxxix, l, 4, 5, 13, 15, 23n, 52, 68, 107 & n, 111, 115n, 140–1, 146, 150, 151, 158, 159–60, 163 & n, 164, 165n,

France (*cont.*)
  172, 174, 188, 195, 196, 197, 207n, 221, 228, 234, 249–50, 266

Gaza: 10n
Genoa, Genoese: 3
Gentz, Friedrich von: 193 & n
George III, King of Great Britain and Ireland: 234 & n
George IV, King of Great Britain and Ireland: xvn, 146n, 234 & n, 253–4
Germany: 196
Ghadames: 9
Gharian: 7n, 8, 148 & n, 162 & n
Great Britain: *See* Britain, British
Greece, Greek: xv, xvii, xxx & n, xxxvi–xliii, xliv, 5–6n, 16, 20, 158, 174, 183, 189 & n, 193–205, 207n, 216–24, 227n, 228, 236–43, 252, 254–6, 261, 263, 265
Gurdji, Mustapha: 7 & n

Hamuda Pasha, Bey of Tunis: 5n
Hanabila: *See* Ahmed ibn Hanbal
Hanafi: *See* Abu Hanifa
Hardenberg, Karl August von: 193 & n
Harrington: *See* Stanhope
Hawe Goi: 5
Hazelwood School: xxix, xxxiv, 52 & n, 150 & n, 151–2
Henry III, King of England: 128–9n
Henry V, King of England: 129n
Henry VII, King of England: 146 & n
Heytesbury: *See* A'Court
Hill, Arthur: 52n, 150n
Hill, Matthew Davenport: 52n, 150n
Hill, Rowland: 52n, 150n
Hill, Thomas Wright: 52n, 150 & n
Hindostan: 11n
Holland, Dutch: *See* Netherlands
Hun: 9
Husain III, Dey of Algiers: 150–1, 159, 175 & n
Hussein Capitan Pasha: 160n

Ibrahim Pasha Kataraghasi: 160 & n
Ireland: 122
Italy, Italian: 3, 172, 196

James II, King of England, Scotland and Ireland: 23n, 127n

Jerbi: 3n
John, King of England: 128–9n, 232 & n
Joseph: 120n

Karamanli, Ahmed: xx, 5–6n, 146–7, 148 & n, 156 & n, 157
Karamanli, Fatima: 5n, 147n
Karamanli, Hassan: xx, 156 & n, 162
Karamanli, Mohammed (d. 1828): xx, 5–6n, 146–7, 154, 156 & n, 157, 162
Karamanli, Mohammed (d. 1835): xx, 156n
Karamanli, Mustapha: xx, 5 & n, 146–7, 148 & n, 156, 157 & n, 160 & n, 161–2
Khalil ibn Ishak, al Djundi: 10 & n
Khangali, Abdallah: 7
Khayr al-Din: 149n
Khoja, Mohammed ibn Hamdan: xxxii–xxxiii, 150–2, 159–60, 180
Korais, Adamantios: xxxvi
Kufa: 10n

Laing, Alexander Gordon: xxxv & n
London: xxxii, xxxiiin, xxxv, xxxvi, xxxvii, xliii, 14, 150, 158, 159, 160, 178
Louis XVIII, King of France: xxxiv & n, 140–1, 158–9
Louriottis, Andreas: xxxvi–xxxvii, xli
Lucas, Simon: 19n
Lyle, Peter: *See* Murad Rais
Lyon, George Francis: 7 & n

Madrid: xxxvi
Malik ibn Anas: 10 & n, 21–2, 33n
Malta: xxx–xxxi, xxxv, 5n
al-Marghinani, Ali ibn Abu Bakr al-Farghani: 11n
Marseilles: xvi, xxxiii & n, 151, 158, 159
Mary II, Queen of England, Scotland and Ireland: 23n
Masalati: 8
Mavrocordato, Alexander: xlin
Medina: 10 & n
Mediterranean Sea: 3, 168, 174, 176, 177
Mehemet Ali, Pasha of Egypt: 147 & n

Metternich-Winneburg, Clemens Wenzel Lothar: 193 & n
Mill, James: xvii
Minorca: 175
Mohammed: xxix, 13, 32, 74–6, 77 & n, 78, 93, 158, 163n, 165n
Mohammed, Pasha of Tripoli: xx
Monroe, James: xxxvii
Montesquieu, Charles Louis de Secondat, Baron de la Brède et de: 240 & n
Morocco: 21, 148–9, 155, 170
al-Mukni, Mohammed: 3n, 7 & n
al-Muntasir, Mohammed: 3n
Murad Rais: 19 & n
Murzuk: 4 & n, 8
Muslim: 77n

Naples, Neapolitan: 165–6n, 216n
al-Nasafi, Abul-Barakat: 10 & n
Netherlands: 146, 151n, 158, 175 & n, 195, 196
Niger, River: xix, xxxv

Olympia: 20n
Orlandos, John: xli
Oudney, Walter: xix
Oxford: 17

Paris: xvi & n, xxxiii, xxxix, 14, 107n, 158, 159
Parr, Samuel: xxxvin, xxxvii, xlii
Parry, William: xliii
Peisistratus: 146 & n
Pellew, Edward, 1st Baron and 1st Viscount Exmouth: 151n
Persia: 11n
Piccolos, Nicolaos: xxxvi
Piedmont: 216n
Place, Francis: 236n
Port Bomba: 3n
Port Mahon: 175
Portugal, Portuguese: xv & n, xvii, 165n, 174, 195, 196, 216n, 217, 228, 229–30, 240, 254n
Prussia, Prussian: 193n, 239–40, 254n

Rabi: 10n
Rome, Roman: 13, 29, 188n, 261
Romilly, Sir Samuel: 159 & n
Russia: 18, 196, 239–40, 254n

Scarlett, James, 1st Baron Abinger: xvi & n, 159 & n
Scillus: 20n
Scotland, Scottish: 17, 19, 245 & n, 253
Scott, John, 1st Baron and 1st Earl Eldon: 13 & n
al-Shafi, Mohammed: 10 & n, 33n
Sinan: 5n
Souza, Don Gerardo José de: xvi
Spain, Spanish: xvi, xxxn, xxxin, xxxvi, xxxix, 165–6n, 172, 174 & n, 175–6, 195, 196, 216–17, 218 & n, 219n, 228, 229–30, 240, 252, 254n
Sparta, Spartans: 196
Stanhope, Leicester, 5th Earl of Harrington: xlii–xliii, 279n, 280n, 282n
Stewart, Robert, Viscount Castlereagh, 2nd Marquis of Londonderry: 193 & n
Sweden: 196

Tajaoura: 16 & n, 17, 111n, 158 & n
Tegerry: 3n
Thomson, Alexander: 67n
Timbuktu: xviii, xix, xxxv
Torrens, Robert: xxx & n
Toughar, Sidi Hammet: 7
Trinity College, Dublin: 17
Tripoli, Tripolitan: xv–xxxvi, xl–xli, 3–22, 32, 36, 40–1, 50–1, 74–102, 104, 109–11, 117n, 129–32, 134–5, 145–9, 153–80
Tripolitza: xli
Tunis: xxvin, 3, 21, 145, 147, 149, 155, 159, 168–70, 176, 180
Turkey, Turkish: xxx & n, xxxiiin, xxxvi, 4 & n, 5n, 10n, 19n, 147, 149 & n, 152, 155 & n, 160n, 168 & n, 169–70, 174

Umar, Dey of Algiers: 151 & n
United States of America: xxxi & n, xxxvii, 23n, 31–2, 50, 52, 57, 82n, 111, 116, 145n, 148 & n, 153, 154 & n, 155, 159, 161 & n, 168, 169, 170–80, 196, 197, 199 & n, 200 & n, 221–3, 225, 227, 229–30, 233–4, 240, 244, 250, 266

Verona, Congress of: xxxn

Warrington, Hanmer: xxxv & n
Washington: 179
Washington, George: 154 & n
Wellesley, Arthur, 1st Duke of Welling-
    ton: xxxn
Wellington: *See* Wellesley
Westminster: 123
William III, King of England, Scotland
    and Ireland: 23n
Wilmot, Robert: xxxiv–xxxv

Xenophon: 20 & n

Yusef, Pasha of Tripoli: xv & n, xx,
    xxxv, 3n, 4–6, 7n, 146–8, 153,
    155–7, 160, 161–4, 166, 172,
    173, 176 & n

Zanzour: 16 & n, 111n, 158 & n